C
as a Second Language

For Native Speakers of Pascal

Tomasz Müldner

Acadia University
Nova Scotia, Canada

Peter W. Steele

Acadia University
Nova Scotia, Canada

Addison-Wesley Publishing Company, Inc.

Reading, Massachusetts Menlo Park, California New York
Don Mills, Ontario Wokingham, England Amsterdam Bonn Sydney Singapore
Tokyo Madrid Bogotá Santiago San Juan

This book is in the Addison-Wesley Series in Computer Science

Michael A. Harrison, Consulting Editor

Library of Congress Cataloging-in-Publication Data

Müldner, Tomasz.
   C as a second language.

   1. C (Computer program language)   I. Steele, Peter W.
II. Title.
QA76.73.C15M85   1988   005.13'3   86–28837
ISBN 0–201–19210–1

Reprinted with corrections June, 1989

DEFGHIJ-HA-89

To Basia, my best friend and wife
Tomasz

To my family and friends
Peter

Preface

C was originally designed in 1972 by Dennis Ritchie at AT&T Bell Laboratories [Rit78]. The first implementation was on a DEC PDP-11; today, C compilers are available for almost all computers, including mainframes, minicomputers, and microcomputers. The popularity of C has grown tremendously over the past years; indeed, it is one of the most popular languages in use today, with a wide variety of applications, such as editors, compilers, databases, and operating systems (in particular, Unix [Rit78]), being written in the language.

This book is called *C as a Second Language* because it is designed for readers who already have experience in programming in Pascal [Jen78] and want to learn to program in C. It is still possible to read the book without knowing Pascal, but a good knowledge of some high-level programming language is necessary.

The book is for students, professional programmers, and computer hobbyists studying C on their own. It is especially suited to students who are either required to study C or who will be entering some high-level computer science courses, such as operating systems or compilers, in which a knowledge of C may be needed.

Our main goal in this text is to show how to write reliable programs in C and how to translate programs from Pascal to C.

A secondary (but not neglected) goal in designing this book was to provide the reader with easy reference to various topics when programming in C.

Another goal is to use a portable C, which in practice means that we have used the Kernighan and Ritchie standard [Ker78]. Many extensions of this standard have appeared, for example, those described in ANSI C [Ans86]: void procedures, enumeration types, and so on. We have described most of the common extensions but have also made it clear that they are nonstandard. (As of the writing of this book, the ANSI C standard has not been completed.)

The first step in learning C is to understand its syntax. We help the reader through this step by comparing C constructs with Pascal's corresponding constructs.

The second step is to understand thoroughly the semantics of the language. Here, our approach is to show several small C programs, explain their semantics, and warn what the typical pitfalls are.

The last step is to develop a programming style. For this, we show larger programs written in a style often used by C programmers. This

v

style is in places concise, but we have avoided "tricky" code even if this could result in less efficient code.

The book has two basic parts. The first part (Chapters 2–11) is an introduction to C that encompasses the goals of the first two steps mentioned above. Since C is likely to be new to the reader, these chapters concentrate on the language itself. The algorithms are fairly simple, sometimes even trivial, so the reader does not have to spend time trying to understand the data structures and algorithms being used.

The second part (Chapters 12–14) assumes a basic understanding of the underlying concepts of C that were introduced in the first part. We continue to discuss programming techniques in C and present additional features of C through examples of larger programs. The topics presented and the data structures and algorithms covered in this part are more advanced.

Important features of the book include:

- **A thorough and detailed description of the C programming language and programming techniques,** including a comparison of C and Pascal constructs and coverage of advanced topics such as the dangling reference problem, heap compaction, and others.
- **Early introduction of pointers and complete,** detailed description of relations between pointers and arrays, functions, and strings (Chapters 7, 8, 10).
- **Implementation in C of data structures and algorithms** such as: linked lists (both pointer based and array based), an array implementation of a stack, an open hash table implementation of a dictionary, an adjacency list representation of a graph, a bit-vector implementation of a set, techniques to manage files containing structured data, memory management with heap compaction, internal and external search techniques, a "virtual" sort that can be applied to arrays of any type of element, and an implementation of an external binary search tree with file compaction.
- **Various implementations** of C under three different environments: Unix, MS-DOS, and the Macintosh. We show how to use specific compilers in each of these environments (Chapter 14). Then through **programming examples,** we discuss such topics as: I/O redirection, error handling, and low-level file I/O under Unix; the ANSI $\mathcal{C}$ standard, MS-DOS services, directories, and file attributes under MS-DOS; window and menu management on the Macintosh.

Pedagogical Aids

Each of the ten introductory chapters begins with a review of Pascal constructs, which describe such concepts as the system stack and the heap as they relate to standard Pascal [Coo83]. Following each review is a glossary of terms, which should be understood before studying the rest of the chapter. In some instances, the reader may start reading a chapter from the glossary, referring to the Pascal review only if needed. (For more detail on the basic concepts of programming languages, refer to "Programming Languages: Design and Implementation" by Pratt [Pra84].)

Our book teaches C through examples. We offer more than 100 complete programs, varying from one as simple as finding the maximum of two integers to one that implements an external binary search tree. Most examples (with the exception of those in Chapter 14 on real systems) are written in a portable style. Each chapter closes with lists of things to remember and common errors made by novice C programmers. We also provide over 100 exercises and give solutions to all odd-numbered exercises.

Chapter 1 gives some basic definitions used throughout the book, such as the run-time system of a language. It also briefly compares Pascal and C. Chapter 2 is on primitive data types and basic terminal I/O. Chapter 3 describes control structures, and Chapter 4 is an introduction to file I/O (which is discussed further in Chapters 12 and 14). Chapter 5 is on preprocessing; Chapter 6 describes functions and scope rules; Chapter 7 is on pointers; and Chapters 8 and 9 define arrays, structures, unions, and enumeration types. Chapter 10 describes C string operations, and Chapter 11, bitwise operations. Chapter 12, a continuation of Chapter 4, discusses additional details of text and binary file I/O. Chapter 13 presents some application programs:

- A calculator program, which shows the implementation of linked lists and open hash tables
- An implementation of Dijkstra's algorithm to find the shortest path in a graph, which also shows the implementation of sets and graphs
- A database program, which shows the implementation of external binary search trees

Chapter 14 describes through several examples the use of C under some real systems—Unix, MS-DOS, and the Macintosh.

Appendices contain a list of C keywords and a complete description of C's syntax (Appendix A), precedence and associativity tables (Appendix B), a detailed description of formatted I/O (Appendix C), and an ASCII table (Appendix D). Appendix E contains solutions to the odd-numbered programming exercises. Appendix F consists of a table comparing Pascal and C, and Appendix G contains a summary of the standard library functions. We provide a program index to allow easy reference to any program in the book.

A disk containing complete source code of all examples may be ordered from the authors. A check for $30 (payable to one of the authors) may be sent to Doctor Tomasz Müldner or Professor Peter Steele, c/o School of Computer Science, Acadia University, BOP 1X0 Wolfville, NS Canada. For classroom adoptions of 25 or more, contact your local Addison-Wesley representative.

Acknowledgments

We wish to thank a number of people who helped us complete our work. Our colleague Dr. Rick Giles carefully read the first draft and made a number of useful suggestions. Many thanks to our students: Bill Nickerson, who helped us debug most of our programs; Donna Cleveland, who helped prepare some of the exercises; Gilbert Verghese and Barbara Müldner, who suggested many corrections in the early versions of the manuscript; Steven Langlois, our last but most thorough proofreader; and finally, the winter 1985 class of Computer Science 2023 at Acadia, the first students we tested our book on. Also, special thanks to our colleague Dr. Wayne Brehaut for his help with many grammatical aspects of the manuscript.

We would as well like to thank the four software companies that allowed us to review their products: Lattice Incorporated for Lattice C; Rational Systems, Inc. for Instant-C; Manx Software Systems, Inc. for Aztec C; and THINK Technologies, Inc. for LightspeedC.

We would also like to express our appreciation to the following reviewers of the manuscripts: Andrew W. Appel, Princeton University; Judith D. Boxler, Vancouver Community College; David Cohrs, University of Wisconsin, Madison; Jon Forrest, Britton Lee, Inc.; Michael A. Harrison, University of California, Berkeley; Raj Nagendra, Ryerson Polytechnical Institute; Paul W. Ross, Millersville University; Henry Ruston, Polytechnic University, Brooklyn.

Nova Scotia   *Tomasz Müldner*
Canada   *Peter Steele*

Contents

1 Introduction

PREVIEW   *This chapter introduces some basic notions that you may need to understand later chapters. First of all, we briefly describe C and then compare Pascal with C. Next, we discuss the representation of the integer and character data types in memory. Finally, we present the concept of a run-time system, include files, and conditional and separate compilation in C.*

1.1   ABOUT C

C is often referred to as a *low-level* high-level language because it provides many tools that allow low-level operations to be performed. As a result, C programs have gained a reputation for being unstructured and difficult to read. In some respects, this reputation may be deserved, but to say it is an exclusive trait of C is unfair. Unreadable programs can be written in any programming language without much difficulty. Furthermore, like a true high-level language, C provides many high-level features, and with some discipline, programs written in C can be as structured and readable as programs written in Pascal. Another important characteristic of C is that most implementations are very efficient.

C provides the typical primitive data types: **character, integer,** and **real**. It also provides structured data types: **arrays, records,** and **unions**. A complete set of control structures is provided, including **conditional**, **selective**, and **iterative** statements. Functions may be recursive, although they may not be textually nested. Programs may be divided into **separately compiled** modules, and a flexible set of scope rules exists to assist in this sort of modularization. One of the main strengths of C is its approach to **pointers,** and many language constructs (such as call by reference) are implemented using pointers. Standard I/O is provided by **run-time libraries**, which makes it easier to port compilers to other machines. C does not provide any high-level data types like those in Ada [Ada83], nor any tools for parallel programming.

For many years, the definition of the C language given by Kernighan and Ritchie [Ker78] was the accepted standard definition. Today, C is being standardized by the American National Standards Institute Subcommittee (ANSI) [Ans86]. Fortunately, most of the proposals in the ANSI C definition are extensions to the Kernighan and Ritchie standard, and most existing implementations today comply with Kernighan and Ritchie, with some newer compilers adopting aspects of ANSI C. Therefore, with a little effort, it is possible to write "almost" portable programs, and only minor changes, if any, are needed to port programs from one machine to another.

1.2   A BRIEF COMPARISON OF PASCAL AND C

In this section, we briefly compare Pascal and C constructs. Our purpose is not to give you detailed information about any specific constructs but to give you a general idea of what the C programming language is like.

Identifiers and Comments
The syntax of **identifiers** is almost identical in both languages except that in C an underscore _ is allowed, and they are *case sensitive*. **Comments** are similar as well:

Pascal	C
`(* comment *)`	`/* comment */`

Program Modules and Scope
A program in C is a sequence of functions. One function must be called `main`; it is from this function that the execution of the program starts. Although the **scope rules** in C are Pascal-like, C functions may not be textually nested; however, they may contain **blocks** (compound statements containing declarations as *well* as statements). Unlike Pascal, subroutines in C are always defined as functions, although any function may be called as a procedure, in which case the value returned by the function is disregarded. As in Pascal, functions in C may be recursive. A simple example:

```
PROGRAM one;

PROCEDURE proc;                    void proc()
BEGIN                              {
    WRITE('Hello');                    printf("Hello");
END;                               }

FUNCTION func : INTEGER;           int func()
BEGIN                              {
    func := 3;                         return(3);
END;                               }
```

```
VAR i : INTEGER;              int i;
BEGIN                         main() {
    proc;                         proc();
    i := func;                    i = func();
    WRITE(i);                     printf("%d", i);
END.                          }
```

The preceding C program has three functions defined: `main`, `proc`, and `func`.

Unlike standard Pascal, C supports **separate compilation** of functions; the keyword `extern` specifies an object that is defined in another file.

Data Types and Declarations, Parameters

Pascal supports the primitive data types **integer**, **real**, **boolean**, and **character**. C supports the types `int`, `float` (which is the same as **real** in Pascal), and `char`. C has no type boolean, although any nonzero integer value is equivalent to true, and zero is equivalent to false. Moreover, C provides a special qualifier `long`, which can be used to define **double precision integers** having approximately twice as many significant digits; similarly, C provides a type `double` to define **double precision reals**.

The syntax of declarations in C is the reverse of that in Pascal; for example,

```
VAR i : INTEGER;              int i;

VAR c : CHAR;                 char c;
```

In C, data can be *initialized* in definitions; for example,

```
int i = 3;
```

Pascal supports structured data types **array**, **record**, and **file**, and C supports the same types, although files are not predefined in the language; instead they are defined in the **system library**.

Examples

```
VAR arr : ARRAY [0..3] OF INTEGER     int arr[4];

rec : RECORD                          struct {
        i : INTEGER;                      int i;
        r : REAL;                         float r;
     END                              } rec;
```

Function definitions are similar, although formal parameter specifications are in different places; for example,

```
PROCEDURE proc(i:INTEGER);    void proc(i)
                              int i;
                              {
VAR j:INTEGER;                    int j;
BEGIN
    j := i + 3;                   j = i + 3;
END                           }
```

Pascal supports two modes of parameter transmission—call by value and call by reference. C supports only call by value; call by reference must be *simulated* using pointers.

Expressions and Statements
Expressions in C are similar to those in Pascal except that types may be freely intermixed with *automatic type conversion* taking place.

Operators and other constructs are similar, but there are some minor syntactic differences:

Equality:	=	==
Inequality:	<>	!=
Logical AND:	AND	&&
OR:	OR	||
NOT:	NOT	!

Assignment:
```
x := 3*(y+6);                 x = 3*(y+6);
```

Conditional statement:
```
IF a>5 THEN a:=a-b            if (a>5) a=a-b;
ELSE b:=a;                    else b=a;
```

Iteration statements:
```
WHILE x>0 DO x:=x-1;          while (x>0) x=x-1;

REPEAT x:=x+2                 do x=x+2;
UNTIL x>100;                  while (!(x>100));

FOR i:=1 TO 10 DO             for (i=1; i<=10; i++)
    x[i] := 0;                    x[i] = 0;
```

Selection statement:
```
CASE i OF                     switch (i) {
1:  j := 3;                   case 1: j = 3;
                                      break;
2:  j := j-1;                 case 2: j--;
                                      break;
END;                          }
```

Compound statement: BEGIN *s1*; ... ; *sk* END   { *s1*; ... ; *sk* }

Return from a function:
```
func := exp;                  return(exp);
end (* function *)
```

Pointer declaration:	VAR p : $^\wedge$INTEGER;	int *p;
Pointer dereferencing:	p$^\wedge$	*p
Access to record fields:	rec.*field*	rec.*field*
Record pointer access:	recpnter$^\wedge$.*field*	recpnter->*field*

A single dimensional array in C is considered a pointer to the memory block allocated for this array. C allows arithmetic on pointers; for example, if x is a single dimensional array, x+1 refers to the second element of the array. A function name without parentheses is also a pointer, in this case a pointer to the code of this function.

Other C Constructs
C supports **macros** with parameters. These macros are expanded before compilation of the program. The C preprocessor also handles **file inclusion** and **conditional compilation**.

1.3   THE COMPUTER'S MEMORY

A computer's memory consists of a number of **words**. Each word consists of a number of **bytes**, and each byte consists of a number of bits (usually 8, though not always). For example, 16-bit words consist of two 8-bit bytes, and 64-bit words consist of eight 8-bit bytes.

For the most part, we assume that each memory location is one byte in size and that a single character may be stored in a byte. This is usually referred to as a **byte-oriented** memory architecture and is the most common architecture in use today, with machines such as the VAX-11 and IBM 360 and their successors using it. Machines that support so-called **word-oriented** architectures are less common. In these architectures, the smallest addressable unit is a word rather than a byte. For example, on the DEC-20, each memory location is 36 bits in size, and on the Cyber 180, each location is 60 bits in size.

From a language designer's viewpoint, the primary difference between a byte-oriented architecture and a word-oriented one is that in a byte-oriented machine, as we mentioned, a single memory location typically can hold only one character value, whereas in a word-oriented machine, a single memory location can hold several characters. For example, on the DEC-20, each memory location can hold five 7-bit characters, with one bit left over. This may cause certain difficulties for a language designer if portability is a concern. Many of the examples in this text should work on any machine regardless of its memory architecture. However, some examples are designed for the more common byte-oriented memory and may have to be modified to work properly on a word-oriented machine.

All data objects—for example, integers or records—are stored during execution in a memory area consisting of several consecutive bytes. The *size* of a data object is the number of bytes this object occupies.

A brief discussion of some of the characteristics of integer and character data is helpful in understanding certain aspects of C. Two types of integer data are supported in C: **signed** and **unsigned**. Codes representing unsigned data are interpreted using **pure binary**, so all bits of a number are used to determine its magnitude.

Pure binary (also called *unsigned*) is a positional representation just like the standard decimal system. Each position in the code has a fixed *weight*, which is used as a multiplying factor to calculate the value of the code. The value of a code is the sum of individual digits, each multiplied by its weight.

In the *decimal* system, weights are powers of 10 (1, 10, 100, and so on, from right to left), whereas in the *binary* system, weights are powers of 2 (1, 2, 4, 8, 16, and so on, from right to left). For example, to determine the decimal value of 1101 binary, the following calculations can be performed:

$$1101 = 1 * 8 + 1 * 4 + 0 * 2 + 1 * 1 = 13 \text{ decimal}$$

```
1101 = 1 * 8 + 1 * 4 + 0 * 2 + 1 * 1 = 13 decimal
│││└────── weight 1
││└─────── weight 2
│└──────── weight 4
└───────── weight 8
```

If n bits are used to encode a number, the largest number possible is $2^n - 1$.

Signed data are trickier. To represent signed data, one bit (usually the high-order bit) is used to indicate the sign of the number; the remaining bits are used to determine its magnitude. Exactly how this magnitude is determined depends on the representation being used; several techniques—including **sign-magnitude**, **one's complement**, and **two's complement**—have been designed, but two's complement is the most common.

The range of values that can be represented using two's complement depends on how many bits are being used. For example, using 8 bits, 256 different binary codes are possible, ranging from 00000000 to 11111111. Using pure binary, these represent decimal values 0 to 255; using two's complement, these represent nonnegative values 0 to +127 (00000000 to 01111111) and negative values −128 to −1 (10000000 to 11111111). Using 16 bits, the possible range of values is from −32768 to

32767. In general, if n bits are used to represent a signed number, the negative maximum is -2^{n-1}, and the positive limit is $2^{n-1} - 1$.

The *character* data type in C is sometimes signed and sometimes unsigned. Most recent implementations of C support both unsigned and signed characters. This means the value -1 assigned to a character may be converted, for example, to 255 (assuming two's complement notation). In other words, the computer may or may not sign-extend characters if they are assigned to integers. **Sign extension** is best illustrated by an example. Assume characters are represented by 8 bits, and integers by 16 bits. If a character variable has the code 10111110 binary and it is assigned to an integer variable, the result will be either 0000000010111110 if sign extension does not take place or 1111111110111110 if sign extension does take place.

Much more can be said about the representation of data, but it is not the subject of this book. If you are interested in more detailed information about this area, see [Ste86].

1.4 PREPROCESSING, COMPILATION, AND LINKING

Three steps are involved in producing an executable program:

- Editing
- Compiling
- Linking

Although exact details may vary from system to system (specific examples are shown in Chapter 14, which discusses some real systems), the usual product of a compiler is an object code program. This program is not yet executable, since it contains only the code of the *user-defined* functions; the *system routines* that may be needed to run the program are not included. To make this object code program executable, it must be combined or *linked* with the code of the system routines used in this program; this task is performed by a program called a **linker** or **loader**. The linker program links the indicated code with the system libraries and reports appropriate errors if any symbols are left undefined when the link is complete (which might happen if a function has been called but not defined or if the wrong library is linked).

The system libraries provide *run-time support* as well as access to various operating system services—typically I/O but sometimes other services, such as floating point routines. The routines that make operating system requests are not normally part of the run-time system.

A language's **run-time system** is the special support code that manages the memory areas called the **stack** (for subroutine calls) and the **heap** (for dynamic memory requests) and other events that take place "behind the scenes" during run time, either by request or automatically. This run-time environment is self-managed and usually apart from the operating system itself. Routines that allow the user to manipulate this environment are often provided in the language's system library.

Both Pascal and C require run-time support to execute recursive functions and procedures and to support operations involving pointers.

In some languages (such as C), the user may split a program into several modules. Each of these is **compiled separately** and must be linked together (along with the required system libraries) to produce executable code. The advantage of using separately compiled modules is that if an error is found, only the incorrect module, not the entire program, has to be changed and recompiled. This corrected module can then be relinked with the other already compiled modules.

Some programming languages support a so-called **preprocessing** feature. This allows the user to specify that certain sequences of text in a source code file are to be replaced by other sequences of text. This task (often referred to as **macro substitution**) is performed by a preprocessor utility and usually takes place before the compilation phase; on many systems, however, the preprocessing is done in tandem with the compilation phase. A related feature supported by many preprocessors is file inclusion, which is specifying that text from another file is to be included as part of the source program during compilation. We describe this in detail in the following section.

1.5 INCLUDE FILES

Usually, the text of a program is stored in a single file. To improve the modifiability of a program, it may be split into two (or more) files, for example, one file containing data structures and another containing the code of the main program. One of these files is considered the principal file and has in it special preprocessor directives indicating that the named files are to be *included* during compilation at the points where the directives occur. When the compiler is compiling a program and an include directive is encountered, it opens the file specified and compiles the text in that file exactly as if the text had appeared at that point in the file it was compiling. When end-of-file is reached on the include file, compilation continues in the main file at the point it was interrupted. When compilation is completed, a *single* object code file is produced, not one for each include file. Thus, from the linker's viewpoint, no difference exists between a program that has include directives specified and one that consists of a single file.

Do not confuse separate compilation with include files. Programs may be divided into separately compiled modules (each of which creates a single object code file when it is compiled), and each module may be further split into several include files (although it is still viewed as one contiguous piece of text by the compiler).

Both macro substitution and include files are supported by most C systems. We describe the standard C preprocessor in Chapter 5.

Glossary   **Byte**   A part of a computer word, normally 8 bits.

Linking   Combining the object code, and possibly some libraries, of several files.

Macro   An in-line procedure expanded during the preprocessing phase of compilation.

Preprocessing   Textual substitution of some parts of the source file.

Run-time system   Support code to manage run-time program requirements.

2 Primitive Data Types and Terminal I/O

PREVIEW

This chapter introduces the primitive data types supported by the C language: int, char, float, *and* double. *We introduce the C assignment operator. We then discuss arithmetic expressions and present some terminal I/O operations. We conclude the chapter by discussing type conversions and defining new data types.*

REVIEW OF PASCAL CONSTRUCTS

In this section, we briefly discuss those Pascal constructs (and some aspects of their implementation) that the corresponding C constructs will be presented for. A similar discussion begins each chapter. We also give definitions of the terms that we use in this and later chapters. Thus this review is also a prerequisite to understanding the rest of the chapter. We provide a glossary at the end of this review to assist you during your study of the main part of the chapter.

Let us start by discussing **lexical structure**. A Pascal program is a sequence of characters put together according to the rules of standard Pascal. These characters combine to form a variety of **tokens**. A token is one of the following:

- Operators, such as +
- Keywords, such as begin
- Identifiers, such as temp
- Literals (numbers and strings), such as 124
- Labels, such as LOOP
- Special symbols, such as [
- Comments

Pascal **identifiers** are composed of letters and digits; they must start with a letter and are *not* case sensitive. That is, the identifier temp is identical to TEMP or Temp. **Comments** start with { and end with }, or start with (* and end with *). In standard Pascal, comments may *not* be nested.

Standard Pascal supports four **primitive data types:** integer, char, boolean, and real. The precision of real arithmetic depends on the implementation and cannot be specified by the programmer.

11

Variables *cannot* be initialized when they are declared. Instead, appropriate statements must be included in the program to perform the desired initializations.

Type checking is **static**. That is, the type of an expression is usually determined when the program is compiled.

Type compatibility is enforced. That is, in an assignment statement, the type of the left-hand side must be the same as the type of the right-hand side; there is *no* automatic type conversion. This is true for input operations as well. The only exception to this rule is that an integer expression will be converted to real if necessary. For example, if the type of the left-hand side of an assignment is real and the type of the right-hand side is integer, the integer value is automatically converted to a real value.

An assignment is a statement rather than an expression, and multiple assignments (for example, x:=y:=2) are not supported.

Terminal I/O is provided by means of four **overloaded** procedures, READ, READLN, WRITE, and WRITELN, each having an indefinite number of parameters. A procedure is said to be overloaded if it can accept parameters of different types, with the exact actions performed by the procedure determined by the parameters specified. For example,

```
READ(x)
```

is overloaded because, depending on the type of x, this procedure reads an integer, a real, or a character value.

A generalized description of terminal input follows. Although the description depends somewhat on the system, it does explain a number of important points. Basically, terminal input may be treated as either

- Buffered/unbuffered
- Echoed/nonechoed

If terminal input is **buffered**, then when Pascal's READ statement is executed, the information typed is not read until the return key is hit. This allows you to edit your input if you make a mistake. For example, if the request

```
VAR c : CHAR;
...
READ(c);
```

is made and you type a but intended to type b, you simply have to press the backspace key to delete the a, and then enter the b. Once you hit return, the input cannot be edited.

In certain applications, this mode of input is not suitable. For example, if you have a menu-driven program and ask the user to type

```
N − edit new file
Q − quit editor
```

as many screen-based editors do, you would probably prefer not to force the user to hit the N or Q and *then* enter return—a single keystroke should do.

Is it possible to have characters read immediately in this fashion? Usually, an internal input buffer is maintained in some manner, and when a READ(c) is executed in Pascal, the value assigned to c is taken from this buffer. If the buffer is empty, you may enter a new line of characters, which is placed in this buffer; nothing is read from the buffer until you press return. This type of input is called buffered input. To have characters read immediately, **unbuffered** or so-called **raw** input is needed. In this mode, there is no buffer; when an input request is issued, the characters are taken directly from the keyboard as soon as they are typed.

Another aspect of interactive input is whether or not the characters typed are echoed on the screen; some implementations of Pascal provide special routines that allow nonechoed input.

The output procedures (WRITE and WRITELN) can be used for formatted or unformatted output. For example,

```
WRITE(x)                    — unformatted
WRITE(x:10)                 — formatted
```

Glossary **Automatic type conversion** The type of an expression is changed by the compiler to satisfy type compatibility requirements.

Buffered I/O I/O operations are performed through an internal buffer.

Overloaded procedure A procedure that can accept parameters of different types, with the exact meaning of this procedure determined by the types of parameters.

Static type A type that can be determined when the program is compiled.

C CONSTRUCTS

2.1 LEXICAL STRUCTURE

The lexical structure of C is similar to that of Pascal in that C is free format, by which we mean a program is viewed as a sequence of tokens separated by whitespace (characters such as spaces, tabs, formfeeds, and newlines are often collectively referred to as **whitespace**). These tokens do not have to appear at specific column boundaries or any other such formatting convention as in some languages (such as Fortran [Mei80]). Appendix A lists the keywords and various special characters that are defined in the language.

C identifiers are built according to the same rules as in Pascal, but they *are* case sensitive. For example, `Temp` and `TEMP` are two *different* identifiers. This case sensitivity applies to the keywords defined in C as well in that they *must* be entered in lowercase, or they will not be recognized as keywords. Moreover, C allows leading, trailing, and embedded underscores. In general, the user should avoid identifiers with leading underscores, since many system libraries use such names for special purposes.

Identifiers may be any length, but in standard C only the first eight characters are significant. However, many implementations do treat more than eight characters as significant. If program portability is a concern, eight is the limit that should be adhered to.

The C language defines four kinds of literals (constants):

- Integers
- Long integers
- Characters
- Doubles

We discuss each of these in detail in Section 2.4.

Comments in C start with /* and end with */; for example,

```
/* this is a comment */
```

Comments may appear anywhere whitespace is legal. Standard C does *not* allow nesting of comments; for example,

```
/* comment and  /* nested comment */ */
```

is illegal.

2.2 PRIMITIVE DATA TYPES, ASSIGNMENT

Declaring Variables

C provides several primitive data types: `char`, `int`, `long int`, `short int`, `float`, and `double`. Unlike Pascal, C provides *no* built-in type boolean. Instead, boolean values are represented with integers: The value 0 stands for false, and any nonzero value stands for true.

Type identifiers in C are similar to those in Pascal:

Pascal	**C**
`INTEGER`	`int`
	`long int`
	`short int`
`CHAR`	`char`
`REAL`	`float`
	`double`

An `int` may be specified as `long` or `short`, with `short int` equivalent to `short` and `long int` equivalent to `long`. Furthermore, `char`, `int`, `short`, and `long` may be specified as `unsigned`. By default, integers are signed; whether characters are signed or not depends on the implementation.

The type specifier `short` denotes integers with generally fewer significant digits than ordinary integers; the actual number of significant digits depends on the implementation. The type specifier `long` denotes integers with generally more significant digits, although the exact number of bytes used to store a long also depends on the implementation.

Variables of type `double` are intended to support roughly twice as many significant digits as variables of type `float` and, of course, may require more memory. They are often called **double precision reals**.

C guarantees that the number of bytes allocated to store an object follows these rules:

Size of `char` is 1 storage unit

Size of `short int` <= size of `int` <= size of `long int`

Size of `unsigned int` = size of `int`

Size of `float` <= size of `double`

Exactly what a **storage unit** is depends on the implementation; traditionally, a storage unit is called a **byte**, and this is the term we use in this text. For an implementation that allocates `short`, `int`, and `long` variables in the same number of bytes, the preceding definition is still correct.

To declare variables, C uses a syntax that is the reverse of that used by Pascal. Moreover, C does not use the Pascal keyword VAR:

Pascal	**C**
`VAR i   : INTEGER;`	`int   i;`
`    c, d : CHAR;`	`char  c, d;`
`    x, y : REAL;`	`float x, y;`

Assignments

An **l-value** is an expression that can be interpreted as an address; for example, a variable is an l-value, whereas a constant is not. Intuitively, an l-value is an expression that can appear on the *left*-hand side of an assignment.

An assignment is an *expression* rather than a statement as it is in Pascal. Its syntax is

Pascal	C
l-value := *expression*	*l-value* = *expression*

An assignment expression in C can be made into a statement by following it with a semicolon; for example,

Pascal	C
`i := 2;`	`i = 2;`
`c := 'a';`	`c = 'a';`
`x := x + 2 * x;`	`x = x + 2 * x;`

Consider the assignment

```
x = x + 2
```

Here, x is an l-value. The occurrence of x on the left-hand side of this assignment represents the address of a memory location, say L, whereas the occurrence of x on the right-hand side represents the current value of x, say V. As a result of the execution of the assignment, the value V + 2 is stored at memory location L. This description also applies to the assignment statement in Pascal.

No colon is used in a C assignment. Perhaps even more troublesome is the equality operator. In Pascal, it is a *single* equal sign =; in C, it is a *double* equal sign ==. These subtle syntactic differences between Pascal and C can cause a lot of hardship.

Since assignment in C is an expression and not a statement, it must yield a value. The value returned by an assignment is the value of the right-hand side. The type of an assignment expression is the type of the left-hand side; for example,

```
i = 8 — integer expression equal to the value 8 and assigning the value 8 to
        the variable i
```

Because an assignment is an expression, multiple assignments are possible; for example,

```
x = y = 3
```

Since the assignment operator = associates from right to left, the preceding expression is equivalent to

```
x = (y = 3)
```

Alternatively, a sequence of assignment statements can be given; for example,

```
x = 3;
y = 4;
```

2.3 THE MAIN PROGRAM

We will now introduce our first C program. The main program's header in C is

Pascal	C
PROGRAM TEST(INPUT, OUTPUT);	main()

There is *no* semicolon in the C header, and the main program does not have a name other than `main`. Actually, as we will see later, the main program is nothing more than a function definition. The only thing that makes it different from other functions is that it is where execution of a program begins. We will fully discuss functions in Chapter 6. The main function can also have parameters, but they are used for purposes different from those in Pascal. See Section 10.5 for a description of how to specify parameters for this function.

Let us now consider a simple program:

Pascal	C
PROGRAM TEST(INPUT, OUTPUT);	main()
VAR	{
i,j : INTEGER;	int i, j;
BEGIN	
i := 1;	i = 1;
j := 3;	j = 3;
i := i + j;	i = i + j;
END.	}

The body of the main program in C starts with a left brace {, followed by the local declarations (if any), followed by instructions (if any), and terminates with a right brace }. In essence, Pascal's

```
BEGIN ... END
```

is replaced in C by

```
{ ... }
```

The braces, however, are used not only to form compound statements but also *blocks*. As you can see in the preceding example, the braces also enclose the declaration of two integer variables, and as in Pascal, a declaration is not considered a statement. A **block**, then, is simply a list of declarations followed by a list of instructions. Distinction between blocks and compound statements is standard (classical) terminology; some books on C, however, regard compound statements and blocks as the same. We discuss blocks further in Section 6.3.3.

Unlike Pascal, C allows you to initialize a variable directly in a declaration; for example,

```
int i = 223;
```

The previous C program can therefore be rewritten

```
main()
{
    int i = 1,
        j = 3;

    i = i + j;
}
```

The convention we use is that variable definitions with initializers are placed on separate lines. In later chapters, we will describe the exact form of a permissible initialization expression. Variables within a block that are not explicitly initialized have *undetermined* initial values.

2.4 CONSTANTS

Integer Constants

A decimal integer constant is in both languages identically defined as a sequence of digits. Unlike Pascal, however, C supports integer constants in three bases:

- Decimal integer constants (base 10):
  Sequence of digits, the first of which is not 0
- Octal integer constants (base 8):
  The digit 0, followed by a (possibly empty) sequence of octal digits (0..7)

- Hexadecimal integer constants (base 16):
  The digit 0, followed by the letter x (or X), followed by a sequence of hexadecimal digits (0..9, a..f, A..F)

Examples

Decimal integer constants:	23, 1
Octal integer constants:	077, 01
Hexadecimal integer constants:	0xA1, 0XCC

Integer constants may be of either type int or type long. Normally, if a constant is small enough to be represented by an integer, its type is int. If the value of a constant exceeds the largest possible integer value, automatic type conversion takes place, and it is converted to long. If the suffix L or l (or, in some implementations, I) is used, the constant is treated as long regardless of its size. For example, both 10L and 3256743L are long integer constants. This explicit conversion is needed in passing actual parameters of type long (see Section 6.2). If the value of a constant exceeds the largest possible long integer value, the result is undefined. Negative integer constants in C are represented in the usual manner with a leading minus sign.

Floating Point Constants
Floating point constants are defined in the same manner as in Pascal except that numbers may also start or end with a decimal point. For example, the following illegal Pascal constants are legal in C:

```
9.
.88
```

Exponents are also specified as in Pascal, with either an e or E representing "ten to the power of." No suffix specifies double values; actually, floating point constants are *always* of type double.

Examples

```
23.
3.1415926
2e3
```

Character Constants
Character constants are the same in C and Pascal, being enclosed by single quotation marks (apostrophes):

```
'x'
```

where x is any printable character. The value of a character constant is its corresponding code, so the type of a character constant is `int`. Most C implementations use ASCII codes, and the examples we use in this text do as well (for a complete ASCII table, see Appendix D).

C provides an alternative method for representing characters using the form

```
'\d'
```

where d is the code of a character expressed as an octal constant of up to three digits. This provides a convenient way to express, in particular, nonprintable characters. For example, the character constant

```
'\015'
```

represents the ASCII character with the octal code 015 (decimal 13). The leading 0 in `'\015'` is not required; that is, `'\015'` is equivalent to `'\15'`. Leading zeros are traditionally used to make a number three digits long, for example, `'\003'`, `'\007'`, and so on.

The backslash character \ is often called an **escape character** because it is used to escape from the usual meaning of the character following it. For example, the expression

```
'015'
```

would be illegal because the quotes should enclose a *single* character, not three characters, unless the quoted string represents an escape sequence. Several escape sequences (in addition to the numeric escape codes) are defined to represent various frequently used nonprintable characters. These are

NEWLINE (LINEFEED)	(LF)	`'\n'`
CARRIAGE RETURN	(CR)	`'\r'`
FORMFEED	(FF)	`'\f'`
TAB	(HT)	`'\t'`
BACKSPACE	(BS)	`'\b'`
NULL CHARACTER	(NUL)	`'\0'`(\ followed by zero)

Two other printable characters also have to be escaped:

BACKSLASH	`'\\'`
SINGLE QUOTE	`'\''`

2.5 ARITHMETIC EXPRESSIONS

As in Pascal, a C expression consists of one or more operands combined in some manner with a variety of operators. Remember, however, that (unlike Pascal) an expression followed by a semicolon becomes a statement. A semicolon by itself represents a *null* statement.

Standard Operators
The following arithmetic operators are defined identically in both Pascal and C:

> **Unary operators:**
>
> Unary minus   −
>
> **Binary operators:**
>
> Addition   +
>
> Subtraction   −
>
> Multiplication   *
>
> Real division   /

There is no unary + in C. (In the proposed ANSI C standard [Ans86] a unary + is defined.)

The other operators differ slightly:

	Pascal	**C**
Integer division	DIV	/
Modulo	MOD	%

As you can see from this table, the division operator / is *overloaded*: If its operands are of type `int`, it performs integer division (with truncation); if its operands are of type `double`, it performs floating point division.

Arithmetic operators in C have the same precedence as in Pascal. (See Appendix B for a complete table of precedence and associativity.)

We describe the boolean operators provided in C in Chapter 3.

Example 2.5.1

```
int i = 3,  j = 7;
j = j / 3;          Integer division, so j gets 2
j = i % 2;          Modulo, j gets 1
```                                                                 ∎

Special Operators
C provides some additional operators for which no equivalents exist in Pascal. These offer a convenient shorthand notation for certain common types of operations:

Increment by one	++
Decrement by one	--

Both operators can be used as either a prefix or a suffix in an expression, with slightly different effects. For example, if ++ is used as a prefix operator, as in

    ++exp

exp is first incremented, and then this incremented value is returned as the value of the expression. The similar

    exp++

returns the original value of *exp* as the value of the expression, and then increments *exp* by one. The effects of this operator are commonly referred to as pre-increment and post-increment. The -- operator is similar: It performs either a pre-decrement or a post-decrement. With both operators, *exp* must be an l-value. For example, both

    `123++`

and

    `--(x * y)`

are illegal.

Example 2.5.2

```
int i = 3,
    j = 2,
    k;

i++;                    i gets 4
j = ++i;                i gets 5, j gets 5
j = i++;                i gets 6, j gets 5
k = (--j + 3);          j gets 4, k gets 7
```
           ■

Other Assignment Operators
C also provides a shorthand notation for some assignment operations. Any assignment of the form

    l-value = l-value op exp

where *op* is a binary operator, can be abbreviated to

    l-value op= exp

Examples of assignment operators that can be formed using this technique are

$$
\begin{array}{ll}
l\text{-}value \mathrel{+}= exp & l\text{-}value = l\text{-}value + exp \\
l\text{-}value \mathrel{-}= exp & l\text{-}value = l\text{-}value - exp \\
l\text{-}value \mathrel{*}= exp & l\text{-}value = l\text{-}value * exp \\
l\text{-}value \mathrel{/}= exp & l\text{-}value = l\text{-}value / exp \\
l\text{-}value \mathrel{\%}= exp & l\text{-}value = l\text{-}value \% exp
\end{array}
$$

Some compilers consider these assignment operators two separate tokens, whereas others treat them as a single token (and so do not accept whitespace between the operator portion and the =). Thus it is better to avoid, for example,

```
i + = 2;
```

Example 2.5.3

```
int i = 1,
    j = 2;

i += j;         i = i+j, so i gets 3
j %= (i++);     j gets 2, i gets 4
j *= i + 1;     j = j*(i+1) = 10, not j = j*i + 1
```

■

We continue the discussion of C expressions in Section 3.1.

2.6   TERMINAL INPUT/OUTPUT

In this section, we introduce the basic tools for **terminal I/O.** Unlike Pascal, standard C does not define any I/O routines as part of the language itself. Rather, a standard library contains several functions that implement I/O. The principal reason for this approach is that since one of the most machine-dependent features of a programming language is its input/output routines, by separating the machine-independent and machine-dependent aspects of a language, it is simpler to adapt it to work on another computer.

The `stdio.h` **Header File**
The basic routines are defined in the standard C library for terminal I/O. It is a good practice to include a special **header** file called `stdio.h` using the C directive

```
#include <stdio.h>
```

since some compilers require it if the standard I/O routines are to be used. Note that the name is enclosed by angle brackets. We describe this command, a part of the C preprocessor, in detail in Chapter 5. In

Chapter 12, we describe the information typically found in the `stdio.h` header.

Single Character I/O

To *output* a single character, C provides the function

```
putchar(c)
```

where c is an integer valued expression representing the code of the character to be output (a more complete description is given in Section 6.2). For *reading* characters, the parameterless int function

```
getchar()
```

is defined, which returns the ordinal value of the character read using buffered, echoed input. A parameterless function must have a pair of empty parentheses ( ) when called.

Example 2.6.1   The following program reads two characters and displays them in reverse order, separated by a tab and terminated by end-of-line:

```
#include <stdio.h>
main()
{
        int c, d;

        c = getchar();
        d = getchar();
        putchar(d);
        putchar('\t');
        putchar(c);
        putchar('\n');
}
```

For example, if the input is

```
af
```

the output would be

```
f    a
```

We have used int variables c and d to store the characters read.   ∎

Formatted I/O

Of course, getchar and putchar provide a very limited form of I/O—they can read and write *single* characters only. C provides two other routines:

```
printf    (stands for print formatted)
scanf     (stands for read formatted)
```

Both routines, though powerful, are somewhat involved. To be able to write working programs, we will therefore now explain only how they can be used to read and write simple data. We give a complete description of these two routines in Appendix C.

To input an integer value, use

```
scanf("%d", &i);
```

where i is an integer variable. Note the ampersand & preceding the variable i. As we explain in Chapter 7, & is the address operator. It returns the address of the memory object specified as its argument and is needed to tell scanf where to store the value it reads. In general, if an argument of a function is to be modified, it has to be preceded by an ampersand.

To output an integer expression *exp*, use

```
printf("%d", exp);
```

No ampersand is required here because the argument *exp* will not be modified.

Example 2.6.2   The following program reads in an integer value and outputs this value incremented by 12:

```
#include <stdio.h>
main()
{
    int i;

    scanf("%d", &i);
    printf("%d", i + 12);
}
```
∎

Example 2.6.3   The following program reads two integer values and outputs the sum and the product of these values:

```
#include <stdio.h>
main()
{
    int i, j;

    scanf("%d", &i);
    scanf("%d", &j);

    printf("%d", i + j);
    printf("%d", i * j);
}
```

For example, if the input is

    3 5

the output would be

    815

The output produced by this program is not very readable because the two output values are not separated.   ∎

The Format Control String

The quoted string argument of `scanf` and `printf` is called a **format control string**. Its contents control the format in which other arguments are input or output. Normally, a format control string contains so-called **conversion specifications**, special character sequences preceded by a %. In `printf`, the control string may also contain character sequences not preceded by a %; these are simply output exactly as they are given. For example, in the preceding `printf` statement, we could use

    printf("The sum is %d ", i + j);

Assuming the value of i + j is 123, this statement would print

    The sum is 123

To print a % sign, the character must be preceded by another percent sign. For example, to print the message

    Mark is 100%

we would use

    printf("Mark is 100%%");

Double quotes are used here rather than single quotes because a format control string is an instance of a **string constant,** and in C, double quotes are used for string constants.

Escaped characters (as described in Section 2.4) can also be used. Thus, the string constant

    "hello\n"

which does not contain any conversion specifications, will be interpreted by `printf` as: Display the letters h, e, l, l, o, and then the character

\n, which means go to the next line. Similarly,

```
printf("hello, world");
```

would display

```
hello, world
```

whereas

```
printf("hello,\nworld");
```

would display

```
hello,
world
```

and

```
printf("hello\tworld\n");
```

would display

```
hello    world
```

To output nonprintable and other special characters in a string constant, they have to be escaped. For example,

```
printf("\007error!");
```

causes the terminal bell to ring when it displays the error message, and

```
printf("\\");
```

outputs a backslash.

Since double quotes enclose string constants, to include a double quote in a string constant, it also *must* be escaped; for example,

```
"a string constant containing a \" character"
```

The number of arguments in the I/O functions may be greater than two, but for each expression, there must be a corresponding conversion specification in the format control string. Not following these rules is a frequent source of errors.

With this more complete definition of `printf`, Example 2.6.3 can be rewritten as follows:

```
...
    int i, j;

    scanf("%d%d", &i, &j);
    printf("The sum of %d and %d is: %d\n", i, j, i + j);
    printf("The product of %d and %d is: %d\n", i, j, i * j)
...
```

If the input was

    62 3

the output produced would be

```
The sum of 62 and 3 is: 65
The product of 62 and 3 is: 186
```

■

Several conversion specifications must be used to output values of different types (so unlike Pascal, I/O operations in C are *not* overloaded).

The following table lists some of the defined conversion specifications. For a complete list, refer to Appendix C.

character	c	
integer	d	
long	ld	
float	f	
double	lf	(long float)
hex	x	(or X)
octal	o	
string	s	

In printf, the conversion specification %f is used to output both floats and doubles, whereas in scanf, %f is used for floats, and %lf is used for doubles. All these conversion specifications *must* be used properly, or the I/O routines will take meaningless action.

Example 2.6.1 can now be rewritten as follows:

```
#include <stdio.h>
main()
{
    char c, d;

    scanf("%c%c", &c, &d);
    printf("%c\t%c\n", d, c);
}
```

In this version, we had to change the declarations of c and d from int to char because the conversion specification %c specifies a character. Character and integer expressions can be freely intermixed in *output* operations. For example, the statement

```
printf("%c\t%d", c, c);
```

outputs the character represented by c followed by the ASCII code of c.

As we explain in Appendix C, scanf skips whitespace looking for the longest data field that matches the specification given in the corresponding control string for all conversion specifications except %c. As an example, assume the user enters the text a12 1.2 when the following program fragment is executed:

```
char c;
int i;
double f;

scanf("%c%d", &c, &i);       Reads the a and the 12
printf("%d%c%c", ++i, ' ', ++c);   Prints 13 b
scanf("%lf", &f);            Reads the 1.2
printf("%f", f);             Prints 1.2
```

Example 2.6.4 The following program reads the number of hours and hourly pay and displays the corresponding salary:

```
#include <stdio.h>
main ()
{
        double pay;
        int hours;

        printf("Enter number of hours and hourly pay: ");
        scanf("%d%lf", &hours, &pay);
        printf("\nThe salary is: %7.2f\n", hours * pay);
}
```

The conversion specification %7.2f specifies a field width of 7, with 2 digits after the decimal. For example, the output might look like

```
The salary is:   638.27                                      ■
```

Finally, another way of displaying string constants is to use the conversion specification %s:

```
printf("%s","hello,world!");
```

We postpone our complete discussion of string I/O until Chapter 10.

2.7   TYPE CONVERSIONS, NEW DATA TYPES: `typedef`

C allows both explicit and implicit type conversion.

Implicit Conversions

The types of operands of C expressions may in some cases be *automatically (implicitly) converted* to other types. Two rules specify these type conversions:

1. In expressions, all values of type `float` are converted to `double` *before* any operation is performed. Thus the `float` type is justified only in arrays and structures (to save memory). Otherwise, `float` is merely a synonym for `double`. Similarly, all `short` and `char` values are converted to `int` in arithmetic expressions.

   Example

   ```
   float f, g;
   ... f + g ...
   ```

   Here, the values of f and g are converted to type `double`; then addition is performed.

2. If two operands of an expression have different types, the type of the operand with the lower priority type is converted to the higher priority type, according to the following hierarchy:

   ```
   int → unsigned → long → double
   ```

   with `int` having the lowest priority and `double` the highest.

   Example

   ```
   int i = 3;
   long j = 4;
   ... i + j ...
   ```

In the preceding expression, i is converted to the type `long` when the addition is performed.

The type of an arithmetic expression is the type of the operand with the highest type precedence.

In an assignment expression, the type of the expression on the right-hand side is converted to the type on the left-hand side, which is the type of the result.

Now consider the following examples:

```
char c;
int i;
float f;
```

(a) c = 2;

Here, 2 is converted to the type char; that is, it becomes the character that has an ASCII code of 2 (control-B). This, then, is the same as Pascal's c := CHR(2). If this assignment was followed by

```
c++;
```

the value c would be 3 (control-C).

(b) ... (c - '0') ...

The value of this expression is the numeric value of character c, assuming it is a digit; in Pascal, ORD(c) - ORD('0').

(c) i = 'a';

In Pascal, i := ORD('a')

(d) i = 'a' + 1;

In Pascal, i := ORD('a') + 1

(e) i = 2.6;

Convert 2.6 to int, truncating, so i gets 2.

(f) f = 2;

Convert 2 to 2.0 and assign it to f.

Converting signed characters to integers may cause some problems because the leftmost bit may, as a result of the conversion, be treated as a sign bit (recall our discussion of sign extension in Section 1.3). Thus in the following example:

```
int i;
char c;
...
i = c;
```

the value of i may be negative after the assignment is done. If it is negative, the reverse assignment,

```
c = i;
```

would not restore the original value of c. For a similar reason, character constants such as '\375' may be treated as negative.

Explicit Conversion

An expression may be explicitly converted to an expression of another type using **type casting.** The type of the cast expression

$$(typ)\ \ exp$$

is converted at *compile-time* to *typ* regardless of the type of *exp*. Here, *typ* may be any type identifier. (We offer a complete description of the allowed forms of *typ* in Section 7.4.4.)

Examples

(int) *charExp*	Ordinal value of character expression *charExp*
(char) *intExp*	Character with the ordinal value of integer expression *intExp*
(int) *floatExp*	Truncates the float expression *floatExp*
(float) *intExp*	Converts the integer expression *intExp* to a float
(double) *floatExp*	Converts the float *floatExp* expression to a double

Casting is *necessary* in a variety of cases. Consider the following example:

```
int i = 10;
double f;

f = sqrt((double)i);
```

Here, we assume sqrt is the square root function. It takes a single double argument, and since no automatic conversion takes place in this context (see Section 6.2), the integer i must be cast to the type double.

Example 2.7.1   The following program reads a double value and displays this value truncated:

```
#include <stdio.h>
main()
{
    double f;

    scanf("%lf", &f);
    printf("The float value %10.2f\t", f);
    printf("truncated is %d\n", (int)f);
}
```

■

A cast expression is not an l-value, which means, for example, the assignment

```
(int)f = 3;
```

is illegal. We will further demonstrate casting in later chapters.

Defining New Types

C provides a tool to define a *synonym* for an existing data type. The syntax is

```
typedef existingType newType;
```

A typedef statement is terminated by a semicolon. (The complete syntax of typedef is more complicated than shown here, so we will discuss it more fully later.) The meaning of this statement is similar to Pascal's TYPE declaration:

Pascal	**C**
TYPE *newType* = *existingType*;	typedef *existingType* *newtype*;

Example

```
typedef int INTEGER;
typedef float REAL;

main()
{
    INTEGER i;
    REAL r;
    ...
}
```

We will give more examples of type definitions in the following chapters.

THINGS TO REMEMBER

All keywords in C are in lowercase.

Division / is overloaded, functioning as integer division with truncation for integer arguments, and real division otherwise.

Assignment is an expression. Any expression becomes a statement if followed by a semicolon.

If the right-hand side of an assignment is of a primitive data type, it is automatically converted to the type of the left-hand side according to C type hierarchy.

Use `float` only if you want to save memory; otherwise, use `double`.

In arithmetic expressions, operands are of one of four types: `unsigned`, `int`, `long`, or `double`. Operands of other types are converted to one of these types.

The number of output expressions in `printf` must match the number of conversion characters.

COMMON ERRORS

`i = +2;`	There is no unary + operator
`main();` `{ ... }`	; should not be here
`i + = 2;`	Avoid whitespace between the operator portion and the = in assignments
`printf("%d%d",i);`	Too few arguments
`int i;` `scanf("%d", i);`	Should be `scanf("%d", &i)`
`char c;` `scanf("%d", &c);`	Should be `scanf("%c", &c)`

EXERCISES

1. Find all syntactic errors in the following programs:

   a.
   ```
   main
   {
       i : integer;
       i := 2;
   }
   ```

   b.
   ```
   main
   {
       integer i = 3; k = 4;
       i = k + 1 = 3;
   }
   ```

2. Determine the decimal value of the following constants:

   a. `02`
   b. `034`
   c. `0x17`
   d. `'\007'`
   e. `'\b'`

3. Given the declarations,

```
int i = 3, j = 5;
```

find the values of the following expressions, and include the values
of the variables i and j after an expression is evaluated.
a. (i / 2) + 4
b. (j % 3) * i
c. (i++) - (--j)
d. j = (i += 2)

4. Given the declarations,

```
int a = 2, b = 2, c = 1, d = 0, e = 4;
```

determine the value of each of the following expressions:
a. a++ / ++c * --e
b. --b * c++ - a
c. -b - --c
d. ++a - --e
e. e / --a * b++ / c++
f. a %= b = d = 1 + e / 2

5. Give the printf statement that produces the following output:

```
J. Bond \ Apt. #645 N.Y.,N.Y. \ "Agent 007"
USA
```

6. Show the output of the following program:

```
#include <stdio.h>
main()
{
     int i = 2,
         j = 5;

     printf("%d ", ++j);
     printf("%d ", i -= ++j);
     printf("%d %d\n", i, j);
}
```

7. Show the output produced by the following program:

```
#include <stdio.h>
main()
```

```
    {
        int   i = 66;
        char  c = 'A';
        float f = 43.5;

        printf("%d %.1f %c\n", i, f, c);
        printf("%d %d %d\n", i, (int)f, c);
        printf("%c %d\n", c + 1 , c);
    }
```

Note the conversion of f to an integer type using (int) casting in
the second printf.

8. Show the output of the following program:

```
#include <stdio.h>
main()
{
    int i = 0,
        j = 1,
        k = 2;

    printf("\nj=%d", j);
    printf("\nk=%d", k);
    j = i == 1;
    printf("\nj=%d", j);
    i = j = k % 3;
    printf("\ni=%d", i);
    j += -i++ + ++k;
    printf("\ni=%d j=%d k=%d", i, j, k);
    printf("\ni=%d j=%d k=%d", i, j, k);
}
```

9. Write a program that inputs a character, increases the ASCII code
   of this character by 1, and then outputs this new character.

   Example: Input :   A   (65 ASCII)
                 Output: B   (66 ASCII)

10. a. Write a program that inputs two characters (both in the range of
       '0'..'9' and 'A'..'F') that represent a hexadecimal number and out-
       puts its equivalent decimal value.

       Example: Input: 3A
                    Output: 58

b. Write a program that inputs an integer greater than 15 and less than 256 and outputs it as two characters that represent its hexadecimal value.

> Example: Input :   58
>   Output: 3A

11. Write a program that prompts the user to enter a float number that represents the price of an item and outputs this price with sales tax included, where the sales tax is 10% of the initial price.

```
Example: Enter the price of the item: 100
         The price including sales tax (10%) is 110.00
```

12. Write a program that prompts the user to enter the base and height of a triangle (both `float` values), computes the area of the triangle, and then outputs this area, along with the data given.

```
Example: Enter base length and height of triangle: 5 6
         The area of a triangle with base = 5 and
         height = 6 is 15
```

13. Write a program that prompts the user for the length and width of a room floor in meters (both `float` values) and outputs the area of the floor and the total cost of the carpet (at $10.00 per square meter) to cover this floor.

```
Example: Enter the length and the width of the floor: 4 5
         The area of the floor is 20 square meters
         The cost for the carpet is $200.00
```

14. Write a program that displays

```
**    **    **    **    **
C AS A SECOND LANGUAGE
**    **    **    **    **
```

15. Write a program that reads a three-letter uppercase word and outputs this word in lowercase.

3 Control Structures

PREVIEW   *This chapter introduces the following C constructs: boolean expressions, the comma and conditional expressions, and statements that control program flow—conditional, iterative, selection, and goto.*

REVIEW OF PASCAL CONSTRUCTS

Pascal provides the following control structures:

- Conditional statement: IF
- Iterative statements: REPEAT, WHILE, and FOR

There is no built-in way of exiting from a loop in Pascal other than to let it eventually terminate when its condition is no longer satisfied (unless a goto statement is used). To control the execution of a loop, Pascal programmers often must introduce additional boolean variables and include them as part of a loop's terminating condition.

- Selection statement: CASE

Standard Pascal requires that every possible value be listed in a CASE statement for a particular variable. It does not provide a clause in the CASE statement—as it provides an ELSE clause in the IF statement—to account for the situation when no match is found.

- GOTO statement

A GOTO statement has the form

```
GOTO label
```

where *label* is an integer. Executing this GOTO statement results in a jump to the statement labeled *label*. There are several limitations to where a jump can be made.

**C
CONSTRUCTS**

3.1   BOOLEAN EXPRESSIONS AND PRECEDENCE RULES

As we explained in Chapter 2, no true boolean type exists in C. Instead, the *integer* type can be used for this purpose, with zero meaning false, and a nonzero value meaning true.

The Relational and Boolean Operators
The relational operators

        <   <=   >   >=

are common to both languages, but other relational and boolean operators differ:

	Pascal	**C**
Equality	=	==
Inequality	<>	!=
Logical and	AND	&&
Logical or	OR	¦¦
Negation	NOT	!

Remember that = and == have quite different meanings; for example, if i is an integer variable,

i = 8   Integer expression equal to the value 8 *and* assigning the value 8 to the variable i.

i == 8   Integer expression yielding 1 (true) if i is equal to 8 and 0 (false) if i is not equal to 8. The value of the variable i is not modified.

Logical **and** and logical **or** have semantics different from Pascal's and are commonly called **short circuits**. The arguments of a logical operator are *evaluated from left to right*, and the evaluation is terminated as soon as the result of the expression can be determined. For example, if the expression

b1 && *b2*

is given, *b2* will not be evaluated if *b1* evaluates to 0 (false), since the expression as a whole will evaluate to 0 no matter what *b2* evaluates to. The same is true for ¦¦ except that in this case the second argument is not evaluated if the first argument produces a nonzero value (true), since this will cause the expression as a whole to evaluate to 1 (true).

This is quite useful in certain types of boolean expressions. For example, in the expression

```
(x != 0  &&  1 / x < 1)
```

if x is zero, the second argument will not be evaluated, and therefore no division by zero error will occur. In Pascal, the equivalent expression

```
((x <> 0) AND (1 / x < 1))
```

could cause a run-time error if x were equal to 0.

Precedence and Associativity Rules

The precedence and associativity rules in C are *different* from those in Pascal (see Appendix B). For this reason, we had to use extra parentheses in the Pascal version of the expression above. The most striking difference is that arithmetic operators and comparisons have higher priority than logical operators, thus the illegal Pascal expression

```
(x <> 0   AND   1 / x < 1)
```

is legal in C:

```
(x != 0   &&   1 / x < 1)
```

Examples

```
int j = 1,
    i;
```

(a) `j = j && (i = 2);`   i gets 2 and j gets 1 since j==1, and the expression i=2 is true

(b) `j = j && (i == 3);`   j gets 0

(c) `j = j || (i / 2);`   j gets 1

(d) `j = !j && (i = i + 1);`   i is *not* increased since !j is 0, and j gets 0

Since == has higher precedence than &&, which in turn has higher precedence than =, the parentheses in assignment (b) may be omitted. However, in assignments (a) and (d) they are essential:

```
j = j && i = 2;
```

would be interpreted as

```
j = ((j && i) = 2);
```

(= associates to the right) which is illegal because (j && i) is not an
l-value. If we use ++i in (d) to replace the assignment to i, that is,

```
j = !j && (++i);
```

the parentheses can be omitted because ++ has higher precedence than
&&.   ∎

Be careful not to confuse the boolean operators && and ¦¦ with the
operators & and ¦. As we shall see in Chapter 11, the latter are used for
performing *bitwise* operations and are quite different from the boolean
operators just discussed.

Conditional Expressions

Pascal supports only conditional statements, not conditional expressions
(at least not in a conventional manner). In C, such a feature is provided:

exp ? *exp1* : *exp2*

This stands for

if *exp* then *exp1* else *exp2*

which means the value of the expression as a whole will be either *exp1*
or *exp2* depending on the value of *exp*.

Example 3.1.1
```
int i, k,
    j = 2;

i = (j == 2) ? 1 : 3;      i gets 1
k = (i > j) ? i : j;       k gets maximum of i and j          ∎
```

The parentheses above are not necessary (the conditional expression has
lower precedence in each case) but may be used for readability. Remember that any expression can be made into a statement by following it
with a semicolon; for example,

```
(i == 1) ? i++ : j++;
```

This usage of a conditional expression is not recommended, since the if
statement (which we describe in the following section) is more readable.
Otherwise, the conditional expression is often useful; for example, the
Pascal statement

```
IF (c >= 'a') AND (c <= 'z')
THEN c:= CHR(ORD(c) - (ORD('z') - ORD('Z')));
```

which converts c to uppercase if it is a lowercase letter, may be coded in

C as

```
c = (c >= 'a' && c <= 'z') ? c - ('z' - 'Z') : c;
```

Comma Expressions

Only four operators guarantee that the left operand is evaluated *before* the right operand. We have already described three of these: `&&`, `||`, and `?:`. The fourth of these operators is the **comma operator**, which is used to build expressions of the form

exp1, exp2

These are often referred to as **comma expressions**. The first operand of the comma operator is always evaluated first, with the result of this evaluation, if any, being discarded. The second operand is then evaluated, and the type and value of the result of the comma expression is the same as that of the second operand. The result is *not* an l-value. Consider the following:

```
int i = 2,
    j = 4;

j = (i++, i - j);
```

Here, i first gets the value 3, and then j gets the value −1. The comma operator has the lowest precedence, so the parentheses in the preceding example are necessary. Comma expressions can be very useful, especially in control statements, although many advocates of C discourage their use.

Other than for these four operators, standard C does *not* guarantee the operands' order of evaluation. This allows the compiler to choose whichever order produces more efficient code. Thus the programmer should avoid expressions such as

```
x = 0;
v = (--x) - (x = 4);
```

If the left operand were evaluated first, v would get the value −5, and x would get the value 4. If, however, the right operand were evaluated first, v would get the value −1, and x would get the value 3.

Example 3.1.2   The following program reads two characters from the keyboard and outputs the character with the larger ordinal value:

```
#include <stdio.h>
main()
{
    int c, d;
```

```
        c = getchar();
        d = getchar();
        putchar(c > d ? c : d);
    }
```

Experienced C programmers tend to write concise code, although this type of code is not necessarily more readable or faster. It is important that C programmers be able to understand others' concisely written code. The preceding program can be rewritten as follows:

```
#include <stdio.h>
main()
{
    int c, d;

    c = getchar();
    putchar(c > (d = getchar()) ? c : d );
}
```

Are all these parentheses necessary? Yes they are because the > operator has higher precedence than the = assignment operator; without the parentheses around the assignment, the grouping of operands with operators would not be what was intended. The rule is to *use parentheses if in doubt.*

The preceding example could have been written as

```
#include <stdio.h>
main()
{
    int c, d;

    putchar( (c = getchar()) > (d = getchar()) ? c : d );
}
```

but the order of evaluation of two arguments in the comparison

```
(c = getchar()) > (d = getchar())
```

is *not* determined. In the rewritten program, this does not matter. In general, however, the order of evaluation may be essential.

3.2 THE if STATEMENT

For the most part, the if statements of Pascal and C are similar. In C, however, the keyword THEN is not part of the syntax.

Pascal	C
IF *booleanExp*	if (*exp*)
THEN *stmt*;	*stmt*

The parentheses specified in the C version are mandatory.

If the expression *exp* evaluates to a nonzero value (that is, true), statement *stmt* is executed; if it evaluates to zero, *stmt* is skipped. Because of the nature of C, evaluating the condition typically produces some side effects, as we illustrate in the example.

Example 3.2.1 The following program reads a character and outputs the numerical value of this character if it is a digit:

```
#include <stdio.h>
main()
{
    int c;

    c = getchar();
    if (c >= '0'  &&  c <= '9')
        printf("%d\n", c - '0');
}
```

This can be shortened to

```
if ((c = getchar()) >= '0'  &&  c <= '9')
    printf("%d\n", c - '0');
```

In this version, the condition is evaluated as follows:

- `getchar()` reads a single character and returns its code.
- This code is assigned to the variable c.
- The first (and possibly the second) argument of && is evaluated.
- The value of the && operation is returned.

Since = has lower precedence than >=, without the parentheses surrounding the assignment

```
c = getchar()
```

the condition expression in the preceding `if` statement would be evaluated as follows:

- `getchar()` reads a character and returns its code.
- This code is compared with '0': If this test returns 0, the evaluation of && terminates, and the value 0 is assigned to c; if the test is nonzero, the second argument of && is evaluated by comparing the (still undefined) value of c to '9', and the result of the && (either 0 or 1) is assigned to c. ∎

Like Pascal, the `if` of C may also have an `else` clause:

Pascal   **C**

```
IF    booleanExp           if (exp)
THEN  stmt1                     stmt1
ELSE  stmt2;               else stmt2
```

Examples

```
IF  x < 1                  if (x < 1)
THEN  y := 2;                   y = 2;

IF  x < 1                  if (x < 1)
THEN  y := 2                    y = 2;
ELSE  y := 3;              else y = 3;
```

Pascal programmers should note the *semicolon* that precedes the else clause in the last example. This can be explained as follows: The *then* clause of an `if` is defined as a single statement; therefore without the semicolon, this assignment would be treated as an expression rather than a statement, which is not allowed. The semicolon then simply converts the assignment expression into a statement. This, as we explained in Chapter 2, can be done with any expression.

A **compound statement** (enclosed by braces) must *not* be terminated by a semicolon:

```
IF    booleanExp           if (exp) {
THEN  BEGIN
          stmt1;               stmt1;
          stmt2;               stmt2;

          ...                  ...
          stmtk;               stmtk;
      END                  }    —N.B: no semicolon here
ELSE                       else
      stmt;                    stmt;
```

If the semicolon were used here, the *then* clause would consist of two statements—the compound statement and the null statement—and this would be incorrect.

Pascal's *dangling else* problem also exists in C and is solved in the same way: The `else` is associated with the closest previous `if`.

Example 3.2.2   The following program reads in three real values and displays the largest value:

```
#include <stdio.h>
main()
{
```

```
          double x, y, z, max;
          printf("Enter three real values: ");
          scanf("%lf%lf%lf", &x, &y, &z);
          if (x > y)
               if (x > z)
                    max = x;
               else max = z;
          else if (y < z)
                    max = z;
               else max = y;
          printf("\nThe largest value is %f\n", max);
     }
```

Example 3.2.3   The following program reads in an integer value, and if it is negative, redisplays this value increased by 2; if the value is nonnegative, it reads in another integer and displays the sum of the two values:

```
#include <stdio.h>
main()
{
     int i, j;

     scanf("%d", &i);
     if (i >= 0) {
          scanf("%d", &j);
          printf("%d\n", i + j);
     }
     else printf("%d\n", i + 2);
}
```

The placement of the opening brace for the compound statement follows the Kernighan and Ritchie layout [Ker78]. Some authors, for example Plum [Plu84], prefer a different layout:

```
if (i >= 0)
{
     scanf("%d", &j);
     printf("%d\n", i + j);
}
else printf("%d\n", i + 2);
```

Example 3.2.4   The following program reads in three real values a, b, and c that represent the coefficients of the equation $ax^2 + bx + c = 0$ and outputs the roots of this equation. To do this, we must use the library function sqrt and thus include the header file math.h.

```
#include <stdio.h>
#include <math.h>
main()
```

```
{
        double a, b, c, delta,
         xr = 0,
         xi = 0,
         yr = 0,
         yi = 0;

    printf("Enter three real values: ");
    scanf("%lf%lf%lf", &a, &b, &c);

    if (a == 0)
        if (b == 0)
            printf("Degenerate equation\n");
        else printf("Only one solution: %f\n", -(c/b));
    else {   /* a != 0 */
        a *= 2;
        c *= 2;
        delta = b * b - a * c;
        xr = yr = - b / a;

        if (delta < 0) {
            delta = sqrt(-delta);
            xi = delta / a;
            yi = -xi;
        }
        else if (delta > 0) {
            delta = sqrt(delta) / a;
            xr += delta;
            yr -= delta;
        }

        printf("\nFirst solution:  %f + i*(%f)\n", xr, xi);
        printf("\nSecond solution: %f + i*(%f)\n", yr, yi);
    }
}
```                                                        ■

Finally, an if statement of the form

```
if (exp != 0) ...
```

where *exp* is an integer expression, can be replaced by

```
if (exp) ...
```

3.3 ITERATIVE STATEMENTS

In C, there are three kinds of **iterative** statements: the while statement, the do statement, and the for statement.

3.3.1   The while Statement

Like Pascal, C also provides a while statement:

Pascal	C
WHILE *booleanExp* DO *stmt*;	while (*exp*) *stmt*

Example

```
WHILE x < 1 DO x := x + 1;    while (x < 1) x++;
```

The semantics of the two versions are identical. Note again the need for parentheses in C's version of the while loop and the absence of the do.

The break and continue Commands
Two special statements in C help to control program flow and are especially useful with iterative statements:

break   Terminates the *innermost* enclosing loop

continue   Jumps to the bottom (end) of the *innermost* enclosing loop, thereby forcing the next iteration of the loop to take place

These statements make it somewhat easier to exit from loops as compared to Pascal. No need is there, as in Pascal, to use artificial boolean variables to control the execution of a loop.

Example 3.3.1   The following program reads ten characters and outputs the ASCII value of the largest input character:

```c
#include <stdio.h>
main()
{
    int c    = 0,
        maxi = 0,
        aux;

    while (c < 10) {
        if ((aux = getchar()) > maxi)
            maxi = aux;
        c++;
    }
    printf("The largest ASCII value: %d\n", maxi);
}
```

This example can be rewritten so that the compound statement is not needed:

```
while (c++ < 10)
    if ((aux = getchar()) > maxi)
        maxi = aux;
printf("The largest ASCII value: %d\n", maxi);
```

Let us modify this program further so that it will stop looking for the maximum value if a control character (any character that has an ASCII code less than 32) is input:

```
while (c++ < 10) {
    if ((aux = getchar()) < 32)
        break;
    if (aux > maxi)
        maxi = aux;
}
printf("The largest ASCII value is: %d\n", maxi);
```

As you can see, no need exists to combine all conditions that control the loop as part of the condition expression. Instead, they can be placed wherever they are logically related to the code. Often useful is a loop with an indeterminate stop condition terminated by the break statement:

```
while (1) {
    if ((aux = getchar()) < 32)
        break;
    if (aux > maxi)
        maxi = aux;
    if (c++ == 10)
        break;
}
printf("The largest ASCII value: %d\n", maxi);
```

If you want to discard nonprintable characters rather than abort the loop when one is read, you could use the continue statement:

```
while (1) {
    if ((aux = getchar()) < 32)
        continue;
    if (aux > maxi)
        maxi = aux;
    if (c++ == 10)
        break;
}
printf("The largest ASCII value: %d\n", maxi);
```                        ∎

The body of a loop may be empty, with the condition itself performing all the required operations. For example, the loop

```
while (getchar() == ' ')
    ;
```

will skip all blanks, and

```
while ((c=getchar()) == ' '  ¦¦  c == '\t' ¦¦ c == '\n')
    ;
```

will skip all whitespace (blanks, tabs, and end-of-lines). To emphasize that the body of the while is empty, the semicolon, representing this *null* statement, is placed on a separate line.

3.3.2   The do Statement

An equivalent of Pascal's REPEAT statement is not directly available in C. However, there is a form of the while statement in which the condition is tested at the *end* of the loop rather than at the beginning.

Pascal	C
REPEAT *stmt*	do *stmt*
UNTIL NOT *cond*;	while (*expr*);

Example

REPEAT i := i − 2	do i −= 2;
UNTIL i <= 0;	while (i > 0);

The do is a keyword, and the terminating semicolon is required. The NOT is included in the REPEAT statement to emphasize an important difference between Pascal's REPEAT statement and C's do statement: In C, the loop terminates when the condition is 0 (false), whereas in Pascal, the REPEAT loop continues to execute until the condition becomes true. Unlike in Pascal's REPEAT statement, the body of C's do statement is a single statement, so braces { . . . } must be used if more than one statement is to be used in the body of the loop.

Example 3.3.2   The following program uses the well-known Euclid algorithm to compute the greatest common divisor of two integer values:

```
#include <stdio.h>
main()
{
    int m, n, k, result;
```

```
        printf("Enter two integers: ");
        scanf("%d%d", &m, &n);
        if (m > 0 && n > 0) {
            do {
                k = n % m;
                if (k == 0)
                    result = m;
                else {
                    n = m;
                    m = k;
                }
            }
            while (k > 0);
            printf("The greatest common divisor is: %d\n",
                    result);
        }
        else printf("Nonpositive values not allowed\n");
}
```

3.3.3 The `for` Statement

The last type of loop we will look at is the `for` statement:

Pascal	C
FOR *controlVar* := *start*	for (*exp1*; *exp2*; *exp3*)
TO *stop*	*stmt*
DO *stmt*;	

Example

FOR i := 1 TO 10 DO	for (i = 1; i <= 10; i++)
WRITE(i);	printf("%d",i);

In general, there is no specific *control variable* as there is in Pascal. Moreover, definitive *start* and *stop* values are not used. The easiest way to describe the semantics of C's for statement is in terms of an equivalent `while` statement:

```
exp1;
while (exp2) {
    stmt
    exp3;
}
```

Thus, *exp1* is evaluated only once before the loop, *exp2* is used to control the execution of the loop and is essentially a stop condition rather than a stop value for the control variable, and *exp3* typically performs some action such as incrementing or decrementing a variable (which is subsequently tested in *exp2*). Any of the three expressions may be omitted. This gives the for statement great power and flexibility. Both break and continue can be used to control the execution of a for loop.

Consider the following:

```
int i = 0;

for (i = 0; i < 10; i++)
    putchar('a' + i);
```

When executed, this loop will display the letters a, b, ..., j. Since i is initialized in the declaration, its initialization in the for loop can be omitted:

```
for (; i < 10; i++)
    putchar('a' + i);
```

The expression i++ can be moved into the body of the loop:

```
for (; i < 10; )
    putchar('a' + i++);
```

or the body could be moved and made part of *exp3*:

```
for (; i < 10; putchar('a' + i), i++)
    ;
```

In this example, the third expression is a *comma* expression: First putchar is called; then i is increased. The value of this comma expression is discarded, and the side effect of its evaluation corresponds to the next step of the for statement. The comma *cannot* be replaced by a semicolon, since the for statement expects three (possibly empty) expressions.

The following loop is yet another version of the maximum character example:

```
for (c = 0; c++ < 10 && (aux = getchar()) >= 32;
    maxi = (aux > maxi) ? aux : maxi)
        ;
```

If a for loop with a body is preferred, the following could be used:

```
for (c = 0; c < 10 && (aux = getchar()) >= 32; c++)
    if (aux > maxi)
        maxi = aux;
```

The two semicolons in the for are *mandatory* even if all the expressions they separate are omitted:

```
c = 0;
for ( ; ; ) {
    if (! (c < 10 && (aux = getchar()) >= 32))
        break;
    if (aux > maxi)
        maxi = aux;
    c++;
}
```

The preceding loop does not have an explicit stop condition and must be exited using a break statement.

The comma operator is often used in for statements. For example, to compute the sum of integers from 1 to 10, we could use

```
int i, sum;

for (i = 1, sum = 0; i <= 10; sum += i, i++)
    ;
```

and to compute the product of all odd integers from 3 to 9, the following would work:

```
int i, product;

for (i = 3, product = 1; i <= 9; product *= i, i += 2)
    ;
```

This example demonstrates the flexibility of C's for statement; Pascal's only allows the control variable to be incremented or decremented by 1.

Example 3.3.3 The following program computes the Newton symbol i over k using the formula

$$\binom{i}{k} = \frac{i!}{k! \, (i - k)!}$$

```
#include <stdio.h>
main()
{
    int i, k, j,
        result = 1;

    printf("Enter two positive integers: ");
    scanf("%d%d", &i, &k);
```

```
        if (i >= k && k >= 0) {
            for ( j = 0;  j < k;  j++)
                result *= (i - j) / (j + 1);
            printf("Newton symbol %d over %d is %d\n", i, k,
                    result);
        }
        else printf("Incorrect data\n");
}
```
■

3.4 THE switch STATEMENT

C's switch statement is equivalent to Pascal's CASE statement, although they have somewhat different syntaxes. An option of the switch statement that standard Pascal does not support is the ability to specify a **default** action. This default action is executed when the switch expression does not evaluate to any of the values specified as case labels:

Pascal	C
CASE *exp* OF	switch (*exp*) {
l1, *l2*, ..., *lk* : *stmt1*;	case *l1* : *stmts1*; break;
...	...
m1, *m2*, ..., *mn* : *stmtp*;	case *mn* : *stmtsp*; break;
END;	default : *stmts*; break;
	}

In the C version, the expression *exp* must be of type int; for example,

```
switch (c = getchar()) {
case 'a' :
case 'b' :
case 'c' :  putchar('1');
case 'd' :  putchar('2');
default  :  putchar('3');
}
```

C's version of the CASE statement employs two separate keywords, switch and case, as well as an optional default. Unlike Pascal's CASE statement, lists of labels are *not* allowed in C, so the case clause has to be repeated:

```
case l1 :
case l2 :
        . . .
case lk :  stmts1
```

Another difference is that whereas Pascal allows only a single statement for each case (which may be a compound statement), C allows a list of statements separated by semicolons to be specified for each case clause (including the default). As in Pascal, no two case labels within a given switch statement may have the same value.

The semantics of the switch statement is as follows: The expression *exp* is evaluated and compared with the consecutive labels. If there is a match, the corresponding statement is executed, and the next, and the next, and so on. The execution actually continues right into the following cases. The only way to exit from a switch statement after the execution starts at a particular case label is to include a break statement as one of the statements logically associated with that case label.

If a switch is performed and there is no match, the default case is executed. Consider the example from above:

```
switch (c = getchar()) {
case 'a' :
case 'b' :
case 'c' :  putchar('1');
case 'd' :  putchar('2');
default  :  putchar('3');
}
```

If the input is a, b, or c, the output is

```
123
```

If the input is d, the output is

```
23
```

For any other character, the output is always

```
3
```

Adding break would limit the output to a single character:

```
switch (c = getchar()) {
case 'a' :
case 'b' :
case 'c' :  putchar('1');
            break;
case 'd' :  putchar('2');
            break;
default  :  putchar('3');
            break;
}
```

Although the last break is not necessary, it is good programming practice to use it anyway. If another case clause is added later, you may forget to include a break in the preceding case if it had been left out. The break statement may occur in the context of a for, while, do, or switch statement, and it relates to the *innermost* statement of one of these types. Thus if a switch occurs in a while, a break within the switch does not terminate the loop.

The default clause is optional and may be omitted. If it is included, it does not have to be the last case of the switch statement although it will be executed only if no other case labels can be selected; for example,

```
switch (getchar()) {
case 'a' :  printf("You typed an 'a'\n");
            break;
default  :  printf("You did not type an 'a' or 'b'\n");
            break;
case 'b' :  printf("You typed a 'b'\n");
}
```

Is this example, the default clause in the middle of the switch will be executed only if neither an a nor a b is read.

Example 3.4.1   The following code reads characters until an asterisk is encountered and redisplays them, replacing each whitespace character (a space or a tab) with a @ and leaving other characters as they are:

```
int c = 0;

while (c != '*')
    switch (c = getchar()) {
    case ' '  :
    case '\t' :  putchar('@');
                 continue;
    case '*'  :  break;
    default   :  putchar(c);
                 break;
    }
```

The preceding construction is a bit tricky. Since c is initially 0, execution proceeds to the switch statement where a character is input. If either a space or a tab is read, a @ symbol is displayed, and then the continue statement is executed. This terminates the switch statement and causes the immediate reexecution of the while loop; since c is not an asterisk, the switch statement is once again executed (thereby reading the next character from the input). If an asterisk is read, the case clause handling this character simply performs a break. Executing this break does *not* terminate the while loop. The switch is the closest surrounding construct that supports break at the point where the `break` is performed; thus the `switch`, not the `while`, is terminated. After exiting from the `switch` statement, the `while` condition is evaluated once again, and because an asterisk was just read, the `while` statement terminates. Any other character would be handled by the `default` clause of the `switch` and therefore be output without change. ∎

This example does not demonstrate a good programming style; our main purpose here is to show how nested constructs behave when `break` and `continue` are used within them. A better algorithm for the preceding problem is as follows:

```
while ((c = getchar()) != '*')
     switch (c) {
     case ' '  :
     case '\t' :  putchar('@');
                  break;
     default   :  putchar(c);
                  break;
     }
```

Example 3.4.2   The following program reads 80 characters from the standard input and outputs the number of blanks, tabs, asterisks, and lowercase letters found:

```
#include <stdio.h>
main()
{
     int i, c,
         cblank = 0,
         ctabs  = 0,
         cstars = 0,
         clower = 0;

     for (i = 0; i < 80; i++)
         switch (c = getchar()) {
         case ' ' : cblank++;
                    break;
         case '\t': ctabs++;
                    break;
         case '*' : cstars++;
                    break;
         default  : if (c >= 'a' && c <= 'z')
                         clower++;
                    break;
         }

     printf("\nNumber of blanks \t%d\n", cblank);
     printf("Number of  tabs \t%d\n", ctabs);
     printf("Number of asterisks \t%d\n", cstars);
     printf("Number of lowercase letters \t%d\n", clower);
}
```
∎

3.5 THE goto AND return STATEMENTS

Like Pascal, C also provides a goto *label* statement that unconditionally transfers control to the statement with the given *label*. A *label* is any identifier followed by a colon, for example,

```
done:
```

The occurrence of an identifier as a label defines this identifier; unlike in Pascal, explicitly declaring labels is not necessary in C. The scope of a goto statement is limited to a single function. If a label is defined to have the same name as an existing identifier, it does not hide the definition of this identifier. Both the label and the other identifier may be referred to without ambiguity because labels can be used only with the goto statement. These identifiers are called *overloaded* in the same sense that procedures are called overloaded. We elaborate on this in Section 6.3.

In Pascal, the goto statement can be used to jump out of a loop so that it is unnecessary to use a boolean variable. We do not support even this use of the goto statement in C because to exit from a loop, C provides the break and return statements. The only justified application of a goto statement is to jump out of a *nested* loop (see the calculator program in Section 13.1.5).

A return statement terminates the execution of the function that contains this statement. If a return is executed in the main program, the program terminates.

Example 3.5.1 The following program reads a list of integer values terminated by a zero and computes their sum, the sum of the positive numbers only, and the sum of the negative numbers only, and then displays the results. It uses four labels: loop, negn, cont, and print.

```
#include <stdio.h>
main()
{
    int n, sum, sumpos, sumneg;

    sum = sumpos = sumneg = 0;
loop:
    scanf("%d", &n);
    if (n == 0)
        goto print;
    if (n < 0)
        goto negn;
    sumpos += n;
    goto cont;
negn:
    sumneg += n;
cont:
```

```
        sum += n;
        goto loop;
    print:
        printf("The total sum is %d\n", sum);
        printf("The sum of positives is %d\n", sumpos);
        printf("The sum of negatives is %d\n", sumneg);
}
```

The goto statement is often used in Pascal to exit from a function by jumping to its final END. This is not recommended in C because the return statement can be used for this.

One of the arguments against using goto's is that the flow of control in a program and its logical structure are not always clear. A structured version of the preceding program makes this obvious:

```
#include <stdio.h>
main()
{
    int n, sum, sumpos, sumneg;

    sum = sumpos = sumneg = 0;
    while (1) {
        scanf("%d", &n);
        if (n == 0)
            break;
        if (n < 0)
            sumneg += n;
        else sumpos += n;
        sum += n;
    }
    printf("The total sum is %d\n",sum);
    printf("The sum of positives is %d\n", sumpos);
    printf("The sum of negatives is %d\n", sumneg);
}
```

THINGS TO REMEMBER

Use = for assignment, == for comparisons.

Logical && and ¦¦ are short circuits.

Use break to implement multiple exits from loops.

For each case in a switch statement, there should be a break statement unless required otherwise.

COMMON ERRORS

Avoid tricky code, for example,

```
i = i++;
```

In general, avoid side effects in expressions in which the order of evaluation is not guaranteed.

`if (condition) then`	then is not a keyword
`if condition`	Missing parentheses

`if (condition)`
`    x = y`
`else`
`    x++;`
	Missing semicolon

`if (x = 1)`	You probably mean if (x == 1)
`if (c = getchar() == '*')`	Should be if ((c = getchar()) == '*')
`while (...) do`	do should not be here
`for (i = 0; i < 10; i++);` `    x += i;`	The semicolon at the end of the line probably should not be there
`printf("%d", i++,j++);`	Incorrect since i++ and j++ would be interpreted as two arguments to printf, not a comma expression. A pair of extra parentheses will solve this problem: printf("%d", (i++,j++)); Constructions like these are best avoided.

EXERCISES

1. Determine the output of the following programs:

   a.
   ```
   #include <stdio.h>
   main()
   {
        int i;
        scanf("%d", &i);
        if (i >= 4)
             while (i--)
                  ;
        printf("%d", ++i);
   }
   ```

   Assume the input value is 5.

   b.
   ```
   #include <stdio.h>
   main()
   {
        int i;
   ```

```
for (i = 1; i <= 5; ++i)
      switch (i) {
      case 1: printf("\ni=1");
              continue;
      case 2: i = 1;
      case 3: printf("\ni=3");
              i += 2;
              continue;
      case 4: printf("\ni=%d", i++);
              break;
      }
}
```

2. Write a program that inputs N integers (prompts the user for the value N) and outputs the sum of the positive integers, the product of the negative integers, and the number of zeros. If there are no positive or negative integers, output 0, respectively, for the sum or product.

3. Write a program that prompts the user to enter four test marks, five assignment marks, and one exam mark (all are float values given as a percentage of 100).

   Compute the final grade knowing the following:

   Tests   = 40% of final

   Assignments = 15% of final

   Exam   = 45% of final

   Compute the final letter grade knowing the following:

   A = 80% to 100%

   B = 70% to 79%

   C = 60% to 69%

   D = 50% to 59%

   E = 0% to 49%

   Remember to round off correctly when determining the letter grade (for example, 79.5% rounds off to 80% = A).

   Finally, output the final grade as a float value, the corresponding letter grade, and depending on the final letter grade, one of the following messages:

A → "excellent"

B → "good"

C → "fair"

D → "poor"

E → "failure"

Example: Enter four test marks: 75 85 83 90
         Enter five assignment marks: 100 90 95 80 50
         Enter exam mark: 87
         Final grade = 87.20% = A = excellent

4. Write a program that inputs a positive integer n and outputs the result of

$$\frac{1*3*\ldots*(2*n-1)}{2+4+\ldots+(2*n)}$$

If n is not positive, reprompt.

5. Write a program that computes the value of any number raised to the power of another number, the latter being a positive integer or 0. If a negative integer is entered, reprompt.
   The following algorithm should be used in the computation:

$$x^n = \begin{cases} 1 & \text{if } n = 0 \\ x & \text{if } n = 1 \\ \text{square}(x^{n/2}) & \text{if } n \text{ is even and } n > 1 \\ x * \text{square}(x^{n/2}) & \text{if } n \text{ is odd and } n > 1 \end{cases}$$

6. Write a program that reads integer values until the value -1 is encountered and then displays the maximum, the minimum, the sum, and the product of the input values.

7. Write a program that reads a positive integer n and outputs n factorial (that is, n! $= 1 * 2 * 3 * \ldots * (n-1) * n$).

8. Write a program that reads two positive integer values a and b and displays all even numbers that are greater than a and less than b.

9. Write a program that converts a positive number in base 10 to an equivalent number in base 16 (hexadecimal). Do not use the %x

control string to do the conversion; instead, implement your own algorithm.

10. Write a program that reads a real number with one decimal digit and no exponential part and writes a sequence of *'s. The number of *'s is equal to the scaled value of the decimal fractional portion of the number. For example, the value 234.7 would result in an output of *******.

11. Write a program that reads characters from the keyboard until an asterisk is encountered and outputs the characters with the largest and smallest ASCII values.

12. Write a program that reads characters from the keyboard until an asterisk is encountered and displays a single character for each pair of identical successive characters. For example, if the character * appears twice in succession, output a single *; if it appears three times, output a single *; if it appears four times, output two * characters; and so on.

13. Write a program to read in a positive integer value N greater than zero, and output the square of the product of the even integer numbers 2 through 2*N.

14. Write a program that prints n Fibonacci numbers defined as follows:

$$f_1 = f_2 = 1;$$

$$f_n = f_{n-1} + f_{n-2} \qquad \text{for } n >= 3$$

15. Write a program that reads a long integer n from the keyboard and prints n rows of the Pascal triangle:

```
            1
          1  2  1
        1   3  3   1
      1  4   6   4  1
    1   5  10 10 5    1
             . . .
```

16. Write a program that inputs a sum of money in cents (less than $1.00) and outputs the least number of coins (quarters, dimes, nickels, and pennies) needed to make this sum.

```
Example:    Input:    97
            Output:   3 quarters
                      2 dimes
                      0 nickels
                      2 pennies
```

4 An Introduction to File I/O

PREVIEW   *This chapter discusses file operations and testing for end-of-line and end-of-file during I/O in the C language.*

REVIEW OF PASCAL CONSTRUCTS

We now describe the basic **file operations** of Pascal, starting with a brief discussion of some aspects of a typical file system.

Although Pascal distinguishes between two kinds of files, **text files** and **binary files**, text files are just files of characters with some special characters defining the line structure.

From the *implementation's* viewpoint, a **file** is a sequence of bytes stored on some medium, such as a hard disk, in several blocks. The blocks are all the same size and do not have to be consecutive on the disk. The operating system manages a file as it is growing or being accessed sequentially or randomly. Thus from the *user's* viewpoint, a file can be considered a sequence of consecutive bytes on a disk.

Interactive I/O, such as reading from a keyboard or writing to a terminal screen, can also be regarded as file I/O.

To use a file in Pascal, the following steps are required:

- Declare a variable of type TEXT for a text file or FILE OF *sometype* for a binary file, for example,

    ```
    VAR f : TEXT;
    ```

- Associate this variable with a file residing on disk. Since this is not defined in Pascal, the actual mechanism may vary from one implementation to another. For example, in some implementations of Pascal the ASSIGN procedure has to be used:

    ```
    ASSIGN(f, 'TEST');
    ```

which associates file variable f with the disk file called TEST. This is not a standard Pascal operation, and different systems may use different methods for specifying the name of an external file.

- Specify whether the access mode is to be *input* or *output* using, respectively,

    RESET(f);

or

    REWRITE(f);

Both of these operations are defined in standard Pascal.

The actual file I/O operations are the same as the terminal I/O operations with an additional argument specifying the file being accessed, for example,

    READ(f, c);

or

    WRITE(f, c);

For the sake of efficiency, file operations are **buffered**. The run-time system of a language maintains a buffer for each file that has been opened, and all I/O operations are carried out through this buffer. This means, for example, writing a character does not immediately write this character to disk; instead, it places it in an appropriate buffer, and this buffer is written to the disk only when it becomes full. Successive write operations will then fill in this buffer starting from its beginning. In most Pascal implementations, when the program terminates, file buffers are not automatically **flushed** (that is, written to the disk). Therefore, using the CLOSE operation is important; for example,

    CLOSE(f);

closes a file when access to this file has been completed. Besides flushing the file's output buffer, the CLOSE operation makes a request to the operating system to update the file's current status so that future attempts to open this file can be handled properly by the operating system (that is, the file is no longer in use by the program so another program can open it).

To test for **end-of-line** and **end-of-file** on input, Pascal provides two standard functions: EOLN and EOF. Exactly what tests these functions perform to determine whether or not the conditions in question are true depends on the system.

Under a few operating systems, special characters denote end-of-file (for example, control-Z under CP/M); however, most operating systems—MS-DOS, Unix, VAX/VMS, and others—do not need terminators because the operating system maintains the length of the file.

When dealing with the end-of-line terminator, the situation is slightly more complicated because several strategies are commonly used. These include

- A single carriage return
- A single linefeed character
- A carriage return followed by a linefeed

In general, a character stored in a file can be interpreted differently in different contexts. Here, again, we need a brief description of the difference between a **return** (also called a carriage return) and a **linefeed**. In the context of terminal *output*, a return moves the cursor left to the beginning of the line (without advancing it vertically); a linefeed moves the cursor down one line (without moving it horizontally).

When you press the return key, a single character code is generated (ASCII 13) by the terminal hardware. However, depending on the program currently running, two characters, return *and* linefeed, are often sent to the screen. If a file is being created in an editor, internally only a single return may be stored, or a linefeed, or both.

C CONSTRUCTS

4.1 FILE OPERATIONS IN C

We now discuss **file operations**. In C, there is only one kind of file: Files are simply *sequences of bytes*. Pascal programmers may be puzzled by the lack of binary (typed) files and wonder, for example, how an array of records could be easily saved in a file using C. We recognize the importance of this technique and describe in Chapter 12 how this can be done.

The following description of C file operations is limited to the *buffered* file operations. We postpone the discussion of *unbuffered* file operations until Chapter 12.

The basic C type specification used for creating and accessing files is

```
FILE *
```

(Note the two components specified: FILE and an asterisk *, which means "a pointer to a FILE type object." We explain this in detail in Chapter 7.) To declare a file variable f, the code

```
FILE *f;
```

would be used. To declare more than one of these variables, the asterisk *must* be repeated, for example,

```
FILE *f, *g;
```

We are not now in a position to explain the reasons for the various requirements in the preceding file declarations; we will provide the necessary explanations in later chapters.

Opening Files

The principal file operations are

Pascal	C
`ASSIGN(f, 'TEST');`	`f = fopen("TEST", "r");`
`RESET(f);`	

As we mentioned, the ASSIGN operation is not defined in standard Pascal, but many implementations do use it, and those that do not usually provide something similar. RESET is standard and opens the file associated with the file variable parameter for input. In the preceding example, the file TEST is opened. These two Pascal operations are replaced in C by a single function with two arguments. The first argument specifies the **filename**, and the second specifies the **access mode**. In the example, r stands for read. To open a file for output, w is specified as the access mode:

Pascal	C
`ASSIGN(f, 'TEST');`	`f = fopen("TEST", "w");`
`REWRITE(f);`	

Various other access modes exist, and these we discuss in Chapter 12.

Basic File I/O Operations

The basic file I/O operations provided in C are as follows:

1. To **read a single character** from the file f:

   ```
   c = getc(f)
   ```

2. To **write a single character** to the file f:

   ```
   putc(c, f)
   ```

3. **Formatted read** from the file f:

   ```
   fscanf(f, "format control string", arguments)
   ```

4. **Formatted write** to the file f:

   ```
   fprintf(f, "format control string", arguments)
   ```

The operation fclose(f) closes the file. In most C implementations, when a program terminates, the file buffers are flushed. However, it is considered poor programming practice not to close files explicitly because the number of files that can be open at one time is limited.

Example 4.1.1   The following program creates a file TEST containing two integer values that are read from the keyboard:

```
#include <stdio.h>
main( )
{
      FILE *f;
      int  i, j;

      scanf("%d%d", &i, &j);
      f = fopen("TEST", "w");
      fprintf(f, "%d %d\n", i, j);
      fclose(f);
}
```
■

Example 4.1.2   The following program assumes the file TEST1 contains three double values, inputs them, and displays the sum of these values on the screen:

```
#include <stdio.h>
main( )
{
      FILE *f;
      double x, y, z;

      f = fopen("TEST1", "r");
      fscanf(f, "%lf%lf%lf", &x, &y, &z);
      printf("%f\n", x + y + z);
      fclose(f);
}
```

As we describe in Appendix C, fscanf is an integer function that returns the number of items successfully read. Thus an additional test could be added to this program to check whether or not the file TEST1 contains three double values:

```
if (fscanf(f, "%lf%lf%lf", &x, &y, &z) == 3)
      printf("%f\n", x + y + z);
else printf("TEST1 does not contain 3 doubles\n");
```
■

Example 4.1.3   The following program reads up to two characters from the file TEST2 and copies them to the file TEST3. The value returned by fscanf is used to check if there are fewer than two characters in TEST2.

```
#include <stdio.h>
main( )
```

```
{
    FILE *f, *g;
    char c, d;

    f = fopen("TEST2", "r");
    g = fopen("TEST3", "w");

    switch (fscanf(f, "%c%c", &c, &d)) {
    case 1 : fprintf(g, "%c", c);
             break;
    case 2 : fprintf(g, "%c%c", c, d);
             break;
    default: break;
    }

    fclose(f);
    fclose(g);
}
```

■

4.2   TESTING FOR END-OF-LINE AND END-OF-FILE

Testing for End-of-Line

To make programs portable, C uses a special character `'\n'` (which stands for **newline**) to represent the end-of-line character. Most often, this corresponds to either a return or a linefeed. Under Unix systems, lines in files are separated by single linefeed characters, so the `'\n'` character corresponds to a linefeed. This may not be the case with all C systems. To conform to the local operating system's conventions, C may *translate* the `'\n'` character to a return followed by a linefeed on output. The same rules would apply to implementations of Pascal under different operating systems.

Unlike Pascal, C does *not* provide any function to test for end-of-line. The function `getchar` is not a boolean function that indicates when end-of-line has been encountered; instead, it always returns the code of the character read, including the code of `'\n'`. Thus to test for end-of-line, the code

```
if ((c = getchar()) == '\n')
    . . .
```

can be used.

Example 4.2.1   The following program copies a single line from the keyboard and redisplays it (including the end-of-line character):

```
#include <stdio.h>
main()
{
    int c;
```

```
        while ((c = getchar()) != '\n')
            putchar(c);
        putchar(c);                        /* to print end-of-line */
}
```
■

Bear in mind that '\n' is a character like any other character, and that it may be used in all contexts where characters are allowed.

Testing for End-of-File
When end-of-file is encountered, getchar returns the value EOF, which is usually defined as -1 in the file stdio.h (see Chapter 12). Thus a check such as

```
if ((c = getchar()) == EOF)
    ...
```

can be used to test if end-of-file has occurred.

Example 4.2.2 The following program redisplays the characters that you type on the keyboard back to the screen. It terminates when the end-of-file condition is detected.

```
#include <stdio.h>
main()
{
    int c;

    while ((c = getchar()) != EOF)
        putchar(c);
}
```

It is easy to see here that the variable c must *not* be declared as a character. If it were, the -1 returned by getchar would be converted to something other than -1 (depending on the implementation), and the loop would never terminate. For example, if c were declared as an unsigned character, the value -1 would be converted to the value 255 (assuming characters were stored as 8-bit bytes).   ■

Example 4.2.3 The following program reads characters from the file TEST and writes them to the file TEST1:

```
#include <stdio.h>
main()
{
    FILE *f, *g;
    int c;

    f = fopen("TEST",  "r");
    g = fopen("TEST1", "w");
```

```
while ((c = getc(f)) != EOF)
    putc(c,g);

fclose(f);
fclose(g);
}
```

■

Both `fopen` and `fclose` are *functions*, and the values returned by these functions can be used to test whether or not they have been successful.

The function `fopen` returns the value NULL if an error occurs:

```
if ((f = fopen("TEST", "r")) == NULL)
    printf("File cannot be opened\n");
```

(Note: NULL is defined in the standard header file `stdio.h` and is usually equal to 0. We explain this in detail in Chapter 12.)

The function `fclose` returns EOF if an error is detected; otherwise, it returns the value 0:

```
if (fclose(f) == EOF)
    printf("File cannot be closed\n");
```

Example 4.2.4   The following program is a rewrite of Example 4.2.3 with additional error checking:

```
#include <stdio.h>
main()
{
    FILE *f, *g;
    int c;

    if ((f = fopen("TEST", "r")) == NULL) {
        printf("File cannot be opened\n");
        return;
    }
    if ((g = fopen("TEST1", "w")) == NULL) {
        printf("File cannot be opened\n");
        return;
    }
    while ((c = getc(f)) != EOF)
        putc(c, g);
    if (fclose(f) == EOF) {
        printf("File cannot be closed\n");
        return;
    }
    if (fclose(g) == EOF)
        printf("File cannot be closed\n");
}
```

■

Example 4.2.5   The following program reads characters from the keyboard and displays the first character from each nonempty input line:

```
#include <stdio.h>
main()
{
     int c;

     while ((c = getchar()) != EOF)
          if (c != '\n')  {
               putchar(c);
               do
                    if ((c = getchar()) == EOF)
                         return;
               while (c != '\n');
          }
}
```

The if statement within the do takes care of the case when end-of-file occurs before the next end-of-line.   ■

The preceding examples may leave you wishing that C had a function like READLN in Pascal. In Chapter 10, we demonstrate how line-oriented processing can be accomplished by using strings, thereby avoiding some of the difficulties encountered in these examples.

The programs just demonstrated show how Pascal's EOF function is expressed in C. C also provides a *function* that can be used to test if end-of-file has been encountered. The function feof(f) returns EOF if end-of-file has been detected, and 0 otherwise. With this function, the loop in Example 4.2.4 could be rewritten as follows:

```
while (1) {
     c = getc(f);
     if (feof(f))
          break;
     else putc(c, g);
}
```

Example 4.2.6   The following program converts all lowercase letters in the input stream to uppercase:

```
#include <stdio.h>
main()
{
     int c;

     while ((c = getchar()) != EOF)
          putchar(c >=  'a' && c <=  'z' ? c + 'A' - 'a' : c);
}
```
                                                                        ■

Example 4.2.7   The following program finds the length of the longest line in the file
TEST:

```c
#include <stdio.h>
main()
{
    FILE *f;
    int c, longest = 0, counter = 0;

    if ((f = fopen("TEST", "r")) == NULL) {
        printf("Cannot open the file TEST\n");
        return;
    }

    while ((c = getc(f)) != EOF)
        if (c == '\n') {
            if (longest < counter)
                longest = counter;
            counter = 0;
        }
        else counter++;

    if (fclose(f) == EOF) {
        printf("Cannot close the file TEST\n");
        return;
    }
    printf("The length of the longest line is %d\n",
            longest);
}
```

∎

The scanf and fscanf functions return the number of items that have
been successfully read and return EOF if end-of-file is encountered (see
Appendix C). Thus these functions can be used to test whether or not
end-of-file has been reached and whether all the data have been successfully read. We demonstrate this in the following example.

Example 4.2.8   The following program reads a list of integer values from the file TEST
and computes their sum:

```c
#include <stdio.h>
main()
{
    int  current;
    long sum = 0;
    FILE *f;

    if ((f = fopen("TEST", "r")) == NULL) {
        printf("Cannot open file TEST\n");
        return;
    }
```

```
    while (fscanf(f, "%d", &current) != EOF)
        sum += current;

    if (fclose(f) == EOF) {
        printf("Cannot close file TEST\n");
        return;
    }
    printf("The sum is: %ld\n", sum);
}
```

We can do further error checking in this example by testing the value returned by fscanf: If it returns 1, a successful read has been performed; otherwise, either end-of-file has been encountered or the input was invalid, for example, a nondigit was encountered:

```
while (1)
    if (fscanf(f, "%d", &current) == 1)
        sum += current;
    else if (feof(f))
        break;
    else {
        printf("error while reading TEST, aborting\n");
        return;
    }                                                          ■
```

Standard Input and Standard Output

In standard C implementations, normally two file identifiers are defined in the header file stdio.h that may be used in a user's program:

```
FILE *stdin;
FILE *stdout;
```

Neither of these identifiers is an l-value and so may not appear on the left-hand side of an assignment. Usually, the identifier stdin denotes the **standard input stream** (the terminal keyboard), and the identifier stdout denotes the **standard output stream** (the terminal screen). Some implementations, including Unix, define a third stream, stderr, which is intended to be used for displaying error messages. Moreover, in some environments, the input/output streams that these identifiers refer to may be (indirectly) changed, which results in **I/O redirection**. Because this is not specifically a feature of the C language, we discuss the topic in Chapter 14, where we look at some particular implementations of C on different systems.

The identifiers stdin and stdout may be used as arguments in any file operation and cause the operation to refer to the terminal. For example,

```
getc(stdin)
```

is equivalent to

```
getchar()
```

and

```
putc(c, stdout)
```

is equivalent to

```
putchar(c)
```

As we explain in Chapter 5, the terminal I/O operations may actually be defined as *macros* that call the appropriate file I/O operations using stdin and stdout (which is the case in most implementations).

Example 4.2.9   The following program shows how file variables may be used in assignments and also demonstrates how some problems caused by buffered input can be handled.

In Pascal, file variables cannot be used as l-values, but in C they can, with the exception of the predefined identifiers stdin and stdout. Thus we can say

```
f = stdout;
```

if f is a file variable, but we cannot say

```
stdout = f;
```

When performing buffered input, the programmer must be aware that although only a single character may be requested in a given operation (for example, using getchar), an entire line actually can be entered. Moreover, even if only a single character is entered, the user must hit return for that character actually to be read. These extra characters, including the end-of-line character, are stored in the input buffer. Whenever an input operation such as getchar is performed, it first checks if there are any characters in this buffer; if there are, it will read from this buffer rather than from the keyboard. Thus if the user wants to force input to come from the keyboard, the buffer first has to be cleared.

This program asks the user whether the characters read from the keyboard should be output to the file TEST or to the standard output stream. If the user chooses to direct the output to the file TEST, the program checks whether or not this file already exists and, if so, asks the user for confirmation before rewriting the file.

```
#include <stdio.h>
main()
{
    FILE *f;
    int c;

    printf("Enter Y to write to the screen, ");
    printf("any other character to write to TEST: ");

    c = getchar();
    while (getchar() != '\n')
        ;
    /* skip the rest of the line */

    if (c == 'y' || c == 'Y')
        f = stdout;
    else if ((f = fopen("TEST", "r")) != NULL) {
        printf("File exists, overwrite? (Y/N) ");
        c = getchar();
        while (getchar() != '\n')
            ;

        if ( !(c == 'y' || c == 'Y') )
            return;
        if (fclose(f) == EOF) {
            printf("error in closing\n");
            return;
        }

        if ((f = fopen("TEST", "w")) == NULL) {
            printf("can't open TEST\n");
            return;
        }
    }

    printf("Enter your text, terminated by end-of-file\n");
    while ((c = getchar()) != EOF)
        putc(c, f);

    if (fclose(f) == EOF) {
        printf("error in closing\n");
        return;
    }
}
```

The loop

```
while (getchar() != '\n')
    ;
```

reads characters until an end-of-line is encountered. Suppose the user entered Y, followed by a return. The Y would be read by the first getchar, and then the loop would read in and discard the end-of-line character. Without this loop, the end-of-line character would be read by the second getchar and would be interpreted as an answer to the confirmation question. Moreover, if the user had entered Yes followed by a return, the while loop would skip both the e and the s, as well as the end-of-line character. ∎

The ungetc Operation

An operation related to buffered input and performed automatically by scanf and fscanf involves restoring the last character read to the input stream (sometimes called a *push-back* operation). This can be performed explicitly by the user with

```
ungetc(c, f)
```

which pushes the character c back on the input stream f. If successful, this function returns the character c; it returns EOF if for any reason the character c cannot be pushed back. Usually, only one character may be pushed back. ungetc is useful in writing routines that need to look ahead one character at a time, such as routines that read digits and convert them to an integer value. The following example demonstrates this. The program fragment uses the function isdigit, which returns true if its argument is a digit, and false if not.

```
int c, value = 0;

c = getchar();
while (isdigit(c)) {
    value = value * 10 + (c - '0');
    c = getchar();
}
ungetc(c, stdin);
```

THINGS TO REMEMBER

Use an integer variable to read characters from a file.

Always test whether file operations fopen and fclose are successful.

Close files as soon as you do not need them.

COMMON ERRORS

```
if (c = getchar() != EOF)        Should be
                                 if ((c = getchar()) != EOF)
```

```
FILE *f;
close(f);                          Should be fclose(f);
```

EXERCISES

1. Write a program that reads in a number of input lines from the keyboard until end-of-file is encountered. Each line is of the form

   1-or-more-blanks salary 1-or-more-blanks name

   where *salary* is a real number, and *name* is a sequence of characters (possibly including spaces). The program displays the sum of the salaries read and the maximum salary.

2. Assume the file TEST contains at least one line of data. Write a complete program to modify this file in such a way that it will contain exactly two lines. The first line is blank, and the second line is a copy of the first line from the file TEST.

3. Write a program that reads text from the file TEST until EOF is encountered and outputs the length of the longest line found and the number of this line. If several lines rate as being the longest, indicate the first line encountered.

4. Write a program that reads text from standard input until EOF is encountered and outputs the number of words beginning with the letter A. Assume a word consists of any characters except whitespace.

5. Write a program that inputs a single character "key" and then reads text from standard input until the key is found or EOF is detected. If the key is found, output the number of the line it was found on, as well as the number of characters preceding the key and the number of characters following the key on this line.

6. Write a program that reads two files, TEST and TEST1, and writes to the file TEST2 the concatenated contents of the two input files.

7. Write a program to simulate the rock, paper, and scissors game. The game is played as follows:

Paper covers rock	→ paper wins
Scissors cut paper	→ scissors win
Rock crushes scissors	→ rock wins

Read lines from the standard input where each line represents a single game and contains any two of the characters P, R, or S, corresponding to paper, rock, and scissors. If the characters are not in this set, output a message indicating an illegal play. Blanks may appear anywhere on the line.

Output the winner of each game, as well as the overall winner (the player who wins the most games).

Example:

Assume the input text contains the following:

```
R P
R    S
  F  S
    S  P
```

Output:

```
RP
Second player wins game 1
RS
First player wins game 2
FS
Play not legal in game 3
SP
First player wins game 4
First player won two games and second player won one game
The overall winner is the first player
```

8. Write a program that reads characters from the standard input and outputs the number of letters, the number of words, the length of the longest line, and the number of double characters in the text. Double characters means the same two characters in a row, for example, curr.

9. Write a program to compare two files. The program should terminate as soon as it finds two characters that differ and write to standard output the number of the offending line, the first position within this line where the characters differ, as well as the culprit characters. If either of these characters is a nonprintable character, its ASCII code should be displayed. If the input files are identical, an appropriate message should be printed. Include full error checking.

For example, assume the two files being compared are TEST1 and TEST2 and their contents are
file TEST1:

```
First line seems to be
OK but :
here we are
...
```

file TEST2:

```
First line seems to be
OK but :
here we are...
```

The compare program would display

```
Files differ on line #3, position #12
Character from TEST1 is a nonprintable character:
     ASCII code: 10
Character from TEST2:
```

   .

10. Write two programs, one to encode a file and one to decode an encoded file in order to obtain its original contents. The encoding algorithm may be a simple one: For each character in the file, add to its ordinal value an integer N, so that $0 < N < 128$, and then store the character with the resulting code in the output file. The value N should be read by the program. The decode program will simply apply the reverse of the encoding algorithm.

11. Write a program that determines the length of the Nth line of the input file TEST. The program should prompt the user to enter the value of N. Include error checking; that is, check whether the file TEST exists and whether the Nth line exists, and perform any other error check that seems appropriate.

12. Modify the program in Exercise 10 so that it first reads a five character password and then applies the above algorithm cycling through the characters of the password to obtain the value to be added to the next input character. That is, the first character of the input is encoded using the ordinal value of the first character of the password, the second character is encoded with the second character of the password, and so on. When the sixth character of the input file is reached, cycle back to the first character of the password to encode it. Repeat this pattern for every group of five characters.

13. Suppose an input file consists of a number of lines, each of the following form:

a single character (P or S) followed by three real numbers where P indicates a product is to be computed, and S indicates a summation is to be computed. Write a complete C program that reads a file of this form and for each line read displays one of the following:

- The product of the real numbers occurring in the line followed by the message PRODUCT if the first character in the input line is P
- The sum of the real numbers occurring in the line followed by the message SUM if the first character in the input line is S
- The error message

```
LINE # i: wrong data
```

if any of the real numbers are negative (i is the line number).

Example:

Assume the input file contains

```
S 1 2.1 3.4
P 2 -1 3
P 0 0 1
P 1 2 3
```

The output produced by your program should be

```
6.5 SUM
LINE # 2: wrong data
0.0 PRODUCT
6.0 PRODUCT
```

14. Consider the file TEST1, where each line is of the form

age name

and write a C program to copy those lines in TEST1 with *age* < 50 to the file TEST2 and to copy the other lines to the file TEST3.

5 The C Preprocessor

PREVIEW   *This chapter introduces the commands supported by the C preprocessor. We cover the subject of macros, particularly as they are used for defining constants. Then, we discuss conditional compilation and file inclusion.*

REVIEW OF PASCAL CONSTRUCTS

In Pascal, depending on the implementation, the occurrences of constant identifiers in the program text will be either replaced by their values or referred to through a constant table (maintained by the compiler). In the former case, the compiler performs direct *textual replacement* of constant identifiers with their corresponding values. Sometimes this activity is called **macro processing**: Constant identifiers are macros, and their replacement is called **macro expansion**, or macro substitution. In Pascal, macro processing is limited to user-defined constants.

In general, a preprocessor processes the source code before the compilation starts. During this stage, new macros may be defined, or existing macros undefined. Macros are very much like procedures: They may have formal parameters, and they are called with a corresponding list of the actual parameters. A macro call, however, causes a textual replacement of the macro name with the defining text. Therefore, macros are sometimes called **in-line functions**.

C CONSTRUCTS

The C preprocessor recognizes lines of the source text that begin with the character # (pound sign). The preprocessor commands are

`#define` *macroName replacementText*	Define a macro
`#undef` *macroName*	Undefine a macro

`#if` *constantExpression*
...
`#else`
...
`#endif`
	Conditional inclusion of some text depending on the value of *constantExpression*

`#include "`*filename*`"` `#include <`*filename*`>`	Include text from the file *filename*

```
#ifdef macroName                        Conditional inclusion of some
...                                      text depending on whether
#else                                    or not the macro is defined
...
#endif

#ifndef macroName                       Conditional inclusion of some
...                                      text depending on whether
#else                                    or not the macro is undefined
...
#endif

#line constantExpression "filename"     Set line number for the
                                         compiler
```

Because of the preprocessing, macro calls are expanded, being replaced by their defining text, and depending on some conditions, additional files may be *included*, or parts of the source file may be *excluded*. The resulting file will be passed on to the compiler. The preprocessor does *not* check the syntax of C constructs; that is the task of the compiler.

5.1 PARAMETERLESS MACROS

In C, named constants are *macros* or, more specifically, parameterless macros. The syntax of this form of macro is

```
#define macroName macroValue
```

The # character must be in the *first* column although in some implementations, it is allowed to be the first non-whitespace character. *macroName* is any identifier. Macro names are traditionally in uppercase, but this is not required. *macroValue* is the text making up the macro constant and starts from the first nonblank character following the macro name and continues to the end of the line. If more than one line is needed, the continuation character \ (backslash) may be placed at the end of the line to cause the subsequent line to be included as part of the macro definition. This can be repeated for as many lines as necessary.

Examples

```
#define PI            3.14
#define PLUS          +
#define SCREENW       80
#define SCREENH       25
#define LONGMACRO      This is a long macro that takes more \
                       than one line!
```

Note that the replacement text for the last macro does not include the backslash. There is no = character between a macro name and its corresponding value, as is required in Pascal constant definitions, and there is no terminating semicolon in a macro definition; if one were included, it would be considered part of the definition:

Pascal	C
PI = 3.14;	PI 3.14

Macro definitions may be placed anywhere in a program. Usually they are defined at the very beginning of a file before any function definitions. In large programs, macro definitions are often placed near the function they are used in. Where a macro definition occurs determines its scope: Macros are defined from the point where their #define is given to the end of the file, or to where they are undefined.

Example 5.1.1

```
#include <stdio.h>
#define PI 3.14
main()
{
      double r;

      printf("Enter a real value: ");
      scanf("%lf", &r);
      printf("%f\n", r * r * PI);
}
```

The occurrence of PI in the main program is replaced by the macro's defining text, that is, 3.14.   ∎

The C preprocessor maintains a table of macro names that have been defined and their corresponding values. If the defining text contains the name of a macro that has been previously defined, this macro will be expanded. That is, before the value of a macro is stored in the table, the defining text is completely evaluated by expanding all macros referenced in it, for example,

```
#define A    (2 + 4)
#define B    (A * 3)
```

If you have an expression such as

```
B + 1
```

it will be expanded to

```
((2 + 4) * 3) + 1
```

rather than

```
(A * 3) + 1
```

This example also shows why macro values that are not simply constants but instead some sort of expression (like 2 + 4) should be enclosed in parentheses. Without parentheses surrounding 2 + 4, A * 3 would expand to 2 + 4 * 3, which is equal to 14 rather than the expected 18.

Since the length of macro names is not limited, one use of macros is to allow identifiers that are longer than the standard eight characters while still adhering to the standard:

```
#define SCREENWIDTH    SCREENW
#define SortRoutine    SortR
```

In a macro definition, the defining text is a *sequence of tokens*, starting from the first character that is not a blank. Thus blanks that separate a macro name from the defining text and those that follow the defining text (up to the end of line) are not part of the defining text. Comments in the replacement text are skipped. For example, in the definition

```
#define  A /* first comment */ 4 /* second comment */
```

the value of A is 4.

Example 5.1.2   Macros can be used to make C programs appear Pascal-like:

```
#include <stdio.h>
#define PROGRAM  main()
#define VAR                   /* an empty macro */
#define BEGIN    {
#define END      }
#define REAL     float
#define PI       3.14
#define PROMPT   printf("Enter a real value: ")
#define READ     scanf("%lf", &R)
#define PRINT    printf("%f\n", AREA)

PROGRAM
BEGIN
    VAR REAL R, AREA;

    PROMPT;
    READ;
    AREA = R * R * PI;
    PRINT;
END
```

The following definitions illustrate further how macros can be used in C to mimic Pascal, in this case, for control structures:

```
#define THEN    )
#define IF      if (
#define BEGIN   {
#define END     }
#define ELSE    else
```

This allows the following to be written:

```
IF x < 1
  THEN BEGIN x = 1;
            y = 2;
        END
  ELSE x = 2;
```

Unfortunately, some constructs may cause problems. For example, if these macros are used to form

```
IF x < 1
  THEN x = 1
  ELSE x = 2
```

a compile error would be generated because a semicolon is missing. There is no simple solution to this problem; if you redefine the ELSE macro to be

```
#define ELSE ; else
```

the last example would work, but the previous one would not. Of course, we are not suggesting that anyone would use macros to simulate Pascal; we are just demonstrating how macros are defined and expanded.

Example 5.1.3   The following program inputs a line of text and redisplays it with control characters printed in the form $^\wedge x$; that is, a control-A is displayed as $^\wedge$A, a control-B as $^\wedge$B , and so on:

```
#include <stdio.h>
#define PRINT    32
#define OFFSET   ('A'-1)
#define EOLN     '\n'
#define CARET    '^'
```

```
main()
{
     int i;

     while ((i = getchar()) != EOLN)
          if (i < PRINT) {
               putchar(CARET);
               putchar(i + OFFSET);
          }
          else putchar(i);
}
```

Macros are *not* expanded within string and character constants. For example, if a macro is defined as

```
#define A 3
```

and then used in expressions

```
"hello A"
```

and

```
'A'
```

it is not expanded. For the same reason, the program

```
#include <stdio.h>
#define STAR *
#define STAR2 **
#define STAR3 ***
main()
{
     printf("STAR\nSTAR2\nSTAR3\n");
}
```

would not display a triangle of asterisks of the form

```
*
**
***
```

as expected. A correct version would be

```
#include <stdio.h>
#define STARS "*\n**\n***\n"
main()
{
     printf(STARS);
}
```

Macros can be used to "hide" error handling; for example,

```
#define ERROR { printf("Out of memory\n"); return; }
```

The only difficulty with this macro is that it must not be followed by a semicolon if it appears before `else`; for example,

```
if (WrongData)
      ERROR                — no ; here
else next statement
```

A macro may be *redefined*, provided it has been previously *undefined:*

```
#undef macroName
```

undefines a macro, for example,

```
#define A 3
#undef  A
#define A 4
```

The effect of

```
#define A 3
#define A 4
```

depends on the implementation, and so should be avoided.

Note that `typedef` is *not* an alternative mechanism for defining macros. We are not yet in a position to provide meaningful examples, but let us try to explain the difference:

- Macros are expanded (textually replaced) in the text of the program wherever they appear.
- `typedef` introduces a synonym for an existing type identifier; the compiler recognizes it as such and does not have to replace it with the type it was derived from.

5.2 MACROS WITH PARAMETERS

Macros may also have *arguments* defined. The syntax is

```
#define macroName(arg1, ..., argk) macroValue
```

where *arg1, ..., argk* are identifiers. There must not be any whitespace between *macroName* and its list of arguments. A macro call with parameters has the form

$$macroName\,(par1,\ ...,\ park\,)$$

and results in the evaluation of *par1*, ..., *park* and a textual substitution of *arg1*, ..., *argk* respectively by them in *macroValue*.
    Consider the macro

```
#define ISLOWER(c)     ((c) >=  'a' && (c) <=  'z')
```

This can be called, for example, as

```
x = ISLOWER(x) ? x - ('z' - 'Z') : x
```

The best way to understand macros with parameters is to expand them manually; for example, the preceding call expands to

```
x = ((x) >=  'a' && (x) <= 'z') ? x - ('z' - 'Z') : x
```

In the definition above, the argument c is enclosed in parentheses to avoid potential errors. The need for parentheses is more obvious in the following example:

```
#define SQR(x)  x * x
```

The call

```
SQR(z + 1)
```

would expand to

```
z + 1 * z + 1
```

which would not evaluate the way it was intended. This problem is solved if the macro is defined as

```
#define SQR(x)  ((x) * (x))
```

Here, both the parameters and the replacement text as a whole are enclosed in parentheses. Using this version, the preceding call would be expanded to

```
((z + 1) * (z + 1))
```

which is correct.

The outer parentheses are also essential. For example, if we use a macro defined as

```
#define READ(c)  c = getchar()
```

in the statement

```
if (READ(c) == 'x') ...
```

it would expand to

```
if (c = getchar() == 'x') ...
```

which because of the precedence of the operators involved, would not evaluate as was intended.

Even with parentheses, there is another pitfall to avoid: If a macro argument appears twice in the defining text, it should *not* be called with an actual argument that produces a side effect when it is evaluated. For example, if a macro is defined as

```
#define isbad(x)    ((x) < 0 || (x) > 100)
```

the call

```
if (isbad(x++))
      ...
```

would expand the text x++ in *two places*, causing the value of x to increase by 2, which is probably not what was intended.

As another example that shows how dangerous it is to call macros whose arguments produce evaluation side effects, consider a macro that tests whether or not a character is a whitespace character:

```
#define WHITE(c) ((c) == ' ' || (c) == '\t' || (c) == '\n')
```

and suppose this macro is called as follows:

```
while (WHITE(x = getchar()))
    ;
```

If a tab is read, the first condition is false, causing the second condition to be evaluated. Since this includes a reference to the macro parameter c, another character will be read (and assigned to x). This problem can be corrected by using a comma expression:

```
while (x = getchar(), WHITE(x))
    ;
```

Generally, evaluating macro arguments should not produce side effects. Macros often are used to simplify common I/O requests:

```
#define INTPRINT(x)    printf("%d", (x))
#define INTREAD(x)     scanf("%d", &(x))
```

It is then possible to write, for example,

```
INTREAD(x);
if (x > 0)
     INTPRINT(x);
```

If a macro is defined as

```
#define PRINT(fmt, x)    printf("%fmt", x)
```

and used, for example, as

```
PRINT(d, x);
```

it may not work because in some implementations macro arguments are not expanded inside quoted strings.

Remember that the actual parameters of macros are evaluated completely as they are being processed in the call. Thus macros may be used as actual parameters in function calls, for example,

```
#define PI 3.14
#define DOUBPRINT(x) printf("%f", (x))
...
DOUBPRINT(2*PI);
```

Pascal programmers may wish to define Pascal-like I/O macros when programming in C, for example,

```
#define WRITELN    putchar('\n')
```

Macros can be used to change the syntax of some control statements, for example,

```
#define FOR(i, start, limit)    for ((i) = (start); \
                                     (i) <=  (limit); (i)++)
```

so that we can write

```
FOR (i, 1, 10)
    printf("%d\n", i);
```

or to define some often used operations such as

```
#define SWAP(value1, value2, temp)    {temp   = value1; \
                                       value1 = value2; \
                                       value2 = temp; }
```

so it is possible to write

```
int  i = 4,
     j = 8,
     temp;

SWAP(i, j, temp)
```

If we define SWAP as

```
#define SWAP(value1, value2)          {int temp = value1; \
                                       value1 = value2;    \
                                       value2 = temp; }
```

using a nested block to declare the variable temp, this version could be used to swap any two integer variables **provided** none of them is called temp; for example,

```
SWAP(a, temp)
```

would not work.

This last macro is a better example of what macros are typically used for in C; ones like WRITELN and FOR above would rarely be used.

Predefined Macros

In many implementations of C, macros are used to define the terminal I/O routines in terms of the corresponding file I/O routines:

```
#define getchar()    getc(stdin)
#define putchar(c)   putc(c, stdout)
```

Most C implementations provide several macros (or, in some implementations, *functions*) for handling characters. Macros that *classify* characters start with is. For example, the macro

```
isdigit(c)
```

is commonly defined and returns 1 if c is a digit, and 0 otherwise. Various macros perform some kind of *conversion*; these macros start with to. For example,

```
c = tolower(c)
```

converts c to lowercase if it is an uppercase letter.

In most systems, these macros are stored in the header file ctype.h. We describe some of these macros below, but Chapter 10 contains a more complete list:

```
isascii(c)
```

returns 1 if c is in the standard 128-character ASCII character set.

```
islower(c)
```

returns 1 if c is a lowercase letter, and 0 otherwise.

```
toupper(c)
```

is a conversion macro that converts a lowercase character to uppercase. Thus we can write, for example,

```
if (islower(c))
    c = toupper(c);
```

You may wonder whether using macros or functions is better. As is often so, there is no single answer. By using macros, the overhead of a function call (stack management) is avoided and the readability of the program text is likely improved. However, because macros expand inline, increased code size is the price of using macros.

Finally, a word of warning about macros: Avoid *recursive* macros because they result in an unbounded expansion when called.

5.3   FILE INCLUSION

One commonly used preprocessor command is the #include command, which specifies that the text of a file is to be included. An included file may itself contain include statements; the maximum level of nesting depends on the implementation.

There are two formats for the include statement:

```
#include "filename"
```

and

```
#include <filename>
```

The two formats differ in how the specified file is to be located if not enough information is provided with the *filename*. The first form is usually defined to first search the *same directory* in which the file containing the #include directive is located and then, depending on the implementation's search rules, to search in other places. The second form is usually defined to search only in certain *special directories* where the standard system include files are located; exactly which directories depends on the system.

File inclusion is a useful mechanism that can be used to increase the readability of programs. For example, all relevant definitions can be grouped in a single file, often called a **header file**, which should be included in the main file:

file `Screen.def`:

```
#define ScrWid 80
#define ScrH   25
```

main file, containing the main program:

```
#include "Screen.def"
main()
{
    ...
}
```

Several *standard* header files are supplied with a typical C compiler. Traditionally, they have the extension `.h`. One of the most commonly used header files, as we have already seen, is

```
stdio.h
```

which contains the basic definitions needed to perform I/O, for example, `getchar`. The actual code of these functions is in the standard system library that will be searched when it is linked with a program; `stdio.h` contains only information that allows the library routines to be accessed properly within a program. The actual contents of `stdio.h` varies from implementation to implementation; if you are curious, examine this file to see what it contains. Two important macros defined in this file are EOF and NULL, which in most cases are defined as (-1) and (0), respectively.

Another standard header file is

```
ctype.h
```

which contains the declarations of several macros (or possibly functions) to test characters, such as the `islower` macro that we mentioned earlier.

The mathematical functions, such as abs and sin, are declared in another file called

```
math.h
```

File inclusion should not be confused with *separate compilation*. Even if a program is divided into several include files, the compiler treats it as *one complete program* and must compile the whole thing.

5.4 CONDITIONAL COMPILATION

In some cases, such as when debugging a program, it is useful to compile a piece of code *conditionally* depending on some conditions specified outside the program.

Conditional compilation means a part of the source file may be skipped during the preprocessing and not be compiled. This conditional exclusion of a part of the source file is controlled by two preprocessor directives. The syntax of the first conditional compilation directive resembles the syntax of an if statement:

```
#if constantExpression
      part1
#else
      part2
#endif
```

The else part may be omitted. If the value of the *constantExpression* is true (nonzero), the text making up *part1* of the file is included; otherwise, *part2* is included. This is often referred to as conditional compilation.

There is a simple yet useful application of the conditional command. As we said in Chapter 2, comments may not be nested. During program development, it is often convenient to exclude a piece of code by placing it within a comment pair. However, if the code contains comments itself, this technique will not work. A simple solution is to use the conditional command shown below:

```
#if 0
      ...
#endif
```

Since 0 is interpreted as false, the code between the #if 0 and #endif commands will be skipped.

Conditional compilation is also frequently used in developing programs that run under different environments, for example,

```
#define IBMPC 1
#if IBMPC              /* if target machine is an IBM PC */
#include <ibm.h>       /* then use IBM specific routines */
#else                  /* else */
#include <generic.h>   /* use machine independent routines */
#endif
```

If IBMPC is not the target machine, the line above could be changed to

```
#define IBMPC 0
```

which would cause the file generic.h to be included rather than
ibm.h when the program is compiled.

Another preprocessor command used for conditional compilation tests
whether or not a macro name has been defined (using the #define
command):

```
#ifdef macroName
        part1
#else
        part2
#endif
```

Here, *part1* is included if *macroName* has been defined; otherwise,
part2 is included. There is a similar command that is the logical negation
of ifdef:

```
#ifndef macroName
        part1
#else
        part2
#endif
```

For *debugging*, you might have a macro name, say DEB, which when
defined, turns debugging on and, when undefined, turns it off. Thus you
can code

```
#define DEB             /* empty, but defined  */
...
#ifdef DEB
      /* some debugging statement, for example */
      printf("value of i = %d", i);
      ...
#else
      /* code which will be executed when NOT debugging */
      ...
#endif
```

This may appear anywhere in a program, and the ifdef command may
be repeated as often as needed. Example 6.4.1 illustrates this tech-

nique. To turn debugging off, you would have to edit your file and make
the definition of the macro DEB a comment, or use the directive

```
#undef DEB
```

to replace it. Since this would require editing the source, many compilers allow the user to define or undefine a macro on the *command line*
used to compile the program; for example, under Unix, the command

```
cc -UDEB filename
```

will undefine the macro DEB when *filename* is compiled, whereas

```
cc -DDEB filename
```

will define it.

When a program consists of several included files, it is easy to inadvertently include the same file more than once, which may be wrong. If
an include file contains only specifications of external functions (see
Chapter 6), it may be safely included in more than one place within the
same file; if, however, a file contains definitions of types, variables, and
functions, and possibly macros as well, it most likely cannot be included
more than once (since doing so would introduce identifiers that are already defined). To avoid doing this, we recommend the following approach: Each include file contains a definition of a macro that indicates
whether or not this file has already been included. For example, an include file screen.h might look like

```
#ifndef SCREENH
#define SCREENH
     . . .
/* contents of the header */
#endif
```

Now consider a file called main.c that includes screen.h:

```
#include "screen.h"
```

If this file has already been included, the preceding command will not
produce any errors because the first inclusion of the header file defines
the macro SCREENH.

Conditional commands may be nested. Newer C implementations provide the C preprocessor command

```
#elif
```

(standing for `else if`), which makes the nesting of conditional commands easier. Note that `#elif` can be used with both `#if` and `#ifdef`. For example,

```
#if condition1
      part1
#else
#if condition2
      part2
#else
      part3
#endif
#endif
```

can be replaced by

```
#if condition1
      part1
#elif condition2
      part2
#else
      part3
#endif
```

Another recently added command is

```
defined (macroName)
```

which can also be written as

```
defined macroName
```

This construct is an expression that returns true if *macroName* is defined and false if it is not. Thus

```
#if defined macroName
```

is equivalent to

```
#ifdef macroName
```

It is more flexible because it can be used in expressions, for example,

```
#if defined(IBM) && debug
```

5.5   LINE NUMBERING

The last preprocessor command we discuss is

> #line *constantExpression* *"filename"*

This command causes the compiler to *think* that it is compiling the file called *filename* and that the current line number is *constantExpression*. The identifier may be omitted, in which case only the current line number changes. For example,

> #line 100 "FILE1"

causes the compiler to assume the number of the next source line is 100, and the name of the file the compiler should associate with it (for example, in error messages) is FILE1. The numbers of subsequent lines read from the current input file will increment from this point. These settings will remain in effect until a new #line directive is given. This command does not actually change the file being compiled, only what the compiler *thinks* it is compiling.

This preprocessor command is useful if the source file being compiled was created by *merging* two or more files. As a rather simplistic example, assume we have the following two files defined:

```
s1.c:
    main()
    {

s2.c:
        integer i;
    }
```

Suppose these two files have been combined as a result of the execution of another program, say P, into a file called s.c:

```
s.c:
    main()
    {
        integer i;
    }
```

If s.c is compiled, the compiler will issue a message that an error occurs on line 3. However, the user may wish to have the compiler indicate where in the files s1.c and s2.c the error is. This can be done by having the program P, which combined these two files originally, insert appropriate #line commands in s.c. Specifically, s.c should look like

```
s.c:
        #line 1 "s1.c"
        main( )
        {
        #line 1 "s2.c"
              integer i;
        }
```

If this file is compiled, the compiler will produce an error message indicating that an error occurred on line 1 of s2.c although it is actually on line 3 of s.c. Exactly this application of the #line command is used by the Yacc program, a *parser generator* available on Unix systems [Joh78].

THINGS TO REMEMBER

All parameters within a macro's defining text should be enclosed by parentheses.

Avoid side effects in evaluating macro arguments.

Use macros to define constants used in the program (this increases the readability and portability of the code).

Use macros with parameters to hide long and complicated expressions (this also increases the readability of a program).

Use conditional compilation to include or exclude debugging statements.

Use conditional compilation to determine whether or not a header file has been already included.

If the compiler complains about some syntax errors that you do not see, use the compiler option (if it exists) that lists a program as it appears after preprocessing. It is likely that some macro is causing problems.

COMMON ERRORS

`#define A = 1`	There should be no =
`#define PI 3.14;`	There should be no ;
`#define INC(x)  x + 1`	Body should be `((x) + 1)`

In a macro definition, do not add a blank between the macro name and the argument list. If you do, the argument list will be considered part of the defining text.

EXERCISES   1. Define a macro W(c) to check if c is a whitespace character, and a
   macro R(x) to read an integer value. The macros should be defined
   so that they can be used as in the following example:

```
while (1)   {
            R(x);
        c = getchar();
        if (W(c))
            continue;
        else break;
    }
```

2. Define macros to implement the following Pascal-like operations:

```
BEGIN
END
WRITE(x)                          where x is a string constant
WRITELN
READ(x)                           where x is of type integer
REPEAT <single instruction>
UNTIL (<condition>)
```

They should be able to be used as in the following example:

```
REPEAT
  BEGIN
    WRITE("Enter an integer please:"); WRITELN;
    READ(x);
  END
UNTIL (x > 2);
```

3. Show the output produced by the following program:

```
#include <stdio.h>
#define LOW         (-2)
#define HIGH        (LOW + 5)
#define PR(arg)     printf("%d\n", (arg))
#define FOR(arg)    for (; (arg); (arg)--)
main()
{
    int   i = LOW,
          j = HIGH;

    FOR(j)
        switch (j) {
```

```
               case 1  : PR(i++);
               case 2  : PR(j);
                         break;
               default : PR(i);
               }
     }
```

4. Define a macro

```
   ISLETTER(c)
```

to determine whether c is a lowercase or an uppercase letter that can be used as in

```
   if (ISLETTER(c))
       . . .
```

5. Define a macro

```
   ISNPRINT(c)
```

to determine whether c is a nonprintable character that can be used as in

```
   if (ISNPRINT(c))
       . . .
```

6. Define a macro

```
   ABS(x)
```

that returns the absolute value of the integer x.

7. Define a macro

```
   GETINT(x)
```

that reads an integer from the keyboard and returns this integer through both the parameter x and GETINT itself so that it can be used, for example, as in

```
   if (k = GETINT(i))
       . . .
```

Hint: Use a comma expression.

6 Functions and Procedures

PREVIEW

This chapter explains how to modularize C programs. In general, there are two ways of encapsulating program modules: using functions and using separate compilation. In both cases, the most essential concept is that of **scope.**

In this respect, C seems to be more flexible than Pascal in that it is possible to define variables whose scope covers precisely the required part of the program without unnecessary overlap with other program regions.

We introduce the syntax of a function definition and call, and we describe the concept of scope. We also discuss the separate compilation of C functions.

REVIEW OF PASCAL CONSTRUCTS

In this section, we present a general definition of the scope of program identifiers and explain how function and procedure calls are implemented.

An identifier in a program is introduced by a clause called an **identifier declaration**. The occurrences of an identifier in the program text are well defined if they can be matched with the defining declaration. The part of the program over which an identifier occurrence refers to a declaration is the **scope** of this identifier. Here, an identifier can denote any object, for example, a variable or a function.

In Pascal, the scope of identifiers is **static**. This means that for any occurrence of an identifier in a program its matching declaration is determined at *compilation time*. (Nearly all programming languages follow this convention; in a few languages, such as LISP and APL, scope is **dynamic**, that is, defined in terms of program execution.) In Pascal, functions and procedures can be textually nested, and names are local to a function or a procedure. A Pascal compiler can distinguish between two objects with the same identifier if they appear at different levels of nesting.

The **lifetime** of an identifier is the interval of time during which a variable may be referenced within its defined scope. A variable identifier must have a storage area bound to it during its lifetime. The action that acquires a storage area is called an **allocation**.

There are two main types of storage allocation: static storage allocation and dynamic storage allocation. **Static storage allocation** means the compiler determines the storage requirements for the variables declared in the main program and in any function or procedure, and the loader allocates this storage at load time (that is, immediately before the start of execution). During program execution, no storage management takes place. The lifetime of any statically allocated variable is from the beginning of program execution to its end; when a function or a procedure is called, its local data may be accessed in the preallocated memory block.

Static storage allocation, though efficient, imposes some limitations on the language; in particular, recursive procedures cannot be implemented. This is because each recursive call to the same procedure requires a fresh block of storage, but the compiler cannot determine how many times a procedure will be recursively called.

A **dynamic storage allocation** technique is needed to implement recursion: The lifetime of a variable starts when the execution enters a subroutine (procedure or function) containing the declaration of that variable and ends when the execution exits that subroutine. Thus storage must be freed in *reverse* order of allocation; therefore, a **stack** is a convenient data structure for this sort of storage allocation. In Pascal, storage allocation is dynamic because Pascal supports recursive procedures.

The scope of a variable is the subroutine containing the declaration of that variable and including all nested subroutines (unless this variable is redeclared in a nested subroutine). Once the execution proceeds beyond the scope of a variable, the memory assigned to this variable is deallocated. Thus if the subroutine where this variable is declared is reentered, the value of the variable is undefined. As a result, a variable that is needed only within a certain procedure, but that must retain its value between calls, has to be declared as a global variable. For example, a seed for a random number generator cannot be defined as a local variable in the procedure; instead, it must be declared as a global variable so that it *retains* its value between successive calls to the generator. Some languages provide a type of variable called **own** or **static** that retains its value even after the subroutine it is declared in is exited. Standard Pascal does not support this type of variable.

Separate compilation means a program may be divided into a number of files containing the declarations of variables and functions. Each file can then be compiled separately, and eventually all files can be linked together. This feature is useful for program development, since a single correction in a large program does not require the recompilation of the entire program but just the file where the correction was made. Moreover, separate compilation facilitates modularization of a program.

Standard Pascal does not support separate compilation, but many of its dialects do. In a program consisting of several separately compiled files, one has to distinguish between the definition of an identifier and the declaration of an identifier. From now on, following the C terminology used by Kernighan and Ritchie [Ker78], we will call the **definition** of an identifier a clause that causes storage to be allocated, and a **declaration** a specification that merely tells the compiler a definition appears elsewhere (usually in another file).

The reason for using a declaration is that the compiler must be given the information that a variable referred to in a program is indeed defined although not necessarily in the file being compiled. Thus a language provides some syntactic means to describe a declaration rather than a definition. In most Pascal implementations that support separate compilation, the clause `extern` specifies a declaration.

Separately compiled files can be linked together using a linker program. The linker checks whether all identifiers declared in a program are *defined* in exactly one file. Clearly, the memory for a variable that is defined in one file and declared in others is allocated only once, and all references to this variable (in various files) refer to this single memory location.

Thus the scope of a variable in a separately compiled setup extends to all files in which this variable is defined or declared. In Pascal implementations that support separate compilation, it is usually not possible to limit the access to a global variable declared in one file from another file. This feature would be useful in the encapsulation of program modules.

Glossary

Declaration of an identifier A specification of this identifier and its type; it does not allocate memory for this identifier.

Definition of an identifier A complete specification of this identifier, including its type; allocates memory.

Dynamic memory allocation The allocation of memory at run time.

Lifetime of an identifier The interval of time during which the program operates on the scope of an identifier.

Scope of an identifier The part of the program over which an identifier occurrence refers to a declaration.

Separate compilation The file containing the program is split into several files, each of which is separately compiled and then linked together.

Static memory allocation The allocation of memory at compilation time.

Static scope The scope is determined at compilation time.

Static variables Variables whose lifetime starts when the defining subroutine is called and ends when the program terminates.

C CONSTRUCTS

A program in C consists of one or more function definitions. One of these functions must be called `main`. The execution of a program starts with the function `main`.

The principal difference between Pascal and C is that in C functions *cannot* be nested (that is, textually enclosed). Therefore, formal parameters and local variables are accessible only within the function in which they are defined and invisible outside. Otherwise, as in Pascal, C uses *dynamic memory allocation* to support recursive function calls.

All subroutines are assumed to be functions, although any function may be called as a procedure, with the value normally returned by the function being discarded.

6.1   FUNCTION DEFINITION

We follow the previously described convention that

- A **definition** of a function specifies a header and a body (this is what Pascal calls a procedure declaration).
- A **declaration** of a function specifies the function name and the type of the value returned by this function. Thus the declaration of a function in C is like a *forward declaration* in some Pascal implementations.

The syntax of a function header is somewhat different from that in Pascal:

- There is no reserved word `function`.
- The type of the value being returned by the function precedes the header.
- A function header includes only formal parameter *names*—the type specification of the formal parameters follows the header.

Pascal	**C**

`FUNCTION` *id* (*mode1 par1* : *typ1* ;
          mode2 par2 : *typ2* ;
 	
          ...
          modek park : *typk*) : *typ;*
	typ id (*par1* , ... , *park*)
	     typ1 par1 ;
	
	     typ2 par2 ;
	     ...
	     typk park ;

`BEGIN`
   ... *body* ...
`END;`
	{
	   ... *body* ...
	}

The header of a function to compute the maximum of two integers may look as follows:

Pascal	C
`FUNCTION max(a, b : INTEGER):` `                  INTEGER;`	`int max(a, b)` `int a, b;`

A function header in C is *not* terminated by a semicolon. Also, there is only one mode of parameter transmission: call by value. Thus the mode of a formal parameter is not specified. (In Chapter 7 on pointers, we explain that call by reference can be achieved by passing the address of the actual parameter.)

In this chapter, we consider only parameters that are of the primitive types, such as `char`, `int`, and `double`. The type of a function may be omitted if it is integer, so the preceding function max could be declared as

```
max(a, b)
int a, b;
```

For clarity, the examples in this book always specify the type of the function (with the exception of the function `main`). Since `char` promotes to `int` in expressions, a `char` function could just as well be defined as `int`.

As for the body of a function, the usual left and right braces { ... } are used the same as in the main program function, and there may be both instructions and optional declarations within the body.

Unlike in Pascal, where a function identifier may appear on the left-hand side of the assignment, in C, the keyword `return` denotes the assignment of a value to a function. The statement

```
return exp;
```

evaluates the expression *exp*, assigns its value to the function, and then *exits* the function. C programmers often enclose *exp* in parentheses:

```
return(exp);
```

The expression *exp* may be omitted entirely, for example, when used to return from a procedure. If an expression is specified, it is converted to the type of the function, if necessary, using an implicit cast.

The complete definition of the function max follows.

Example 6.1.1

Pascal	C
`FUNCTION max(a, b : INTEGER):` `                  INTEGER;`	`int max(a, b)` `int a, b;`

```
BEGIN                                  {
    IF a > b THEN                          return(a > b ? a : b);
       max := a                        }
    ELSE max := b
END;
```
                                                                              ∎

Functions are called in the same way as in Pascal, unless the function does not have any parameters. The preceding function `max` could be called, for example, using

```
x = max(10 * a, b - 15);
```

A function that does not have any formal parameters must *still* include a pair of parentheses when it is defined. For example, the following function reads two integer values from the keyboard and returns the sum of these integers:

```
int addtwo()
{
    int a, b;

    scanf("%d%d", &a, &b);
    return (a + b);
}
```

This function could be called using a statement such as

```
j = addtwo();
```

A pair of parentheses *must* be included when a parameterless function is called.

Procedures
Strictly speaking, C does not support procedures. However, any function, regardless of its result type, can be called as a procedure (in the same fashion as in Pascal), in which case the value normally returned by the function is simply discarded. For example, C compilers would allow the functions `max` and `addtwo` to be called in a fashion such as

```
max(a+3, b);
addtwo();
```

In both cases, the result of the function call is discarded.

Some recent implementations of C have introduced a special type `void` to denote functions always called as procedures, for example,

```
void showletter(c)
char c;
```

If a programmer wants to follow this convention but the type void is not supported by the compiler being used, it could be defined as int using typedef:

```
typedef int void;
```

To be precise, however, the type void is intended to denote an empty set of values, and this is exactly how the ANSI C standard defines it.

Example 6.1.2   The following program shows a simple procedure that reads a character value from the keyboard and displays its ASCII code:

```
#include <stdio.h>
void ascii()
{
    char c;

    scanf("%c", &c);
    printf("The ASCII code of %c is %d\n", c, c);
}

main()
{
    ascii();
}
```

Many modern compilers are beginning to be more strict about the distinction between functions and procedures. For example, if a function is defined as

```
int cube(d)
int d;
{
    return (d * d * d);
}
```

some compilers may not allow it to be called as a procedure, such as

```
cube(5);
```

Instead, if a function is to be called as a procedure, its result must be cast as void:

```
(void) cube(5);
```

This approach also complies with ANSI C recommendations.

Functions in C may be recursive, as we illustrate in the following example.

Example 6.1.3   The following program shows a function that computes the factorial of a number recursively (this version returns 1 if n <= 0) :

```
int fact(n)
int n;
{
    return (n < = 0 ? 1 : n * fact(n - 1));
}
```
■

Let us now consider a function that returns a noninteger value.

Example 6.1.4   The following program shows a function that takes a double value as a parameter and returns this value increased by 15 percent:

```
double increase(x)
double x;
{
    return x * 1.15;
}
```
■

Function Declarations

As we mentioned, a function may not be *defined* within another function, but of course it may be *called* from another function. If the type of value returned by a function is other than integer and the function is called before it is defined, the calling function should *declare* the type of the called function. This type of declaration consists of a type identifier followed by a function identifier with a pair of parentheses. For example,

```
double increase();
```

would be used to declare the function increase. In this context, these declarations play the same role as forward declarations in Pascal.

Now consider a function that calls increase. The function display below reads in a value from the keyboard, calls the function increase to increase this value by 15 percent, and then displays the result:

```
void display()
{
    double increase();
    double x;

    scanf("%lf", &x);
    x = increase(x);
    printf("%f\n", x);
}
```

The declaration

```
double increase();
```

may also be written as

```
extern double increase();
```

with the keyword `extern` indicating that the specified function is defined elsewhere. If this function is called *before* it is defined or declared, the compiler assumes it is an integer function. For example, without the declaration of `increase`, the compiler would assume `increase` is an integer function, and so the assignment

```
x = increase(x);
```

would essentially be incorrect (`increase` returns a `double` value, but the main program thinks it returns an integer and would therefore interpret the result incorrectly).

If the function `increase` is *defined* before the function `display` is defined, it does not have to be declared. When the definition of the function `display` is processed, the compiler will know the type of the value returned by the function `increase`. We recommend that a function be declared, whether or not it is necessary, to better document the program and to help prevent errors. If a function definition is moved during program development, a declaration of the function may be required in another function where it was not required before. If a function is declared to return a particular type, say `int`, then defined later to return a different type, the compiler will generate an error.

This discussion also applies to procedures. That is, if a procedure (a function returning `void`) is called *before* it is defined, the C compiler will assume it is an integer function. Thus when a function that has not been defined or declared is referenced in a program, its result type is assumed to be `int`, even if it is being referenced as a procedure. When the procedure is later defined (as a `void` function), the compiler will complain that the function type (`void`) is not the same as what it thinks it should be (`int`). This problem can be solved by declaring the procedure before it is used, specifying that its result type is `void`.

Consider Example 6.1.2. If the definitions of the routines `ascii` and `main` were exchanged, then when `ascii` is called in `main`, the compiler would assume `ascii` is an integer function. Therefore, when `ascii` is defined following `main` to be, in fact, a `void` function, the compiler would complain. If these routines are indeed defined in the order suggested, this problem can be solved by adding the declaration

```
extern void ascii();
```

in the function `main`.

Example 6.1.5   In the following example, the function `getreal` reads in a sequence of characters from the standard input that represent a real number and returns the corresponding numeric value. If the first non-whitespace character cannot be interpreted as a real number, the value returned is undefined. To write this function, we use the macros `isdigit` and `isspace`, which in most implementations of C are defined in the header file `ctype.h` (see Chapter 10).

```c
#include <stdio.h>
#include <ctype.h>

double getreal()
{
    double power = 1,
           val   = 0;
    int    sign  = 1,
           c;

    /* skip whitespace  */
    while (c = getchar(), isspace(c))
        ;
    /* check current character */
    switch (c) {
    case '-' :  sign = -1;
    case '+' :  c = getchar();
    case '.' :  break;
    default  :  if (!isdigit(c))      /* error */
                    return 0;
    }

    while (isdigit(c)) {
        val = val * 10 + (c - '0');
        c = getchar();
    }
    if (c == '.')
        while (c = getchar(), isdigit(c)) {
            val = val * 10 + ( c - '0');
            power *=  10;
        }
    if (c != EOF)
        ungetc(c, stdin); /* return last character */
    return sign * val / power;
}
```

Library functions do not have to be declared if the appropriate header files are included. For example, the declaration

```c
FILE *fopen();
```

appears in the file `stdio.h`.

Function Result Conversion

Recall that the type of the return expression of a function does *not* have to be identical to the type of the function. Consider the definition

```
typ f(...)
{
    ...
    return exp;
    ...
}
```

When the `return` is executed, the expression *exp* is implicitly cast

```
(typ) exp
```

Consider, for example,

```
int convert(d)
double d;
{
    return d;
}
```

If this function is called as

```
k = convert(4.5);
```

the value 4.5 is cast (truncated) on return and then assigned to the integer variable k.

6.2 FUNCTION PARAMETERS

C supports only one mode of parameter transmission: *call by value*. Other modes, however, can be simulated using pointers; these we explain in Chapter 7.

Unlike Pascal, typical implementations of C do not check whether or not the number of actual parameters is the same as the number of formal parameters. Actually, there are various library functions such as `printf` that accept a *variable* number of parameters. Users may write functions like these although to do so requires a detailed knowledge of the calling convention of the particular implementation (that is, a knowledge of how parameters are passed on the stack). Thus this technique is neither portable nor recommended. Generally speaking, if a function is defined with, say, two parameters, and a call to the function specifies only one parameter, unpredictable events are likely to occur.

Formal Parameter Conversions

The type of an actual parameter should match that of the corresponding formal parameter because no implicit type conversion takes place, with the exception of the following types of formal parameters that *are* implicitly promoted:

```
char  to int
short to int
float to double
```

These implicit conversions also affect the manner in which formal parameters are implemented in C. For example, if a function is defined as

```
void test(c)
char c;
```

it is usually implemented as if it were defined as

```
void test(c)
int c;
```

Similarly, formal parameters of type short are treated as if they were of type int, and float type formal parameters are treated as if they were of type double.

In the preceding list of conversions, an int value is not promoted to double (or to float), so for the function increase defined as

```
void increase(x)
double x;
```

the call

```
increase(4)
```

will likely produce a meaningless result and should be replaced by

```
increase(4.0)
```

Similarly, if x is defined as an int variable, the call

```
increase(x)
```

should be replaced by the call

```
increase( (double)x );
```

Moreover, if a long integer is to be passed as a parameter, the suffix L must be used. For example, if the function mlalloc expects a long argument and is to be called with an actual parameter of, say, 10000, it must be called as

```
p = mlalloc(10000L);
```

C makes no attempts to check the validity of parameters in a function call (although some recent compilers give warnings); it is entirely up to the programmer to ensure that the types of actual and formal parameters match.

Example 6.2.1   The following program reads a positive integer and outputs the prime number nearest to this integer. If there are two prime numbers equidistant from the input number, it outputs the first one found.

We define a macro ODD(n) and use this to test if n is an odd or even integer. We also use the library function sqrt and so include the header file math.h. The function sqrt expects a double argument, thus a type conversion must be performed if the argument p is of type int:

```
sqrt( (double)p )
```

The function prime tests whether or not its argument is a prime number:

```c
#include <stdio.h>
#include <math.h>

#define ODD(n) ((n) % 2 == 1)

#define TRUE   1
#define FALSE  0
typedef int bool;

bool prime(p)
int p;
{
    int root, divisor;

    if (p < 4)
        return (p >= 1);
    else if (!ODD(p))
        return (FALSE);
    else {
        root = sqrt((double) p) + 0.5;
        for (divisor = 3; divisor <= root &&
                               p % divisor != 0;)
            divisor += 2;
        return (divisor > root);
    }
}
```

The main program starts searching for a prime number close to the input value n. In each step of the main loop, we check whether or not numbers n+1, n+3, and so on are prime if n is even, and we try n+2, n+4, and so on if n is odd.

```
main()
{
    int n, k;

    printf("Enter an integer: ");
    scanf("%d", &n);
    printf("\nNearest prime to %d is ", n);
    if (prime(n))
        printf("%d\n", n);
    else {
        if (ODD(n))
            k = 2;
        else k = 1;
        while (TRUE) {
            if (prime(n + k)) {
                printf("%d\n", n + k);
                return;
            }

            if (prime(n - k)) {
                printf("%d\n", n - k);
                return;
            }
            k += 2;
        }
    }
}
```

∎

ANSI C Function Declarations

The ANSI C standard [Ans86] suggests a more detailed function declaration syntax that lists the *types* of the formal parameters, for example,

```
extern double increase(double);
```

This type of declaration enables a compiler to verify that the number and types of the actual parameters given in a function call correspond to the formal parameter specifications. Several recent compilers support this feature, and we discuss it further in Section 14.2.1.1.

Actual Parameter Evaluation

The order that actual parameters are evaluated in is *not* guaranteed by the definition of the C language. Thus the result of a call such as

```
printf("%d %d", i, ++i);
```

is undefined. The general rule is to avoid using actual parameters that produce *side effects*.

6.3 SCOPE

This section discusses the concept of the scope of variables and other identifiers (for example, those defined by `typedef`) as it pertains to C. We first consider the case of a program contained within a single file, and then we consider the case of separately compiled files.

The **scope** of an identifier is the region of the program over which occurrences of this identifier can be matched with the defining declaration.

C's implementation of scope is a mixture of Pascal's concept of scope and Fortran's concept of scope (see [Mei80]). Since functions cannot be nested, the formal parameters and local variables of a function f (that is, variables declared within the function) are visible *only* within f.

However, the user may define *global* variables which have a scope that encompasses the entire file. Thus global variables in C can be used for communication between functions in the same way as in Pascal.

6.3.1 Global Variables

The basic organization of declarations in a program is

Global declarations and definitions
Function definition
Function definition
...

Global declarations are declarations of variables that are *defined* in separate files. Since these declarations in C are specified using `extern`, they are also called `extern` declarations. We deal with global declarations later when we discuss separate compilation. **Global definitions** define variables whose scope is from the point of their definitions to the end of the file. These definitions occur *outside* the bodies of any functions in the file, for example,

```
int i;

A()
{
    /* function A */
    ...
    /* end of A */
}
```

```
int j;

B()
{
     /* function B */
     ...
     /* end of B */
}

C()
{
     /* function C  */
     ...
     /* end of C */
}

/*  end of file */
```

The scope of the variable i is from the definition of function A to the end
of the file, and the scope of the variable j is from the definition of function B to the end of the file.

In terms of Pascal, global variables are like variables declared in the
main program and thus visible in other functions (here, however, these
variables are defined outside the main function; variables defined inside
main are *not* considered global).

It is illegal to have the same identifier denoting different objects (in
the same scope), with the following two exceptions:

- Statement labels (see Section 3.5)
- Structure and union tags (see Chapter 9)

As in Pascal, identifier definitions within functions may supersede the
definitions of global identifiers with the same names. Consider the following example:

```
int i1, i2;
A()
{
     int i1, j1;
     ...
}

int j1, j2;
B()
{
     int i1, j1, k1;
     ...
}
```

Within the function A, the global identifier i1 is superseded by the local
identifier with the same name. Thus within this function, the global

identifier i2 and the local identifiers i1 and j1 can be used. Within the function B, the global identifiers i2 and j2 and local identifiers i1, j1, and k1 are visible.

To further illustrate the scope of variables in a C program, consider the following example:

```
int i = 5;
void subr(j)
int j;
{
      int x = 10;

      j = 0;
      printf("%d %d %d\n", i, j, x);
      i = 10;
}

main()
{
      int x = 7, i = 6;

      printf("%d %d\n", x, i);
      subr(x);
      printf("%d %d\n", x, i);
}
```

The output of this program would be

```
7 6
5 0 10
7 6
```

Example 6.3.1   The following program finds the length of the longest line in the file TEST. It uses a global variable f and four functions—opentest, closetest, getline, and main. Since f is global, it is accessible in all four functions.

```
#include <stdio.h>
#define ERROR(mes)    { printf("%s\n", mes); return; }
#define EOLN          '\n'
FILE *f;

int opentest()
/* returns 1 if TEST can be opened, 0 otherwise */
{
      return (f = fopen("TEST", "r")) != NULL;
}

int closetest()
/* returns 1 if the file f can be closed, 0 otherwise */
{
      return fclose(f) != EOF;
}
```

```
int getline()
/* returns length of an input line,
   or EOF if end-of-file is encountered*/
{
    int len = 0,
        c;

    while ((c = getc(f)) != EOF)
        if (c == EOLN)
                return len + 1;
        else len++;
    return EOF;
}

main()
{
    int longest = 0,
        current;

    if (!opentest())
        ERROR("Cannot open TEST")

    while ((current = getline()) != EOF)
        longest = (current > longest) ? current : longest;

    printf("Length of longest line is %d\n", longest);
    if (!closetest())
        ERROR("Cannot close TEST");
}
```
■

Associated with the issue of local and global identifiers is the issue of
variable *initialization*. Local variables are *not* automatically initialized
and so have undefined initial values. Global variables, however, are implicitly initialized to "zero"—that is, integer variables will have initial
values of 0, reals will be initialized to 0.0, and so on. We describe explicit initialization in Section 6.5.

6.3.2 Storage Classes

Besides a type, variables in C can be designated to have a particular
storage class. The **storage class** of a variable determines how the compiler allocates memory to that variable. Four storage classes are defined
in C:

- auto
- extern
- static
- register

If a variable declared within a function has no explicit storage class indicated, auto is used by default. Thus the keyword auto is rarely specified, and so the declaration

```
func()
{
     auto int i;
     . . .
}
```

would normally be written as

```
func()
{
     int i;
     . . .
}
```

The storage class extern is mainly used along with separate compilation, which we discuss in Section 6.4.

The **lifetime** of a variable is the period during which memory is allocated to the variable. *Local* variable lifetime, as in Pascal, starts when a function containing the definition of this variable is called and ends when this function terminates. *Global* variable lifetime, which is the lifetime of the program, starts when the program starts execution and ends when the program terminates.

Static local variables are variables that *retain* their values between calls. The lifetime of a static local variable starts when the function containing its definition is called for the first time and ends when the program terminates. Static variables are not allocated on the stack but in a so-called global data segment and exist for the lifetime of a program.

Static variables are defined by preceding the type specification with the keyword static, for example,

```
void f()
{
     int x = 2;
     static int i = 0;

     printf("f is called %d-th time, x is %d\n", i, x);
     i++;
     x++;
}
```

In this function, x is a local (automatic) variable, and i is a local static variable. Every time f is called, x is allocated a new memory location, and so its value from the previous call is lost; i, however, *retains* its location, and so its value is the same as it was when the previous call to f terminated. If f were called three times in a loop such as

```
for (j = 0; j < 3; j++)
    f();
```

the output would be

```
f is called 0-th time, x is 2
f is called 1-th time, x is 2
f is called 2-th time, x is 2
```

If an initializer is specified in the definition of a static variable, it has an effect only the *first* time the function containing the static variable is called. The only difference between global and static variables is that the scope of global variables is the entire file, whereas the scope of static variables is limited to the function they are declared in. Their lifetime is identical.

Functions and global variables may also be specified as static. The effect of doing so we describe in Section 6.4.

The fourth storage class is `register` variables. Since C is a *low-level* high-level language, it provides the user with the option of defining variables that may be allocated in machine *registers* rather than in ordinary memory. Variables allocated in registers have a shorter access time than variables allocated in regular memory. Usually, few, if any, registers are available in a specific implementation. There are also various limitations; for example, the address operator may not be applied to a register variable. The keyword `register` preceding a variable definition specifies that it should be allocated in a register:

```
register int i;
```

If no register is available, the variable is allocated in the usual fashion.

6.3.3   Blocks

A block is a feature not supported by Pascal and seems to be used rarely by C programmers. A **block** contains both declarations and statements. These declarations are nested within the enclosing function (or within another compound statement), and all scope rules described earlier apply. Variables declared in a block may be either `auto` or `static`.

Example 6.3.2   The following program reads a single `int` value, and if this value is positive, another `int` value is read and the sum of the two values is output.

Otherwise, a `double` value is read and the product of the two values is output.

```
#include <stdio.h>
main()
{
    int i;

    scanf("%d", &i);
    if (i > 0) {
        int j;              — j declared in an inner block
        scanf("%d", &j);
        printf("%d\n", i + j);
    }
    else {
        double f;           — f declared in an inner block
        scanf("%lf", &f);
        printf("%f\n", i * f);
    }
}
```

A possible justification for the use of nested blocks is that, in theory, memory is not allocated for the variables within a block until the block is entered during execution; however, in practice, this depends on the implementation and may not always be the case. Another reason for their use might be to improve the clarity of the code.

Sometimes we want to define macros that need local variables to perform their actions. In these cases, we can use blocks in macro definitions, for example,

```
#define SWAP(x, y) {double f; f = (x); (x) = (y); (y) = f;}
```

6.4 SEPARATE COMPILATION

We now discuss *multiple-file* programs. In this kind of program, the scope of a global variable extends over the file in which it is *defined* and over all files in which it is *declared*. In this case, we do not use the `#include` command to include the contents of another file, since a C compiler can process an incomplete part of a program provided all type definitions are given and all variables are either defined or declared.

The storage class `extern` specifies the declaration of a variable, not the definition of a variable. As an example, consider a file A containing

```
int x;
extern double f;

int fun()
```

```
{
      return(x + (int) f);
}
```

Here, x is *defined* and f is *declared*. Without the declaration of f, this identifier cannot be used in the file A.

Now let us consider a file B containing the declarations of the variable x and the function fun and also the definition of the variable f:

```
extern int x;
extern int fun();
double f;

main()
{
      x = 3;
      f = 3.5;
      printf("%d\n", fun());
}
```

This program prints the value 6.

The extern specification

```
extern int fun();
```

in this program may be omitted (since its result type is int), but this is not considered a good practice. Different implementations of C may approach problems related to assumed extern declarations in different ways (see [Har84]).

The scope of the variables x and f, and also the function fun, is the file A *and* the file B.

Because external identifiers must be processed by linkers, they are subject to additional limitations. Some systems restrict the number of significant characters in external identifiers to seven (or fewer) characters (such as the VAX/VMS); other systems do not distinguish between uppercase and lowercase (such as the IBM 360/370). Thus we recommend that external identifiers be kept short and case insensitive.

Static Global Variables

The scope of a global identifier can be limited by specifying that this identifier is **static**. Thus the keyword static has two different meanings depending on whether it is applied to local or global variables. Static global identifiers are *hidden* from other modules, and so can used in encapsulating program modules.

Both variables and functions may be defined as static; an identifier defined as static cannot be declared as external in another file—it is accessible *only* within the file where it is defined. For example, consider a file A containing the following code:

```
static int x;
extern double f;

static double fun(x)
double x;
{
    return(x);
}

int fun1()
{
    return((int) fun(f) + x);
}
```

Here, x is defined as a `static int` variable, and `fun` is defined as a `static double` function. Thus their scope is limited to the file A.

Now consider a file B:

```
extern int x;
double f;
extern int fun1();

main()
{
    x = 3;
    f = 3.5;
    printf("%d\n", fun1() );
}
```

If this file is compiled and linked with the preceding file A, the linker will complain that the variable x is not *defined:* The static definition of x in the file A does not extend over the file B, so no definition of x matches the declaration of x in the file B.

A direct call to `fun` cannot be made in the main program because this function is visible only in the file A.

Example 6.4.1   The following program is made up of two separately compiled modules, as well as a header file. In this example, we demonstrate how conditional compilation can be used to produce two versions of this program, one with debugging statements and one without.

This program consists of two main files. One file, `fileops.c`, contains several file processing functions, such as `words` to find the number of words in a file. The other file, `filepgm.c`, is the main program and contains the function `help`, which displays a list of available file processing functions, the function `menu`, which reads a single character from the keyboard and calls the required function, and the function `main`, which initiates and eventually terminates the program.

Both files include the header file `fileops.h`:

```
#define TRUE 1
#define FALSE 0
```

```
typedef int bool;
extern bool parentheses();
extern long words();
extern long lines();
extern long count();
```

The function `parentheses(f)` returns `TRUE` if the parentheses in the file `f` are balanced; otherwise, it returns `FALSE`. The functions `words(f)` and `lines(f)` return, respectively, the number of words and the number of lines in the file `f`. The function `count(f, c)` returns the number of occurrences of the character `c` in the file `f`.

The actual definitions of these routines are in the file `fileops.c`. Since these functions are used to perform a variety of operations on the same file, we must make sure the file input pointer is positioned at the beginning of the file *each time* one of these functions is called. Although this could be done by closing and opening the file each time, a better way is to use the function

```
rewind(f)
```

We describe this function in detail in Chapter 12.

We start by discussing the function `parentheses`. This function assumes the text it is searching represents a C program. Since we want to determine only if the parentheses within the code portion of this text are balanced, any parentheses found within comments or quoted strings must be ignored. If end-of-file is encountered while a comment or string is being skipped, the program treats this as the end of the comment or string. Our solution uses a number of macros, both to improve readability and to test your understanding of Chapter 5.

The first group of macros is used to recognize the beginning and the end of a comment and also to skip a comment:

```
#define COMMENT1(c)        ((c) == '/')
#define COMMENT2(c)        ((c) == '*')
#define endCOMMENT(c, d)   ((c) == '*' && (d) == '/')
#define skipCOMMENT        { int c=getc(f), d=getc(f); \
                             while (!endCOMMENT(c, d)   \
                                    && !feof(f))        \
                                 { c=d; d=getc(f); }}
```

The second group of macros is used to skip quoted strings:

```
#define startQUOTE(c)      ((c) == '\'' || (c) == '"')
#define skipQUOTE(quote)   { int c;                     \
                             while ((c=getc(f))!=quote  \
                                    && !feof(f))        \
                                 if (c=='\\') getc(f); }
```

Note that `skipQUOTE` skips escaped characters within strings. The last group of macros is used to count parentheses:

```
#define ISLEFT(c)           ((c) == '(')
#define ISRIGHT(c)          ((c) == ')')
#define TRY(c)              if (ISLEFT(c)) ParCount++; else \
                            if (ISRIGHT(c)) ParCount--;
```

The complete code of the function `parentheses` follows:

```
bool parentheses(f)
FILE *f;
{
    int ParCount = 0,
        c;

    rewind(f);
    while ((c = getc(f)) != EOF)
        if (COMMENT1(c)) {
            c = getc(f);
            if (COMMENT2(c))
                skipCOMMENT
            else ungetc(c, f);
        }
        else if (startQUOTE(c))
            skipQUOTE(c)
        else TRY(c)
    return ParCount == 0 ? TRUE : FALSE;
}
```

The second function we discuss is the function `words`. The code itself is rather straightforward, but take note of the use of *conditional compilation*; this conditional code was used in the actual development of the program:

```
long words(f)
FILE *f;
{
    bool flag = TRUE;
    long WordCount = 0;
    int c;

    rewind(f);
    while ((c = getc(f)) !=EOF)
        if (isspace(c))
            flag = TRUE;
        else if (flag) {
            flag = FALSE;
            WordCount++;
```

```
#ifdef DEB
                        printf("\nword #: %ld\n", WordCount);
                        fputc(c, stderr);
#endif
                }
#ifdef DEB
                else fputc(c, stderr);
#endif

        return WordCount;
}
```

The implementations of the remaining file processing functions we leave for you as an exercise. To finish this example, let us now describe the file filepgm.c:

```
#include <stdio.h>
#include "fileops.h"
#define EOLN '\n'
```

The first function is menu:

```
void menu(f)
FILE *f;
{
    int c;
    extern void help();

    while (1) {
        printf("> (h for help): ");
        c = getchar();
        while (getchar() != EOLN)
            ;
        switch (c) {
        case 'h': case 'H':
            help();
            break;

        case 'w': case 'W':
            printf("The number of words is %ld\n",
                    words(f));
            break;

        case 'l': case 'L':
            printf("The number of lines is %ld\n",
                    lines(f));
            break;

        case 'c': case 'C':
            printf("Enter a character: ");
            c = getchar();
            while (getchar() != EOLN)
                ;
```

```
                        printf("%c occurs %ld times\n", c,
                                count(f, c));
                        break;

                case 'p': case 'P':
                        printf("Parentheses are %sbalanced\n",
                                parentheses(f) ? "" : "not ");
                        break;

                case 'q': case 'Q':
                        return;

                default:
                        printf("\nUnknown command\n");
                        break;
                }
        }
}
```

You should take note how the preceding function skips the rest of the input line after reading in the next command.

The function help displays a list of available functions:

```
void help()
{
        printf("Enter\n\tH for help\n\tW to count words\n\t");
        printf("L to count lines\n\tC to count characters\n\t");
        printf("P to check parentheses\n\tQ to quit\n");
}
```

Finally, the main program is as follows:

```
main()
{
        FILE *f;

        if ((f = fopen("TEST", "r")) == NULL) {
                printf("Cannot open TEST\n");
                return;
        }
        menu(f);
        if (fclose(f) == EOF)
                printf("Cannot close TEST\n");
}
```

A major limitation of our program is that it always opens the same file for processing. However, it is easy to modify it so that the name of the file to be examined is read at the beginning of execution rather than having this name constant. In Chapter 10, on strings, we explain how this is done.   ∎

We present more examples of this type in Chapter 13.

6.5   INITIALIZATION

Local variables with *simple types* may be explicitly initialized. If they are not explicitly initialized, their initial values are undefined, unless they are specified as static, in which case they are set to zero, for example,

```
void f()
{
    int x;
    static int y;
    static int z = 8;
    . . .
}
```

Here, x has an undefined initial value, and y is set to 0.

A *global* variable may be explicitly initialized regardless of its type. If it is not initialized, it is set to zero.

Initializers of *automatic* variables may be arbitrarily complex expressions, whereas initializers of *static* and *global* variables must be constant expressions. **Complex expressions** may contain variables or even function calls, that is, anything that can appear on the right-hand side of an assignment. A **constant expression** is an expression made up of constants combined with various operators so that its value can be determined at compilation time.

Assuming c is an automatic variable and k is a local static variable, the following are legal:

```
int c = getchar();
static int  k = 5 * 1024;
```

Remember that for a program consisting of several separately compiled files, there must be *at most one* explicit initialization (in the definition). We continue this discussion in Chapter 8.

THINGS TO REMEMBER

Functions may not be nested.

A function that returns a noninteger value must be declared in the function it is called in. An alternative solution is to declare functions called in other modules in a header file and to include this file in whichever modules needed.

Use void to specify functions that do not return values. (If void is not supported in your implementation, use typedef to define it as int.)

The types of formal parameters and actual parameters must be identical. Note, however, that all `chars` and `shorts` are passed automatically as `ints`, and all `floats` are passed as `doubles`.

Use static variables to limit their scope whenever appropriate.

External identifiers should be short and case insensitive.

Make sure external variables are initialized only once.

EXERCISES

1. Define a function `up(c)` that returns via up the character c converted to uppercase if c is a lowercase letter, and c unchanged otherwise. In a short but complete main program, show how this function may be called.

2. Write a function to compute the Least Common Multiple (LCM) of a pair of real numbers A and B using the formula

   ```
   LCM(A, B) = (A * B) / GCD(A, B)
   ```

3. Write a function with two parameters—a real r and an integer n— that prints a table of powers of r, from 1 to n. Test this function in a main program.

4. Write a function that prints the prime factorization of a number. For example, $68 = 2 * 2 * 17$.

5. Write a function that has a character parameter c and an integer parameter n and displays a triangle of c's with one c in the first row, two c's in the second row, and so on.

6. Write a function that returns 1 if the file TEST exists and 0 otherwise.

7. Write a function with two parameters—a file variable f and a character c. This function assumes the file f is open for input and returns the number of occurrences of the character c in the file. Test this function in a main program for a file called TEST.

8. Write a function that returns the maximum integer value stored in the file TEST. Write a short program to test your function.

7 Pointers

PREVIEW   *Almost all Pascal texts discuss pointers near the end of the book. In C, however, pointers play an important role. Arrays, strings, and even parameters passed by variable are all intimately associated with pointers. Discussing these topics would be impossible without first providing information on pointers. This chapter therefore introduces pointers.*

We begin by describing pointer types. Then, we discuss the address and dereferencing operators. The concept of memory alignment, which often causes portability problems, we next present. We continue the discussion of functions, address the problem of dangling references, and then describe two additional modes of parameter transmission: passing variables by reference and passing functions as parameters. This we follow with a presentation of permissible function and pointer declarators; we continue this subject in the following chapters where we describe array, structure, union, and enumeration declarators. Next, we discuss pointer arithmetic. We also present memory allocation and deallocation. We conclude the chapter with two examples that show how records and arrays can be simulated using pointers.

In the following review, we describe not only how pointers are declared and used in Pascal but also the concept of pointers in general. Pointers are the heart and soul of the C language, so an understanding of this material is essential. We also describe the relation between the system stack and heap.

**REVIEW OF
PASCAL
CONSTRUCTS**   Pointers are often somewhat confusing for novice programmers. In this section, we review how to define pointers and how to use them properly. The most important aspect to remember about a pointer is that it is like any other variable except that the value stored in it has a different interpretation: It is the *address* of some memory location. Thus whenever we talk about a pointer, we are referring to a variable that holds a memory address. Let us explain our terminology with an example:

```
VAR p : ^INTEGER;
```

In this declaration, p is defined as a variable of the type pointer to integer, or simply, a pointer. Assume at some point, the value 17 is stored in p. We interpret this value as a memory address. If the contents of memory location 17 is 31, we say the **value** of p is 17, and p **points** to the value 31:

To make the relation between the value of the pointer and the value pointed to by a pointer more clear, we use the following graphical representation:

Sometimes the address stored in a pointer is not important, and we use the abbreviated representation

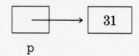

Let us summarize this example:

- p is a pointer.
- p's *value* (in this case) is 17.
- The value 17 is interpreted as an *address*.
- p *points to* the value 31 (assuming memory location 17 contains 31).

What about the address of the variable p itself? This information is not essential in the preceding example, but to make our discussion complete, we explain it now. When a variable is declared, sufficient memory space is allocated to hold one value of whatever type the variable is defined as. This is true for pointer variables as well. Specifically, when a pointer is declared, enough memory is allocated to hold an address. Exactly where in memory this space is allocated is usually not important. As for the example, assuming the space for pointer p is allocated at memory location 53, we have the following:

We have introduced a minor extension of our graphical representation:

   p: 53

denotes that the memory location with the address 53 has been allocated for the variable p; in other words, the value 17 is stored at memory location 53. In Pascal, the address of a variable cannot normally be accessed by a programmer.

   Since the value stored in a pointer is a memory address, the language has to provide the user with some sort of **dereferencing** mechanism, that is, a mechanism that can be used to access the value pointed to by the pointer. Pascal implements dereferencing by following the pointer variable with a caret symbol $^\wedge$:

   $p^\wedge$ has the value 31.

The expression $p^\wedge$ is an integer and may be used wherever an integer variable may be used. Graphically, we have

```
┌──────┐        ┌──────┐
│  17  │ ────▶  │  31  │
└──────┘        └──────┘
  p: 53          p^: 17
```

How are pointers initialized? Is the statement

   $p^\wedge := 1;$

allowed immediately after the declaration of p? The answer is no: The initial value of a variable, including a pointer variable, is undetermined. As an example, let us assume the initial value stored in p is 17:

```
┌──────┐        ┌──────┐
│  17  │ ────▶  │ ...  │
└──────┘        └──────┘
   p             p^: 17
```

If the statement

   $p^\wedge := 1$

is given, this causes the value 1 to be stored in memory location 17:

```
┌──────┐        ┌──────┐
│  17  │ ────▶  │  1   │
└──────┘        └──────┘
   p             p^: 17
```

This arbitrary location would be part of the user's address space or the operating system itself. In either case, memory is being indiscriminately modified, which could cause unpredictable results.

As we show in later examples, it is often useful to be able to arbitrarily create a pointer to *any* type of variable, including attributes of records and elements of arrays. The fact that the address of a variable cannot be accessed in standard Pascal can therefore be a limitation.

Memory Allocation and Deallocation

We now briefly discuss memory allocation and deallocation. In Chapter 1, we described the **run-time system** of a programming language as a set of routines that support the execution of a program. These routines provide operations that have to be performed when a program is running—operations whose requirements cannot be determined at compile time. A good example is the NEW operation in Pascal. The call NEW(p) is used to *allocate* a block of memory and assign the base address of this block to the pointer p. At the machine level, this statement is translated into a call to the run-time system routine that handles requests for memory. The amount of memory that this routine will allocate depends on the size of the object that p is defined to point to, and this size can be determined at compile time. For example, if p is declared as

```
VAR p : ^REAL;
```

a NEW(p) request would allocate enough memory to hold a real value. However, although the amount of memory that will be needed is known at compile time, the logic of the program while it is running determines whether the request will ever be made. For that reason, run-time support for memory requests is essential.

The Heap

The NEW routine reserves a block of memory of the requested size in a pool of free memory called the **heap**. Assuming p is declared as before, the call

```
NEW(p)
```

would allocate a block of memory large enough to hold a real value. If the value of p is later changed and there is no longer a pointer pointing to this block, the memory is called "garbage." The run-time systems of some programming languages provide so-called **garbage collectors** which can determine when a block of memory is no longer needed and return it to the heap. Automatic garbage collection is expensive in terms of CPU time, and therefore many languages (including Pascal and C) do not provide this feature. A more common approach is to delegate the task of garbage collection to the programmer by providing a special routine that may be called to deallocate memory when it is no longer needed. In Pascal, this routine is called DISPOSE. The call

```
DISPOSE(p)
```

deallocates the block of memory pointed to by p and returns it to the pool of available memory blocks (the heap). In this scheme, it is entirely the programmer's responsibility to ensure that unused memory is deallocated properly. If unused memory is not restored to the heap, a later request for memory (via NEW) may fail even though technically free memory is available.

Two separate data storage areas are used by the program during run time: the stack and the heap. The lifetime of data stored on the *stack* is relative to the lifetime of the subroutine that the data are defined in. The lifetime of data stored on the *heap* starts with the execution of the allocation procedure NEW and ends when the deallocation procedure DISPOSE is called. As we show in Example 7.4.1, it is wrong to make global pointers point to stack allocated data because those values disappear as soon as the procedure that contains them terminates. This is usually referred to as the **dangling reference** problem.

Parameter Transmission Modes

Finally, let us look at modes of parameter transmission in Pascal. There are three modes of parameter transmission:

- Call by value
- Call by reference (also known as call by var)
- Passing functions and procedures as parameters

We now briefly describe the implementation of these modes.

Call by value is used to pass a value from the caller to the called procedure. The actual parameter is evaluated, and its *value* is assigned to the formal parameter before the execution of the procedure (or function) starts. Thus an actual parameter may be any expression provided its type is compatible with the type of the formal parameter. The value of the actual parameter cannot be changed as a result of the call.

Call by reference is used to establish a two-way communication between a procedure (or function) and the calling subroutine. When a procedure with a VAR type formal parameter is called, the *address* of the actual parameter and not its value is passed to the called procedure. Any reference within this procedure to the formal parameter is indirectly passed to the actual parameter. The actual parameter must be an l-value, that is, a simple, indexed, or dotted variable (so its address may be determined).

In some implementations of Pascal, compound objects may be passed both by value and by reference; there is an important difference between the two. For example, passing an array X by value means the whole array must be copied (and so X cannot be modified as a result of the call); passing X by reference means only the address of X will be copied, and any update of the formal parameter changes the value of X.

To explain passing functions and procedures as parameters, let us consider an example. A root of a function f is an element x of the domain of f such that

$$f(x) = 0$$

To write a function that computes a root of a function f in the interval $[a, b]$ with the accuracy *eps*, that is, to find a point x in this interval so that the condition

$$abs(f(x)) <= eps$$

holds, we need a function $root(f,a,b,eps)$ that returns a point that satisfies the estimation. The first parameter of the function $root$ is a **function parameter**. Technically speaking, passing a function parameter means passing the address of the code of this function. If one treats a function as the address of the code of this function, this mode of parameter transmission becomes a version of call by value. When a call is made, the value of the formal parameter becomes the value of the actual parameter, which represents the address of the code of the "actual function."

Standard Pascal supports passing functions and procedures as parameters, but many compilers do not implement it.

Glossary

Allocation of memory   The action of acquiring a block of memory from the heap.

Dangling reference   A reference to an object whose lifetime is over.

Deallocation of memory   The action of returning a block of memory to the heap.

Dereferencing of a pointer's value   The value pointed to by a pointer.

Heap   A pool of free memory. Dynamic memory requests allocate memory from this area.

Pointer   A variable whose value is interpreted as a memory address. A pointer points to the value stored in the location at that address.

C CONSTRUCTS

7.1 DECLARING POINTERS

We are now ready to compare the definitions of pointer type variables in Pascal and C. In both languages, the syntax of a pointer definition is the same as an ordinary variable or type definition with the addition of a special symbol to qualify it as a pointer definition. In Pascal, a caret or circumflex (commonly called an up-arrow) is used; in C, an asterisk is used.

Variable definition:

Pascal	C
VAR *id*: ^*typ*;	*typ* *id;

In Pascal, the $^\wedge$ precedes the type *typ*, whereas in C, the * precedes the identifier *id*, for example,

Pascal	C
VAR p : ^INTEGER;	int *p;

Alternatively, a **pointer type** could be defined and then used to define a variable:

Pascal	C
TYPE pint = ^INTEGER;	typedef int * pint;
VAR p : pint;	pint p;

Consider the following definition:

```
int *ip;
```

This defines `ip` as a pointer to integer. The space between the `int` and the `*` is not essential. This definition may also be written as

```
int* ip;
```

or

```
int * ip;
```

The layout we use

```
int *ip;
```

suggests `*ip` is an integer.

The separate definitions of an integer and a pointer to integer may be shortened to a single definition:

```
int *ip, i;
```

In this case, the * applies only to ip. This also explains why in Chapter 4 on files we had to use an asterisk for each file variable defined, for example,

```
FILE *f, *g;
```

A macro could also be used:

```
#define PINT int *
PINT ip;
```

This would define ip as a pointer to integer. But using this macro can be misleading; for example, consider

```
PINT pi, pj;
```

Although it appears that both pi and pj are being defined as pointers, only pi is. The reason for this is obvious if the macro is expanded:

```
int * pi, pj;
```

pi is a pointer variable, and pj is an integer variable. There is no way to define a pointer "type" using a macro that avoids this problem. The correct way of introducing pointer types is to use typedef:

```
typedef int * PINT;
PINT pi, pj;
```

Visually, the definition of pi and pj is the same as the preceding example, which uses a macro. However, in this version, *both* pi and pj, not just pi, are defined as pointers to integers. The difference is subtle but important.

A pointer may point to a pointer:

```
typedef int   *  PINT;
typedef PINT  *  PPINT;
PINT p;
PPINT pp;
```

In this example, p is a pointer to integer, and pp is a pointer to pointer to integer.

7.2 DEREFERENCING POINTERS AND THE ADDRESS OPERATOR

Dereferencing refers to accessing the value that a pointer points to. For this, C again uses an asterisk prefix. In this context, the asterisk is treated as a unary operator that interprets its single argument as an address and returns the contents of the address as the value of the operation. In Pascal, the circumflex is used for dereferencing, but it follows the variable being dereferenced.

Pascal	C
p$^\wedge$	*p

C, unlike Pascal, provides an operator that may be applied to a variable to determine the *address* of that variable—that is, the first location in memory that the variable has been allocated. The ampersand & is the symbol used, and it is called the **address operator**. Consider the following definitions:

```
int   i = 1,
      *j;
```

Here, j is a pointer to integer. Assume i and j are allocated memory cells at addresses 10 and 20, respectively. Graphically, we have

```
+-------+       +-------+
|   1   |       |  ...  |
+-------+       +-------+
 i: 10           j: 20
```

This means the value of &i is 10, and the value of &j is 20.

7.3 POINTER ASSIGNMENTS AND CONVERSIONS

7.3.1 General Concepts

Any pointer variable is an l-value. The * operator can be applied to any pointer expression *exp*, and

exp

is also an l-value. On the other hand,

&*exp*

is well defined only if *exp* is an l-value. Clearly, a construct such as

```
&123
```

is wrong, since no memory location is associated with an integer constant. Moreover, &*exp* itself is not an l-value. We describe pointer expressions in Section 7.5.

Pointer Assignments

As is true for any language construct, there are two aspects of pointer assignment correctness: static (compile-time) correctness and dynamic (run-time) correctness.

For an assignment, **static correctness** means the type of the left-hand side must be compatible with the type of the right-hand side. For example, if we have

```
int   p, *pp;
```

the assignments

```
p   = 3;
*pp = 4;
p   = *pp;
*pp = p;
pp  = &p;
```

are all statically correct (including the second one because the type of pp is pointer to integer, and so the type of *pp is integer). Thus the value 3 will be stored in the memory location allocated to the variable p, the value 4 in the location pointed to by pp, and so on. On the other hand, the assignments

```
pp = 3;
p  = pp;
p  = &pp;
```

are not statically correct (although some compilers may accept them).

The concept of **dynamic correctness** deals with the dynamic allocation of memory to pointers, such as is done via the NEW procedure in Pascal. Neglecting to properly allocate memory to pointers is a common cause of errors when programming in C; even experienced programmers often make this mistake. For example, the statement

```
*pp = 4;
```

is incorrect.   ■

Unless special provisions are made, variables in C are not automatically initialized, just as they are not in Pascal. For example, if the definitions

```
int  i = 1, *j, *k;
```

are given, the initial values of j and k are unknown and could be anything. These variables are often referred to as undefined. Consider the following examples:

1. `j = &i;`
   This assigns to the pointer j the address of integer variable i; that is, j now points to i. Assuming the addresses of i, j, and k are 10, 20, and 30, respectively, graphically, we have

   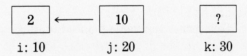

2. `*j = 2;`
   This statement stores 2 in the memory location pointed to by j, which in this case is memory location 10.

   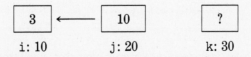

   As a side effect of the assignment, the value of integer variable i has been changed to 2.

3. `i = *j + 1;`
   This assigns to i the contents of the location pointed to by j, incremented by 1.

   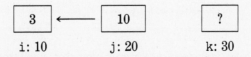

   Here, * has higher precedence than +, so

   ```
   *j + 1
   ```

is equivalent to

```
(*j) + 1
```

On the other hand, ++ has higher precedence than *, so

```
*j++
```

is equivalent to

```
*(j++)
```

and increments j rather than the value pointed to by j (which is correct but has a different meaning; see Section 7.5 on pointer arithmetic).

4. k = &i;
   Now, both k and j have the address of i as their value; that is, they both point to i. The assignment k = j would have the same effect.

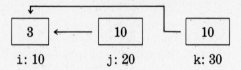

3	←	10		10

i: 10   j: 20   k: 30

5. printf("%d",*k);
   This prints the value pointed to by k, which in this case, is 3.

Example 7.3.1 The following program reads in two integers and then prints the larger of the two values using an auxiliary pointer:

```
#include <stdio.h>
main()
{
    int i, j, *pi;

    scanf("%d%d", &i, &j);
    pi = i > j ? &i : &j;
    printf("%d\n", *pi);
}
```
■

Now consider a pointer variable used in an input operation such as scanf:

```
int i, *pi = &i;                  -pi points to i
scanf("%d", pi);
```

This statement reads an integer value into the variable i because pi points to the variable i. Since pi is a pointer, the & operator is not needed here; we explain this fully in Section 7.4.1.

In Pascal, the value of a pointer cannot be printed directly (it would have to be done using a variant record); in C, it is allowed. For example,

```
int *pi;
printf("%u", pi);
```

is syntactically correct. The value displayed by this statement is the value of pi, which is an address. Since in most implementations addresses are unsigned integers, we have used the %u conversion character in the preceding example. Usually, a pointer is treated as either an unsigned int or an unsigned long; if the size of a pointer is long, a %lu conversion would be required in the printf. The ANSI C standard [Ans86] proposes that a %p control string be defined for this purpose, but few compilers now implement this. We assume addresses are *unsigned*.

The NULL Pointer

Like Pascal, C defines a special *nil* value that can be assigned to a pointer to indicate that its value is defined but that it does not point to anything. In Pascal, the value that nil corresponds to may vary in different implementations. In C, the nil pointer is called NULL and is usually equal to 0. The macro

```
#define NULL 0
```

is defined in the standard header file stdio.h to represent this value. On some systems, NULL may be defined as

```
#define NULL 0L
```

if the size of pointers is the same as the size of longs. This is primarily done because otherwise there may be a problem when NULL is passed uncast as a parameter to a function.

A convenient way to set the initial value of a pointer to NULL is in the definition itself, as in the following example:

```
int *pi = NULL,
    *pj = NULL;
```

Pointers are sometimes useful for accessing *absolute* memory addresses, especially on microcomputers. The following example demonstrates this:

```
typedef char * BYTE;
BYTE add;
add = (BYTE) 0x80;
```

This assigns the absolute memory address 80 hexadecimal to the pointer add. Note the casting used: 0x80 is of type int, and add is defined as a pointer to char; thus it has to be cast. The value of the expression *add would be the contents of memory location 80 hexadecimal.

If, in the preceding example, the assignment was done as

```
add = 0x80;
```

it may not be correct since *integers are not pointers*, and the actual conversion that would take place depends, in this case, on the implementation.

7.3.2 Pointer Conversions

Let us now discuss conversions of pointer types. In many cases, pointer conversion, either explicit (by casting) or implicit, is nonportable. We describe why this is so and specify which conversions are portable.

A pointer is defined to point to a particular type of object, and different objects may require different amounts of memory in which to be stored. Similarly, as we describe in Section 7.3.2.2, pointers pointing to different types of objects may themselves be of *different* sizes and use different internal representations.

Some compilers allow the assignment of one type of pointer to another type of pointer and perform the necessary type casting implicitly. For example, if we have the definitions

```
char *pc;
int  *pi;
```

and write

```
pc = pi;
```

this may be allowed, being implicitly converted into

```
pc = (char *)pi;
```

Many compilers will give a warning message in a case like this, and some may not allow it at all. To be safe, explicit casting should be used, although even this may not be completely portable as the following discussion illustrates.

7.3.2.1 Memory Alignment

Any data type S has a so-called **alignment modulus**. The address of any object of type S must be a multiple of its alignment modulus. For example, on the PDP-11, the alignment modulus for the type int is 2. On other machines, the alignment modulus for type int is 4.

The type T is called more **restrictive** (or stringent) than the type S if the alignment modulus for T is greater than or equal to the alignment modulus for S. For example, if the alignment modulus for the type char is 1, and the alignment modulus for the type int is 4, int is more restrictive than char.

Each machine has a particular type that is most restrictive; often, it is char, although on some machines it is int or possibly double.

In this regard, pointer conversions may create problems. For example, assume the alignment moduli for char and int are 1 and 4, respectively. If we assume the preceding definitions, and pc is initialized in some manner to 1001, what would be the value of

```
(int *)pc
```

The conversion of pc to an *integer* pointer type may require an adjustment to an address that is divisible by 4 either by scaling down to 1000 or scaling up to 1004. The C language does not specify whether the adjustment is backward or forward, so both possibilities should be considered. Whatever the case, because this scaling takes place, the value of

```
(int *)pc
```

differs from the value of

```
pc
```

A third possibility is that no address adjustment is performed when pointers are converted from one type to another. If this is how the conversion is handled, an expression involving dereferencing of that converted pointer, for example,

```
*( (int *)pc )
```

may result in the operating system aborting the program because of illegal addressing (an integer at an address not divisible by 4).

In general, pointers to the type S may be safely converted to pointers to the type T and back if S is *more restrictive* than T. For example, referring to our earlier discussion, pointers to int can be converted to pointers to char and back without the value of the pointer involved being changed, as the following illustrates:

```
pc = (char *)pi;
pi = (int *)pc;
```

In this example, after the second assignment is performed, the value of pi should be unchanged since no scaling takes place. However, the *reverse* of this is not necessarily true:

```
pi = (int *)pc;
pc = (char *)pi;
```

In this case, the initial assignment of pc to pi may cause scaling to occur, and as a result, the reassignment of pi to pc may change the original value of pc. Of course, if a particular implementation does not perform scaling of pointers, these assignments would not cause the values of pointers to change; however, subsequent dereferencing may cause a run-time error to occur. The NULL pointer can *always* be safely used in pointer expressions, since its value can be converted to any pointer type regardless of any memory alignment restrictions.

7.3.2.2 The Representation of Pointers

A problem related to the nonportability of pointer assignments deals with general pointer representation. Strictly speaking, we cannot assume pointers to different types are identical either in size or in internal representation. This is particularly important when dealing with the NULL pointer.

In general, the NULL pointer value is special in that it may be used with any pointer type and will be automatically converted to a representation compatible with that type. For example, if we have the definitions

```
char *c;
int *p;
```

it is *not* necessary to cast NULL when it is assigned to either of these pointers:

```
c = (char *)NULL;
p = (int *)NULL;
```

These assignments are correct, and for clarity, some programmers may cast NULL in situations like this. However, the assignments

```
c = NULL;
p = NULL;
```

are also correct, even if character pointers and integer pointers have different representations, since NULL is always converted to the appropriate type *when it is used in a pointer context*.

One situation where NULL *does* have to be cast is when it is passed as an actual parameter to a function. This is because most C compilers do not check the types of parameters and thus will simply pass NULL as an integer rather than a pointer. For example, if we have a function defined as

```
void test(c)
char *c;
...
```

where the formal parameter c is specified as a pointer to char, if NULL is to be passed as an actual parameter, test should be called using

```
test((char *)NULL);
```

where NULL is explicitly cast as a char pointer.

On most byte-oriented architectures, pointers to different types are the same size and representation, and in these cases, this casting would not be needed. On many word-oriented architectures, pointers to different types do have different representations. Therefore, to avoid potential problems, NULL should be cast when it is used as an actual parameter.

This rule should also be followed when passing pointers other than NULL as actual parameters. Specifically, if the type of an actual pointer parameter is not the same as the type of the corresponding formal parameter, it should be cast to the type of the formal parameter.

7.4 POINTERS AND FUNCTIONS

In this section, we explain the dangling reference problem, how to express call by reference in C, how to define pointers to functions, and how to pass functions as parameters.

7.4.1 The Dangling Reference Problem

The lifetime of an auto variable is limited to the time when the function that contains a definition of this variable is active. Thus a global pointer set to point to an auto variable during the execution of a function should *not* be dereferenced once the function terminates. This is illustrated in the following example.

Example 7.4.1

```
#include <stdio.h>
int *pi;

void f()
{
     int i = 2;

     pi = &i;
     printf("Inside f the value pointed to by pi is %d\n",
            *pi);
}

void confuse()
{
     int x = 5;
}

main()
}
     f();
     printf("After f terminates this value is %d\n", *pi);
     confuse();
     printf("After confuse terminates this is %d\n", *pi);
}
```

In function f the pointer pi is set to point to the value allocated on the *stack* for the local variable i. When f terminates, the pi is still pointing to this location and the value there may still be equal to 2. After confuse is called the stack has been modified as a result of allocation and subsequent assignment to the local variable x. Thus the value pointed to by the pointer pi may also be changed. On most systems the output from this program would be:

```
Inside f the value pointed to by pi is 2
After f terminates this value is 2
After confuse terminates this is 5
```

This is usually referred to as the **dangling reference problem**.   ∎

7.4.2 Call by Reference

As we explained in the review, **call by reference** means the *address* of a variable is passed to the called function. Thus formal parameters called by reference must be defined as pointers, and the calling function must be provided with the addresses of the actual parameters (using the & operator) unless the actual parameter already is a pointer. As an example, consider the function swap below, which exchanges the values of its parameters:

```
void swap(x, y)
int *x, *y;
{
     int temp;

     temp = *x;
     *x = *y;
     *y = temp;
}
```

A rule of thumb is that parameters called by reference appear within the function body in the form *identifier*.

If we want to exchange the values of integer variables i and j, swap should be called as

```
swap(&i, &j);
```

We now trace this call using the graphical representation introduced earlier. Remember that call by value in this context means when the execution enters the body of swap, its formal parameters are initialized as if the following two assignments are executed:

```
x = &i;
y = &j;
```

Assuming the initial values of the variables i and j are 3 and 4, respectively, the memory map before the call has been made would be

Immediately after the call has been initiated, the memory map would be

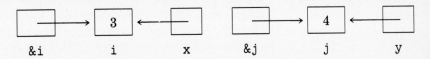

After the execution of temp = *x:

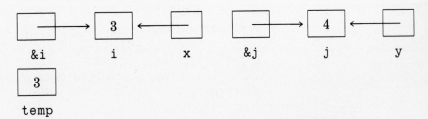

After the execution of *x = *y:

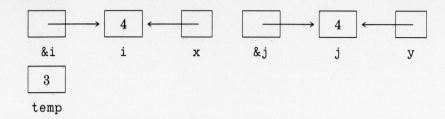

After the execution of *y = temp:

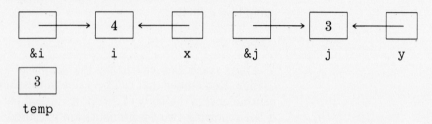

Many programming errors are caused by calls to functions that do not specify actual parameters as addresses. For example, the call

```
swap(i, j)
```

treats the values of i and j (3 and 4 in the preceding example) as *addresses* and produces meaningless results. ∎

It should now be clear why in Chapter 2 we used & in scanf: Since as a result of the call to scanf its actual parameters are to be changed, they have to be passed by reference, and so must be preceded by &.

Example 7.4.2   Suppose we want to read a single line from the keyboard and count the number of whitespace characters and the number of lowercase letters that occur in this line. In the following program, we write a "boolean" function called get that returns 1 if it can read a nonempty line; otherwise, it returns 0. In the former case, get also returns, through parameters, the number of whitespace characters and the number of lowercase letters.

```
#include <stdio.h>

int get(ws, lc)
int *ws, *lc;
{
    int c;
```

```
           *ws = *lc = 0;
           while ((c = getchar()) != EOF)
                switch (c) {
                case ' ' :
                case '\t': (*ws)++;
                           break;
                case '\n': return 1;
                default  : if (c >= 'a' && c <= 'z')
                                (*lc)++;
                           break;
                }
           return 0;
      }
```

In this version, if end-of-file is encountered before end-of-line, get returns 0. Recall that in (*lc)++ parentheses *are* necessary. A main program that uses this routine might look like

```
main()
{
     int ws, lc;

     if (get(&ws, &lc) != 0) {
          printf("There are %d whitespace characters", ws);
          printf("\nand %d lowercase letters\n", lc);
     }
     else printf("unexpected end-of-file\n");
}
```

If ws and lc were defined as

```
int *ws, *lc;
```

get should *not* be called as

```
get(ws, lc)
```

because no memory has been allocated to these pointers. If memory were allocated to the pointers ws and lc, the call would be correct. If a variable is already a pointer and it is used as an actual parameter, there is *no* need to use an & in a function call. This explains why we can use

```
scanf("%d", pi)
```

if pi is a pointer. ∎

7.4.3   Pointers to Functions and Functions as Parameters

A function can return a pointer type. Moreover, the user can define pointers to functions. Logically, a pointer to a function is the address of the function's code in memory, but this may differ from one implementation to another.

Example

```
extern double f();
double (*fp) ();
```

Function declarators have higher precedence than pointer declarators; thus the parentheses here are necessary. The example *declares* a double function f and a pointer fp to a double function. To assign a value to the pointer fp, an assignment of the form

```
fp = f;
```

should be used. An assignment like this, an initializer for a function pointer definition, and the actual parameter corresponding to a function pointer formal parameter are the only contexts where a function identifier may appear without parentheses; in the preceding example, it is converted to a pointer to a double function.   ∎

Generally, a function name f may appear in three constructs:

- In a definition or declaration of f
- In a call to f, with parameters (if any) enclosed within parentheses
- Without parentheses as in the preceding two contexts

A function name is *not* an l-value.

A pointer to a function may be dereferenced, using a *, and this denotes the function itself. Thus to call the function pointed to by the pointer fp the following can be used:

```
...  (*fp)(actual parameters) ...
```

Parentheses surrounding *fp are again needed because of the precedence mentioned earlier. The same expression without parentheses,

```
...  *fp(actual parameters) ...
```

would be interpreted as "take the value pointed to by the pointer that is returned by the call to the function fp." Here, fp is *not* a function, but rather a *pointer* to a function, so the expression would not be correct.

A graphical representation may be helpful. Assume the code of the function f is stored starting at address 100:

> code of function f

100

An occurrence of f, followed by parentheses, initiates execution of the code at address 100. A pointer to a function, like any other pointer, does not have any special initial value. After the assignment

    fp = f

we have

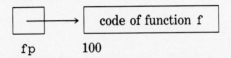

fp   100

Therefore, *fp refers to the origin of the code for f. (Note, however, that the actual contents of memory at this address depends on the implementation.)   ■

Example 7.4.3 The following program consists of functions representing the two polynomials $x^2 - 2$ and $x^3 - 2x + 5$:

```
double pol1(x)
double x;
{
     return (x * x - 2);
}

double pol2(x)
double x;
{
     return (x * x * x - 2 * x + 5);
}
```

and a main program in which we want to tabulate these functions, say, in the interval $[-1, +1]$ with a step of 0.001. Instead of writing code to produce the tabulation of one function and duplicating the code to tabulate the other function, we can use the same piece of code to tabulate both functions by using a pointer to a function:

```
#include <stdio.h>

#define LOW    (-1.0)
#define HIGH   1.0
#define STEP   0.001

main()
{
    int    i;
    double x,
           (*fp)();      /* pointer to function */

    for (i = 0; i < 2; i++) {
        /* first assign a pointer fp */
        if (i == 0)
            fp = pol1;
        else fp = pol2;
        /* now tabulate */
        for (x = LOW; x <= HIGH; x += STEP)
            printf("%13.5lf %20.10lf\n", x, (*fp)(x));
    }
}
```

To illustrate how this works, let us assume the code for function pol1 begins at address 400 and the code for function pol2 begins at address 800.

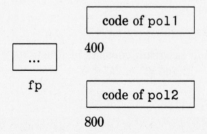

On the first iteration of the outer for loop, i is equal to 0; therefore, fp is assigned the value 400, the base address of function pol1. That is, fp is pointing to function pol1. Thus in the tabulation for loop, each time the expression (*fp)(x) is evaluated, code at address 400 (function pol1) will be executed. On the second iteration of the outer for loop, fp takes on the value 800, the start address of function pol2. Therefore, when the tabulation loop is executed on this iteration, code at address 800 will be executed (function pol2).

Actually, it would be more appropriate in this particular example to use a function that takes as a parameter the function to be tabulated, and in Example 7.4.4 we show how these can be done. There are, however, situations where direct assignment of different functions to a pointer to function is useful.   ∎

Example 7.4.4   The following shows how the function tabulation example (Example 7.4.3) can be generalized to tabulate any function by using a procedure with a function parameter.

```
void tabulate(low, high, step, f)
double low, high, step, (*f)();
{
    double x;

    for (x = low; x <= high; x += step)
        printf("%13.5f %20.10f\n", x, (*f)(x));
}
```

The function passed as a parameter is specified as

```
double (*f)();
```

This looks like a declaration of a pointer to a function, and this is exactly how C treats functions passed as parameters. Since f is a pointer to a function, *f is a function, and thus

```
(*f)(x)
```

is a call to *f with the actual parameter x.

The function tabulate can be called, for example, as

```
tabulate(-1.0, 1.0, 0.0001, pol1)
```

to tabulate function pol1, or as

```
tabulate(-2.0, 2.0, 0.002, pol2)
```

to tabulate pol2. Writing tabulate in this manner allows us to use it to tabulate any function, not just pol1 and pol2— provided, of course, the function takes a single parameter like pol1 and pol2 so that when it is invoked in tabulate via the expression (*f)(x), the number of parameters is correct for that function. Only the *name* of a function is specified when it is passed as an actual parameter.   ∎

Example 7.4.5   The following program is the one we described at the beginning of the chapter in the review of Pascal: a function that computes the root of a function f, that is, a point x such that f(x) = 0. We now implement this function in C. It will compute the root of a function f in the interval [a, b], using the *bisection* algorithm. The routine assumes a root exists within this range. The library function fabs is used to obtain the absolute value of a number.

```
#include <math.h>
#include <stdio.h>

double root(f, a, b, e)
double (*f)(), a, b, e;
{
      double c, fabs();

      c = (a + b) / 2;
      while (fabs( (*f)(c) ) >= e) {
            if ((*f)(c) * (*f)(a) > 0)
                  a = c;
            else b = c;
            c = (a + b) / 2;
      }

      return(c);
}
```

To complete this example, the main program uses this function to find a root of the function $f(x) = 2x^3 - x$:

```
double f(x)
double x;
{
      return( 2 * x * x * x - x);
}

main()
{
      double a, b, eps,
             f(),
             root();

      printf("Enter ends of interval and accuracy: ");
      scanf("%lf%lf%lf", &a, &b, &eps);
      printf("\nThe root is %f\n", root(f, a, b, eps));
}
```

In the main program, the actual parameter in the call to function root is the function f.

Another practical use of functions as parameters is in writing a generalized sorting routine. Consider the function header

```
sort(array, siz, numb, compare)
```

where array represents an array of numb elements, each siz bytes in size, and compare is a function pointer used to compare two elements of the array to determine which is larger. Because a comparison routine is provided as a *parameter* to the function, sort could be used to sort the elements of *any* type of array in whatever order the compare function is designed to order them. In Chapter 8 on arrays, we give a complete implementation of this kind of a sort routine (see Example 8.1.8).

7.4.4   Declarators—Part 1

Function declarators can be combined with other declarators. In this section, we provide a description of a declarator that is limited to function and pointer types; in the following chapters, we expand this description to include array and structure types.

A **type-specifier** is either a primitive type identifier, such as `int` or `float`, or a type identifier introduced by `typedef`. A **declarator** is defined recursively as

> *declarator:*
> > *identifier*
> > (*declarator*)
> > *declarator* (*formals*)
> > * *declarator*

This is read as "a *declarator* is either an *identifier*, or it is of one of the forms (*declarator*), *declarator* (*formals*), or * *declarator*." The *identifier* in the first of these forms is a variable identifier or a function identifier. The second form uses parentheses to change default precedences. The third form is used in function declarations; the *formals* specification in this form represents a function's formal parameter list and is optional. The fourth form of a *declarator* is used in pointer declarations. Using this, the complete form of an **identifier definition** can be formally stated as

> *type-specifier declarator*

for example,

```
int x;
float *y;
double *z();
int *(*v)();
```

We now explain how these definitions are interpreted, that is, how to derive the type of an identifier from a given definition. To help us describe the semantics of C type definitions, we introduce some terminology. The term **type-prefix** we define as

> *type-prefix:*
> > *empty*
> > *pointer to type-prefix*
> > *function returning type-prefix*

The term *empty* means an "empty" symbol, and in actual constructions it will be omitted; for example,

> *pointer to empty*

will be written as

> *pointer to*

Using the term *type-prefix*, the **type** of an identifier can be stated formally as

> *type-prefix type-specifier*

Some examples of types derived in this fashion are

```
int
```
> *pointer to* `double`
> *function returning pointer to pointer to* `int`

To determine the *type-prefix* of an identifier, we use the following rules:

I. If D is a declarator of the form

> `x`

(an identifier), its type-prefix is *empty*. Thus the definition

> *TS* `x;`

where *TS* is a type-specifier, defines x to be of type

> *empty TS*

or simply *TS*.

II. The second rule is recursive: Let D be a declarator that defines an identifier x to have a type-prefix *TP1*. Then
(a) the declarator

> `*D`

defines x to have a type-prefix *TP2* of the form

> *TP1 pointer to*

(b) the declarator

$(D)(\ )$

defines x to have a type-prefix *TP2* of the form

TP1 function returning

This may seem rather complicated, but the following examples should clarify the issue.

1. `int x;`
   According to rule I, the type-prefix of x is *empty*, and so the type of x is `int`.

2. `float *y;`
   Since the type-prefix of y is *empty*, according to rule IIa, the type-prefix of y in

   `*y`

   is

   pointer to

   and the type of y is

   type-prefix type-specifier

   or

   pointer to `float`

3. `double *z( );`
   Since ( ) has higher priority than *, this definition is equivalent to

   `double * (z( ));`

   According to rule IIb, the type-prefix of z in

   `z( )`

   is

   function returning

Therefore, according to IIa, the type-prefix of z in

```
* (z())
```

is

function returning pointer to

and the type of z is

function returning pointer to double

4. `int *(*v)();`
   This definition is equivalent to

```
int * ( (*v)() );
```

The type-prefix of v in

```
(*v)
```

is

pointer to

and so the type-prefix of v in

```
(*v)()
```

is

pointer to function returning

and the type-prefix of v in

```
* ( (*v)() )
```

is

pointer to function returning pointer to

Thus the type of v is

pointer to function returning pointer to int   ∎

Using a similar approach, we now give a more formal definition of the syntax of `typedef` (again, we give the complete definition in later chapters):

> `typedef` *type-specifier declarator*

The identifier that appears in the *declarator* is the identifier of the new type being introduced (a synonym of the existing type). The rules given earlier can also be applied here to determine what the existing type being used is. For example, in

```
typedef float * FLOAT;
```

the type of the identifier `FLOAT` is

> *pointer to* `float`

and so `FLOAT` is a synonym of this type. Similarly, in

```
typedef double (*FUNC)();
```

`FUNC` is a synonym of the type *pointer to function returning* `double`. Having this type defined, we can say

```
FUNC f;
```

to define a pointer to a function. A function of this type could also be defined:

```
FUNC g()
{
      return(sqrt);
}
```

When called, this function would return a pointer to the `double` function `sqrt`. To actually call g, and then call the function `sqrt` returned by g, an expression such as

```
(*(g()))(10.0)
```

could be used. In this example, the square root of 10 would be calculated. ∎

The following constructs are *illegal* in C:

- An array of functions (see Section 8.1.6)
- A function returning an array type (again see Section 8.1.6)

- A function returning a function
- A function returning a pointer to void (that is, void *)

The last case, if allowed, would be a definition such as

```
void *f( );
```

We continue this discussion in Section 8.1.6, where we describe the relations between function types and array types.

Type-names
Related to the concept of declarators is the term **type-name**, which we define as

> *type-name*:
>   *type-specifier abstract-declarator*

where *abstract-declarator* has a definition similar to that of a declarator except that it does not introduce an identifier:

> *abstract-declarator*:
>   *empty*
>   (*abstract-declarator*)
>   * *abstract-declarator*
>   *abstract-declarator* ( )

(we discuss this definition further in Section 8.1.6). The term *type-name* allows us to formally define the syntax of a **cast expression** as

> (*type-name*) *exp*

The type specified by an *abstract-declarator* can be derived using the notion of a type-prefix. For example, the *abstract-declarator*

```
(*)( )
```

represents

> *pointer to function returning*

and so a cast of the form

```
(int (*)( )) exp
```

means *exp* is cast to

> *pointer to function returning* int

As an example, suppose we have a pointer to integer function defined as

```
typedef int (* PIFUN)();
PIFUN p;
```

If we have a `double` function `f`

```
double f(...)
...
```

to make p point to f we can say

```
p = (PIFUN) f;
```

To correctly call f via p is somewhat involved. We cannot use

```
(*p)(...)
```

because `*p` is interpreted as an integer function, not a `double` function. Instead, we have to cast p to the type

pointer to function returning `double`

using the *type-name*

```
(double (*)())
```

and so the call will look like

```
(*(double (*)())p)(...)
```

If we introduced a *type* using

```
typedef double (*PDFUN)();
```

the syntax of the call could be simplified:

```
(*(PDFUN)p)(...)
```

This form, though probably more readable, would not have to be done in this fashion unless many of these calls are to be made.

7.5   POINTER ARITHMETIC

In this section, we describe a useful feature of C: pointer arithmetic. In Pascal, the values of two pointers may be compared only for equality or inequality and only if the pointers are of the same type. C is more flexible, allowing both addition and subtraction of pointer values, as well as general comparisons. Valid operations on pointers are

- The **sum** of a pointer and an integer
- The **difference** of a pointer and an integer
- Pointer **comparison**
- The **difference** of two pointers

Other pointer operations are not valid and may produce undetermined results.

The `sizeof` Operator

When dealing with pointers, it is often useful to know the size of the object pointed to by a pointer. This can be done using the `sizeof` operator. Its syntax is

```
sizeof(type-name)
```

or

```
sizeof expression
```

where *type-name* is described in the previous section.

The `sizeof` operator returns the number of bytes required to store a value of the type of the specified argument. Note that `sizeof` is a compile-time operator; that is, the *type* of its argument (and not the value) determines the result. Consider the following example:

```
int i;
float f;

i = sizeof(int) + sizeof(f);
```

Here i is assigned the number of memory cells required to store an `int` value plus the number of cells required to store a `float`; the actual result of this expression depends on the implementation.

When pointers are used, the same rules apply. For example, if we have the definitions

```
int i, *p;
```

then

```
i = sizeof(p);
```

would yield the number of bytes required to store a pointer (an address), whereas

```
i = sizeof(*p);
```

would yield the number of bytes required to store an object of the type pointed to by p, in this case an integer. In both cases, the type of the expression is used to determine the value returned by sizeof. The type of the value returned by sizeof is not defined in C, and so depends on the implementation. Most often, this type is unsigned int or unsigned long.

7.5.1 The Sum of a Pointer and an Integer

The expression

```
p + n
```

yields a pointer to the nth object beyond the one that p currently points to. The *address value* of this pointer is equivalent to

```
(char*)p + sizeof(*p) * n
```

that is, the value n is scaled according to the type of the object that p points to:

$$p \qquad p+1 \qquad p+2 \qquad\qquad\qquad p+n$$

If p is a pointer to type T, p may point to any object of type T. Each such object is sizeof(T) or sizeof(*p) bytes in size. Thus the expression

```
p + n
```

does *not* point to the nth address beyond that equal to p; instead, it points to the nth *object* of type T beyond p. If p is cast as a character pointer, that is,

```
(char*) p + n
```

the value of n will not be scaled as the type of p has been changed. (Actually, n *will* be scaled, but since sizeof(char) is 1, the result of the scaling will not change the value of n.)

To illustrate how different types affect scaling, consider the following definitions:

```
char    *pc;
int     *pi;
float   *pf;
```

Assume `sizeof(char)` is 1, `sizeof(int)` is 2, and `sizeof(float)`
is 4. Further assume pc, pi, and pf all equal 10.

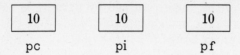

Then

    pc + 1

is 11,

    pc + 2

is 12, and so on. This is so because the type of pc is a pointer to char,
and

    pc + 1 = (char*)pc + sizeof(char) = 10 + 1 = 11

Now consider pi. The expression

    pi + 1

is equal to 12, being equivalent to

    (char*)pi + sizeof(int) * 1 = 10 + 2 = 12

The expression

    pi + 2

is equal to 14,

    (char*)pi + sizeof(int) * 2 = 10 + 4

and so on. Similarly,

    pf + 1

is equal to 14,

    10 + sizeof(float) * 1

and

    pf + 2

is equal to 18,

```
10 + sizeof(float) * 2
```

and so on.

Now suppose we do not have a character pointer available. It is still possible to sequence through the memory one byte at a time by using *casting*. For example, the expression

```
(char *)pi + 1
```

is equal to

```
10 + sizeof(char) * 1 or 11
```

and similarly

```
(char *)pf + 5
```

is equal to 15. In each case, the pointer involved has been cast as a character pointer, so the offset is calculated with respect to this type.

Since adding an integer to a pointer yields a pointer value, such an expression may be assigned to a pointer, for example,

```
pc = pc + 5
```                                                        ∎

Example 7.5.1   The following program reads in a double value and displays the successive bytes of that value in hexadecimal:

```
#include <stdio.h>

typedef char* MEMPTR;

main()
{
     double  val;
     MEMPTR  pointer;
     int     count;

     printf("Enter a real value: ");
     scanf("%lf", &val);
     for (count = 0, pointer = (MEMPTR) &val;
          count < sizeof(double);  pointer++, count++)
        printf("%d-th byte in hex is %02x\n", count, *pointer);
}
```

Note the need for casting in

```
pointer = (MEMPTR) &val
```

If characters are treated as signed integers, the definition of MEMPTR should be changed to

```
typedef unsigned char* MEMPTR;
```
∎

Example 7.5.2   This example shows an application of static variables. Consider a memory block containing a sequence of characters terminated by the ASCII null character. We want to print these characters on a single line, separated by blanks, and enclosed in square brackets, for example

```
[ a b c d ]
```

It is fairly easy to write an *iterative* solution:

```
void print(p)
char *p;
{
    printf("[ ");
    for (; *p; p++)
        printf("%c ", *p);
    printf("]\n");
}
```

A *recursive* version is somewhat more involved. An initial attempt might look like

```
void rprint(p)
char *p;
{
    printf("[ ");
    if (*p) {
        printf("%c ", *p);
        rprint(++p);
    }
    printf("]\n");
}
```

This is incorrect because it will output an open bracket before every character and follow the whole list with an equivalent number of closing brackets. A solution to this problem is to print the left square bracket only in the first call to print and the right square bracket only in the last call to print. Local automatic variables are of no help because they cannot be used to pass information to the recursively called function. A local static variable is what we need:

```
void rprint(p)
char *p;
{
    static int first = 1;
```

```
        if (first) {
            printf("[ ");
            first = 0;
        }
        if (*p) {
            printf("%c ", *p);
            rprint(++p);
        }
        else {
            printf("]\n");
            first = 1;  /* reset first for next call */
        }
    }
```

■

Example 7.5.3   The following function reads in a sequence of characters and converts it to a real value. This example is similar to Example 6.1.5, but instead of reading from the keyboard as was done in that example, this version assumes the parameter of the function getreal is a pointer to a memory area containing a sequence of characters that represent a real value. The function processes these characters and returns the corresponding real value.

```
#include <ctype.h>

double getreal(arr)
char *arr;
{
    double power = 1,
           val = 0;
    int    sign  = 1;

    while (isspace(*arr))
        arr++;
    switch(*arr) {
    case '-'  :  sign = -1;
    case '+'  :  arr++;
    case '.'  :  break;
    default   :  if (!isdigit(*arr))   /* error */
                    return(0.0);
    }
    while (isdigit(*arr))
        val = val * 10 + (*arr++ - '0');
    if (*arr++ == '.')
        while (isdigit(*arr)) {
            val = val * 10 + (*arr - '0');
            power *= 10;
            arr++;
        }
    return(sign * val / power);
}
```

■

7.5.2   Difference of a Pointer and an Integer

The expression

```
p - n
```

is essentially the same as the sum of a pointer and an integer. In this case, the evaluation follows the formula

```
(char*)p - sizeof(*p) * n
```

giving the address of the nth object *before* p, with scaling again being used relative to the size of the object that p points to.

Example

Suppose p is a pointer and the statement

```
for (i = 0; i < LIM; i++)
    p++;
```

has been executed (and LIM is nonnegative). How would the value of p prior to executing this loop be determined? The expression

```
p - LIM
```

is one possible solution, since the execution of the loop does nothing more than

```
p += LIM
```

■

7.5.3   Pointer Comparison: <, <=, >, >=, ==, !=

If p and q are pointers, an expression such as

```
p < q
```

is well defined if p and q both point to objects within a *contiguous* memory segment. Two pointers point to the same memory segment if, for example, they point to elements of the same array or structure. If this is the case, the expression yields 1 if the value of p (an address) is less than the value of q (also an address); otherwise, it yields 0. The reason for this restriction on pointer comparison is that, in some systems, memory may be physically divided into several separate segments; therefore, the comparison of pointers that do not point to objects in the same segment is meaningless. Moreover, on some computers, pointer comparisons are signed, whereas on others they are unsigned. Thus values such as -1 should *not* be assigned to pointers.

As a consequence of the preceding discussion, pointers to different types should *not* be compared. The only exception to this rule is the NULL pointer, which can be used with any type of pointer.

Example

Suppose p and q are pointers to characters and p points to a block of memory LIM bytes in size. How would q be tested to determine whether or not it is pointing to a value within this block? The expression

```
(q >= p  &&  q < p + LIM)
```

is one possible solution.   ■

As another example, assume we have the definitions

```
char *pc, *pd;
int *pi;
```

and the current values of pc and pd are 10 and 19, respectively. Now consider the loop

```
for ( ;  pc <= pd;  pc++)
    printf("%c", *pc);
```

This prints the character values contained in ten consecutive memory cells starting at address 10 and ending at address 19. Suppose that sizeof(int) is 2 and those ten cells represent five integer values rather than ten character values. How could these integers be printed? Consider the following attempt:

```
for ( ;  pc <= pd;  pc++)
    printf("%d", (int)*pc);
```

This version will print ten integers made up of overlapping pairs of bytes. That is, the first integer will be made up of bytes 10 and 11; the second integer, of bytes 11 and 12; and so on. That is *not* what is wanted. To correct this problem, we should have used integer casting on the increment operation. The use of an int pointer, for example,

```
for (pi = (int *)pc;  pi <= (int *)pd;  pi++)
    printf("%d", *pi);
```

should work on most machines, but it is not completely portable because the *memory alignment* restrictions that we discussed in Section 7.3 may cause problems when pc is assigned to pi.   ∎

Example 7.5.4   By using pointer comparison, we can rewrite Example 7.5.1 without using the integer variable count:

```
#include <stdio.h>

typedef char* MEMPTR;
#define ADD(v)      (MEMPTR) &(v)

main()
{
    double val;
    MEMPTR fpoint;

    printf("Enter a real value please: ");
    scanf("%lf", &val);
    printf("The bytes of this number are:\n");
    for (fpoint = ADD(val);
            fpoint < ADD(val) + sizeof(double); fpoint++)
        printf("%02x ", *fpoint);
    putchar('\n');
}
```

In the for statement, fpoint is initialized to point to the first byte of memory allocated to the float type variable val. The loop stops when fpoint points to an address greater than the last cell allocated. Thus only the cells within these two bounds are examined.   ∎

Example 7.5.5   Pointer arithmetic can be used for a *fast copy* of a block of memory. Assume we have

```
char *p, *q, *aux;
```

and p is pointing to a memory block N bytes in size, and we want to copy these N bytes to the place pointed to by q:

```
for (aux = p; aux < p + N; *q++ = *aux++)
    ;
```

The basic step is

```
*q++ = *aux++
```

which does the following:

First, the assignment

```
*q = *aux
```

copies the current contents of the location pointed to by aux to the location pointed to by q.

Next, both pointers are incremented,

```
q++
aux++
```

so that they will point to successive locations.

In this version, after the termination of the loop, the pointer q is pointing to the byte following the *end* of the copied memory block. If this is undesired, another pointer may be used, or pointer/integer subtraction (see Section 7.5.2) may be used to reset q:

```
q -= N;
```                                                    ■

7.5.4 Pointer Subtraction

If p and q are defined as pointers, the expression

```
p - q
```

yields the number of objects between p and q, including p and excluding q, and is evaluated according to

```
((char*) p - (char*) q) / sizeof(*p)
```

This expression is therefore meaningful *only* if p is greater than q and both are of the same type.

Pointer arithmetic should be used carefully because *wraparound* could occur. Though the odds of this happening are low, you should be aware of it. Suppose sizeof(int) is 2 and we have two pointers defined as

```
int *p, *q;
```

If pointer p is initialized to 1, the loop

```
for (q = p + 10;   q >= p;   q--)
    printf("%d", *q);
```

which is supposed to print the values of the integers stored between
p+10 and p, would iterate more times than was intended. This is because q is defined as a pointer to integer, and so each time it is decremented, its address value is decreased by 2, sequencing through values
11, 9, 7, and so on. As a result, when q becomes equal to 1, on what
should be the last iteration of the loop, and is decremented, a wraparound occurs (that is, q−1 is equal to MAXINT, *not* −1). Thus the loop
will not terminate on this iteration. We assume addresses are treated as
unsigned integers ranging from 0 to MAXINT; if a C system treats addresses as signed values, this loop may in fact work.

Example 7.5.6   Suppose a pointer p is pointing to the block of ten characters. The following loop prints the position of the first ? character in that block, or
−1 if ? does not occur. Assume p and q are defined as pointers to character.

```
for (q = p;  *q != '?' && q < p + 10;  q++)
    ;
printf("%d\n", q < p + 10 ? q − p + 1 : −1);
```

As a final comment on pointer arithmetic, note that the sum of two pointer
values is *not* defined.

7.6   MEMORY ALLOCATION AND DEALLOCATION

We continue this chapter by discussing how to allocate and deallocate
memory for pointers. In Pascal, this is accomplished with the procedures NEW and DISPOSE. In C, several variations of these basic routines allow both a high-level and a low-level approach to memory allocation and deallocation. Adopting a high-level approach is less likely to
cause errors but is less efficient; low-level management of memory improves efficiency but is more difficult to debug. In this section, we describe only how to use the high-level memory management routines. In
Chapter 14, we describe the other routines that are available in some
systems.

The Function malloc
A philosophy of C is to place system-dependent routines in libraries.
Memory architectures vary from system to system, so memory manage-
ment routines depend on the system. To **allocate** memory, the standard
C library provides the function malloc which takes an unsigned integer
argument and returns a pointer to character, for example,

```
char *p;
p = malloc(10);
```

The function `malloc` allocates from the heap a block of memory consisting of a specified number of bytes and returns the base address of this block as the result of the function. If there is no block of the required size in the heap, NULL is returned.

The Function `free`

To deallocate memory, C provides the procedure `free(p)`. The parameter p is assumed to point to a block of memory allocated from the heap. Calling `free` causes the indicated block of memory to be returned to the pool of free memory on the heap.

As in Pascal, where DISPOSE(p) does *not* change the value of p, in C, `free(p)` also does not update p. This pointer is still pointing to the memory area that has been deallocated, and it is the user's responsibility not to access that area.

A similar programming error is to free a memory area and then use another pointer to access this area. For example, if p and q are two pointers that point to the same address,

```
free(p);
```

should be followed by

```
p = q = NULL;
```

Examples

```
char c, *pc;
int  *pi,
     i = 0;
char *malloc();
```

Remember that the function `malloc` must always be declared as shown here because it returns a pointer to character.

Since initially the value of a pointer type variable is undefined, the statement

```
*pc = 'a';
```

would be incorrect. We could assign to pc the address of another variable (such as c), or we could *dynamically* allocate memory for it with `malloc`:

```
pc = malloc(1);
```

To be perfectly safe, you should include a check to test if the call to `malloc` was successful:

```
if ((pc = malloc(1)) == NULL) {
     - no memory available, perform
        some action, for example abort
     . . .
}
```

This check could also be performed as

```
if (!(pc = malloc(1))) ...
```

if NULL were equal to 0 (because it would be interpreted as false).

Assuming the call to malloc allocated one cell at memory location 10, the statement

```
*pc = 'a';
```

would store the value a at location 10. If the call

```
pc = malloc(20);
```

were now made, it would replace the value in pc by the address of this new block, and location 10 would therefore become *inaccessible*. To be correct, the memory should be properly deallocated before malloc is called:

```
free(pc);
```

If we assume two consecutive bytes are required to store one integer, we could allocate memory for an integer pointer pi using

```
pi = malloc(2);
```

Since this statement depends on the system, it would be better to use

```
pi = malloc(sizeof(int));
```

However, this is still incorrect because the type of the left-hand side of the assignment and the type of right-hand side are incompatible. A correct solution is

```
pi = (int *) malloc(sizeof(int));
```

The casting of the value returned by malloc is safe; that is, even though the value returned by malloc is a character pointer, it may be converted to any other pointer type without worrying about possible memory alignment problems. In other words, `malloc` returns an address that can be used to store an object of the *most restrictive* type.

If preferred, a new type could be introduced with `typedef`:

```
typedef int * PINT;
PINT pi;
```

and then used in the allocation request:

```
pi = (PINT) malloc(sizeof(int));
```

Note that

```
pi = (PINT) malloc(sizeof(PINT));
```

may be incorrect: The size of a *pointer* is not necessarily the same as the size of an *integer*. A correct version is

```
pi = (PINT) malloc(sizeof(int));                        ∎
```

Remember that pointers and integers are two *different* data types and must not be mixed except in the cases we have described. Experienced C programmers may know ways to bend these rules, but the resulting code is not likely to be portable.

The Function `calloc`

In some applications, it is convenient to allocate n objects of the given size rather than n bytes. The function `calloc(n,siz)` allocates memory in the heap to hold `n*siz` consecutive bytes and, like `malloc`, returns the address of the origin of this memory area. All bytes in the allocated area are cleared to zero.

To free a memory area that has been allocated by `calloc`, the function `cfree` must be used in some systems. That is, if the call

```
p = calloc(n, m);
```

was made, the call

```
cfree(p);
```

must be used to free the memory.

Frequent memory allocation and deallocation may lead to heap *fragmentation* (see Chapter 13), and, as a result, memory allocation requests may fail. To help prevent fragmentation, C provides the function realloc(p, siz). Here, p points to a memory area allocated by a previous call to malloc, and siz is the size of the new area required. A pointer to an area of the requested size is returned. This call reallocates the area previously allocated (that is, it attempts to increase or decrease its size), and so, if reduction of heap fragmentation is a concern, it should be made rather than calling free(p) and malloc(siz).

Other Memory Management Functions
The remaining memory operations are almost identical to those we have already described, except the arguments n and siz are of the type unsigned long so that they can be used to deal with objects larger in size than the maximum unsigned integer value:

mlalloc(n)   Allocates memory objects of n
                                    bytes in size

clalloc(n, siz)   Allocates memory for n*siz
                                    bytes

relalloc(p, siz)   Reallocates memory

These routines may not be available on all systems.   ∎

In the following examples, we consider functions that have parameters that are pointers to blocks of memory.

Example 7.6.1   The following program reads ten double values, stores them in a memory block, and then finds the product of these values. The program consists of three functions and a main program.

The first function creates a memory block and returns the base address of this block; if the memory cannot be allocated, the function returns NULL. Thus the returned value of this function will be a pointer to double. Later, we show how to write a procedure-based version of this function that returns the base address through a parameter.

```
#define SIZE 10
double *init()
{
    char *malloc();

    return (double *)malloc(SIZE * sizeof(double));
}
```

The second function initializes the memory block (obtained by calling init) by reading values from the keyboard. Thus this function takes a pointer to double as a parameter.

```
void readin(a)
double *a;
{
    int i;
```

```
        printf("Please enter %d values: ", SIZE);
        for (i = 0; i < SIZE; i++)
                scanf("%lf", a + i);
}
```

The formal parameter is a pointer, and the function modifies the contents of the memory block with the base address specified by the value of the actual parameter; it does not modify the value of the actual parameter.

The third function returns through the parameter result the product of the elements stored in the memory block.

```
void product(arr, size, result)
double *arr;
int size;
double *result;
{
        for (size--, *result = *(arr + size); --size >= 0;
                        *result *= *(arr + size))
                ;
}
```

The last parameter, result, must be passed by reference, so we use a pointer. As we demonstrated in function swap (see Section 7.4.2), in the body of the function product we use *result as if it were a double variable. The product is computed by first taking the last value in the array and then successively multiplying it by each of the previous elements.

Finally, the main program is as follows:

```
#include <stdio.h>
main()
{
        double *x, res, *init();

        if ((x = init()) == NULL)
            /* error */
            return;
        readin(x);
        product(x, SIZE, &res);
        printf("Their product is: %10.2f\n", res);
}
```

When readin is called, its actual parameter is x rather than &x because x is defined as a pointer. On the other hand, the third actual parameter is &res because res is a double variable, and here a pointer to double is required.

Alternatively, a procedure-based version of the init function could be used. What we want to achieve is a modification of the *value* of the pointer, so the only solution is to pass this pointer by reference. To do this, we have to specify the formal parameter as a *pointer to pointer*. The following function init returns (through a) the value NULL if it fails; otherwise, it returns a pointer to a memory block.

```
#define SIZE 10
void init(a)
double **a;
{
    char *malloc();

    *a = (double *)malloc(SIZE * sizeof(double));
}
```

In the main program, init would be called as follows:

```
main()
{
    double *f;

    init(&f);
    ...
}
```

It is important that you have a thorough understanding of why a pointer to pointer to double is passed and why the version with a pointer to double would not work. Some diagrams may help. Immediately after the call to init, the situation is

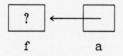

(The value of f is not initialized, and as a result of the call, a takes on the value &f, meaning a points to f.) After the call to malloc:

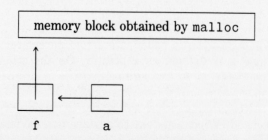

After init terminates:

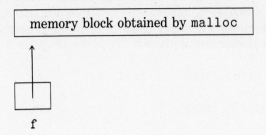

f

7.7 SIMULATING ARRAYS AND RECORDS

Blocks of memory allocated using malloc can be used in the same way as a Pascal programmer would use arrays and records. Although we describe genuine C arrays and records in later chapters, we demonstrate now in these examples how they can be simulated using pointers.

Example 7.7.1 The following program reads and saves in memory ten characters, then makes a copy of them, and eventually displays them in reverse order:

```
#include <stdio.h>

typedef char * STRING;
#define LIMIT 10
#define ERROR { printf("Out of memory\n"); return; }

main()
{
    STRING p, q, aux;
    char *malloc();

    if ((p = malloc(LIMIT)) == NULL)
        ERROR

    /* read in data to fill this block    */
    for (aux = p;  aux < p + LIMIT;  *aux++ = getchar())
        ;

    /* now make a copy of these characters */
    if ((q = malloc(LIMIT)) == NULL)
        ERROR
    for (aux = q;  aux < q + LIMIT;   *aux++ = *p++)
        ;

    /* display them */
    for (aux--; aux >= q; aux--)
        printf("%c", *aux);
    putchar('\n');
}
```

Example 7.7.2   The following program creates a linked list of integers from 1 to 9 and then prints these values. (We assume you are familiar with linked lists.)

Clearly, to implement the algorithm, records are desirable. We actually need a memory block to store an integer value and a pointer to the next element on the list. Thus the program will be allocating

```
sizeof(int) + sizeof(char *)
```

bytes by calling

```
p = malloc(...)
```

where p is a pointer to character. Here, p is pointing to a memory block that simulates a record:

```
p →  | int data | next |
```

How can the components of this "record" be accessed? Since the first component lies at the beginning of the block, we can access it directly using p, cast appropriately:

```
*(int *)p
```

As we mentioned before, a cast is not an l-value. Therefore we *cannot* use

```
(int *)(*p) = ...
```

However, a * can be applied to some types of expressions that are not l-values, including casts, and the result is an l-value.

To access the second component, we can use pointer arithmetic; specifically,

```
p + sizeof(int)
```

is needed.

The remaining problem is to create links. In Pascal, we would use

```
NEW(p);
p^. data := 1;
FOR i := 2 TO 9 DO
BEGIN
   NEW(p^.next);
   p := p^.next;
   p^.data := i;
END;
```

Once we have created the first element, our problem is to express

```
NEW(p^.next);
```

The solution is to increment p,

```
p += sizeof(int);
```

so that it will point to the second component and then to do

```
*(char **)p = malloc(size of a "record")
```

because this will store the address of a newly obtained memory block in the second component of a memory block pointed to by p. The conversion to char ** makes it possible to treat the value pointed to by p as an address. Our solution is machine dependent because we cannot guarantee that the memory for the pointer next is properly aligned.

The complete program follows:

```
#include <stdio.h>

#define INTSIZE sizeof(int)
#define RECSIZE sizeof(int) + sizeof(char *)
#define LIM     10
#define ERROR   { printf("error\n"); return; }


main()
{
    int i;
    char *p, *q, *first, *malloc();

    /* allocate memory for the first element */
    if ((p = malloc(RECSIZE)) == NULL)
        ERROR
    first = p;
    *(int *)p = 1;  /* store 1 in the first element */
    p += INTSIZE;   /* make p point to the "next" field */
    for (i = 2; i < LIM; i++, p += INTSIZE)
        if ((q = malloc(RECSIZE)) == NULL)
            ERROR
        else {
            *(char **)p = q;/* store link to the next */
            p = q;          /* p now points to next */
            *(int *)p = i;
        }
    *p = NULL;              /* last link is NULL */
    /* now print the list */
    for (p = first; p; p += INTSIZE, p = *(char **)p)
```

```
                    printf("%d ", *(int *)p);
              putchar('\n');
    }
```

Fortunately, C supports records.   ■

THINGS TO REMEMBER

Pointers are *not* integers.

To have portable programs, convert pointers of type *S* only to a pointer of a more restrictive type, that is, requiring an object of a smaller size.

Always use casting to enforce type compatibility.

Use `sizeof` to determine the size of an object pointer to by a pointer.

Always test whether or not memory allocation requests are successful.

Always declare `malloc` and cast its call appropriately when assigning to a pointer (that is not a pointer to `char`).

Only memory that has been allocated using `malloc` (or the related routines) should be freed.

Remember that `free(p)` makes all pointers having the same value as p undefined (that is, they should be reset before reuse).

Do not depend on the number of bytes in a word or on their order.

To pass a parameter by variable, specify this parameter as a pointer, and precede the actual parameter with a &.

To update the value of the actual parameter that is a pointer, use a pointer to pointer.

Always cast the NULL pointer when it is passed as an actual parameter.

COMMON ERRORS

```
int *p = 2;        Wrong, or at least nonportable            ■

main()
{
      int i = 2;

      printf("%d\n", add(i));                                ■
}
```

```
int *add(i)
int i;
{
    return(&i);
}
```

The function `add` should be declared in the main program:

```
int *add();
```

```
void example(i)
int *i;
    ...

main()
{
    int j;
    ...
    example(j);
    ...
```

The call should be

```
example(&j);
```

```
void example(i)
int *i;
    ...

main()
{
    int *j;
    ...
    example(j);
    ...
```

Memory must be allocated for `j`:

```
j = (int *) malloc(sizeof(int));
```

```
main()
{
    int *p;
    p = malloc(4);
    ...
```

Should declare

```
char *malloc();
```

and use casting:

```
p = (int*)malloc(4);
```

EXERCISES

1. Describe what is wrong, if anything, with each line of the following
   program.

   ```
   main()
   {
           int j = 2,
               *p, i;
           char *malloc();

           *i = 1;
           *p = 1;
           p = malloc(sizeof(int));
           *p = &i;
           p = &j;
           *p = i;
           *p = j++;
   }
   ```

2. Declare `pint` as a pointer to `int` type and `pfloat` as a pointer to
   `float` type. Use these types to write a program that reads in an integer `i` and a `float f` and stores them in the memory locations
   pointed to, respectively, by an integer pointer `pi` and a `float`
   pointer `pf`.

3. Assume `sizeof(char)` is 1, `sizeof(int)` is 2, and `sizeof`
   `(float)` is 4. Given the following definitions, determine the values
   of the assignments. For each assignment, the results of the previous
   assignments should be taken into consideration.

   ```
   char *pc;                Assume pc = 900
   int *pi1, *pi2;          Assume pi1 = 1000 and pi2 = 1012
   float *pf1, *pf2;        Assume pf1 = 1100 and pf2 = 1112

   pc += 6;
   pi1 += 6;
   pf1 += 6;
   *pf1 = pi1 - pi2;
   *pi1 = pf1 - pf2;
   pi1 -= *pi2;
   ```

4. Given the following definitions and assuming the variables are in the
   memory locations indicated, show the contents of the locations after
   each of the assignment statements.

   ```
   int x = 1, y = 2, *px = &x, *py = &y, **ppx = &px;
   ```

Memory addresses

```
x    = 100
y    = 102
px   = 104
py   = 106
ppx  = 108
```

```
px = py;
ppx = &py;
y = *px;
x = **px + 1;
```

5. Write a complete C program to read in 15 float values, store them in a block of memory using pointers, then output the sum of these values and the minimum value.

6. Write a complete C program to read in ten characters, store them in memory using pointers, then copy these ten characters to a separate block of memory (again using pointers), and finally print the integer position of the first occurrence of the ? character in that block (or −1 if there is no ?).

7. Consider the following fragment of a C program:

```
#include <stdio.h>

typedef unsigned* POINT;
#define NEW(x,y)  ((POINT) malloc( (x) * sizeof((y)) ))
#define SIZE      40

main()
{
      POINT p1, aux,
            *p2 = &p1;
      char *malloc();

      p1 = NEW(SIZE, unsigned);
      printf("%u\n", p2);
      ...
```

Assume the current value of p1 is 200, sizeof(unsigned) is 4, sizeof(POINT) is 2, and the preceding printf statement prints the value 400.

a. Draw a memory map that shows the state of memory.
b. Write a statement to read in SIZE unsigned values from the keyboard and store them in the memory area starting at the current value of p1. Do not define more variables than those al-

ready defined. If this statement changes the values of p1 or p2, follow it with another statement to restore their original values.

c. Assume the first four values read from the keyboard are

    3   1   8   9

Draw a memory map that shows where these values are stored (include the current values of all program variables).

d. Show the output produced by each of the following statements:

```
printf("%u\n", p2);

printf("%u\n", *p2);

printf("%u\n", **p2);

printf("%u\n", p2 + 2);

printf("%u\n", (*p2) + 2);

printf("%u\n", (**p2) + 2);

printf("%u\n", *((*p2) + 2));

aux = p1 + 3;
printf("%u", aux - p1);
```

8. Write a program that inputs a string of at most 25 letters, terminated by \n and outputs the letters sorted in alphabetical order.

9. A palindrome is a word that reads the same both forward and backward. Write a program that reads a sequence of words, each word being no more than ten characters long, and outputs all the palindromes.

10. Write a program that reads in a string no more than ten characters long terminated by \n and, depending on the value of the last character, does one of the following:

    A → sort characters in ascending order
    D → sort characters in descending order
    E → reverse the string
    S → sum the digits in the string
    X → read another string
    else → output the length of the string

11. Write a program that reads in a list of at most ten integers, terminated by a zero; sorts them in ascending order; and then outputs the

sum of the first, third, fifth, seventh, and ninth elements, followed by the product of the second, fourth, sixth, eighth, and tenth elements.

12. Write a program that reads a word and then searches subsequent input text for all occurrences of this word and either outputs the line numbers it was found on or indicates it was not found. Assume there are at most 50 lines of input, there is at least one word in the text, and all words are no more than ten characters long.

13. Write a program that reads a sequence of words and outputs in the reverse order in which they occur in the input those words that begin with an uppercase letter. Assume there are no more than 50 words each consisting of ten or fewer letters. It may help to store a \0 character to denote the end of a word.

14. Consider an input file called TEST, every line of which is of the form

   integer   blank   sequence-of-characters

   The first *integer* represents the number of characters in the *sequence-of-characters* (excluding the end-of-line), for example

   ```
   13 Hello how are
   5 oh no
   0
   23 the above line is empty
   ```

   First, read in the file to determine the number N of nonempty lines. Then allocate a block B of memory to store N memory addresses. Next, reread the file, line by line, and for each nonempty line

   • Allocate memory for the characters in the line, including the end-of-line character \n.
   • Store the address of this block in the next position in B.
   • Store the characters in the memory block.

   For example, if the input file contained the information in the preceding sample, we would end up with

   N = 3

   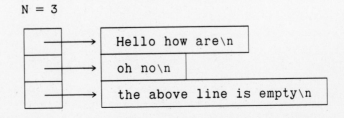

Finally, output the lines from the last line to the first line. For the example, this would produce

```
the above line is empty
oh no
Hello how are
```

15. Write a function alter(x,y) that changes the value of x to x+y and the value of y to x*y, where x and y are of type double. Test this function in a main program.

16. Write a boolean function readfl(f) that reads in a real value and returns this value through the parameter f and returns 1 through readfl if f is positive and 0 otherwise. Test your function in a main program.

17. Write a function graph(f, a, b, step) that plots the function f in the interval [a, b] in increments of step. Test graph in a main program for the function $f(x) = x^3$ with

```
a = -1.0,
b = 1.0, and
step = 0.1
```

To simplify the problem, assume the x axis is vertical and the y axis is horizontal.

18. Define a procedure up(c, d) that returns via parameter d the character c converted to uppercase if c is a lowercase letter, and c unchanged otherwise. Show in a short but complete main program how the procedure may be called.

8 Arrays

PREVIEW

This chapter introduces arrays in C. Although our discussion is limited primarily to one- and two-dimensional arrays, the concepts apply to any number of dimensions. We also give several complete C programs, including binary search and sort programs. We discuss dynamic arrays in C as well as functions that operate on arrays. As usual, we begin with a review of arrays in Pascal and, in particular, describe the representation of arrays in memory. This discussion is needed to understand the concept of arrays in C.

REVIEW OF PASCAL CONSTRUCTS

Arrays are **homogeneous** structures. That is, they consist of elements of the same *type*. An array type is declared as

```
TYPE T1 = ARRAY [idtyp] OF basetyp;
```

where *idtyp* specifies the range of indices used to access elements in the array, and *basetyp* specifies the base type of those elements. The index type *idtyp* must be an ordinal type and is of the form

```
LB..UB
```

where *LB* is the lower bound of the index type, and *UB* is the upper bound. The values of the expression *LB* and *UB* must be known at compile time; thus arrays in Pascal are **static**.

Like simple variables, array variables cannot be initialized within a declaration. To initialize an array declared as

```
X : ARRAY [1..3] OF REAL;
```

so that all elements are zero, the following loop could be used:

```
FOR i := 1 TO 3 DO X[i] := 0;
```

Arrays of the same type may be assigned directly, allowing whole arrays to be transferred in a single operation. For example, if two arrays

195

X and Y are declared as

```
TYPE ARR = ARRAY [1..50] OF INTEGER;
VAR  X, Y : ARR;
```

the following assignment is correct:

```
X := Y;
```

This makes a *copy* of the information in array Y in array X. Whole array operations like this are allowed only if the arrays are declared to be of the *same* type.

Some comments on the implementation of arrays (specifically, single-dimensional arrays) are appropriate. Each array variable is allocated a contiguous memory block large enough to hold all the elements of the array. For example, if an array A is declared as

```
TYPE T = ARRAY [2..10] OF INTEGER;
VAR  A : T;
```

a block of memory to hold nine integer values is allocated. Assuming an integer value is stored in 2 bytes and this block starts at location 100, a total of 18 bytes are allocated for the array A:

98   100   102   104   106   108   110   112   114   116   118

| | | | | | | | | |

A[2] A[3] A[4] A[5] A[6] A[7] A[8] A[9] A[10]

Internally, the variable A is represented by the address 100. This address is called the **base address** of A. The address of each indexed element is determined with respect to this base address. Specifically, the calculation

address of A[i] = base address of A − lower bound scaled + i scaled

is used. The index i essentially represents an **offset**, which is added to the base address to obtain the actual address of the memory location allocated for the element A[i]. The scaling is done by multiplying the value to be scaled by the number of bytes required to store a value of the base type:

lower bound scaled = 2 * sizeof(integer) = 2 * 2 = 4

So for this specific case, the address of `A[i]` is equal to

100 − 4 + i scaled

or

100 − 4 + 2 * i

For an access such as `A[i]`, the value of the index expression should be within the defined bounds of the index type:

2 <= i <= 10

Thus `A[i]` is in the range

100 − 4 + 4 .. 100 − 4 + 20

or

100 .. 116

and this is exactly the range of memory allocated to A in the diagram.

Examples

address of `A[3]` = 100 − 4 + 2 * 3 = 102
address of `A[8]` = 100 − 4 + 2 * 8 = 112

If the lower bound of an index type is zero, the formula to compute `A[i]` can be simplified:

address of `A[i]` = base address of A + i scaled   ■

Since index expressions may contain variables, these computations must clearly be performed at *run-time*. Thus if the Pascal run-time system is to control whether the value of the index is in the range of the index type, it must be able to determine the values of the lower and upper bounds of the array. Typically, these values are stored in a so-called **array descriptor**, which is generated by the compiler. However, because range checking slows execution and uses extra memory, most compilers offer a switch to specify whether or not index range checking is to be performed. This saves memory space (no descriptors are needed) and improves the speed of array accesses. If range checking is not used, it is the programmer's responsibility to ensure that the index is in the allowed range.

Glossary **Address of an indexed variable** Base address − lower bound scaled + index scaled.

Base address The address of the origin of memory area allocated for the array.

C CONSTRUCTS

In C, arrays are *static*, and the lower bound of an array is *always* zero. Arrays are implemented in this manner in C mainly for efficiency; as we mentioned earlier, the formula to calculate the address of an array element is simpler if the lower bound is zero. C simplifies the situation even further by allowing only integer indices, unlike Pascal, which permits any ordinal type to be used as an index type.

8.1 SINGLE-DIMENSIONAL ARRAYS

8.1.1 Array Definitions and Indexed Variables

C's syntax of an array definition is quite different from Pascal's. First of all, consider **array variables**:

Pascal	C
VAR x: ARRAY [0..*size*−1] OF T;	$T\,x[size]$;

The syntax of the Pascal declaration is shown in this way to better illustrate the meaning of C's corresponding syntax. In C, the lower bound of an array is always zero, and the definition $x[size]$ allocates a block of memory for *size* objects of type T with indices ranging from 0 to *size*−1. Thus the value specified in an array definition in C is *not* the upper bound of the array but rather the number of elements in the array.

As in Pascal, the size of arrays defined in this manner is static. This implies that the value of *size* must be known at compile time. In C, this value is allowed to be a *constant expression*. In Pascal, there is no alternative to static allocation of arrays, but in C there *is*. This we discuss later; for now, we deal only with static arrays.

Examples

```
#define MAX 10

int    x[MAX], y[MAX * 2], z[MAX * 3 + 5];
int    v[4], w[4];
char   s1[2], s2[1];
float  f[10];
```

Array types are similarly defined:

Pascal	C
`TYPE` *newID* `= ARRAY [0..`*size*`-1]` `OF` *knownID*`;`	`typedef` *knownID* *newID*`[`*size*`]`;

The size of the array is specified along with *newID* rather than *knownID*. We give the complete syntax for `typedef` using arrays in Section 8.1.6.

Examples

Type definitions:

Pascal	C
`VEC5 = ARRAY [0..4] OF INTEGER;`	`typedef int   VEC5[5];`
`VEC3 = ARRAY [0..2] OF INTEGER;`	`typedef int   VEC3[3];`
`FVEC = ARRAY [0..9] OF REAL;`	`typedef float FVEC[10];`

The only difference between an array variable definition and an array type definition is the addition of the keyword `typedef`.

Variable definitions using above types:

```
v5  : VEC5;                    VEC5 v5;
v3  : VEC3;                    VEC3 v3;
f   : FVEC;                    FVEC f;          ■
```

The syntax of indexed variables is the same in both languages, for example,

```
v[3]
```

Clearly, indexed variables are *l-values*.

C does *not* make any attempt to check if the index is in the specified range or not, and this leads to many programming errors. For example, if an array is defined as

```
int x[3];
```

the C compiler will not issue an error if you use

```
x[3]
```

which actually refers to the object beyond the end of the block of memory allocated to the array x.

In the next two examples, we show some simple programs using single-dimensional arrays.

Example 8.1.1   The following program reads ten integer values, stores them in an array, and then searches this array to find the maximum and minimum of these values:

```
#include <stdio.h>
#define SIZE 10
main()
{
      int a[SIZE], i, max, min;

      printf("Enter 10 integers:\n");
      for (i = 0; i < SIZE; i++)
          scanf("%d", &a[i]);

      max = min = a[0];
      for (i = 1; i < SIZE; i++) {
          if (max < a[i])
              max = a[i];
          if (min > a[i])
              min = a[i];
      }

      printf("Maximum value is: %d\n", max);
      printf("Minimum value is: %d\n", min);

}
```
■

Example 8.1.2   In the following program, an integer representing a number in base 10 and an integer representing a base are read, and then the first number is redisplayed in the specified base. For example, if the input were

127 16

the output would be

7F

The program is as follows:

```
#include <stdio.h>
main ()
{
      char digit[30];
      int  k, i, base, val, aux;
```

```
      printf("Enter value and base:");
      scanf("%d%d", &val, &base);
      if (base < 2 || val < 1) {
          printf("incorrect data\n");
          return;
      }

      for (k = 0; k < 30 && val > 0; k++) {
          aux = val % base;
          digit[k] = ((aux >= 0 && aux <= 9) ?
                  (aux + '0') : (aux + 'A' - 10));
          val /= base;
      }

      for (i = k - 1; i >= 0; i--)
          putchar(digit[i]);
      putchar('\n');
  }                                                              ■
```

Remember that C does *not* specify whether in an assignment the left-hand side or the right-hand side is evaluated first. Thus the effect of

```
a[i] = i++;
```

depends on the implementation.

8.1.2 Arrays and Pointers

In this section, we describe how C interprets arrays. In our discussion on the internal representation of arrays in Pascal, we explained that an array variable is represented by a memory address. This address is the base address of the memory block allocated to the array variable. Assuming the lower bound is zero, the address of the indexed element `x[i]` is

```
&x[i] = base address of x + i scaled
```

Arrays in C are represented internally in the same manner, but the fact that *an array variable is a memory address* is exploited. Since (as we mentioned in Chapter 7) a pointer is a memory address, it follows that an array variable is a pointer, and that is exactly how C treats arrays. Arrays and pointers are similar. Consider the following definitions:

Array	**Pointer**
typ avar[size];	*typ *pvar;*

Both *avar* and *pvar* are pointers of type *typ*. They differ in that

- *avar* is a *constant*, implying its value cannot be changed. That is, an array identifier is not an l-value. The value of *avar* is the address of the block of memory allocated to the array.
- *pvar* is a *variable* with an undetermined initial value. Eventually, an address may be assigned to it through a call to `malloc`:

pvar = (*typ* *)malloc(sizeof(*typ*));

This discussion also applies to indexed variables. That is, an access such as

```
x[i]
```

is *exactly* the same as

```
*(x + i)
```

This is because x + i is the address obtained by adding the scaled value of i (the offset) to the base address of the array. Applying the dereferencing operator * fetches the contents of that location.

These two expressions are completely interchangeable; deciding which to use is entirely up to the programmer. That is,

```
x[i]
```

may be used even if x is defined as a pointer, and

```
*(x + i)
```

may be used even if x is defined as an array.

If p is defined as a pointer to integer and initialized using `malloc`,

```
int *p;
p = (int *) malloc(4 * sizeof(int));
```

p can be considered an array consisting of four elements, so both expressions in each of the following pairs are equivalent:

```
p[0]   *p
p[1]   *(p + 1)
p[2]   *(p + 2)
p[3]   *(p + 3)
```

If a program contains several calls to `malloc` of this form, a macro can be defined to improve readability:

```
#define CREATE(SIZE) (int *) malloc((SIZE) * sizeof(int))
```

and then the allocation request will look like

```
p = CREATE(4);
```

Consider the following example:

```
typedef int INT4[4];

INT4 x;
```

Assuming the base address of `x` is 100 and `sizeof(int)` is 4, the memory allocated to `x` is mapped as follows:

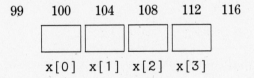

It follows that the expressions

```
x[0]     *(x + 0)     *x      *(100)
```

are all equivalent. Likewise,

```
x[1] = *(x + 1 scaled) = *((char *)x + sizeof(int)*1) = *(104)
```

and so on.

The address operator `&` may be applied to any indexed variable as well:

```
&x[0] = &*(x + 0) = x
&x[1] = &*(x + 1) = x + 1
```

and in general

```
&x[i] = x + i
```

In the definitions,

```
int  x[1],
     *px;
```

the variable x is a constant pointer, and so it cannot be modified. However, *x is not a constant, and since x points to an allocated memory block, the assignment

```
*x = 2;
```

is valid (and equivalent to x[0] = 2). On the other hand, the pointer px has not been initialized, and though the statement

```
*px = 2;
```

is syntactically correct, it is logically invalid since px points to an unknown location. To initialize px, we could say

```
px = (int *)malloc(sizeof(int));
```

which would make px point to a new block of memory. It would also be correct to write

```
px = x;
```

which would make px point to the block of memory allocated to the array x. This initialization could be performed in the definition itself:

```
int x[1],
    *px = x;
```

The indirection operator * applies to the definition part, and the assignment is made to px rather than to *px; therefore, px is initialized to point to the base of array x.

Unlike Pascal, C does *not* support whole array operations. For example, if x and y are defined as

```
int x[10], y[10];
```

the statement

```
x = y;
```

would not be correct because x is a constant. Instead, the elements have to be transferred using a loop:

```
for (i = 0; i < 10; i++)
    x[i] = y[i];
```

Likewise, there is *no* built-in test for equality of arrays—the expression x==y merely compares two pointers. Thus it is necessary to explicitly traverse the arrays to check whether or not they are equal:

```
for (i = 0; i < 10; i++)
    if (x[i] != y[i])
        break;
```

Examples 8.1.1 and 8.1.2 used Pascal-like traversals of arrays. Recall from Chapter 7 that pointers may be compared if they point to members of the same array. Thus if we have, for example, an array x and a pointer px defined as

```
double x[size];
double *px;
```

px points to an element of x if

```
x <= px < x + size
```

Therefore, to sequence through the elements of an array, it is possible to use either integers (to index into the array as in the preceding examples) *or* pointers:

```
double b[3];
...
for (p = b; p < b + 3; p++)
    printf("%dth component: %f\n", p - b, *p);
```

This traversal can also be done in the reverse direction:

```
for (p = b + 2; p >= b; p--)
    ...
```

The following modified versions of the array *copy* and *compare* loops illustrate this pointer-based approach of traversing arrays:

```
int x[10], y[10], *p, *q;
```

To copy y into x:

```
for (p = x, q = y; p < x + 10; )
    *p++ = *q++;
```

To compare x and y:

```
for (p = x, q = y; p < x + 10; )
    if (*p++ != *q++)
        break;
```

Traversals like this may be more efficient than the traditional indexed approach because, depending on the compiler and the machine, calculating the address of an element of the array is usually less involved.

Example 8.1.3   The following program demonstrates a similar rewrite of Example 8.1.1 to find the maximum and minimum elements of an array.

```
#define SIZE 10
main()
{
    int x[SIZE],
        *i   = x,
        *max = x,
        *min = x;

    printf("Enter 10 integers:\n");
    for (; i < x + SIZE; i++)
        scanf("%d", i);

    for (i = x + 1; i < x + SIZE; i++) {
        if (*max < *i)
            max = i;
        if (*min > *i)
            min = i;
    }

    printf("Maximum value is: %d\n", *max);
    printf("Minimum value is: %d\n", *min);

}
```

Example 8.1.4   The following code shows how to output an array's memory map:

```
float   b[3];
int     i;

b[0] = 0.5;
b[1] = 1.5;
b[2] = 2.5;

for (i = 0; i < 3; i++)
    printf("%dth component:\n\taddress: %u\tvalue: %f\n",
        i, &b[i], b[i]);
```

Assuming the base address of b is 100 and each `float` value occupies 4 bytes, the output of this program is

```
0th component:
     address: 100      value: 0.5
1th component:
     address: 104      value: 1.5
2th component:
     address: 108      value: 2.5
```

The `sizeof` function works differently with respect to arrays and pointers. For example, if we had two variables defined as

```
int x[10], *y;
```

and allocate memory to y using

```
y = (int *)malloc(10 * sizeof(int));
```

for the most part, x and y can be treated identically as ten-element integer arrays. However, `sizeof` does not treat them the same. In the call

```
sizeof(x)
```

x is treated as a ten-element integer array, and the value returned by this call is

```
10 * sizeof(int)
```

On the other hand, in the call

```
sizeof(y)
```

y is treated as a *pointer*, and the value returned by this call would be whatever size an address is on the machine in question. In this case, the size of the memory block pointed to by y is not considered at all.

In some applications, it is useful to have a macro such as

```
#define DIM(array)  (sizeof((array)) / sizeof((array)[0]))
```

to have a portable way of computing the size of an array. This works only if `array` is a genuine array, *not* a pointer. Another example of a macro that might be useful is

```
#define ENDOF(array)  ((array) - 1 + DIM((array)))
```

which computes the address of the last element of the specified array. ∎

Strings

We present a complete discussion of strings in Chapter 10, but it is appropriate to briefly introduce them here. A **string** in C is an array of characters with a null (zero) byte as the last character to indicate the end of the string. Consider the following example:

```
char *s;
s = "Hello!";
```

In this example, s is defined as a pointer to char. The quoted string assigned to s is a **string constant** and represents a *constant* pointer pointing to a block of memory containing the specified characters. Assuming this block of memory starts at location 100, the memory map of this string is

99	100	101	102	103	104	105	106	107
	H	e	l	l	o	!	\0	

Note the null character \0 at the end of the string. Assigning this string to s does *not* copy the characters; it simply assigns to the pointer s the address of the memory block containing the characters, in this case 100. Since a string constant is considered a character array, when sizeof is applied to a string constant, it returns the number of characters in the constant plus one (for the terminating null character), for example,

```
sizeof("datal")
```

is 6.

Example 8.1.5 The following program shows another application of the scanf function. As we mentioned before, scanf returns the number of data that have been successfully read. We use this feature of scanf to implement a simple version of a calculator that accepts expressions of the form

$$n \; bbb \; op \; bbb \; n$$

where n is a double value, *op* is some operator, and *bbb* represents zero or more blanks. The program will also do some error checking to verify whether or not the input data are correct.

```
#include <stdio.h>
#define ERROR(m) { printf("%s\n", m); return; }
main()
{
    double f, s;
    char oper[2];
```

```
        printf("Enter expression: ");
        if (!scanf("%lf", &f)    ||      /* read first value */
              !scanf("%1s", oper) ||     /* read an operator */
              !scanf("%lf", &s))         /* read second value */

              ERROR("Incorrect input")


        switch (oper[0]) {
        case '+' : f += s;
                   break;
        case '-' : f -= s;
                   break;
        case '*' : f *= s;
                   break;
        case '/' : if (s != 0) {
                      f /= s;
                      break;
                   } else ERROR("Cannot divide by zero")
        default  : ERROR("Unknown operator")
        }

        printf("The result is %f\n", f);
    }
```

If any of the calls to scanf fails (for example, if a double value is not
encountered), the execution is aborted. There is an important reason
why we used the specification %1s to read in the operator character.
Consider a sample input line of the form

    12   +3

If we used

    scanf("%c", &c);

where c is of type char, this call would not skip the blanks before the +
sign, and the value of c would therefore be a blank. Likewise, if we
used

    scanf("%s", oper);

the string +3 would be read in and stored in the array oper. Thus we
need to use %1s to read in exactly one character while skipping leading
blanks. The array oper has been defined as an array of size 2 because
scanf with the control character %s appends a terminating null character \0, and we have to provide space for this character.   ∎

8.1.3 Dynamic Arrays

As we mentioned, the size of an array in Pascal *must* be specified in the definition, and once the array is defined, the amount of space allocated to it cannot be changed. This is also true for arrays in C that are defined, for example, as

```
int   x[20], b[30];
char name[15];
```

The sizes of these arrays are *static* and cannot be changed. However, by using pointers to simulate arrays, it is possible to have **dynamic** arrays which can change in size.

Example 8.1.6 Suppose we have a program in which initially we want to have an array X large enough to hold 10 integers, and during the program's execution, every time the array becomes full, we want to increase the size of the array to allow another 10 elements. In addition, as elements are removed from the array, and whenever there are more than 20 free elements in X, we want to decrease its size so that it will have at most 10 free elements.

As we mentioned, this type of dynamic array must be created as a *pointer* rather than a static array. Thus X would be defined as

```
int *X;
```

The initial allocation of 10 integers would be done using

```
X = (int *)calloc(10, sizeof(int));
```

It is now possible to access the individual elements using array indexing, for example,

```
X[5] = 20;
X[1] = X[5] * 2;
```

When X becomes full, we define an auxiliary pointer to allocate more memory, then copy the existing array to the new block, and eventually free the space occupied by the old array. For example, suppose the current dynamic size of the array is held in the integer variable size. The following code demonstrates how the array X can be increased to hold 10 more integers:

```
int *aux, *point1, *point2;
...

aux = (int *)calloc(size + 10, sizeof(int));
```

At this point, `aux` points to the new array space, and the old contents can be copied:

```
point1 = X;
point2 = aux;
while (point1 < X + size)
      *point2++ = *point1++;
size += 10;
```

Now, we free the space allocated to the old array:

```
cfree((char*)X);
```

The new array is 10 elements larger. To make X point to the new array, we write

```
X = aux;
```

To *decrease* the size of the array, a similar sequence of operations is required. This we leave for you to do as an exercise.   ■

Example 8.1.6 shows that though in one respect arrays in C are static, because pointers can be used like arrays, dynamic arrays can also be created.

8.1.4 Arrays as Function Parameters

To illustrate some points about array parameters, consider the following function, which finds the maximum element in an array of `size` real values:

```
double maxi(arr, size)
double arr[];
int size;
{
      double *max = arr, *temp;

      for (temp = arr + 1; temp < arr + size; temp++)
          if (*temp > *max)
              max = temp;
      return (*max);
}
```

As this example shows, a **formal array parameter** is specified by following its identifier with a pair of empty square brackets. Thus the specification of the formal parameter

```
double arr[];
```

is *equivalent* to the specification

```
double *arr;
```

because array identifiers are pointers; if the size of the array is needed, it must be passed as another parameter. There is no way to dynamically determine the size of an array parameter in a function. In the preceding example, sizeof(arr) returns the size of a pointer, whereas sizeof(*arr) would return the size of a single double. That is, a formal parameter specified as an array, like arr, loses its array status, and even if the user specifies the size, the complier neglects it. For example,

```
double arr[10];
```

in the parameter specification is *still* equivalent to the specification

```
double *arr;
```

Another important characteristic of a formal array parameter is that it is *not* a constant pointer, as is a normal array, and it may be used as an l-value.

The following example demonstrates how the function maxi can be called. The main program first initializes an array and then displays the maximum value.

```
#include <stdio.h>
main()
{
     double a[10],
            maxi();
     int i;

     printf("Enter 10 real values: ");
     for (i = 0; i < 10; i++)
         scanf("%lf", &a[i]);
     printf("\nThe maximum value is: %f\n", maxi(a, 10));
}
```

If we wished to find the maximum of a *slice* of this array, say from the third to the sixth elements, we could call the function maxi as

```
maxi(a + 2, 4);
```

Let us now rewrite this function as a procedure. Let us also use a pointer to traverse the array:

```
void maxi(arr, size, max)
double *arr;
int    size;
double *max;                            /* returned value */
{
     double *temp;

     *max = arr[0];
     for (temp = arr + 1; temp < arr + size; temp++)
          if (*max < *temp)
               *max = *temp;
}
```

Note the difference between the function and procedure versions of this routine as far as the usage of the pointer variable max is concerned. In the *function* version, each time a new maximum is found, max is set to point to that value in the array. When the traversal is complete, the value *max is returned. In the *procedure* version, the pointer max is a formal parameter called by reference; thus its value is the address of the actual parameter passed when maxi was called. Since this actual parameter is intended to receive the result of the function, it would be incorrect to make an assignment to max such as

```
max = temp
```

This would overwrite the address contained in max, and we could not update the actual parameter. To avoid this problem, rather than updating max to point to a new maximum value, a copy of this value is placed in *max (the actual parameter).

The main program needed for this procedure version would look like

```
#include <stdio.h>
main()
{
     double x[10],
            max;
     int i;

     printf("Enter 10 real values: ");
     for (i = 0; i < 10; i++)
          scanf("%lf", &x[i]);

     maxi(x, 10, &max);

     printf("\nThe maximum value is: %f\n", max);
}
```

An alternative way of reading in values is to use an auxiliary pointer to traverse the array:

```
double *aux;
for (aux = x; aux < x + 10; aux++)
    scanf("%lf", aux);
```

Example 8.1.7   The following functions implement two techniques for searching an integer array for a particular value. In the first method, we assume the array is sorted and use a *binary search*. The function given returns a pointer to the element b in the array x, or NULL if b does not occur in x.

```
int *binsearch(x, b, size)
int x[], b, size;
{
    int start = 0,
        end   = size - 1,
        middle;

    while (start <= end) {
        middle = (start + end) / 2;
        if (x[middle] == b)
                return &x[middle];
        else if (x[middle] > b)
                end   = middle - 1;
        else start = middle + 1;
    }
    return NULL;
}
```

A binary search can also be implemented using recursion:

```
int *binsearch(x, b, size)
int x[], b, size;
{
    int start = 0,
        end   = size - 1,
        middle;

    if (start <= end ) {
        middle = (start + end) / 2;
        if (x[middle] == b)
                return &x[middle];
        else if (x[middle] > b)
                return binsearch(x, b, middle);
        else return binsearch(x + middle + 1, b,
                    size - (middle + 1));
    }
    else return NULL;
}
```

The linear search version could be written as

```
int *linsearch(x, b, size)
int x[], b, size;
{
    int i;

    for (i = 0; i < size; i++)
        if (x[i] == b)
            return &x[i];
    return NULL;
}
```
■

Example 8.1.8   As another example on single-dimensional arrays, consider the function

```
sort(array, siz, numb, compare)
```

where `array` points to a block of memory containing numb elements, each of size `siz`, and sorts these elements using a function `compare` to determine whether one element is greater than another. It might be said that this function sorts a "virtual" array because the type of elements in the array is not specified.

Let us first give the header of the function `sort`, then some applications, and finally its definition.

```
typedef int bool;
#define TRUE   1
#define FALSE 0

void sort(array, siz, numb, compare)
char *array;
int siz, numb;
bool (*compare)();
```

The parameter `compare` is defined as a pointer to an integer function and will have to be passed as this when `sort` is called. When the `compare` function is called, it will need two parameters that point to the elements being compared. For example, to sort an array of integer values, we would need a function to compare two integers:

```
bool intcmp(e1, e2)
char *e1, *e2;
{
    return( *(int *)e1 < *(int *)e2 );
}
```

The parameters e1 and e2 are defined as character pointers and cast as integer pointers before they are dereferenced. If we wanted to use our `sort` routine to sort, say, an array of `double` values, the comparison routine in this case would have to cast the char pointer parameters as pointers to doubles.

Next, we define the initialization function that creates a *dynamic* array of siz integers and reads values from the keyboard to initialize this array:

```
bool init(block, siz)
int **block;
int siz;
{
    int  *aux;
    char *malloc();

    if ((aux = (int*)malloc(siz * sizeof(int))) == NULL)
        return(FALSE);
    printf("Enter %d integer values: ", siz);
    *block = aux;

    while (siz--)
        scanf("%d", aux++);
    return(TRUE);
}
```

Before the code for the sort routine itself is given, we will take a look at the main program; remember that we want to sort an array of integer values.

```
#include <stdio.h>
#define SIZE 10
main()
{
    int *arr, i;

    if (!init(&arr, SIZE)) {
        printf("Cannot allocate memory\n");
        return;
    }
    sort((char *)arr, sizeof(int), SIZE, intcmp);
    for (i = 0; i < SIZE; i++)
        printf("%d\n", arr[i]);
}
```

Note the parameters that are passed in the call to sort; to use this function to sort real values, we would have to modify the initialization routine and write a comparison function to handle reals.

In the sort function that follows, we make use of a macro that swaps two memory blocks, each of size siz; its definition is

```
#define SWAP(e1, e2, siz) { char *a1, *a2, c; int i = 0;\
          for (a1=(char*)(e1),a2=(char*)(e2); i<(siz);\
                  c=*a1,*a1++=*a2,*a2++=c,i++); }
```

We have used a nested block in this macro to define local variables needed to swap two memory blocks.

The sort function itself follows; for simplicity, we have implemented a *bubble sort*:

```
void sort(array, siz, numb, compare)
char *array;
int siz, numb;
bool (*compare)();
{
    int i, j;

    for (i = 0; i <= numb - 2; i++)
        for (j = numb - 1; j >= i + 1; j--)
            if ((*compare)(&array[j*siz], &array[(j-1)*siz]))
                SWAP(&array[j*siz], &array[(j-1)*siz], siz)
}
```

Alternatively, we could have used pointers in the for loop rather than integers:

```
{
    char *i, *j;

    for (i = array; i <= array+(numb-2)*siz; i += siz)
        for (j = array+(numb-1)*siz; j >= i+siz; j -= siz)
            if ((*compare)(j, j - siz))
                SWAP(j, j - siz, siz)
}
```

In either version of this routine, character pointers are used when it calls compare (which in our case, corresponds to intcmp). If you recall the implementation of intcmp, these character pointers are cast as integer pointers before they are used. As we pointed out in Chapter 7, converting a character pointer to an integer pointer may cause problems if integers have an *alignment modulus* greater than that of characters. However, in this particular case, we can do this safely because the method used to derive the character pointers ensures that they are pointing to objects (integers in this case) at their proper alignment boundary. Thus they can be converted to integer pointers without creating any problems. This would be the case no matter what type of data were being sorted. ∎

8.1.5 Another Dangling Reference Problem

In Example 7.4.1, we showed one way in which a dangling reference can occur. In Example 8.1.9, we present another situation that can result in a dangling reference.

Example 8.1.9   Assume we want to set a pointer p to point to an array of five real values read from the keyboard, using the function init:

```
void init(p)
double **p;
{
        double arr[5];
        int i;

        printf("Enter 5 double values: ");
        for (i = 0; i < 5; i++)
                scanf("%lf", &arr[i]);
        *p = arr;
}

main()
{
        double *p;

        init(&p);
        . . .
}
```

After the call to init is made, p is pointing to the memory area containing five real values. The problem is that this memory area is allocated on the stack when init is entered and is not *retained* when init is exited. Thus successive calls to functions will allocate memory on the stack and so overwrite this same memory area. Any reference to the array p in the main program, for example,

```
p[1] = . . .
```

is incorrect, since it references memory that has been deallocated. A solution to this problem is to allocate memory on the *heap* rather than on the stack:

```
void init(p)
double **p;
{
        double *arr;
        char *malloc();
        int i;

        arr = (double*) malloc(5 * sizeof(double));
```

```
for (i = 0; i < 5; i++)
    scanf("%lf", &arr[i]);
*p = arr;
}
```

In this version, the memory for the variable `arr` (which is subsequently passed on to p) is allocated on the heap so that it will not be deallocated after `init` terminates. An alternative solution is to use an array specified as *static*, since such an array would be allocated in a special data segment reserved for static variables. (The only problem with this solution is that there would be no way to free the memory allocated to the static array.) ∎

8.1.6 Declarators—Part 2

In this section, we extend the description of a declarator given in Section 7.4.4 and provide a complete definition. A **declarator** is defined recursively as

declarator:
    identifier
    (*declarator*)
    declarator (...)
    * *declarator*
    declarator [...]

A **type-prefix** is defined as

type-prefix:
    empty
    pointer to type-prefix
    function returning type-prefix
    array of type-prefix

The **type** of an identifier is of the form

    type-prefix type-specifier

To derive the *type-prefix* of an identifier, we use the following rules:

I. If D is a declarator of the form

    x

(an identifier), its type-prefix is empty, and the definition

    TS x;

where *TS* is a type-specifier, defines x to be of the type

empty TS

or simply *TS*.

II. The second rule is recursive: Let *D* be a declarator. If this declarator defines an identifier x to have a type-prefix *TP1*,
(a) the declarator

*D

defines x to have a type-prefix *TP2* of the form

TP1 pointer to

(b) the declarator

(D)( )

defines x to have a type-prefix *TP2* of the form

TP1 function returning

(c) the declarator

(D)[ ]

defines x to have a type-prefix *TP2* of the form

TP1 array of

Examples

1. `double (*f[])();`
An array declarator `[ ]` has higher precedence than a pointer declarator `*`, so the preceding expression is equivalent to

```
double ( (* (f[])) )();
```

The type-prefix of `f` in

```
f[]
```

is

array of

in

    * (f[])

is

   array of pointers to

and in

    ((* (f[])))()

is

   array of pointers to functions returning

Thus the type of f is

   array of pointers to functions returning double

2. `double (*f())[];`
   This expression is equivalent to

    double (*(f())) [];

The type-prefix of f in

    *(f())

is

   function returning pointer to

and so the type of f in the example is

   function returning pointer to array of double

3. `double * (f[]) ();`
   The type-prefix of f in

    (f[])()

is

   array of functions returning

which is illegal.

4. `double *f()[];`

The type of f is a *function returning array of pointers to* `double`, which again is illegal.

A possible application of an array of pointers to functions would be in a **menu-driven** program. Each command from the menu could be associated with an index into an array and a function pointed to by this array entry. Once a command is given and its index determined, the function defining the actions of that command could be called directly.

Another application of this construct is for generating intermediate code in a so-called stack machine (see [Ker84]).

The definition of `typedef` to include arrays is identical to that given in Section 7.4.4 except the definition of a declarator has a clause to describe arrays (as listed above).

Example

```
typedef double (* f[])();

typedef f *g();
```

The type f is a synonym for

array of pointers to functions returning `double`

and the type g is a synonym for

function returning pointer to f

or

function returning pointer to
    array of pointers to functions returning `double`   ∎

To close this section, we give a complete definition of an **abstract-declarator**, which we introduced in Section 7.4.4:

abstract-declarator:
    empty
    (*abstract-declarator*)
    * *abstract-declarator*
    abstract-declarator ( )
    abstract-declarator [*index*]

where the term *index* is a constant expression and may be omitted.

Example

```
(*)[3]
```

The type-prefix of this abstract-declarator is

array of pointers to   ■

Recall that declarators and abstract-declarators are used with type-specifiers to define types and type-names. The definition of type-specifiers given in Section 7.4.4 is not complete—it does not include structure, union, and enumeration types. We complete this definition in Section 9.4.

Example 8.1.10   As an exercise on arrays of pointers, let us consider a simple menu-driven program that uses an array of pointers to functions. The program is interactive and reads lines from the keyboard that have the following form

command-character integer real real ... real

The command character specifies the operation that will be performed on the values in the line. The integer following the command character indicates how many `double` values are on the line.

In this example, each command is implemented by a separate function. These functions all have two parameters: an array of `double`s and the size of this array. The actions of these functions are described as follows:

`add`	Display the sum of all elements in the array
`greatest`	Display the maximum value in the array
`least`	Display the minimum value in the array
`product`	Display the product of all elements in the array
`sort`	Display the sorted contents of the array; leave the array parameter unchanged

The declarations of these functions will be stored in the header file `menu.h`:

```
extern void add();
extern void greatest();
extern void least();
extern void product();
extern void sort();
```

and their definitions will be given in the file `functions.c`. The header file also contains the definition of a macro which computes the end of an array:

```
#define END(v, s)  ((v) + (s) - 1)
```

The definitions of the menu function and the main program are given in the file menu.c. This file also contains the definition

```
typedef void (*cmdarr)();
```

which specifies the type cmdarr to be a pointer to a function returning void.

The functions are selected by their corresponding command characters. Two arrays are used for this purpose: an array of pointers to functions and an array of characters:

```
cmdarr cmd[] = { add, greatest, least, product, sort};
char names[] = { 'a', 'g',      'l',   'p',      's'};
```

(These definitions illustrate how arrays can be initialized when they are declared. We present this topic in detail in Section 8.3.) To select the required function, we perform a binary search on the array names (note that this array is sorted). This is done using the function

```
cmdarr menu(c)
int c;
```

The parameter c is the command character the function is to look for. If the search is successful, menu returns the corresponding function pointer stored in the parallel array cmd; if the command does not exist, menu returns NULL.

The function main reads from the keyboard until end-of-file is encountered. For each input line, it uses the function menu to determine whether the command indicated by the first character in that line is in the array names. If it is not, the appropriate message is issued and the rest of the offending line skipped. Otherwise, the integer following the command character is read, a dynamic array of this size is created, and the list of doubles is read and stored in this array. After the values have all been read, the indicated command is executed.

```
#include <stdio.h>
#include "menu.h"

typedef void (*cmdarr)();
cmdarr cmd[]   = { add, greatest, least, product, sort };
char   names[] = { 'a', 'g',      'l',   'p',      's' };

#define nofcmd     sizeof(names)

cmdarr menu(c)
int   c;
{
    char *b, *t, *m;
```

```
        /* binary search on names */
        b = names;
        t = END(names, nofcmd);
        while (b <= t) {
                m = b + (t - b)/2;
                if (c < *m)
                        t = m - 1;
                else if (c > *m)
                        b = m + 1;
                else return cmd[m - names];
        }
        return NULL;
}

main()
{
        int c, i, count;
        double *cd;
        char *malloc();
        cmdarr cp = NULL;

#define SKIP   while ((c = getchar()) != '\n') if (c==EOF)\
                        return;

        while (1) {
                printf(">> ");
                if ((c = getchar()) == EOF)
                        return;
                if ((cp = menu(c)) == NULL) {
                        printf("<< unknown option: %c\n", c);
                        SKIP
                        continue;
                }
                if (scanf("%d", &count) != 1) {
                        printf("<< wrong line\n");
                        SKIP
                        continue;
                }
                if ((cd = (double *)malloc(count*sizeof(double)))
                                == NULL) {
                        printf("out of memory\n");
                        return;
                }

                for (i = 0; i < count; i++)
                        scanf("%lf", &cd[i]);
                SKIP
                (*cp)(cd, count);
                free((char *)cd);
        }
}
```

The macro SKIP has been defined within the body of the function main.
As we stated in Chapter 4, a macro can be defined at *any* place in a program, and its scope is from the definition to the end of the source file.

As we mentioned, the actual definitions of the command functions are given in the file functions.c. We implement only two of these functions, add and sort; the rest we leave as exercises for you to do. Since all the functions need an auxiliary variable, we chose to define a global variable rather than having to define it in each function. This variable is specified as *static*, since its scope is limited to the file functions.c.

```c
#include <stdio.h>
#include "menu.h"

static double *aux;

void add(L, s)
double L[];
int s;
{
    double sum = 0;

    for (aux = L; aux <= END(L, s); aux++)
        sum += *aux;
    printf("<< The sum is: %f\n", sum);
}
```

We assume the sorting routine does not modify the original array but instead copies it to an auxiliary array, sorts it, displays the result, and then deallocates the auxiliary array. The function uses *shell sort* to sort the array. (For a description of this sorting algorithm, see [Aho83].)

```c
void sort(L, s)
double L[];
int s;
{
    double *pd, temp;
    char *malloc();
    int gap, i, j;

    if ((pd=(double*)malloc(sizeof(double)*s)) == NULL) {
        printf("out of memory\n");
        return;
    }
    for (aux = L; aux <= END(L, s); )
        *pd++ = *aux++;
    pd -= s;

    for (gap = s/2; gap > 0; gap /= 2)
        for (i = gap; i < s; i++)
            for (j=i-gap; j>=0 && pd[j]>pd[j+gap];j-=gap) {
                temp = pd[j];
                pd[j] = pd[j + gap];
                pd[j + gap] = temp;
            }
```

```
    printf("<< The list sorted is\n");
    for (i = 0; i < s; i++)
        printf("%f\t", pd[i]);
    putchar('\n');
    free((char *)pd);
}
```
■

8.2 MULTI-DIMENSIONAL ARRAYS

It is possible to have arrays with more than one dimension in C, just as
in Pascal. Most of the examples in this section deal with two-dimensional arrays, but much of the discussion applies as well to arrays of dimension greater than two.

8.2.1 Array Definitions and Indexed Variables

To define a **two-dimensional** array, both the number of rows and the
number of columns, in that order, must be specified. Both values must
be enclosed by square brackets. For example,

Pascal	C
`VAR X : ARRAY [0..1, 0..2] OF INTEGER;`	`int x[2][3];`

shows definitions in Pascal and C of an integer array with two rows and
three columns.
    Two-dimensional array types can be created from a primitive type us-
ing `typedef`, for example,

Pascal	C
`TYPE TWO = ARRAY [0..2, 0..3]` `        OF INTEGER;`	`typedef int TWO[3][4];`

A two-dimensional array type can also be created from an existing one-
dimensional array type:

Pascal	C

`TYPE SINGLE = ARRAY [0..4]`
`            OF INTEGER;`
`     TWO    = ARRAY [0..3]`
`            OF SINGLE;`
	`typedef int SINGLE[5];`
	
	`typedef SINGLE TWO[4];`

Indexed variables follow the same syntax as array definitions, with each index specified in a *separate* set of square brackets rather than being separated by commas as they are in Pascal. For example,

```
int table[5][10];

table[1][0] = 55;
table[4][9] = 0;
```

Arrays of dimension greater than two are defined and accessed similarly to two-dimensional arrays by specifying the appropriate number of square brackets. Some examples are

```
int    cube[5][6][4];       A three-dimensional array
float data[3][4][9][2];     A four-dimensional array

cube[0][1][3] = 20;
data[1][0][5][1] = 0.0;
```

The examples in the remaining part of this section deal only with one- and two-dimensional arrays.

8.2.2 Representation of Arrays in Memory

Two-dimensional arrays in C are stored by rows. This means the array x defined as

```
int x[2][3];
```

is allocated a single block of memory consisting of 2*3 elements, or 2*3*4 bytes (assuming `sizeof(int)` is 4), and the base address (say 100) of that block is assigned to x:

```
100         112
row #0      row #1
```

or, more precisely:

```
  100         104         108         112         116         120
┌───────┐  ┌───────┐  ┌───────┐  ┌───────┐  ┌───────┐  ┌───────┐
│       │  │       │  │       │  │       │  │       │  │       │
└───────┘  └───────┘  └───────┘  └───────┘  └───────┘  └───────┘
 x[0][0]    x[0][1]    x[0][2]    x[1][0]    x[1][1]    x[1][2]
```

C is consistent in its approach to arrays: A two-dimensional array in C is a *pointer* to the first row. Therefore, the type of the array x is a three-element integer array, and the size of this type is 12 bytes.

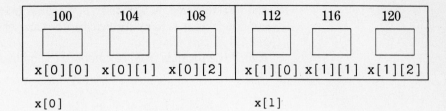

Thus

    x

and

    x[0]

have identical values (that is, they both point to the same location in memory). However, although their values are equal, they have *different types*.

In this example, the type of x is a pointer to the first row, whereas the type of x[0] is a pointer to integer. Moreover, x[0][0] is an integer. Thus in pointer arithmetic, scaling will be different. As a result,

    x + 1

and

    x[0] + 1

are different: The first represents a pointer to row 1 of the array x, and the second represents a pointer to element 1 of row 0. Similarly,

    x[i]

is a pointer to the origin of the ith row and is the same as

    *(x + i)

For example,

    *(x + 1) = x[1] = 112

Note how the value 1 is scaled. As we explained previously, scaling is performed by multiplying the value in question by the size of the base type, which in this case, is the size of a row, or 12. On the other hand,

    *(x[0] + 1) = *(104)

(assuming the size of a pointer is 4 bytes) because different scaling is used: The value 1 is multiplied by the size of the type pointer to integer—4 in this example.

Recall the formula used to compute the address of an indexed variable y[i]:

&y[i] = base address of y + i scaled = y + i

For a two-dimensional array defined as x[size1][size2], the formula to compute the address of an element x[i][j] is

```
&x[i][j]  =   base address of x + i scaled + j
          =   base address of the ith row + j
          =   x[i] + j
```

since

```
x[i] = *(x + i)
```

is the base address of the ith row. Thus the *address* of the indexed variable is

&x[i][j] =   x[i] + j =   *(x + i) + j

and so its *value* is

x[i][j] =   *(x[i] + j) =   *(*(x + i) + j)

This formula is used by a C compiler wherever index expressions occur.

Example 8.2.1   The following code demonstrates how a two-dimensional array could be initialized:

```
int x[2][3], i, j;

for (i = 0; i < 2; i++)                  /* for each row     */
    for (j = 0; j < 3; j++)              /* for each column  */
        x[i][j] = i + j;
```

Assume the base address of x is 100; the following code displays a memory map of this array:

```
for (i = 0; i < 2; i++) {
    printf("memory map of the %dth row:\n", i);
    for (j = 0; j < 3; j++)
        printf("\tcolumn # %d\n\t\taddress %u\tvalue %d\n",
                        j, (x[i] + j), x[i][j]);
    putchar('\n');
}
```

The output would be

```
memory map of the 0th row:
    column # 0
        address 100      value 0
    column # 1
        address 104      value 1
    column # 2
        address 108      value 2

memory map of the 1th row:
    column # 0
        address 112      value 1
    column # 1
        address 116      value 2
    column # 2
        address 120      value 3
```

8.2.3   Two-Dimensional versus Single-Dimensional Arrays

When programming in C, you must understand that two-dimensional arrays can be regarded as single-dimensional arrays. Consider a two-dimensional array x defined as x[size1][size2] and the expression

```
x[i]  =  *(x + i)
```

Since the type of *x is a pointer to the type of the array, the preceding expression is equivalent to

```
*x + i * size2
```

Thus

```
x[i][j] = *( x[i] + j )
        = *(*x + i * size2 + j)
        = (*x)[i * size2 + j]
```

This formula (note the absence of the number of rows) illustrates how to translate an expression with two indices into a version with only one index. In Section 8.2.4, we demonstrate the use of this transformation for functions with array parameters.

8.2.4   Alternative Representations of Two-Dimensional Arrays

Consider the following definitions:

(a) A two-dimensional array declared as, for example,

```
float xa[2][3];
```

(b) An array of pointers, for example,

```
float *xb[2];
```

(c) A pointer to array, for example,

```
float (*xc)[3];
```

(d) A pointer to pointer, for example,

```
float **xd;
```

These four constructs can all be used as two-dimensional arrays although, as we point out, there are subtle but important differences among them.

Construct (a)
The first of these constructs is, of course, a true two-dimensional array, and as we have explained, the elements of a two-dimensional array are stored contiguously by rows. If we consider the array xa, we can picture it as

```
xa  →   ┌─────┬─────┬─────┬─────┬─────┬─────┐
        │  a  │  b  │  c  │  d  │  e  │  f  │
        └─────┴─────┴─────┴─────┴─────┴─────┘
```

In this, elements a, b, and c belong to the first row, and elements d, e, and f belong to the second row. If we assume xa is allocated at location 100 and floats require 4 bytes, element a would be stored at location 100, element b at 104, element c at 108, and so on. The assignments

```
xa[0][0] = 5.8;
xa[1][0] = 1.4;
```

would store 5.8 in element a and 1.4 in element d.

To illustrate the differences between this construct and the other three, several things should be pointed out. First of all, the values of

```
xa
address of xa[0]
address of xa[0][0]
```

are equal (although their types are different). Similarly,

```
xa + 1 = address of xa[1] = address of xa[1][0]
```

As we said, the array identifier xa is a *constant* pointer, and a value may not be assigned to it (since it is not an l-value). In this case, xa is equal to 100 (the address of the first row), and xa+1 is equal to 112 (the address of the second row). The scaling factor used in this second case is equal to sizeof(row of xa), which is 12. This scaling factor is used because the type of xa is pointer to row. Similarly, xa[0] is *not* an l-value—it is a constant pointer to the first row of xa. The type of xa[0] is pointer to float, so clearly, the value of xa[0]+1 is 104 because the scaling factor used is sizeof(float), which is 4.

Construct (b)

Now consider construct (b): an array of pointers, such as,

```
float *xb[2];
```

The variable xb is not a two-dimensional array; rather, it is a two-element, single-dimensional array of pointers to float. However, if xb is initialized properly, it may be used as a two-dimensional array in exactly the same fashion as xa in construct (a).

If we want to initialize xb so that it represents a 2 by 3 array of floats, the following steps would be needed:

```
xb[0] = (float *)malloc(3 * sizeof(float));
xb[1] = (float *)malloc(3 * sizeof(float));
```

Both xb[0] and xb[1] now point to memory blocks large enough to hold three float values. We can picture this as

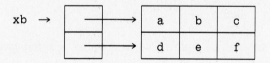

This diagram illustrates a single-dimensional array of pointers to "rows," where each row is a single-dimensional array holding three values. With this setup, it is possible to use an expression such as

```
xb[1][2] = 5.2;
```

which would store 5.2 in element f as denoted. To show that xb[1][2] does indeed refer to element f, recall that the array reference

```
xb[1][2]
```

is equivalent to

```
*(*(xb + 1) + 2)
```

Since the type of xb is pointer to pointer to float,

```
*(xb + 1)
```

points to the second row, and since the type of this is pointer to float,

```
*(*(xb + 1) + 2)
```

is the third element in this row. Similarly,

```
xb[0][0] = 1.6;
```

would store 1.6 in element a.

Although this structure may now be accessed as a two-dimensional array, there are important differences between it and the true two-dimensional array xa:

1. The elements denoted by a through f are not necessarily stored contiguously as they are in xa. Rather, because separate calls to malloc are used to allocate the two rows pointed to by xb, these rows are stored in separate areas of memory. This means elements a through c are contiguous, and elements d through f are contiguous, but elements a through f are *not* contiguous.
2. The values of the expressions

```
xb
address of xb[0]
address of xb[0][0]
```

are *not* all equal. The first value is a constant pointer pointing to the first element of the single-dimensional array xb. This element of xb is *not* a row as it was in the case of xa; rather, because xb is an array of pointers, the first element of xb is a pointer. The second expression, address of xb[0], is equal to the address of the first element of xb, which is the same as the value of xb. Unlike xa[0], xb[0] is an l-value. The third expression, address of xb[0][0], is not equal to xb. Intuitively, this expression translates as the address of the first element of the first row of the two-dimensional array represented by xb; in our case, this is the address of element a, and that is exactly what this expression is equal to. As an actual example, assume the array xb is allocated at location 200, the first call to malloc allocated a memory block at location 500, and the second call to malloc allocated a memory block at location 600. Then

```
xb = 200
address of xb[0] = 200
address of xb[0][0] = 500
```

Moreover, if we assume pointers require 2 bytes, then

```
xb+1 = 202
address of xb[1] = 202
address of xb[1][0] = 600
```

The value of xb+1 is the address of the second element of the single-dimensional array xb. Note the difference between this expression and the equivalent expression using xa; in that case, the scaling factor used was sizeof(row), whereas here the scaling factor used is sizeof (pointer to float).

Construct (c)

Next, consider construct (c): a pointer to array, such as,

```
float (*xc)[3];
```

Here, we are defining xc as a pointer to an array of three floats. Its value is initially undetermined and must be defined using, for example, malloc. To initialize it properly so that it can be treated as, in our example, a 2 by 3 array, it must be made to point to a block of memory holding not one three-element array of floats, but two three-element arrays of floats stored contiguously:

```
xc = (float(*)[])malloc(2 * 3 * sizeof(float));
```

We can picture this as

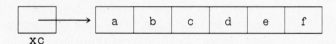

where xc is pointing to an area of memory holding six float values. With this setup, we can write, for example,

```
xc[0][2] = 2.5;
xc[1][1] = 3.2;
```

Note that xc is not a pointer to float; it is a pointer to an array of three floats. Thus if xc is equal to, say, 100, xc+1 is equal to 100 + 1 * sizeof(3 floats), or 112, which is the address of the second group of three floats allocated to the pointer xc or, more precisely, the address of the second row of the array.

This is exactly the same as the first construct. In fact,

```
xc = address of xc[0] = address of xc[0][0]
```

is the same as for the true array xa. The main difference between construct (a) and construct (c) is that the array identifier xa is a *constant* pointer, whereas the identifier xc is a *variable* pointer (an l-value). Thus the expression

```
&xa
```

is invalid, but

```
&xc
```

is valid and represents the address of this pointer variable. In both cases, the expressions

```
&xa[0]
&xc[0]
```

are invalid, since neither xa[0] nor xc[0] are l-values.

Construct (d)
Finally, consider construct (d): a pointer to pointer, such as,

```
float **xd;
```

In this case, xd is defined as a pointer to pointer to float. This means the type of *xd is a pointer to float, and the type of **xd is a float. A construct such as this can also be used as a two-dimensional array if it is initialized properly. Three steps are required to do this. The variable xd itself is a pointer to pointer to float, but in this application, we want to make it point to an area of memory large enough to hold as many pointer to floats as there are rows in our array, which in this example, is 2:

```
xd = (float **)malloc(2 * sizeof(float *));
```

The result of this we can picture as

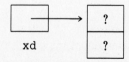

This illustrates that xd is pointing to an array of two pointers whose values are as yet undetermined. To finish the initialization, we must define each of these pointers to point to an array of three floats, corresponding to the rows of our array:

```
xd[0] = (float *)malloc(3 * sizeof(float));
xd[1] = (float *)malloc(3 * sizeof(float));
```

This gives us

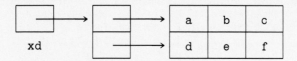

We can now write, for example,

```
xd[0][1] = 3.14;
xd[1][2] = 5.5;
```

which would set element b to 3.14 and element f to 5.5.

This construct is almost identical to construct (b). The primary difference is that whereas the array identifier xb is a *constant* pointer and cannot be assigned to, the identifier xd is a *variable* pointer (an l-value) and must be assigned to before it can be used. The other comments made about xb also apply to xd.

Many of the points made about the differences among these constructs can be reduced to considering whether or not an expression is an l-value. Specifically,

- Neither xa nor xa[0] is an l-value.
- xb is not an l-value, but xb[0] is.
- xc is an l-value, but xc[0] is not.
- Both xd and xd[0] are l-values.

Looking at the differences in this manner, and recalling that an array reference such as

```
arr[i][j]
```

is equivalent to

```
*(*(arr + i) + j)
```

we can see that all these constructs are consistent in the way in which C represents arrays.

What are the advantages and disadvantages of these different array representations?

Construct (a) is most efficient in terms of memory required because no extra pointers are needed to represent the array; thus the evaluation of indexed expressions would probably be more efficient than the other representations.

Constructs (b) and (d) are useful for creating so-called **ragged arrays** where the rows of an array are not all the same size. Consider the following program fragment:

```
int *xx[3];

for (i = 0; i < 3; i++)
    xx[i] = (int *)malloc(sizeof(int) * (i + 1));
```

If this code were executed, a "triangular" array would be created:

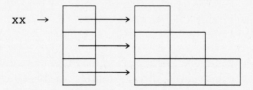

The individual elements would be accessed as

```
xx[0][0], xx[1][0], xx[1][1], xx[2][0], xx[2][1], xx[2][2]
```

The reference

```
xx[0][1]
```

would also be syntactically legal but logically invalid because row 0 does not technically have an element with index 1. This is also true for `xx[1][2]` and `xx[2][3]`. Ragged arrays would be useful for saving space in an application that did not require all elements of all rows to be defined.

Construct (a) is a *static* array, since its size must be specified at compile time. Constructs (b) through (d), however, allow us to create various types of *dynamic* arrays:

1. Construct (b) allows us to create arrays with a fixed number of rows but with a dynamic number of columns, even to the extent that some rows are of lengths different from other rows (a ragged array).
2. Construct (c) allows us to create arrays with a fixed (static) number of columns but with a variable number of rows.
3. Construct (d) allows us to create completely dynamic two-dimensional arrays with any number of rows and any number of columns (including ragged rows).

Generalized code could be designed to create dynamic arrays of each of these types. Example 8.2.2 demonstrates how this could be done for arrays represented using construct (d).

Example 8.2.2 The following code implements a routine that can be used to create dynamic two-dimensional arrays of integers with any number of rows and any number of columns.

```
int **Create(rows, cols)
int rows, cols;
{
    int **x, i;
    char *malloc();

    x = (int **)malloc(rows * sizeof(int *));
    for (i = 0; i < rows; i++)
        x[i] = (int *)malloc(cols * sizeof(int));
    return(x);
}
```

This function could be used as

```
int **x, **y;

x = Create(3,11);
y = Create(8,4);
```

The variable x now represents a 3 by 11 array, and variable y represents an 8 by 4 array. ∎

If we had the definitions

```
int **x, y[4][7];
```

we could not make the assignment

```
x = (int **)y;
```

and then use x to access the elements of y because, clearly, x has not been initialized correctly for using a pointer to pointer as a two-dimensional array.

The concepts introduced in this section can be generalized to arrays of dimension greater than two, but we leave this as an exercise for you to do.

8.2.5 Two-Dimensional Arrays as Function Parameters

A two-dimensional array may also be specified as a function parameter. In this case, the size of the first dimension may be omitted (and is ignored by the compiler even if given by the user), but the specification of the size of the second dimension is mandatory and *must* be a constant expression.

As with single-dimensional arrays, a two-dimensional array parameter is converted to a pointer when it is passed. In this case, the conversion will be to the type pointer to a row. For example,

```
double x[3][4];
```

in a parameter specification is converted to

```
double (*x)[4];
```

and so it is equivalent to

```
double x[][4];
```

Both bounds must not be omitted in the specification of a formal two-dimensional array parameter; for example,

```
double x[][];
```

is illegal.

Since the size of a row is known within a function, an expression such as

```
x + 1
```

may be accordingly scaled. As we explained in a previous section,

```
x[i][j] = (*x)[i * number of columns + j]
        = *(*x + i * number of columns + j)
```

Thus to generate a correct *address mapping*, the compiler does not need to know the size of the first dimension, but it does need to know the size of the second dimension. For arrays of dimension greater than two, all bounds except the first must be specified.

Example 8.2.3   Consider the following function to find the maximum element in a two-dimensional array:

```
double maxi(arr, size)
double arr[][4];
int size;
{
    double temp = arr[0][0];
    int    i, j;
```

```
      for (i = 0; i < size; i++)
           for (j = 0; j < 4; j++)
                if (arr[i][j] > temp)
                      temp = arr[i][j];
      return temp;
}
```

The size specified for a two-dimensional array parameter must be a constant. That is, we *cannot* write

```
double maxi(arr, size1, size2)
double arr[size1][size2];
int size1, size2;
```

because the compiler will complain that the size specified for the first dimension is not a constant. There is, however, a way to get around this problem: Transform the two-dimensional array into a single-dimensional array:

```
double maxi(arr, size1, size2)
double arr[];
int size1, size2;
{
     double temp = arr[0];
     int    i, j;

     for (i = 0; i < size1; i++)
          for (j = 0; j < size2; j++)
               if (arr[i * size2 + j] > temp)
                     temp = arr[i * size2  + j];
     return temp;
}
```

The only change we made is replacing

```
arr[i][j]
```

with

```
arr[i * size2 + j]
```

In the main program, a call to this function must take into account the transformation applied. For example, for the two-dimensional array

```
double b[5][6];
```

the call will be

```
maxi(*b, 5, 6)
```

because *b represents a pointer to double.

Finally, we cannot replace the definition of the formal parameter arr with

```
double **arr;
```

as an alternative implementation of maxi and still use this function to find the maximum element of a true two-dimensional array. We saw in the previous section that although a pointer to pointer can be used as a two-dimensional array, the way in which such an array is represented in memory is different from the way in which true two-dimensional arrays are represented; thus the two cannot be freely intermixed as formal and actual parameters.   ∎

8.3 INITIALIZATION OF ARRAYS, EXTERNAL ARRAYS

An array may be initialized if it is a local static or global array; local auto arrays may not be initialized.

We now describe a form of initializer that varies slightly depending on the type of variable. An initializer can always be enclosed by braces, but in the case of simple values (not arrays or structures), it is not necessary.

A single-dimensional array initializer is a list of initializers enclosed in braces, that is, of the form

```
{ I1, I2 ,..., Ik }
```

where In is an initializer for the nth element of the array. An initializer must be a static expression, for example,

```
double f[3] = { 1.5, 3.0, 1.88 };
```

Note the following:

• In the example, each simple initializer can be enclosed in braces, but as we indicated, this is not necessary:

```
double f[3] = { {1.5}, {3.0}, {1.88} };
```

- The size of the array may be omitted, since the compiler can determine the size from the initializer:

```
double f[] = { 1.5, 3.0, 1.88 };
```

- If the size of the array is specified and the number of provided initializers is less than the size, the remaining elements of the arrays are set to zero:

```
double f[3] = { 1.5, 3.0 };
```

Here, f[2] is zero.

- It is incorrect to specify more initializers than the size of the array:

```
double f[1] = { 1.5, 3.0 };
```

Multi-dimensional arrays may be initialized in the same way, using nested braces, for example,

```
double f[][2] = {
                 { 1.5,   3.0 },
                 { 2.66,  1.0 },
                 { 1.9,   1.0 }
                }
```

The last dimension—the number of columns—*must* be provided. This also applies to arrays of dimension greater than two; all bounds but the first must be specified.

If the sizes are provided explicitly in the definition, braces do not have to be nested. For example, the preceding declaration could be rewritten as follows:

```
double f[3][2] = { 1.5,   3.0,
                   2.66,  1.0,
                   1.9,   1.0
                  }
```

String constants may be used in definition initializers. For example, the definition

```
char *x[] = { "C", "programming", "language" };
```

introduces an array of three pointers to strings. Thus

```
printf("%s\n", x[1]);
```

outputs

```
programming
```

and

```
printf("%c\n", x[2][1]);
```

outputs the letter

```
a
```

(the first a in language). The definition

```
char xx[2][10] = { "C", "language" };
```

introduces an array of two strings, each of which has 10 bytes allocated and initialized with the strings provided. In the previous example, the length of each row has been determined by the compiler from the actual length of the strings occurring in the definition.

Arrays may also be specified as extern. For extern arrays, the specification of the size in the first dimension is *optional*; if it is omitted, it must contain a pair of square brackets, for example,

File A:

```
int x[10];
float y[7][5];
```

File B:

```
extern int x[];
extern float y[][5];
```

The second dimension in the extern declaration of y must be specified. For arrays of dimension greater than two, all bounds except the first must be specified.

THINGS TO REMEMBER

An array identifier is a constant pointer.

A formal parameter array identifier is a variable pointer.

Arrays are stored by rows.

Let x be a two-dimensional array of type *typ*. Then

- The type of x is a pointer to a row.
- The type of *x is a pointer to *typ*.
- In the expression x + i, i is scaled by the size of the row.
- In the expression *x + i, i is scaled by the size of *typ*.
- *x = x[0].
- **x = *(x[0]) = x[0][0].
- x[i] = *(x + i) = *x + i * *number of columns*.

If x is a single-dimensional array of type *typ* passed as parameter to a function, x may be declared as

   typ x[ ];

or, equivalently,

   typ *x;

In the first form, the size of x may be specified, but it is neglected.

If x is a two-dimensional array of type *typ* passed as parameter to a function, x may be declared as

   typ x[ ][*size2*]

and the specification of the constant *size2* must not be omitted.

COMMON ERRORS

```
int b[3];
b[3] = 4;
```
Indices of b are in 0..2

```
int b[3];
b = 3;
```
b is a constant

```
int b[3];
   ... &b ...
```
b is not an l-value

```
f(b)
double b[][];
```
For a two-dimensional array, the number of columns must be specified

```
f(b)
float b[];
{
   ...sizeof(b)...
}
```
This does not return the size of array b, but the size of a pointer

EXERCISES

1. Write a program to read in a line of characters and store them in an 80-element character array. If end-of-line has not been detected before 80 characters are read, input should be stopped in this case as well. Then redisplay the characters on a new line with all blanks and digits removed.

2. Write a program that reads characters from the keyboard until end-of-file is encountered or 80 lines are read, saving the lengths of the lines in an array. After the lines have been read, the program should print the sum of line lengths and the minimum and maximum lengths.

3. Write a program that reads a sequence of `float` values, terminating when either 50 values have been read or 0 has been encountered and stores them in a `float` array. Then the program should display the sum and the product of the `float` values.

4. Write a program that reads the current position of the bishop on a chess board (its row and column) and prints a character grid representing the board, marking with an asterisk all squares that the bishop can move to from the input position.

5. Suppose the file TEST contains a number of lines describing marks for students in sections B and C of a course, each of the following form: an integer representing a mark, followed by a single blank, followed by a character representing a student's last name initial, for example,

   50 K

   The first 100 or fewer lines of the file describe students from section B; this group is terminated by a line of the form

   0 X

   Following this line is an indeterminate number of lines for students in section C (there may be more than 100).
   The marks for students in section B are in ascending order, as are the lines for the students in section C. You may assume no two marks are the same.

   Example

   20 G
   30 H

```
 0  X
 4  V
 6  A
60  D
```

Your program should merge these two groups, that is, produce a combined ordered list of marks and initials. If a line represents a student from section B, the character B should be printed after the initial; otherwise, a C should be printed. For the sample input file, the output would be

```
 4  V  C
 6  A  C
20  G  B
30  H  B
60  D  C
```

Assume there is at least one line for both sections, and the data are in sorted order within each group. The 100 (or fewer) students from section B should be read into arrays, then merged with the students from section C directly (that is, do not store the students from section C in arrays).

6. Write a complete C program that reads a number of lines from standard input, each no more than 80 characters long, and outputs these lines prefixed by their length, followed on the next line by asterisks beneath each digit in the line output.

Example

Input file:

```
How are you Mr. 007?
Just fine. I made $30,000 a day in 1985.
```

Output file:

```
20: How are you Mr. 007?
                   ***
40: Just fine. I made $30,000 a day in 1985.
                 ** ***            ****
```

7. Write a function FIND that takes three parameters,

```
An integer n
A float array F (more than n elements in size)
A float x
```

which returns 1 if x is in the array F, and 0 otherwise. Assume F is sorted, and use a binary search.

8. Consider the following program:

```
#include <stdio.h>
int x[][3] = { {1,   4,   2},
               {15,  17,  202}
            };
main()
{
    int i, *p;

    p = x[0];
    for (i = 0; i < 6; i++) {
        printf("%dth: %u\n", i, p);
        p++;
    }

    p = x[1];
    for (i = 0; i < 3; i++) {
        printf("%dth: %d\n", i, *p);
        p++;
    }
}
```

Assume the first output is

```
0th: 8515
```

and sizeof(int) is 2. Show the complete output produced by this program. Use the table below.

```
0th: 8515
1th:
2th:
3th:
4th:
5th:
0th:
1th:
2th:
```

9. Write a function PRO that takes three parameters,

```
An integer n
A float array F (more than n in size)
A float x
```

and returns through x the product of all the elements in F from positions 0 through n. Show how this function should be called.

10. Write a function `MAXI` that takes three parameters,

    ```
    An integer n
    A float array F (more than n in size)
    A float x
    ```

    and returns in x the maximum element in array F from position 0 to position n. Define MAXI as a boolean function that returns 1 (TRUE) if the maximum element is positive.

11. Write a function

    ```
    shrink(x)
    float *x[];
    ```

    that shrinks array x by two elements each time it is called. By shrink, we mean decrease the size of the memory block allocated to the array. This can be done by allocating a new (smaller) memory block, copying the desired part of the original array to it, deallocating the space assigned to the array, and then making the array point to the new memory area. For example, if the initial size of x is 10, the first time shrink is called, x will be shrunk to 8 elements (with elements 9 and 10 removed); the second time shrink is called, x will be shrunk to 6 elements; and so on. shrink must have only one parameter, and must not use any global variables.

    Write a short main program that creates and initializes (reading values from the keyboard) an array of size 10, calls shrink three times on this array, and then outputs the size of the array and the remaining elements.

12. Write a complete C program consisting of two functions and a main program. The function

    ```
    init(x, N)
    ```

    should read in N float values and store them in the two-dimensional array x of float values, which has five columns (the number of rows is not known here). The function

    ```
    find(x, f, i, j)
    ```

returns through i and j the row index and the column index of the float value f in the two-dimensional float array x. If f is not in x, i and j should return −1. Assume x has four rows and five columns. If f occurs more than once in x, find should return its last occurrence.

Example

x:	1.88	3	5.6	1.222	9.98
	0	0	1	4	4
	.2	.55	1.43	12	33
	.67	2.3	22.1	−32	−.4

```
find(x, 1.43, &i, &j);
```

assigns 2 to the variable i and 2 to the variable j.
In the main program,

- Define a two-dimensional array y (four rows and five columns).
- Call init to read in 20 float values.
- Call find to search for the value 1.99.
- Output the position (row and column indices) of where this value was found or a message if the value 1.99 was not found in y.

13. Write a function mult(a, b, n) that performs component-by-component multiplication of two n-element single-dimensional arrays of float values (that is, each component of the result is the product of the corresponding components of the two arrays) and returns the result through mult. Test this function in a main program.

14. Write a function mult(a, n1, n2, b, m1, m2, c) that multiplies two two-dimensional arrays of float values. Here, a is an array with n1 columns and n2 rows, and b is an array with m1 rows and m2 columns. The result should be returned through c. The function returns the value 1 if the multiplication can be performed, and 0 otherwise.

15. Write a function value(x, p, n) that finds the value of a double polynomial p of degree n at point x, using Horner's rule:

```
p(x) = p[0] + x(p[1] + x(p[2] + ... + x(p[n])...))
```

where the coefficients of the equation are passed in the array p. For example, if

```
p[0] = 1.0
p[1] = 2.0
p[2] = 3.0
```

this represents the polynomial $1 + 2x + 3x^2$ and the call

```
value(2.0, p, 2)
```

would yield the value 17.

9 Structures, Unions, and Enumeration Types

PREVIEW   *This chapter introduces structure, union, and enumeration types in C and compares these with related constructs in Pascal. We continue our discussion on functions by presenting functions with structure parameters and structures containing pointers to functions. Several examples show how to translate Pascal programs that use records and records with variants to C.*

REVIEW OF PASCAL CONSTRUCTS

Records

Pascal records can be used to create **nonhomogeneous structures**, which, unlike arrays, may contain components of different types. Internally, the representation of a record is similar to that of an array in that a single *contiguous* memory block is allocated for a record variable, with the size of the block being large enough to hold the values of all record components. Consider the following example:

```
TYPE REC = RECORD
             A : INTEGER;
             B : REAL;
             C : CHAR;
           END;

VAR X : REC;
```

Assuming integers require 2 bytes, reals 4 bytes, and characters 1 byte, a memory block 7 bytes in size would be allocated to the record variable X. (Note: In all examples in this section we assume no memory alignment is required.) If the base address of this memory block is 100, we have

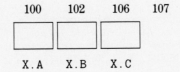

```
     100     102     106     107
    ┌───────┬───────┬───────┐
    │       │       │       │
    └───────┴───────┴───────┘
      X.A     X.B     X.C
```

The address of a dotted variable is computed by adding to the base address of the record the offset of the component being accessed, which the compiler determines by the relative position of the component within the record:

```
address of X.A  =  100 + 0  =  100
address of X.B  =  100 + 2  =  102
address of X.C  =  100 + 6  =  106
```

The *types* of the components are used to determine their relative offsets; thus the offsets can be determined at compilation time.

Variant Records

Records with **variants** are represented in a different way to reflect that different variants are *not* allocated separate memory blocks. Instead, a single memory block large enough to hold the largest variant is allocated, and all variants map onto this same address space. Consider the following example:

```
TYPE REC = RECORD
                A : INTEGER;                     (* 2 bytes *)
                CASE B : BOOLEAN OF              (* 1 byte  *)
                TRUE    : ( C : REAL;            (* 4 bytes *)
                            D : INTEGER; );
                FALSE   : ( E : INTEGER;
                            F : REAL;
                            G : CHAR; )          (* 1 byte  *)
           END;

VAR X : REC;
```

The size of the TRUE variant is 2 bytes for the integer A, 1 byte for the boolean B, 4 bytes for the real C, and 2 bytes for the integer D, for a total of 9 bytes. The size of the FALSE variant is 10 bytes because this variant has an additional character variable G. Therefore, a memory block 10 bytes in size is allocated to the variable X. If we map this address space using the TRUE variant, assuming the base address of X is 100, we have:

```
100     102     103     107     109
┌─────┬─────┬─────┬─────┬─────┐
│     │     │     │     │     │
└─────┴─────┴─────┴─────┴─────┘
 X.A     X.B     X.C     X.D
```

If the FALSE variant is used, the space is mapped as

```
100     102     103     105     109     110
```

```
X.A     X.B     X.E     X.F     X.G
```

The current value of the variant selector (the tag field) is used to determine which variant is "active." An attempt to access an attribute of the nonactive variant would be considered illegal and cause a run-time error. However, because this type of access control is expensive (both in memory requirements and execution time), it is often not implemented. Pascal also provides a type of variant record in which the control of variants is left entirely to the programmer. In this type, the name normally assigned to the variant selector may be omitted:

```
TYPE REC = RECORD
              A: INTEGER;
              CASE BOOLEAN OF
              TRUE  : ( F   : TEXT );
              FALSE : ( DAT : ARRAY [1..14] OF BYTE;
                        FIB : ARRAY [1..32] OF BYTE )
           END;

VAR X : REC;
```

With this structure, the programmer may freely access both variants. Moreover, since no tag variable is specified, no memory is allocated for one. This type of variant record is also called a **free union**.

Finally, consider the use of procedures or functions as fields in records. This capability could be useful in encapsulating data structures, for example, when writing a device driver. Unfortunately, Pascal does not support this construct.

Enumeration Types

Pascal supports enumeration types where the range of the type is defined either by enumerating (listing) all values or by specifying a subrange of an already known type. The elements of the range, called **enumeration constants**, have implicit ordinal values starting from 0. For example, in

```
TYPE COLOR = ( blue, red, green, yellow );
```

blue has the value 0, red 1, and so on. These values may be accessed using the function ORD. The variables of an enumeration type may be assigned values and compared for equality, for example,

```
VAR c, d : COLOR;

c := blue;
d := green;
IF c <> d THEN
    WRITELN(ORD(c));
```

Moreover, two predefined functions SUCC and PRED, respectively, can be used to obtain the value succeeding and preceding the given enumeration value, for example,

```
c := PRED(d);
```

An enumerated type and an integer type are two *different* types and may not be mixed in expressions, for example,

```
c := 0;
```

is incorrect.

C CONSTRUCTS

9.1 STRUCTURES

Records in C are called **structures**. The syntax of **a structure variable** definition is

Pascal	**C**

VAR A: RECORD
            components;
         END
	struct {
	            components;
	         } a;

The form of record definition shown here is not used often in Pascal since no name for the record type is defined. Still, it is syntactically correct, and we use it to begin our discussion on structures.

A structure definition always starts with the keyword struct and is followed by a list of components enclosed in braces, for example,

```
struct {
    int age;
    float salary;
} john;
```

This definition allocates a block of memory large enough to hold the specified attributes (an integer and a float), and the base address of that block is assigned to the variable john. As in Pascal, more than one variable may be defined by specifying a list of names:

```
struct {
    int age;
    float salary;
} john, mary, george;
```

Structure types may also be defined in C:

Pascal	**C**
TYPE *typ* = RECORD	struct *typ* {
components;	*components*;
END;	};

This definition introduces *typ* as a **type identifier** even though typedef has not been used. As in Pascal, the identifier *typ* can be used to define variables, but it *must* be preceded by the keyword struct; for example,

```
struct student {
    int age;
    float salary;
};

struct student john, george;
struct student ringo;
```

This defines john, george, and ringo as student type structures. The expected form

```
student john, george;
```

is incorrect.

A structure type definition may include variable definitions. For example, the preceding example can be shortened to

```
struct student {
    int age;
    float salary;
} john, george, ringo;
```

Bear in mind that the identifier following the keyword struct is a *type identifier*, whereas the identifiers following the final } are *variable identifiers*.

By using typedef, a new type can be introduced that incorporates the word struct as part of the type:

```
typedef struct student STUDENT;
```

or, alternatively,

```
typedef struct student {
            int age;
            float salary;
        } STUDENT;
```

This eliminates having to use the word `struct` in future definitions:

```
STUDENT john, george, ringo;
```

In the definition of type STUDENT, the structure identifier `student` serves no purpose and can be eliminated:

```
typedef struct {
            int age;
            float salary;
        } STUDENT;
```

Structure fields are accessed in the same way as in Pascal using a dot:

```
STUDENT s, t;

s.age    = 100;
t.age    = s.age;
t.salary = 11.2;
```

An equivalent of Pascal's `WITH` statement is not provided in C. Moreover, in earlier implementations, structure variables could not appear in assignment statements, but many systems today do allow it. For example, the statement

```
s = t;
```

where s and t are defined as structures means the structure t is copied to the structure s. There is no test for equality of whole structures, so they have to be compared component by component.

Structures may be combined with arrays, for example,

```
struct student {
    char name[30];
    int StudNum;
} Stats[100];
```

or, alternatively,

```
struct student {
    char name[30];
    int StudNum;
};

struct student Stats[100];
```

The word `struct` is again required here. This defines

```
Stats
```

as an array of `struct student`, and

```
Stats[i]
```

is of the type `struct student`. Using `typedef`, this would be done as follows:

```
typedef struct student {
            char name[30];
            int StudNum;
        } STUDENT;

typedef STUDENT CLASS[100];
CLASS Stats;
```

This is equivalent to the following Pascal definitions:

```
TYPE STUDENT = RECORD
                  NAME    : ARRAY[0..29] OF CHAR;
                  STUDNUM : INTEGER;
               END;
     CLASS    = ARRAY[0..99] OF STUDENT;

VAR Stats : CLASS;
```

In the C version,

```
STUDENT
```

is a type identifier denoting a `struct student`, and

```
CLASS
```

is a type identifier denoting an array of STUDENT. This type identifier can be used to define arrays, as in

```
CLASS Stats;
```

Recall from Chapter 8 that an array variable cannot be assigned another array variable (it must be copied element by element). This is another case where structures with nested arrays can be useful. For example, if we have

```
struct student s, t;
```

and perform the assignment

```
s = t;
```

which is allowed, it effectively copies the array nested in the structure in a single operation.

C does not permit **self-referential** structure definitions. For example,

```
struct data {
    struct data d;
        . . .
};
```

is illegal.

Finally, structure type identifiers can be *overloaded* with other type identifiers even in the same scope. A useful application of this rule would be to define, for example,

```
typedef struct student {
            char name[30];
            int StudNum;
        } student;
```

Now the meaning of the identifier student depends on the context: It may denote a structure type or a synonym for `struct student`. Similarly, it is correct to define

```
struct student {
    char name[30];
    int StudNum;
} student[100];
```

9.1.1 Structures and Pointers

Pointers to structures are defined in the usual way, for example,

```
struct student {
    char name[30];
    int StudNum;
} s, *ps;
```

This defines s as a structure and ps as a pointer to a structure. The variable ps can be initialized in two ways:

- ps can be made to point to s:
  ps = &s;

- `malloc` can be used to allocate memory for `ps`:

  ```
  ps = (struct student *)malloc(sizeof(struct student));
  ```

Note the need for *casting*. This allocation statement can be made clearer if `typedef` is used:

```
typedef struct student {
          . . .
        } STUDENT;

STUDENT s, *ps;

ps = (STUDENT *)malloc(sizeof(STUDENT));
```

A structure pointer type could be defined using, for example,

```
typedef STUDENT * PSTUDENT;
```

or alternatively

```
typedef struct student {
          . . .
        } STUDENT, *PSTUDENT;
```

This definition introduces *two* type identifiers:

- STUDENT is shorthand for

  ```
  struct student
  ```

- PSTUDENT is shorthand for

  ```
  struct student *
  ```

A self-reference in a structure definition is allowed if it refers to a pointer. For example,

```
struct example {
    struct example *e;
    . . .
}
```

is correct.

You must be careful when using `typedef` in the preceding context: An identifier used in a `typedef` must be defined previously. For example,

```
typedef struct {
            int val;
            ITEM *next;
        } ITEM;
```

is incorrect because `ITEM` is used to define the attribute `next` before `ITEM` itself is defined. The solution to this problem is to introduce a structure type identifier:

```
typedef struct item {
            int val;
            struct item *next;
      } ITEM;
```

In general, the only context in which a structure type T may be used before it is defined is the definition of a pointer of type T. This is because if a variable of type T was defined *before* type T was defined, the compiler would not know the size of the structure T. Thus if a structure is used in more than one file, its definition must appear in each of these files.

In the case of pointers that point to structures, there has to be some way to access the individual fields of the structure. Consider the following definitions:

```
STUD  s;
PSTUD ps;
```

If ps is initialized to point to s,

```
ps = &s;
```

an initial attempt to access the fields of the structure s through ps might be

```
*ps.StudNum
```

however, . has higher precedence than * so the expression would be interpreted as

```
*(ps.StudNum)
```

and is therefore wrong. To get around this problem, we can use parentheses:

```
(*ps).StudNum
```

An alternative notation that is equivalent to the preceding expression and that avoids the need for parentheses,

```
ps->StudNum
```

may also be used. Compare this with the corresponding Pascal construct:

Pascal	**C**
`pointer^.field`	`pointer->field`

In Pascal, an up arrow (circumflex) and a dot are used in place of the right-pointing arrow (a hyphen followed by a greater than character) in C.

Example 9.1.1   Assume that data about factory employees are stored in an array called `factory`, defined as

```
struct address {
     char street[20];
     int number;
};

struct person {
     char name[20];
     char department[10];
     struct address addr;
     float salary;
};
struct person factory[1000];
```

and we want to print the address of the person who has the best salary. Further assume the name of each street consists of at most 20 characters and is terminated by the character \0:

```
int    i, who = 0;
float most = 0,
      aux;

for (i = 0; i < 1000; i++)
    if ((aux = factory[i].salary) > most) {
        most = aux;
        who = i;
    }
```

Another version of this portion of the program makes use of pointers to increase the efficiency of memory address calculations:

```
float most = factory[0].salary;
struct person *aux, *who;

for (aux = who = factory; aux < factory + 1000; aux++)
    if (aux->salary > most) {
        who = aux;
        most = aux->salary;
    }
```

Note how the two pointers are initialized:

- `most` is the salary field of the 0th employee.
- `aux` is pointing to the base address of the array, so it also points to the 0th structure.

In each step of the loop, the current value of `most` is compared with the `salary` field of the current record. The operation

```
aux++;
```

moves `aux` to the next record because the increment is scaled by the size of the structure `person`. We encourage you to compare the efficiency of the two versions. This is the same approach used in Chapter 8 to traverse arrays of simple elements (such as `int`s or `float`s), and this technique cannot be used in Pascal because a pointer cannot be made to point to a particular element of an array.

To print the address of the employee having the highest salary, we can use

```
printf("%d %s\n", who->addr.number, who->addr.street);   ∎
```

Structure Component Allocation
In C, components of a structure are assigned increasing memory addresses in left-to-right order. Consider the structure

```
struct example {
    int  i, j, k;
} e;
int *point, i;
```

The following loop performs a component-by-component traversal of this structure:

```
for (i = 0, point = (int*) &e; i < 3; point++, i++)
    . . .
```

This example may seem somewhat artificial, but it does illustrate some points. In particular, recognize that this loop will work only if the components are of the same type and that even then it may not work. This is because structure components may have to be aligned, requiring that *padding* be used. Consider the following example, which assumes a structure must start on an even byte boundary. C requires that a structure terminate on the same alignment boundary it started on. Assuming a character takes 1 byte and an integer takes 2 bytes, the structure

```
struct example {
     char c;
     int i;
};
```

would occupy 4 bytes—3 bytes make up the actual components, and an extra byte is added so that the structure terminates on an even byte boundary.

Example 9.1.2 The following program is on linked lists (this time using real structures, not an imitation, as in Chapter 7). The program creates a linked list of N integer values (ranging from 1 to N), then traverses this list deleting every value that can be divided by 3, and finally displays the values that are left.

```
#include <stdio.h>
#define NEW(PP)  ((PP) = (PITEM)malloc(sizeof(ITEM)))
#define TEST(PP) if (NEW(PP) == NULL) \
                             { printf("memory error\n"); return; }


typedef struct item {
              int val;
              struct item *next;
           } ITEM, *PITEM;

main()
{
     int i, n;
     PITEM current, first, prev;
     char *malloc();

     printf("Enter a positive integer value: ");
     scanf("%d", &n);
     if (n < 1) {
          printf("number must be positive\n");
          return;
     }

     /* create the list */
     TEST(first)
     current = first;
     first->val = 1;
     for (i = 2; i <= n; i++) {
          TEST(current->next)
          current = current->next;
          current->val = i;
     }
     current->next = NULL;
```

```
                /* remove elements divisible by 3 */
                for (prev = current = first; current != NULL;
                        prev = current, current = current->next)
                            if (current->val % 3 == 0 ) {
                                    prev->next = current->next;
                                    free((char *)current);
                                    current = prev
                            }
                /* display what is left */
                for (current = first; current != NULL;
                        current = current->next)
                            printf("\n%d\n", current->val);
        }
```

When removing elements divisible by 3, we traverse the list maintaining two pointers—one that points to the current element, and one that points to its predecessor. This way we can easily free the required element. ■

9.1.2 Structures and Functions

Functions may return pointers to structures, and they may have parameters that are pointers to structures.

Example 9.1.3 The following program shows a function that creates a new object for the structure

```
        struct student {
            long StudNum;
            char name[20];
        };
```

and returns a pointer to this object:

```
        struct student *new()
        {
            struct student *aux;
            char *malloc();

            aux = (struct student *)malloc(sizeof(struct student));
            if (aux == NULL)
                printf("Out of memory\n");
            return (aux);
        }
```

To rewrite the function as a procedure, we have to pass a *pointer to pointer* to structure:

```
void new1(s)
struct student **s;
{
     char *malloc();
     struct student *aux;

     aux =  (struct student*)malloc(sizeof(struct student));
     if (aux == NULL)
          printf("Out of memory\n");
     else *s = aux;
}
```

You may wish to trace a call to new1 using the graphical representation introduced in the previous chapters.

The following program shows how the preceding two functions can be used:

```
#include <stdio.h>
main()
{
     struct student s, *ps, *ps1,
                         *new();

     /* allocate memory for ps using new  */
     ps = new();

     /* allocate memory for ps1 using new1  */
     new1(&ps1);

     /* now all the variables have memory allocated */
     /* and component access is well defined */
     s.StudNum = 821366;
     ps->StudNum = s.StudNum + 1;
     ps1->StudNum = 877744;
     ...
}
```
■

In newer C implementations, a function may return a structure, and structures may be passed as parameters.

Example 9.1.4   The following code demonstrates how structures could be used to represent complex numbers and how functions for operations such as addition of complex numbers could be implemented. The basic definition needed is

```
typedef struct {
            double re, im;
        } complex;
```

This structure defines complex numbers in terms of a real part and an imaginary part. If we had variables defined as

```
complex x, y, z;
```

an operation such as

```
z = x + y;
```

would not be allowed. Instead, we would have to implement the required operations in terms of functions. Addition, for example, could be implemented as follows:

```
complex add(x, y)
complex x, y;
{
    complex z;

    z.re = x.re + y.re;
    z.im = x.im + y.im;
    return(z);
}
```

The structure z in this function is allocated on the stack when the function is called, and it is released when the function terminates. If the function add is called as

```
v = add(x1, y1);
```

where v, x1, and y1 are variables of type complex, the value returned by the function (the contents of the structure z) is copied into the structure v, and even though the memory allocated for z has been released, the data representing z on the stack is still intact because the assignment to v is done immediately. If, however, the function add is called as

```
pv = &(add(x1, y1));
```

where pv is a pointer to complex, a *dangling reference* occurs. That is, pv is pointing to an area on the stack that may be reused on a subsequent function call. This is true for any type of function, and the general rule is that the address operator should not be applied to a function result.

Another operation that would be useful in this application is a function that initializes the fields of a complex structure:

```
void init(px, r, i)
complex *px;
double r, i;
{
    if (px) {   /* px is not NULL */
        px->re = r;
        px->im = i;
    }
    else  /* undetermined result */
        return;
}
```

The parameter px is a pointer to complex. To call init, we would use, for example,

```
init(&v, 3.0, 6.0);
```

Recall the necessity of passing 3.0 and 6.0 rather than 3 and 6.

Other operations on complex numbers, such as subtraction, multiplication, and division we leave as exercises for you to do. ∎

If a function is designed to *modify* the components of a structure passed as a parameter, this parameter must be defined as a *pointer to structure* (as it was in init). Even if the components are not intended to be changed, it is still better to use a pointer to structure; otherwise, the entire structure is duplicated by the system when a function call is made (as is always done when call by value is used). This is true for any type of parameter, not just structures.

Example 9.1.5   Let us now modify the definition of complex numbers to include a "virtual" function norm that computes the norm of a complex number. We call norm virtual because at this stage it is not determined:

```
struct complex {
    double re, im;
    double (*norm) ();
};
```

Note that norm is a *pointer*, and so it can be defined in the structure. We now define two functions in the main program and assign them to two pointers.

The first function uses the formula

$$\sqrt{re^2 + im^2}$$

whereas the second uses the formula

$$|re| + |im|$$

We assume `fabs` and `sqrt` are library functions that return the absolute value of a `double` and the square root of a `double`, respectively.

```
#include <math.h>
typedef struct complex complex, *pcomplex;

double norm1(x)
pcomplex x;
{
     return (fabs(x->re) + fabs(x->im) );
}

double norm2(x)
pcomplex  x;
{
     return (sqrt(x->re * x->re + x->im * x->im));
}
```

Having defined these functions, we can initialize the attribute `norm` of a variable of type `complex`, for example,

```
complex x;

x.norm = norm1;
```

But how can the function `norm` of the structure x be called? Since

```
x.norm
```

is a pointer to a function, the expression

```
(*(x.norm))(...)
```

is a *call* to this function (note how we use parentheses). Pointers may be used similarly:

```
pcomplex px;
... initialization of px ...
px->norm = norm2;
```

The function may be called using

```
(*px->norm)(...)
```

The main program is not particularly useful; its purpose is to show some sample calls to the norm functions:

```
#include <stdio.h>
main()
{
        complex x, y;
        pcomplex px = &x, py = &y;
        extern double norm1(), norm2();
        double f1, f2, f3, f4;

        x.re = 1;
        x.im = 2;
        y.re = 3;
        y.im = 4;
        x.norm = norm1;
        y.norm = norm2;

        /* ready for calls, first using structures  */

        f1 =  (*(x.norm))(&y);
        f2 =  (*(y.norm))(&x);

        /*  now using pointers */
        f3 =  (*px->norm)(py);
        f4 =  (*py->norm)(px);

        /* output results */
        printf("f1= %f,  f2= %f,  f3= %f,  f4= %f\n",f1,f2,f3,f4);
}
```

The following pictures may help you understand these structures:

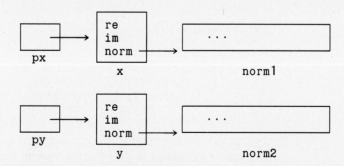

The proposed ANSI C standard suggests that function pointers may be called as functions directly. For example, instead of

```
fp = (*(x.norm))(&y);
```

the statement

```
fp = x.norm(&y);
```

could be used. This causes no ambiguity in C's syntax and can make the
code considerably more readable.   ■

9.1.3 Initialization of Structures

Structures may be initialized similarly to how arrays are initialized by
providing a list of initializers enclosed in braces. For example,

```
struct table {
    int i;
    double f;
};

struct table c = { 1, 1.99 };
```

This may be combined with arrays or nested structures, as shown in the
following examples:

```
struct table1 {
    struct table p;
    int p1[2];
};

struct table1 c1 = {
                { 2, 2.3 },   /* p initializer */
                { 1, 2 }      /* p1 initializer */
            };

struct address {
    char *city;
    int phone;
} book[] = {
            "Wolfville", 5423333,
            "New York",  7883210,
            "Halifax",   4555231
        };
```

The number of elements in the array can be computed as

```
#define SIZE (sizeof(book) / sizeof(struct address))
```

because these values are known at compilation time.

The rules describing the cases of too many or too few initializers for
arrays apply to structures as well.

Remember that structures and arrays may *not* be explicitly initialized unless they are static. For example,

```
struct example {
    ...
};

void f()
{
    struct example e = { ... };
    ...
}
```

is an incorrect initialization (e is a local automatic variable). This can be corrected by specifying e as a static variable:

```
struct example {
    ...
};

void f()
{
    static struct example e = { ... };
    ...
}
```

or by making it a global variable:

```
struct example e = { ... };

void f()
{
    ...
}
```

9.2 UNIONS

Unions in C are similar to variant records in Pascal that do not specify a tag field (**free unions**). The syntax of unions is almost identical to the syntax of structures with the exception of the keyword union:

Pascal	C
TYPE *typ* = RECORD	union *typ* {
common attributes;	
CASE *varTyp* OF	
val1 : (*variant1*);	*variant1*;
...	...
valk : (*variantk*);	*variantk*;
END;	}

Since C does not support **discriminated unions** (that is, unions with common attributes), this translation is not entirely faithful. We now show in more detail how Pascal's variant records can be translated into C.

To define union type variables, the keyword union must be repeated, as demonstrated in

```
union UnionType x, y;
union UnionType z;
```

or typedef can be used to introduce a synonym for

```
union UnionType
```

for example,

```
typedef union UnionType UNIONTYPE;
UNIONTYPE x, y, z;
```

union type identifiers can be *overloaded* with other identifiers within the same scope in the same fashion as structure type identifiers. Thus

```
typedef union UnionType UnionType;
```

is correct.

The memory block allocated for a variable of type

```
union typ
```

is large enough to store the largest component of the union and is *aligned* to an address suitable for all elements of this union. That is, a union is a structure in which all elements are at offset zero. Thus it is the user's responsibility to properly access the components of a union—the run-time system will not issue an error if you access a component of the union that you did not intend to.

To access union components, the syntax is identical to that of structure components, for example,

```
union CharInt {
    char c;
    int i;
} x, *px = &x;

...
x.i = 3;
px->c = 'a';
```

Variant Records versus Unions

There are various differences between the Pascal and C versions of free
unions. Unlike Pascal, unions in C do not have a common attribute part.
For example, the following Pascal declaration of a free union (that is, a
record without a tag field),

```
TYPE TYP = RECORD
              A, B : INTEGER;
              CASE BOOLEAN OF
                TRUE  : (variant1...);
                FALSE : (variant2...);
           END;
```

does not have a direct translation to C. Moreover, each variant in C is
just a single variable (either simple or complex). As a first step, let us
translate the simpler Pascal declaration

```
TYPE VARIANTS = RECORD
                   CASE BOOLEAN OF
                     TRUE  : (I, J : INTEGER);
                     FALSE : (K, L : REAL);
                END;
```

Structures would have to be defined first:

```
typedef struct {
           int i, j;
        } VARIANT1;

typedef struct {
           float k, l;
        } VARIANT2;
```

and then these used to define the union:

```
typedef union {
           VARIANT1 v1;
           VARIANT2 v2;
        } VARIANTS;
```

Alternatively, we could nest the structures representing the variants directly in the definition of the union:

```
typedef union {
           struct {
              int i, j;
           } v1;
           struct {
              float k, l;
           } v2;
        } VARIANTS;
```

In this version, v1 and v2 are variables of anonymous types, but this is sufficient; for example, if a variable is defined as

```
VARIANTS x;
```

the component i can be accessed using

```
x.v1.i
```

How would a common set of attributes be introduced into the union? One possible solution would be to define a structure where one component is a union (like the one shown) that represents the variant part, and where additional attributes represent the fixed part. For example, in the following structure, x and y correspond to the fixed part, and v corresponds to the variant part:

```
typedef struct {
             int x, y;
             VARIANTS v;
        } VREC;
```

This same approach could be used to implement an equivalent of Pascal's tag field by using a variable in the fixed part to indicate which variant is currently in use.

Example 9.2.1   The following program reads ten values from the keyboard. Each of these values is read from a new line and is preceded by either an I or a C to indicate whether the value to be read is an integer or a character, respectively. These values are stored in a linked list and then redisplayed. The integer variable what is equal to 1 if the data stored in the union is a character; it is equal to 0 otherwise. Thus it serves as a *tag selector*.

```
#include <stdio.h>


#define INTEGER    'I'
#define CHARACTER  'C'
#define LIMIT      10
#define NEW(PP)    ((PP) = (PITEM)malloc(sizeof(ITEM)))
#define ERROR      {printf("Error, aborting\n"); return; }
#define SKIP       while (getchar() != '\n') ;

typedef union {
             char c;
             int i;
        } CHARINT;
```

```
typedef struct item {
            CHARINT val;
            int what;
            struct item *next;
        } ITEM, *PITEM;

main()
{
    int   i;
    PITEM p, temp;
    char *malloc();

    if (NEW(p) == NULL)
        ERROR
    temp = p;
    for (i = 0; ; i++) {
        switch (getchar()) {
        case INTEGER    : p->what = 0;
                          scanf("%d", &(p->val.i));
                          break;
        case CHARACTER  : p->what = 1;
                          scanf("%c", &(p->val.c));
                          break;
        default         : ERROR
                          break;
        }
        SKIP
        if (i == LIMIT - 1)
            break;
        else {
            if (NEW(p->next) == NULL)
                ERROR
            p = p->next;
        }
    }

    for (i = 0, p = temp; i < LIMIT; p = p->next, i++)
        if (p->what)
            printf("%c ", p->val.c);
        else printf("%d ", p->val.i);
}
```

We have used a macro SKIP to skip characters until the end of line is reached. ∎

The earlier description of structure component layout and possible alignments apply to unions as well. This—to force alignment on the appropriate memory boundary—is one possible application of unions. For example, in a memory management system, we need to be concerned about alignment: The function that allocates memory (such as malloc) must return the storage aligned for the objects that later will be stored in it. Recall that each computer has its own *most restrictive type*, that is, a type whose value must be stored at a particular address multiple.

Assuming the type `long` is the most restrictive type, we can force alignment using unions:

```
union align {
    long whatever;
    struct {
        /* aligned with long */
        . . .
    }
}
```

In Section 13.3, we show an example of a program that uses this technique. More advanced applications of unions are also given in Section 13.2, where we present a hash table that can contain both variables and functions, and in Section 13.5, where we demonstrate an external binary search tree.

Standard C does not allow initialization of unions in definitions.

9.3   ENUMERATION TYPES

The syntax of enumeration types is similar to the syntax of structures and unions, for example,

```
enum color {
    blue, red, green, yellow
} c, d;
```

No terminator follows the last enumeration value.

As in Pascal, the variables of an enumeration type may be assigned values that are enumeration constants and may be compared for equality:

```
c = blue;
d = green;
    . . .
if (c == d)
    . . .
```

In general, enumeration constants are not l-values. Enumeration types are a fairly recent addition to C, so unfortunately, no standard for them yet exists. Most C compilers implement enumeration constants as integers even to the degree of allowing an explicit initialization of these constants:

```
enum color1 {
     blue = 0,
     red  = 1,
     green = 3,
     yellow
} c1, d1;
```

In the preceding example, the enumeration constants are *not* consecutively valued. This means that if c1 is equal to red, for example, the result of the statement

```
++c1;
```

depends on the implementation, and is not necessarily green. Some compilers do not allow this construct at all.

An enumeration constant not explicitly initialized receives a value 1 greater than the value of the preceding constant. In the example, the value of yellow is 4.

An initializer for a variable of an enumeration type must be an expression of that type, for example,

```
enum color {
    blue, green, red
} c = blue;
```

Enumeration types are defined in the usual manner, for example,

```
typedef enum color {
          blue, green, red
       } color;
```

Enumeration type identifiers can be overloaded with other identifiers in the same way as structure and union identifiers.

Some implementations (for example, 4.3BSD Unix C) do not treat enumeration constants as integers and do not allow enumeration variables to be incremented, compared (except for equality and inequality), and so on. In particular, to iterate over enumeration ranges is impossible unless integer casting is used. Consider the following example:

```
typedef enum values { a, b, c, d } values;
```

The functions succ and pred, defined below, are effectively the same as those defined in Pascal (and as in Pascal, they are undefined if their arguments are, respectively, the largest or the smallest enumeration value).

```
values succ(x)
values x;
{
      return (values)((int)x + 1);
}

values pred(x)
values x;
{
      return (values)((int)x - 1);
}
```

The following main program shows how these functions could be used:

```
main()
{
      values  v = a;

      while (1) {
            if (v == d)
                  break;
            printf("%d\n", (int)v);
            v = succ(v);
      }
      for (v = d; (int)v > (int)a; v = pred(v))
            printf("%d\n", (int)v);
}
```

To print the value of the enumeration variable v, we have cast it to int. This example is somewhat of a programming "trick"; the actual application of enumeration types is to designate objects and to improve error handling (see Example 12.2.1).

Example 9.3.1   Consider an implementation of a linked list whose elements contain either an integer value or a pointer to a list. Assume a list has a header cell that contains the length of the list and a pointer to the first element. Typically, we have an enumerated type that determines the kind of each element in a list:

```
typedef enum {
            IntItem, ListItem
      } KIND;
```

and a structure with two variants:

```
typedef struct velem {
        KIND kind;
        struct velem *next;
        union {
                struct {
                        struct velem *first;
                        int length;
                } head;
                int value;
        } variant;
} VELEMENT, *PVELEMENT;
```

An alternative definition of this structure is

```
typedef struct {
        struct velem *first;
        int length;
} HEAD;

typedef union {
        HEAD head;
        int value;
} VARIANT;

typedef struct velem {
        KIND kind;
        struct velem *next;
        VARIANT variant;
} VELEMENT, *PVELEMENT;
```

A variable of type VELEMENT is either a list element containing an integer or a list header cell pointing to another list. This is determined by the value of the field kind. For example,

```
VELEMENT x, y;

x.kind = IntItem;              set kind to IntItem
x.variant.value = 500;         set its value to 500
y.kind = ListItem;             y is a list variant
y.variant.head.first = NULL;   list is empty
y.variant.length = 0;
y.next  = &x;
```

Combining these variants allows us to set up lists of lists. For example, the list diagrammed as

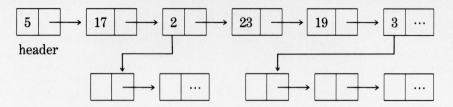

represents a list containing five elements. The very first element of the list is a header, so it stores the current length of the list—5. The second, fourth, and fifth elements are of type `IntItem`, and they store the values 17, 23, and 19, respectively. The third and sixth elements are of type `ListItem`, and they represent lists containing 2 and 3 elements, respectively. The code needed to actually create these lists we leave for you to do as an exercise.   ∎

9.4 DECLARATORS—PART 3

In this section, we complete the definition of a type-specifier. As we described in Section 7.4.4, a *type-specifier* is the name of a predefined primitive data type, such as `int` or `double`. Moreover, a type-specifier can be a `structure`, `union`, or enumerated type specifier. We provide the complete syntax for a type-specifier in Appendix A; here we give several examples:

```
struct complex;
struct complex { double re, im; };
union { int ivar; char cvar; };
enum { intItem, listItem };
```

These type-specifiers can be used in any of the contexts described in Sections 7.4.4 and 8.1.6; for example, to declare a function returning a structure:

```
extern struct { double re, im; } add();
```

THINGS TO REMEMBER

Structures are stored in blocks of consecutive memory locations with padding if memory alignment is required.

Structure assignments and passing a structure as a parameter involves copying the entire structure.

Unions are structures in which all elements are at offset 0. There is no
tag field, and structures with nested unions must be used to implement
it.

**COMMON
ERRORS**

```
struct test {
     int a, b;
};
test x;                          Should be struct test x;

typedef struct link {
          LINK *next;            Should be struct link *next;
     } LINK;

struct test {
     int a, b;
} x, *px = &x;
*px.a = 3;                       Should be px->a = 3;

enum { a, b; }                   Should be enum { a, b }
```

EXERCISES

1. Write complex number routines for multiplication, division, and subtraction, using the same structures as defined in Example 9.1.4.

2. Consider the following definitions:

```
typedef struct {
     float marks[20];
     int   numMarks;
     char  name[25];
} STUDENT;
```

where numMarks is the number of marks in the array marks, and name
is the student's name. Write a procedure TopMark(s, tm) that returns through parameter tm the highest mark of the student s.

3. Consider the following definitions:

```
struct secret {
     int age;
     enum {
          male, female
     } sex;
};
```

```
struct agent {
      struct secret friends[10];
      struct secret enemies[10];
};
```

Write a procedure info(a, fage, eage) that returns through fage the age of the youngest female friend of agent a and through eage the age of the oldest male enemy. Return −1 if there are no female friends or male enemies.

4. Consider the following definitions:

```
struct secret {
      int age;
      enum {
            male, female
      } sex;
};

struct agent {
      enum {
            friend, enemy
      } tag;
      union {
            struct secret friends[10];
            struct secret enemies[10];
      } a;
};
```

Write a procedure info(a, fage, eage) that returns through fage the age of the youngest female friend of agent a and through eage the age of the oldest male enemy. Return −1 if there are no female friends or male enemies.

5. Consider the following definition:

```
struct el {
      int x;
      char y[10];
      float f;
}
```

a. Write a function newel() that allocates memory for this structure and returns a pointer to it.
b. Repeat the above, this time using a procedure version that returns the pointer through a parameter.

6. Consider the following definitions:

```
typedef struct line {
            char li[80];
            int length;
        } LINE, *PLINE;
PLINE text[100];
```

Write a program that reads lines of characters, until either end-of-file is encountered or 100 lines have been read, and stores the lines along with their lengths in the array text. The program should then redisplay the lines prefixed by their lengths.

7. Consider the following definitions:

```
typedef struct employee {
            int age;
            float salary;
        } *PEMP;
PEMP company[100];
```

Write the following two functions:

a. update, which takes four parameters—array company, integer id (which is an index into company), integer age, and real salary—and creates a new employee structure at position id of company, with its age and salary attributes set to the corresponding parameters. For example, the call

```
update(company, 20, 39, 30000.0)
```

creates a new employee at position 20 with age set to 39 and salary to 30000.

b. total, which takes one parameter company, an array of PEMP, and returns the sum of the salaries of all employees at least 50 years old.

8. Consider the following definitions:

```
typedef struct employee {
            float salary;
            char name[20];
            long EmpNumber;
        } EMPL, *PEMPL;
PEMPL factory[100];
```

Assume all 100 records have been initialized, and write a function

```
show(factory)
```

that returns a pointer to the structure of the employee who makes the highest salary (assuming all salaries are different).

9. Write a program to find prime numbers less than N using the Eratosthenes sieve algorithm:

create a sorted linked list containing numbers 2 to N;

for (num = 2; num <= n; num = next list element if any)
*   delete from the list all numbers that are multiples of num;*

numbers left in list are prime;

10 Strings

PREVIEW   *Because standard Pascal's string facilities are rather limited, most implementations extend the language in some manner to make strings more usable. Unfortunately, these extensions usually vary from system to system, sometimes substantially, thus making programs difficult to port. To describe all these implementations here would be impossible, so to generalize the discussion, this chapter presents the concept of the data type string along with a collection of routines defined to operate on values of that type. We then elaborate on a specific implementation of strings popularized by the well-known UCSD Pascal system (which is now used in several Pascal compilers) [Bow77]. Following this, we present a detailed description of strings as they are implemented in C. Finally, we discuss macros and functions designed to manipulate single characters.*

REVIEW OF PASCAL CONSTRUCTS

The Data Type STRING

By a STRING, we mean an ordered sequence of characters, with a first character, second character, and so on. The length of a string is the number of characters in the string. Typically, a set of operations in the form of procedures and functions is defined to manipulate strings. The procedures commonly provided are

DELETE(s,i,n)	Deletes n characters from the string s, starting from the ith character
INSERT(s1,s,i)	Inserts the string s1 into s at position i
CHANGE(s1,i,s2)	Replaces LENGTH(s2) characters in s1, starting from the ith position, by the characters from the string s2

The functions defined to operate on strings are

LENGTH(s)	Returns the current length of string s
EXTRACT(s,i)	Returns the character at position i in s
COPY(s,i,n)	Returns a copy of a substring of s starting from position i and consisting of n characters

CONCAT(s1,s2)	Returns a new string consisting of s1 followed by s2
POS(s1,s2)	Returns the position of the first occurrence of s1 in s2 or 0 if s1 does not exist in s2
LESS(s1,s2)	Returns TRUE if s1 is lexicographically less than s2

Similar functions are defined for the other types of comparisons, for example, EQUAL and GREATER.

String constants are represented by enclosing them in single quotation marks. A string constant may appear either on the right-hand side of an assignment statement or as an argument in one of the string operations (provided that this argument does not change as a result of the operation). String variables may also appear in I/O statements.

Strings in Standard Pascal

In standard Pascal, a small subset of these basic operations is provided. The string data type itself is represented by a character array. For example, the declaration

```
VAR STR : PACKED ARRAY[1..8] OF CHAR;
```

defines STR as a string variable for strings eight characters long. A value may be assigned to it, as in

```
STR := 'Hello!  ';
```

but the length of the quoted string must be *exactly* as declared. In this example, it was necessary to pad the string on the right with spaces to make it eight characters long. A string variable may be assigned to another string variable if it is of the same type. For example, if S1 and S2 are defined as

```
TYPE STR10 = PACKED ARRAY[1..10] OF CHAR;
VAR  S1, S2 : STR10;
```

it is correct to say

```
S1 := S2;
```

However, the statement

```
STR := S1;
```

where STR is declared as before, would be incorrect.

A string variable may be compared to either another string variable of the same type or a string constant of the correct length. For example,

```
IF S1 = 'Hello men!' THEN ... ;
IF S2 < S1 THEN ... ;
```

and so on. All the comparison operators defined in Pascal are allowed.

Individual characters of a string variable may be referenced using array indexing:

```
S1[10] := '?';
...
S2[1]  := S1[5];
...
FOR i := 1 TO 10 DO S1[i] := S2[11 - i];
```

No other string operations are defined in standard Pascal.

Extensions to Pascal Strings

As we mentioned, because of the limitations of standard Pascal's strings, many implementations provide an extended form of string. The most common approach is to introduce a predefined type STRING, which represents a string as an array of characters with the addition of a length attribute often stored as the zeroth component of the array. This length field allows strings to vary in size up to some maximum length. For example, to define a string type for strings up to ten characters long, the definition

```
TYPE STRIN10 = STRING[10];
```

would be given.

String variables would be declared as expected:

```
VAR S : STRIN10;
```

Each variable of type STRIN10 is represented in memory by an array of 11 bytes:

```
S[0] S[1] S[2]              S[10]
 _____         _____
|     |     |     |   ...    |     |
|_____|_____|_____|          |_____|
```

Initially, the individual bytes in S are undefined; they can be initialized, for example, by executing

```
S := 'Today is';
```

The string constant does not have to be exactly ten characters long.

This assignment replaces the current values of characters 1 through 8 of S and updates S[0] to reflect the length of the string. In this case, the value stored in S[0] is the character whose ordinal value is 8 (in ASCII, this is control-H):

S[0]   S[1] S[2] S[3] S[4] S[5] S[6] S[7] S[8] S[9] S[10]

ctrl–H	T	o	d	a	y		i	s	?	?

The characters at positions 9 and 10 in S are still undefined—this assignment affects only the first eight elements of the array. The currently defined length of the string is 8, as indicated by the value in position 0. This value is a *character*, not an integer, and it would be incorrect to say

```
IF S[0] = 8 THEN ... ;
```

To be valid, it is necessary to state this as

```
IF ORD(S[0]) = 8 THEN ... ;
```

UCSD Pascal [Bow77] (as well as various other implementations, including Turbo Pascal [Bor85]) uses this approach to represent strings. Moreover, it provides operations equivalent to most of the operations listed. Each of these routines uses the length field to determine how much of the string to access and updates this field if necessary. The programmer should never have to directly refer to position 0 of a string variable; rather, the LENGTH function should be used:

```
IF LENGTH(S) = 8 THEN ... ;
```

One instance where the length field is not used is when the string is treated strictly as a character array. For example, if the loop

```
FOR i := 1 to 10 DO
   READ(S[i]);
```

is executed, ten characters are read in and stored in consecutive elements of the string. However, manipulating a string in this manner does not update the length field. This can be corrected by adding the statement

```
S[0] := CHR(10);
```

after the loop, but a better approach is as follows:

```
VAR c : CHAR;
. . .
S := '';              (* to clear a string *)
FOR i := 1 to 10 DO
BEGIN
  READ(c);
  S := CONCAT(S, c);
END;
```

In this version, the length of the field is updated automatically by the CONCAT operation.

C CONSTRUCTS

10.1 STRINGS IN C

Rather than storing a length, an alternative way of implementing strings is to store a special *terminating* character in a string. If we choose the character that has an ordinal value of 0 (denoted by \0 in C and pronounced "null") to be the terminal character, the string in the preceding example would be stored internally as

S[0] S[1] S[2] S[3] S[4] S[5] S[6] S[7] S[8] S[9]

T	o	d	a	y		i	s	\0	?

This is precisely the approach used by C to represent strings: A string is an array of characters, with a \0 indicating the end of the string. If this terminating character is inadvertently overwritten, the operations defined to work on strings that rely on this value will produce unpredictable results.

In the implementation of Pascal strings that we described in the review, the length of a string can be computed by a single access to the array. In C, however, to determine the length of a string, it is necessary to scan the array until the null character is encountered. An advantage to this implementation is that if s is a string and i any integer between 0 and the length of s, then s+i is a string (specifically, a substring of s starting at position i):

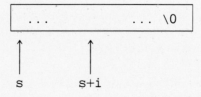

Moreover, the declaration of a Pascal string is static in that the maximum size of the string is specified when it is declared and must be a constant. In C, the definition of a string as a pointer to character allows the possibility of *dynamic* (run-time) specification of the string's length. The price is that the run-time system does not check whether the user operates on elements within the specified bounds.

10.1.1   How to Define Strings

A string can be defined as a character array:

```
char str[10], str1[30];
```

The number of characters that may be stored in a string is *one less* than the defined size of a string, since one position is always used for the terminal character. In the example, `str` can hold up to 9 characters and `str1` can hold up to 29 characters.

The string `str` could also be defined as a pointer to character rather than as an array:

```
char *str;
```

In this case, it is first necessary to allocate a sufficient amount of memory using, for example,

```
str = malloc(10);
```

or on input the characters read will overwrite memory.

In many of the examples in this chapter, we use a type identifier called `STRING`:

```
typedef char * STRING;
```

It is important to distinguish between null *pointers* and null *strings*: Null pointers are equal to NULL (which is usually 0), whereas null strings are strings whose first character is the null character. For example,

```
STRING nullPoint, nullString;
nullPoint = NULL;
nullString = malloc(10);
nullString[0] = '\0';
```

10.1.2   Formatted String I/O

To perform formatted string input, `scanf` can be employed; the call

```
scanf("%s", x);
```

stores characters read from the standard input in memory starting at the address equal to the value of x and then appends the terminating null character to these characters. When the %s specification is used in `scanf`, it skips whitespace looking for the first non-whitespace character, and then reads in characters until a whitespace character is encountered.

In the example, x is not preceded by an ampersand &, as is normally used when reading, for example, integers or reals. This is because `scanf` requires pointers to the objects it is reading values for and an array identifier *is* a pointer.

To perform formatted string output, `printf` should be used; the call

```
printf("%s", x);
```

writes to the standard output all the characters stored in the memory block originating at the address equal to x up to the terminating \0.

Example 10.1.1   The following program inputs a string no greater than 10 characters in length and then outputs it:

```
#include <stdio.h>
main()
{
    char str[11];

    printf("Enter a string: ");
    scanf("%s", str);
    printf("The string is: %s\n", str);
}
```

The declared size is 11, but strings in this example cannot exceed 10 characters, or they will *overwrite* the memory cells following the block allocated to str. It would probably be safer to use a %10s rather than %s to limit the width of the input field. The %s specification in `scanf` is not oriented toward line processing. We demonstrate the proper technique for reading an entire line of characters in Section 10.3.

In the program, the space for str is statically allocated; the program can be rewritten so that the memory space for the string is allocated dynamically:

```
#include <stdio.h>
typedef char* STRING;
main()
{
    STRING str, malloc();

    str = malloc(11);
    printf("Enter a string: ");
    scanf("%s", str);
    printf("The string is: %s\n", str);
}
```

The header file `string.h` can be included if string operations are being used. This file contains declarations of the available string operations. On some systems, however, this header file does not exist, and so the user would have to declare noninteger string functions explicitly. ∎

Example 10.1.2   The following program shows one more application of string I/O.

```
#include <stdio.h>
main()
{
    char word[21],
        *current = word;

    printf("Enter a string: ");
    scanf("%20s", current);
    while (*current)
        printf("%s\n", current++);
}
```

Assume the input is

```
Hello
```

These characters, along with a terminating \0, will be stored in the array `word`. Each time the `printf` statement is executed, all characters starting from the current value of the pointer `current`, up to (but not including) the \0, will be output. Thus the output will be

```
Hello
ello
llo
lo
o
```

∎

The format control argument of `printf` and `scanf` is a string, and so it is correct to say, for example,

```
char *format[] = { "%c", "%d", "%ld", "%f", "%f", "%s"};
#define CHAR      0
#define INT       1
#define LONGINT   2
#define FLOAT     3
#define DOUBLE    4
#define STRIN     5
```

and then use

```
printf(format[STRIN], "hello\n");
```

We continue the discussion of string I/O in Section 10.3.

10.1.3   String Constants

As we have seen, a string constant is enclosed by double quotes, *not* single quotes as in Pascal:

```
"Example of a string in C"
```

The compiler always appends a terminating zero to the string. String constants are actually constant pointers to the memory blocks containing the specified characters.

Unlike Pascal, string constants may *not* be assigned to string variables defined, as in the following example, as character arrays:

```
char str[9];
str = "Today is";
```

This is because an array identifier is not an l-value (that is, it may not appear on the left-hand side of an assignment). However, if a string is defined as a pointer to character rather than as an array, this is allowed. If we have

```
STRING str;
```

it could be initialized using

```
str = "Hello how are you";
```

or directly in the definition:

```
STRING str = "Hello how are you";
```

Any character, including escaped characters, may be specified in a string constant. Recall that an escaped character sequence is of the form

ch

where *ch* is one of n, t, b, r, f, v, \, ', or ", and that a numeric escape code is of the form

d

where *d* is an octal code. When a numeric escape code is used in a string constant, the octal code terminates either after three octal digits are found or when a nonoctal digit is encountered. For example, the string

```
"A\128B\n"
```

consists of the character A, followed by the character with an ASCII code of 12 octal, followed by the characters 8B, followed by the newline character.

String constants may be continued on more than one line, using the continuation character \, for example,

```
"This is a very long string constant that exceeds one line \
so it is continued on the second line"
```

The expressions

```
"a"
```

and

```
'a'
```

are *not* the same. Specifically, the first expression is a constant pointer to 2 bytes of memory storing the characters a and \0, whereas the second expression is simply a single character and not a pointer at all.

10.2   IMPLEMENTATION OF STRING OPERATIONS

The C language does not define any string operations as part of the language. Most implementations, however, do provide a reasonably standard set of string operations in the system *library* (although they may differ slightly from one implementation to another). The routines described here are provided in most implementations. Some correspond directly to the STRING routines already described and some do not.

There is also a relatively complete set of macros and functions defined in most C systems designed to manipulate single characters. These are closely related to string processing, and we describe them in Section 10.6. Many of the string routines return noninteger values and would therefore have to be declared.

Traditionally, the names of string routines in C start with str. The most common ones are

`int strlen(s)` `STRING s;`	Returns the number of characters in STRING s; preceding the terminating \0
`STRING strcpy(s1, s2)` `STRING s1, s2;`	Copies s2 to s1 and overwrites s1. Returns a pointer to the first character in the new s1
`STRING strcat(s1, s2)` `STRING s1, s2;`	Appends s2 to s1. Returns a pointer to the first character in the concatenated string

`int strpos(s, c)`
`STRING s;`
`char c;`
	If the character c occurs in s, the position of the first occurrence is returned; otherwise −1 is returned

`STRING strchr(s, c)`
`STRING s;`
`char c;`
	Returns a pointer to the first occurrence of the character c in s, and NULL if c does not occur. Sometimes called index

`int strcmp(s1, s2)` `STRING s1, s2;`	Returns 0 if s1 is equal to s2, a negative value if s1 is lexicographically less than s2, and a positive value otherwise

Moreover, for each of these functions, a similar function with an additional integer parameter max specifies that the operation is to be performed on only the first max characters rather than on the whole string. Traditionally, the names of those operations start with strn. For example,

```
strncpy(s1, s2, max)
```

copies at most max characters from the string s2 to the string s1.

For the sake of completeness, we provide the remaining string operations defined in the run-time library:

`STRING strrchr(s, c)`
`STRING s;`
`char c;`
	Same as strchr, but returns a pointer to the last position of c in s or NULL if c is not in s. Sometimes called rindex

`int strrpos(s, c)`
`STRING s;`
`char c;`
	Same as `strpos`, but returns the integer position of the last occurrence of c in s

`STRING strpbrk(s1, s2)` `STRING s1, s2;`	Same as `strchr`, but looks for any character from s2 (thus s2 is a string that is considered a set) skipping over characters that are not in s2, and returns a pointer to the first occurrence of such a character, or NULL if no character from s1 occurs in s2
`STRING strrpbrk(s1, s2)` `STRING s1, s2;`	Same as `strpbrk`, but returns a pointer to the last occurrence, or NULL
`int strcspn(s1, s2)` `STRING s1, s2;`	Same as `strpbrk`, but returns the length of the longest initial segment of s1 that consists of characters not found in s2. If no characters from s1 appear in s2, `strlen(s1)` is returned
`int strspn(s1, s2)` `STRING s1, s2;`	Same as `strcspn`, but skips over characters in the set s2 and returns the longest initial segment of s1 that consists of characters found in s2. If every character of s1 appears in s2, `strlen(s1)` is returned

Note: If the string arguments used in these routines overlap in memory, the result of an operation is unpredictable.

Example 10.2.1   A routine that does not appear on this list but is often defined by programmers is one that allocates several bytes for a string and then initializes it to an empty string:

```
void init(s, size)
STRING *s;
int size;
{
    char *malloc();

    if ((*s = malloc((size + 1) * sizeof(char))) == NULL)
        error(...);
    **s = '\0';
}
```
■

10.2.1   Implementation of Standard C String Operations

In this section, we illustrate how the string operations described in Section 10.2 are actually implemented in C. This is a good exercise on functions and pointers.

Example 10.2.2   First, we define `strlen`, a function that computes the length of a string:

```
int strlen(s)
STRING s;
{
     int i;

     for (i = 0; s[i] != '\0'; i++)
          ;
     return (i);
}
```

When this loop terminates, the value of i is the current length of s. The stop condition can be made simpler because the value \0 can be interpreted as false:

```
int strlen(s)
STRING s;
{
     int i;

     for (i = 0; s[i]; i++)
          ;
     return(i);
}
```

Since s is a pointer, the function can be rewritten as

```
int strlen(s)
STRING s;
{
     int i;

     for (i = 0; *s; i++, s++)
          ;
     return(i);
}
```

For those who prefer pointers, another solution is

```
int strlen(s)
STRING s;
{
     STRING p;

     for (p = s; *p; p++)
          ;
     return(p - s);
}
```

Example 10.2.3   Now we define strcpy(s1, s2), a function that makes a copy of s2 in s1:

```
void strcpy(s1, s2)
STRING s1, s2;
{
     STRING p1 = s1, p2 = s2;

     while (*p2)
          *p1++ = *p2++;
     *p1 = '\0';
}
```

The while statement copies s2 to s1 character by character until the terminating \0 is encountered. In each step, a single character is copied and both pointers are updated.

Auxiliary pointers are used in an attempt to avoid modifications of the actual parameters. For example, if the main program has the statement

```
STRING t1, t2;
...
/* initialization of t1 and t2 */
...
strcpy(t1, t2);
```

it would be desirable to have both t1 and t2 pointing to the beginning of the strings. Now, consider a version of the preceding example with the auxiliary pointers removed:

```
void strcpy(s1, s2)
STRING s1, s2;
{
     while (*s2)
          *s1++ = *s2++;
     *s1 = '\0';
}
```

When the call

```
strcpy(t1, t2)
```

is made, the values of t1 and t2 are assigned to s1 and s2, respectively. Thus modifications of s1 and s2 within the body of strcpy do not affect the values of the actual parameters, and so the auxiliary pointers are not necessary. It is the usual lesson: When a formal parameter called by value is modified, the corresponding actual parameter is not changed.

The last problem with the implementation of strcpy is the assignment that has to be made outside the loop because the loop terminates as soon as s2 points to zero. Moving the body of the loop to the loop's condition eliminates the need for an extra assignment:

```
void strcpy(s1, s2)
STRING s1, s2;
{
    while (*s1++ = *s2++)
        ;
}
```

Here, all characters in s2, including the terminating zero, are copied to s1.

In some implementations, the system library contains strcpy implemented as a function rather than a procedure and returns the copied string as the result of the function:

```
STRING strcpy(s1, s2)
STRING s1, s2;
{
    STRING aux = s1;

    while (*aux++ = *s2++)
        ;
    return(s1);
}
```

This may be preferable, since a function may be used in expressions.

We do need an auxiliary variable here; otherwise, in

```
while (*s1++ = *s2++)
    ;
return(s1);
```

we would have changed the value of s1 and, thus, would have returned a pointer to the *end* rather than the beginning of the resulting string.

In all these versions of strcpy, it is assumed memory has been allocated for s1 *before* the call is made. Inexperienced C programmers often write

```
STRING source, dest, malloc();

source = malloc(10);
scanf("%s", source);
strcpy(dest, source);
```

This will not work because no memory is allocated to the string dest.

To correct this problem, memory should be allocated before `strcpy` is called, for example

```
dest = malloc(10);
```

■

Example 10.2.4   Another possibility is to write a version of `strcpy` that assumes no memory is allocated to the first argument and that allocates it itself. We have also modified `strcpy` to make it a boolean function, returning TRUE or FALSE depending on whether or not `malloc` is successful:

```
typedef int    bool;
#define TRUE   1
#define FALSE  0

bool strcpy1(s1, s2)
STRING *s1, s2;
{
     STRING aux, malloc();

     if ((aux = malloc(strlen(s2) + 1)) == NULL)
          return(FALSE);
     *s1 = aux;
     while (*aux++ = *s2++)
          ;
     return(TRUE);
}
```

Since this routine makes a copy of s2 in s1, the first step is to allocate a block of memory for s1 to hold those characters. When the space is allocated, the copying can be performed.

The way in which the first parameter is passed must be taken into consideration in the main program:

```
STRING source, dest;

source = malloc(10);
scanf("%9s", source);
if (!strcpy1(&dest, source))
     error(...);
```

As in the previous example, we may ask whether we need an auxiliary pointer. Consider a modified version of `strcpy1`, without an auxiliary variable:

```
*s1 = malloc(strlen(s2) + 1);
if (*s1 == NULL)
     return(FALSE);
while (**s1++ = *s2++)
     ;
return(TRUE);
```

and a main program in which we have

```
STRING t1, t2;
```

and then the statement

```
t2 = "hello";
```

Assume the address of t1 is 100 and the value of t2 is 200:

Now consider the call

```
strcpy1(&t1, t2);
```

The first statement

```
*s1 = malloc(strlen(s2) + 1);
```

is correct—it allocates memory for *s1, which is the same as t1. Assume the memory area obtained by malloc starts at address 300:

However, the loop is incorrect, since the assignment

```
**s1++ = *s2++
```

increments s1, causing the contents of s2 to be copied to the memory area starting at address 100 rather than to the memory area allocated as the result of the call to malloc (starting at address 300).

What if we increase *s1?

```
*((*s1)++) = *s2++;
```

This *does* solve the problem—the contents of memory locations starting at address 200, which is the value of t2, are copied to the memory area allocated for s1; however, the actual parameter is consequently updated and no longer points to the beginning of the copied string. This is the reason we have used an auxiliary pointer. ▪

Example 10.2.5   It might be better to define strcpy as a function that takes one string parameter and returns a copy of it, allocating the necessary memory. We call this function strsave because it saves the string passed as a parameter.

```
STRING strsave(s)
STRING s;
{
      STRING p, malloc();

      p = malloc(strlen(s) + 1);
      if (p != NULL)
            strcpy(p, s);
      return(p);
}
```

In this version, testing whether or not the returned value is NULL can be performed in the calling routine:

```
STRING source, dest, malloc();

source = malloc(10);
scanf("%9s", source);
dest = strsave(source);
if (dest == NULL)
      error(...);
```
  ▪

Example 10.2.6   In all the preceding examples, the only error checking we have implemented is related to memory allocation. It is the programmer's responsibility to make sure, for example, in a call such as strcpy(dest, source), that the string source has been correctly initialized—that is, that it contains a terminating \0 somewhere within its defined memory space. The implementation of strncpy shown here avoids this problem by specifying the maximum number of characters to process.

```
STRING strncpy(s1, s2, max)
STRING s1, s2;
int max;
{
      int i;

      for (i = 0; i < max && (s1[i] = s2[i]) != NULL; i++)
            ;
      return(s1);
}
```

In this routine, the terminating zero may not be copied.   ■

Error checking in `str` operations is limited, since the size of the memory block allocated to the string cannot be obtained at run time; thus it is the programmer's responsibility not to go beyond that block; in `strn` operations, the maximum number of characters that may be accessed is specified.

Example 10.2.7 Next, we look at `strcat(s1, s2)`. This is sometimes implemented as a function that returns a new string consisting of s2 appended to the end of s1 through both s1 and the function result, and it is sometimes implemented as a procedure that appends s2 to s1 and returns an updated s1 only through a parameter. This latter version could be implemented using

```
strcpy(s1 + strlen(s1), s2)
```

provided the two string arguments do not *overlap*. The following version works for any case:

```
void concat(s1, s2)
STRING s1, s2;
{
    int i;

    for (i = strlen(s1); *s2; i++)
        s1[i] = *s2++;
    s1[i] = '\0';
}
```

Alternatively, pointers could be used exclusively:

```
void concat(s1, s2)
STRING s1, s2;
{
    s1 += strlen(s1);
    while(*s1++ = *s2++)
        ;
}
```

Both of these versions have the side effect that if the strings do overlap, s2 will be modified as a result of the operation.   ■

10.2.2   Implementation of Other String Operations

The additional Pascal STRING operations that we discussed earlier are implemented in the following examples.

Example 10.2.8 To implement DELETE(str, start, number), the characters in the string str beyond the last character of the substring to be deleted (that is, starting at position start and ending at position start+number) up to the end of the string (including the \0) must be shifted left to the position of the first character to be deleted. This can be done using strcpy:

```
bool DELETE(s, i, n)
STRING s;
int i, n;
{
    if (i >= 0  &&  n > 0  &&  n + i < strlen(s)) {
        strcpy(s + i, s + i + n);
        return(TRUE);
    }
    else return(FALSE);
}
```

This version is incorrect because the two parameters of strcpy overlap. To solve this, a terminating \0 character can be inserted at the end of the first string and strcat used instead of strcpy:

```
bool DELETE(s, i, n)
STRING s;
int i, n;
{
    if (i >= 0 && n > 0 && n + i < strlen(s)) {
        s[i] = '\0';
        strcat(s, s + i + n);
        return(TRUE);
    }
    else return(FALSE);
}
```

A specific example may be helpful. Consider the call

```
DELETE(s, 6, 2);
```

where the value of the string s is 10 (that is, it points to location 10), and it represents the string value

```
"Today isMonday"
```

The resulting string should be

```
"Today Monday"
```

Consider the following memory map:

10	11	12	13	14	15	16	17	18	19	20	21	22	23	24
T	o	d	a	y		i	s	M	o	n	d	a	y	\0

After replacing i at position 6 with \0, we have

```
s                           s+i+n
↓                           ↓
```

10	11	12	13	14	15	16	17	18	19	20	21	22	23	24
T	o	d	a	y		\0	s	M	o	n	d	a	y	\0

The string s now has the value "Today ". The value of s+i+n is
10 + 6 + 2 = 18, so this string may be interpreted as a string with the
value "Monday".

After concatenating the strings s and s+i+n, we have

```
s                           s+i+n
↓                           ↓
```

10	11	12	13	14	15	16	17	18	19	20	21	22	23	24
T	o	d	a	y		M	o	n	d	a	y	\0			∎

Example 10.2.9 To implement the operation INSERT (s1, s, i), a substring of s starting from position i and consisting of strlen(s1) characters must be
shifted right to make room for the new string; then, the new string
must be copied to that space. This copying cannot be done using
strcpy because it would insert a \0 in the middle of s. One possible solution is

```
bool INSERT(s1, s, i)
STRING s1, s;
int i;
{
    int j, k;

    j = strlen(s1);
    if (i >= 0 && i <= strlen(s) && j > 0) {
        for (k = strlen(s) - i; k >= 0; k--)
            s[i + j + k] = s[i + k];
        s += i;
        while (*s1)
            *s++ = *s1++;
        return(TRUE);
    }
    else return(FALSE);
}
```

Again, a specific example may be helpful. Assume the string "how " is
to be inserted into the string "Hello are" at position 6:

10	11	12	13	14	15	16	17	18	19	20	21	22	23	24
H	e	l	l	o		a	r	e	\0					

```
                    s[6]
```

In this example, i=6, j=4, and s=10. Thus s+i is the string "are ", and it is copied to the string originating at address 20. The string s after the first loop is

10	11	12	13	14	15	16	17	18	19	20	21	22	23	24
H	e	l	l	o		a	r	e	\0	a	r	e	\0	

The string s after the second loop is

10	11	12	13	14	15	16	17	18	19	20	21	22	23	24
H	e	l	l	o		h	o	w		a	r	e	\0	

        ■

Example 10.2.10
The function POS(s1, s2) searches for the first occurrence of the string s1 in the string s2. If s1 does not appear in s2, POS returns the value −1 rather than 0 (as it does in Pascal) because 0 is a valid position in C:

```
#include <stdio.h>
#include <string.h>
typedef char * STRING;


int POS(s1, s2)
STRING s1, s2;
{
     STRING aux1, aux2,
            prevs2 = s2;

     for (aux1 = s1, aux2 = s2; *aux2; aux2++)
          if (*aux1 == *aux2) {        /* there is match */
               aux1++;
               if (!*aux1)      /* end of search, found */
                    return aux2 - s2 - (aux1 - s1) + 1;
          } else {
               aux1 = s1;          /* miss, reset aux1 */
               aux2 = prevs2++; /* reset aux2, update prevs2 */
          }
     return -1;
}
```

The pointer aux1 is moved along the string s1, and the pointer aux2 is moved along the string s2. In each step of the loop, the characters pointed to by aux1 and aux2 are compared, and if they are equal, the search continues with both pointers pointing to the successive characters in the strings. If the two characters differ, the pointer aux2 is reset to the value saved in prevs2.   ■

Example 10.2.11
The implementation of CHANGE(s1, i, s2) replaces length(s2) characters in the string s1, starting from the ith position, with the

characters in the string s2:

```
bool CHANGE(s1, i, s2)
STRING s1;
int i;
STRING s2;
{
     int j, s1l, s2l;

     s1l = strlen(s1);
     s2l = strlen(s2);
     if ((s1l == 0) !! i < 0 !! i > s1l)
          return FALSE;                        /* error ... */

     if (s2l == 0)
          return TRUE;            /* nothing to replace */
     if (s2l > s1l - i + 1) {
          s1[i] = '\0';
          strcat(s1, s2);
     }
     else {
          s1 += i;
          for (j = 0; j < s2l; j++)
               *s1++ = *s2++;
     }
     return TRUE;
}
```

Though C libraries often provide other routines, we do not discuss these routines here. If you are interested in these, check the documentation of the system you are using for details.

10.3 ADDITIONAL STRING I/O ROUTINES

Versions of the formatted I/O operations we introduced in Section 10.1.2 (scanf and printf) are defined to read from *strings*. This means the contents of a string can be converted according to the specification given in a format control string and then stored in arguments. The syntax and semantics of these operations are almost identical to fscanf and fprintf, but the first letter is s rather than f to signify string I/O, and the first argument is a string rather than a file:

```
sscanf(s, "format control string", arg1, ..., argk);
sprintf(s, "format control string", arg1, ..., argk);
```

Example 10.3.1   The following program reads in a string of at most four digits and outputs the corresponding numerical value of this string:

```
#include <stdio.h>
main()
{
    int i;
    char s[5];

    scanf("%4s", s);
    sscanf(s, "%d", &i);
    printf("%d\n", i);
}
```

The first input statement reads from the standard input, whereas the
second input statement reads from the string s. Because the format
control string specifies integer conversion, the string is converted to an
integer value and stored in the variable i.   ∎

Example 10.3.2   The following program reads in a hexadecimal integer value of at most
four digits and outputs a string of characters derived from this integer
corresponding to each digit:

```
#include <stdio.h>
main()
{
    int i;
    char s[5];

    scanf("%4x", &i);
    sprintf(s, "%x", i);
    printf("%s\n", s);
}
```

The first input statement reads a hexadecimal integer value and stores
it in the integer i. The first output statement, sprintf, outputs the
value of i in hexadecimal to the string s. Then this string is sent to the
standard output.   ∎

The function sprintf is also useful if you want to initialize an array
of characters with some string constant. For example, if we have

```
char buf[128];
```

an attempt to assign a string constant to this array using the statement

```
buf = "some string";
```

would be incorrect because buf is *not* an l-value. Instead, the statement

```
sprintf(buf, "%s", "some string");
```

or simply

```
sprintf(buf, "some string");
```

could be used.

In Appendix C, we offer a complete description of all formatted I/O operations.

Line-Oriented Terminal I/O

Formatted input operations are limited when applied to strings: With the %s specification, the input field ends at the *first* non-whitespace character. Thus to read an entire line using these operations, substrings must be read until the end-of-line is encountered. There are two additional I/O string operations to read or write *entire* lines. The specifications of these I/O routines are

```
STRING gets(s)
STRING s;

int puts(s)
STRING s;
```

In some respects, the routine gets is similar to READLN in Pascal. It reads in a line of characters from standard input and stores it in s (with the exception of the terminating \n). The result is returned in two ways: through gets and through s. The value NULL is returned if no string can be read. A terminating null character is appended to the string s. As usual, it is the user's responsibility to allocate enough memory for the string s to receive the characters that are read and one more byte for the terminating null character. If end-of-file is encountered immediately (before any characters have been read), gets returns a null pointer and does not store *anything* in the string s (not even a null character).

The puts operation is like WRITELN in Pascal: It outputs the string s and then prints a \n character. Of course, puts expects a terminating null character in s and does not stop until it reaches one. This means if the string s contains any special characters—for example, an end-of-line character—as a result of the call to puts, more than one line may be output. If an error occurs, puts returns EOF; otherwise, it returns a value other than EOF.

An entire line can be read from standard input and written to standard output using

```
char line[80];
if (gets(line) != NULL)
    puts(line);
```

The variable line could also be defined as

```
char *line;
```

However, if this is used, it is necessary to allocate memory explicitly.

Consider a pointer to a structure containing two string attributes, name and address. The following program first creates a structure containing two strings read from the standard input and then reads a third string and compares it with the first field of the structure. If the two strings are identical, the second field is replaced by the string "GONE".

```
typedef struct {
            STRING name, address;
        } *person;

person ex;
STRING third;
```

First, create a structure:

```
ex = (person)  malloc(sizeof(*ex));
ex->name = malloc(10);
ex->address = malloc(10);
third = malloc(10);
```

Now, read in the strings:

```
gets(ex->name);
gets(ex->address);
gets(third);
```

Then, compare:

```
if (!strcmp(ex->name, third)) {
    free(ex->address);
    ex->address = "GONE";
}
```

Example 10.3.3 The following program reads lines from standard input until an empty line is encountered and then outputs the longest line. We assume a line cannot be longer than 80 characters:

```
#include <stdio.h>
main()
{
    char longest[81],
         current[81];
    int  curlen, lonlen;
```

```
        if (gets(longest) == NULL)
            return;

    lonlen = strlen(longest);
    while (gets(current) != NULL && (curlen = strlen(current)))
        if (curlen > lonlen) {
            strcpy(longest, current);
            lonlen = curlen;
        }

    puts(longest);
}
```

The stop condition in the while statement is evaluated as follows: A line is input and stored in the array current. If no line is available from the standard input, gets returns NULL, and the while loop stops. Otherwise, the length of the current line is computed and stored in the variable curlen. If this value is 0, the second argument of the logical *and* evaluates to 0, and thus the while terminates.

If the loop does not terminate, the length of the line just read is compared to the length of the longest line, and if it is greater, the current line is copied to the array longest.   ∎

Line-Oriented File I/O

Two other operations are defined for line-oriented string file I/O:

```
STRING fgets(s, max, f)
STRING s;
int max;
FILE *f;

int fputs(s, f)
STRING s;
FILE *f;
```

Like gets and puts, fgets reads a line from the file f, and fputs writes a line to the file f. Here, fgets reads at most max characters, and if *end-of-line* occurs, it is stored in the string s (this differs from how gets works). Thus fgets is useful even if it reads from standard input, that is,

```
fgets(s, max, stdin)
```

since gets does not provide a way to limit the number of characters read. Similarly, fputs does *not* supply an extra end-of-line character after writing the string s. Clearly, if there is such a character in the string, it will be output. As with puts, fputs returns EOF if an error occurs; otherwise, it returns a value other than EOF.

As we mentioned, these routines facilitate line-oriented processing of files. We demonstrate this by the following code, which copies the file f to the file g (assuming both files have been opened). Each line in the file is assumed to have at most 80 characters.

```
char line[81];
...
while (fgets(line, 80, f))
     fputs(line, g);
```

Recall that scanf pushes the last character it has read back on the input stream. If this character happens to be an end-of-line character, and the next statement is a gets statement, the result of the program may not be what was intended:

```
int i;
char line[81];

scanf("%d", &i);
printf("\n%d\n", i);
if (gets(line)[0] == '\0')
     puts("empty input line");
else puts(line);
```

If the input stream is

```
123
Hello there
```

the output will be

```
123
empty input line
```

The solution to this problem is to skip the rest of the first input line:

```
scanf("%d", &i);
printf("\n%d\n", i);
gets(line);
if (gets(line)[0] == '\0')
     puts("empty input line\n");
else puts(line);
```

10.4 ARRAYS OF STRINGS

Some applications use arrays of strings. For example, in an editor, text can be stored using an array of strings representing the individual lines. We discuss this issue next. Consider the following definition:

```
STRING textarr[4];
```

From the discussion in Chapter 7, it should be clear that the type of textarr is a pointer to string. Memory is allocated for four pointers (so, assuming a pointer takes 2 bytes, 8 bytes are allocated). Since each element of this array is an *address* (a pointer to a string), clearly, the strings pointed to can be of different lengths.

We demonstrate this in the following example. The first two elements are initialized with two string constants of different lengths, and the remaining elements are read from the standard input:

```
textarr[0] = "first";
textarr[1] = "second";
textarr[2] = malloc(10);
gets(textarr[2]);
textarr[3] = malloc(20);
gets(textarr[3]);
```

Assuming the input strings are

```
third
fourth
```

and the value of textarr is 100, the memory map will look like

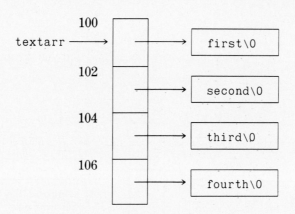

Characters from the first string could be accessed using

```
textarr[0][0], textarr[0][1],
```

and so on, or by using an auxiliary pointer:

```
STRING aux;

aux = textarr[0];
while (*aux++) ...
```

A pointer to string could also be used for the auxiliary pointer:

```
STRING *paux = textarr;
```

In this case, the value of *paux represents the string stored in the ze-roth row of the array, so

```
puts(*paux)
```

would output the value

```
first
```

Using further dereferencing, the value of **paux is the first (or zeroth) character from the zeroth string, which in this case, is an f.
    What is the output produced by

```
puts(++*paux)
```

Since the type of *paux is STRING, the addition is scaled by the factor of sizeof(char). Therefore, the value of ++*paux is a pointer to the zeroth string with the first character skipped; thus the output is

```
irst
```

A memory map may be helpful for you to understand what has hap-pened:

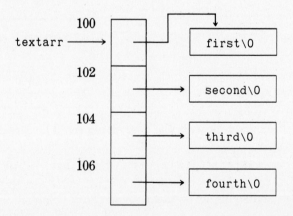

Specifically, the value of textarr[0] has been changed as a side effect of the preceding output statement. If we follow this statement with the loop

```
for (i = 0; i < 4; i++)
    puts(*paux++);
```

the output would be

```
irst
second
third
fourth
```

In this case the pointer paux itself is being incremented rather than
*paux, and since the type of paux is a pointer to pointer to character,
on each iteration of the loop paux is incremented by sizeof(char*).

As we mentioned, the type of **paux is char. We encourage you to
confirm that the output of the loop

```
for (paux = textarr; **paux; )
    printf("%c\n",  *++*paux);
```

is

```
r
s
t
```

Example 10.4.1 The following code demonstrates a function that reads a sequence of
strings from a file, stores them as an array of strings, and then sorts
them using an *insertion* sort. We chose this sorting algorithm for simplicity rather than efficiency. Sorting an array of *pointers* to character
arrays is more efficient than sorting an array of character arrays because, to swap two entries, only pointers have to be copied, not whole
arrays.

We assume the lines are at most LINELEN characters long:

```
#define LINELEN 81
```

and no more than MAXLINE lines are read from the file:

```
#define MAXLINE 1000
```

The lines read are stored in a global string array defined as

```
char *text[MAXLINE];
```

The function input reads the file and initializes the array text. It returns the number of lines read from the file, or −1 if it fails. To simplify
the code, error checking is limited:

```
#include <stdio.h>
int input(fname)
char *fname;              /* reads from the file fname */
{
   FILE *f;
   int lineNo, lineLen;
   char line[LINELEN + 1],
        *malloc();

   f = fopen(fname, "r");    /* assume it is successful */
   for (lineNo = 1; lineNo < MAXLINE &&
            fgets(line, LINELEN, f) != NULL; lineNo++) {
       if ((text[lineNo]=malloc(lineLen=strlen(line)))==NULL)
           return(-1);
       line[lineLen - 1] = '\0';
       strcpy(text[lineNo], line);
   }

   fclose(f);                 /* assume it is successful */
   returnlineNo - 1;
}
```

The terminating end-of-line character stored by the call to `fgets` is removed by the code. And to simplify the insertion sort, the zeroth element of the array is not used to store a line from the file; instead, this array element is initialized to be an empty string using

```
text[0] = "";
```

so that the comparison in the following insertion sort is guaranteed to find a string less than the one the loop is currently moving into place:

```
#define SWAP(p, q)       { char *temp; \
                            temp=(p); (p)=(q); (q) = temp; }
void InsSort(lineNo)
int lineNo;
{
    int i, j;

    for (i = 2; i < lineNo; i++)
        for (j = i; strcmp(text[j], text[j - 1]) < 0; j--)
            SWAP(text[j], text[j - 1]);
}
```

■

10.5   MAIN FUNCTION ARGUMENTS

As we mentioned in Chapter 6, a program in C consists of a number of functions. The main program is also a function, and the execution of a program always starts from this function. Moreover, the main function may have two or three parameters (or none). In most implementations, two parameters are allowed, but under Unix three may be specified. Here, we discuss the first case; in Section 14.1, we deal with features specific to Unix.

Traditionally, the formal parameters are called `argc` and `argv`, and so the header of `main` may look like

```
main(argc, argv)
```

The purpose of these parameters is to interface the program with its environment by passing values specified on the command line. For example, if the executable code of a program is stored in the file `test`, the command

```
test argument1 argument2
```

passes the values *argument1* and *argument2* to the program.

The first parameter `argc` is initialized to the number of actual parameters appearing in the command line, and the second parameter `argv` is an array of `argc` strings that corresponds to the actual parameters. Thus the specification of the formal parameters is

```
int argc;
char *argv[];
```

Although this specification of `argv` is equivalent to

```
char **argv;
```

the first version is used more often only to stress that `argv` is actually an array of strings. The name of the file containing the executable code is considered the zeroth parameter, so `argc` is *always* greater than or equal to 1. Thus in the previous example,

```
argc        = 3
argv[0]     Points to the string "test"
argv[1]     Points to the string "argument1"
argv[2]     Points to the string "argument2"
```

A command line argument enclosed in double quotes is counted as a single argument, for example, if the command is entered as

```
test "hello how" are "you doing"
```

then

```
argc        = 4
argv[0]     Points to the string "test"
argv[1]     Points to the string "hello how"
argv[2]     Points to the string "are"
argv[3]     Points to the string "you doing"                    ∎
```

Example 10.5.1   The following program displays the number of arguments on the command line, followed by each of these arguments:

```c
#include <stdio.h>
main(argc, argv)
int argc;
char *argv[];
{
    int i;

    printf("This program has %d arguments\n", argc);
    for (i = 0; i < argc; i++)
        printf("%s\n", argv[i]);
}                                                               ∎
```

Example 10.5.2   The following program expects zero, one, or two arguments on the command line, representing, for example, file names. If arguments are specified, they should be copied to character arrays for future use in the program; if no arguments are given, they should be read from the keyboard:

```c
#include <stdio.h>
#define NAMELEN 20
main(argc, argv)
int argc;
char *argv[];
{
    char name1[NAMELEN], name2[NAMELEN];

    switch (argc) {
    case 1:  if (gets(name1) == NULL)
                 return;
             if (gets(name2) == NULL)
                 return;
             break;
    case 2:  strcpy(name1, *++argv);
             if (gets(name2) == NULL)
                 return;
             break;
    case 3:  strcpy(name1, *++argv);
             strcpy(name2, *++argv);
             break;
    default: printf("usage: %s [name1] [name2]\n", argv[0]);
             return;
    }
    ...
}
```

Prefix incrementation of `argv` gives access to the first argument, skipping the name of the executable file. ∎

Example 10.5.3   Often programs are executed with various options specified on the command line. Consider a program `compare` to compare two files; let us assume this program may have two options:

-t   To compare *text* files and display the number of the first line that differs in the two files

-b   To compare *binary* files and display the position in the file of the first characters that differ

This program may therefore be invoked using either

```
compare -t file1 file2
```

or

```
compare -b file1 file2
```

Again, `argv` can be used to check which option is specified:

```c
#include <stdio.h>
#define TEXT        't'
#define BINARY      'b'
#define LINELEN     81
#define ERROR(mes)  { printf("%s\n", mes); return; }

main(argc, argv)
int argc;
char *argv[];
{
    extern void comptext();
    extern void compbin();

    if (argc != 4 || **++argv != '-')
        ERROR("usage: compare -{t|b} f1 f2\n")

    switch (*++*argv) {
    case TEXT   : comptext(argv[1], argv[2]);
                  break;
    case BINARY : compbin(argv[1], argv[2]);
                  break;
    default     : ERROR("usage: compare -{t|b} f1 f2\n")
                  break;
    }
}
```

Since

```
*++argv
```

is a pointer to the first argument on the command line,

```
**++argv
```

is the first character in this argument, which should be −. Then

```
*++*argv
```

increments *argv before taking the value, so it represents the second character in the first argument. At this point, argv has been increased by 1, so argv[1] points to the second argument in the command line, and argv[2] points to the third argument.

The two compare functions are as follows:

```
void comptext(fname1, fname2)
STRING fname1, fname2;
{
    char line1[LINELEN+1], line2[LINELEN+1];
    FILE *f1, *f2;
    long count;

    if ((f1 = fopen(fname1, "r")) == NULL ||
            (f2 = fopen(fname2, "r")) == NULL )
        ERROR("Cannot open input files")

    for (count = 0; fgets(line1, LINELEN, f1); count++)
        if (fgets(line2, LINELEN, f2) != NULL ||
                    strcmp(line1, line2)) {
            printf("Files differ at line %ld\n", count);
            count = -1;
            break;
        }
    if (count > -1 && fgets(line2, LINELEN, f2) == NULL)
            printf("Files differ at line %ld\n", count);
    if (fclose(f1) == EOF || fclose(f2) == EOF)
        ERROR("Cannot close input files")
}

void compbin(fname1, fname2)
STRING fname1, fname2;
{
    long c1, c2, count;
    FILE *f1, *f2;

    if ((f1 = fopen(fname1, "r")) == NULL ||
                    (f2 = fopen(fname2, "r")) == NULL )
        ERROR("Cannot open input files")
```

```
for (count = 0; (c1 = fgetc(f1)) != EOF; count++)
    if ((c2 = fgetc(f2)) == EOF !! c1 != c2 ) {
        printf("Files differ at character %ld\n", count);
        count = -1;
        break;
    }

if (count > -1 && (c2 = fgetc(f2)) != EOF)
    printf("Files differ at character %ld\n", count);

if (fclose(f1) == EOF !! fclose(f2) == EOF)
    ERROR("Cannot close input files")
}
```

10.6 CHARACTER PROCESSING MACROS AND FUNCTIONS

C implementations provide several routines for character processing. These routines are implemented either as functions or as macros. Therefore, the programmer should be cautious and use the routines as if they were macros, avoiding, for example, *side effects* in the evaluation of the actual parameters. Using character processing routines is recommended because they facilitate portable code. User-defined macros may depend on the implementation.

To use these character processing routines, the appropriate library must be included; the name of this library should be given in your system's documentation. We provide a list of the most common routines, all of which take one parameter of type char; thus the specification of the type of the parameter in the descriptions is omitted.

The first group of routines includes boolean functions that return the value non zero value or 0:

int isalnum(c)	Returns non zero value if c is an alphanumeric character (letter or digit), and 0 otherwise
int isalpha(c)	Returns non zero value if c is a letter, and 0 otherwise
int isascii(c)	Returns non zero value if c is a standard ASCII character, and 0 otherwise
int iscntrl(c)	Returns non zero value if c is a nonprintable character, and 0 otherwise
int isdigit(c)	Returns non zero value if c is a digit, and 0 otherwise
int isodigit(c)	Returns non zero value if c is an octal digit, and 0 otherwise
int isxdigit(c)	Returns non zero value if c is a hexadecimal digit, and 0 otherwise
int isgraph(c)	Returns non zero value if c is any printable character but a space, and 0 otherwise

inr isprint(c)	Returns non zero value if c is any printable character including a space, and 0 otherwise
int isspace(c)	Returns non zero value if c is a whitespace character, and 0 otherwise
int islower(c)	Returns non zero value if c is a lowercase letter, and 0 otherwise
int isupper(c)	Returns non zero value if c is an uppercase letter, and 0 otherwise

The second group includes routines that perform some kind of conversion:

int toascii(c)	Returns the low-order 7 bits of c
int toint(c)	Returns the decimal value of the hexadecimal digit c, or −1 if c is not a hexadecimal digit
int tolower(c)	If c is an uppercase letter, returns the corresponding lowercase letter, otherwise c
int toupper(c)	If c is a lowercase letter, returns the corresponding uppercase letter, otherwise c

Example 10.6.1   The following code implements a routine to perform a hexadecimal dump of a sequence of max characters originating at the address given by the pointer p. It displays the ASCII codes of each of the characters in hexadecimal, separated by blanks, and then the characters themselves, with nonprintable characters being displayed as dots.

```
void hex(p, max)
char *p;
int max;
{
      int aux;
      char *paux;

      for (aux = max, paux = p; aux; paux++, aux--)
          printf("%02x ", *paux);
      putchar('\n');

      for (aux = max, paux = p; aux; paux++, aux--)
          putchar(iscntrl(*paux) ? '.' : *paux);
      putchar('\n');
}
```

The conversion specification %02x causes the hexadecimal value to be displayed with a leading zero if it is less than 0x10.   ∎

Example 10.6.2   The following code can be used to *undo* the hexadecimal dump. The function unhex expects a pointer to a memory block containing pairs of ASCII characters (separated by whitespace) representing hexadecimal numbers. It converts these character pairs to their corresponding numeric values and stores them as bytes (characters) in a file; unhex terminates when the first nonhexadecimal digit is encountered.

```c
#include <stdio.h>
#include <ctype.h>
#ifndef toint  /* toint is unavailable on some systems  */
#define toint(i) ((i) >='0' && (i)<='9' ? (i)-'0' : (i)-'A'+10)
#endif

void unhex(p, fname)
char *p, *fname;
{
    FILE *f;
    int i;

    if (p == NULL || fname == NULL ||
                 (f = fopen(fname, "w")) == NULL) {
        printf("invalid parameters\n");
        /* error */
        return;
    }

    while (*p) {                   /* until end-of-string */
        if (isspace(*p)) {      /* skip space */
            p++;
            continue;
        }
        if (isxdigit(*p) ) {
            i = toint(*p);  /* convert a hex digit to ASCII */
            p++;               /* take the next hex digit */
            if (isxdigit(*p)) {
                fputc(i * 16 + toint(*p), f);
                p++;
            }
            else break;
        }
        else break;
    }

    if (fclose(f) == EOF)
        printf("cannot close %s\n", fname);
}
```

THINGS TO REMEMBER A string is terminated by the ASCII character null; remember this when specifying the size of a string array or when calling malloc to allocate memory for a string.

Include `string.h` when using string operations.

Remember to allocate memory when using string functions.

COMMON ERRORS

```
char c;
scanf("%1s", &c);     c is not a string
```

Avoid memory overlapping in string operations.

EXERCISES

1. Write a procedure `strip(s,t)` that returns through `t` the string `s` with all leading blanks removed. Assume `t` has been allocated enough space to hold the new string.

2. Write an integer function `replace(str,old,new)` that replaces the first occurrence of the string `old` in the string `str` with the string `new` and returns the result in `str`. If `old` is not found in `str`, the function returns 0; otherwise, it returns 1.

3. Implement the string comparison function `strcmp`.

4. Write a program to convert Roman numerals to Arabic numerals and back.

5. Write a program that expects a filename with extension `.c` in the command line and displays the message `OK` if the file with the same base name and the extension `.o` exists, and displays the message `NO OBJECT FILE` otherwise.

6. Write a program that reads a file containing long integer values and creates a file containing strings representing these integers. Then write a program to perform the conversion in the opposite direction.

7. Write a program that reads a file whose lines are of the form

   First-Name Last-Name

   and displays this file with each line output as

   Last-Name Initial

8. As we discussed, strings in C are arrays of characters terminated by `\0`. In many implementations of Pascal, a different approach is

used, with the zeroth byte containing the length of the string and
with no terminating character being stored. Using this approach,
implement in C the STRING routines introduced at the beginning of
this chapter. For this, implement the routine

```
STRING pnew (i)
int i;
```

which allocates i+1 bytes for a string of i characters and length
byte and returns a pointer to this block. The type STRING is defined
as usual:

```
typedef char * STRING;
```

9. Consider the following program:

```
#include <stdio.h>

typedef char * STRING;
STRING b[4] = {"test-number","three","for-2023","section"};

main(argc, argv)
int argc;
STRING argv[];
{
     STRING x, *px;
     int i;

     x = *b;
     for (i = 0; i < 4; i++) {
          puts(x);
          x++;
     }
     px = argv + 1;
     for (i = 0; i < argc - 1; i++) {
          puts(*px);
          px++;
     }
}
```

Find the output produced by this program, assuming the command
line contains the following arguments:

```
I like to program
```

10. Assume an arbitrary length string has been placed at absolute ad-
    dress 128. Write a procedure

```
save(s)
```

that finds the length of the string at location 128, then allocates memory for the string s, and finally copies the string at 128 to s. Show how `save` can be called in a short (but complete) main program.

11. Show the output produced by the following program:

```
#include <stdio.h>
#define lim 10
char s[lim];

int find(c)
char c;
{
        static int posi = 0;

        while (s[posi] != c) {
                if (posi == lim - 1)
                        return(0);
                posi++;
        }
        return(1);
}

main()
{
        gets(s);
        if (find('a'))
                puts("fine");
        else puts("bad");
        if (find('b'))
                puts("fine");
        else puts("bad");
        if (find('a'))
                puts("fine");
        else puts("bad");
}
```

Assume the input is

```
be aware
```

12. Show the output produced by the following program:

```
#include <stdio.h>
#define lim 10
char s[lim];

int find(i)
```

```
         int i;
         {
                 return(s[i++]);
         }

         void inter()
         {
                 int k;

                 gets(s);
                 for (k = 0; k <= 2; k++)
                         main();
         }

         main()
         {
                 static int i = 0;
                 int c;

                 if (i == 0) {
                         i++;
                         inter();
                 }
                 c = find(i++);
                 putchar(c);
         }
```

Assume the input is

```
finalexam
```

13. Write a program that expects one or two filenames on the command line and produces a hexadecimal dump of the file passed as the first argument. If the second argument is present, the dump is stored in the file whose name is passed as this argument; otherwise, the dump is displayed on the screen. The format of the dump should be as demonstrated:

```
0000: 70 72 6F 67 72 61 6D 20 3B 0A 62 65 67 69 6E 0A program ;.begin.
0010: ...
```

The first 4 columns are the current character offset in hexadecimal and should increment by 0x10 for each line. Each line contains 16 hexadecimal ASCII codes of the next 16 bytes from the file. The last 16 columns are used to display the corresponding characters, with each nonprintable character being displayed as a dot and other characters unchanged.

11 Bitwise Operations and Bit Fields

PREVIEW *This chapter discusses bitwise operations that operate on individual bits of a computer word. We also introduce the concept of a bit field.*

REVIEW OF PASCAL CONSTRUCTS

Standard Pascal does not provide bitwise operations or bit fields. As usual, many implementations provide special extensions to the language so that these features are available; however, since there seems to be no generally accepted standard, we do not discuss any here.

C CONSTRUCTS

Up to now, you have learned about high-level, Pascal-like features of C, as well as some low-level, assembly-like features. In this chapter, we discuss additional low-level tools that can be useful in certain applications.

11.1 BITWISE OPERATIONS

In many system programs, it is desirable to access individual **bits** of a computer word. For example, in an MS-DOS environment, some bits in the keyboard flag byte may have to be accessed, or in a Unix environment, it may be necessary to mask incoming characters to ensure that all characters are positive. For this purpose, C provides several **bitwise** operations:

bitwise *and*	&
bitwise *or*	¦
bitwise xor	^
left shift	<<
right shift	>>
one's complement	~

The arguments for these operations may be neither `float` nor `double`, since they are converted to a binary form immediately before an operation is performed. Standard C defines bitwise operations for *unsigned* arguments only, and for portability, signed arguments should be avoided.

Bitwise And

The ith bit of the result of the bitwise *and*

```
x & y
```

is 1 if the ith bit of both x and y is 1; otherwise, this bit is 0. Thus each bit of the result is obtained by taking the logical *and* of the two corresponding bits of the operands.

The bitwise *and* operation could be used to implement a macro isodd, which tests whether an integer x is odd or not:

```
#define isodd(x)    (1 & (unsigned)(x) )
```

As another example, consider input operations on the LSI 11/02 [Com84], where a word is 16 bits long. An incoming character is retrieved from the Serial Line Unit buffer, where the high-order nibble of the high-order byte has bits set to 1 if any errors occurred, and the low-order byte contains the character itself (a nibble is 4 bits):

	High nibble	Low nibble	
x:	Error bits		character
	High byte	Low byte	

To retrieve the character from the word, we have to mask off the high-order byte. The value 0xff in binary is

```
0000000011111111
```

so the mask operation can be performed using

```
x = x & 0xff;
```

or simply

```
x &= 0xff;
```

This clears the high-order byte.   ∎

The result of a *logical* and operation (&&) and a *bitwise* and operation (&) may differ.

Bitwise Or
The ith bit of the result of the bitwise *or* operation

```
x | y
```

is 1 if the ith bit of at least one of the two arguments is equal to 1.

Whereas bitwise *and* is useful for setting bits to 0, bitwise *or* is useful for setting bits to 1:

```
x |= MASK
```

sets those bits in x for which the corresponding bits in MASK are 1. For example, assuming a word is 16 bits in length, to set the high-order bit of a character x, the operation

```
x |= 0x80
```

could be used.

Bitwise Exclusive-Or
The ith bit of the result of the bitwise *xor* operation

```
x ^ y
```

is 0 if the ith bits of x and y are identical; otherwise, it is 1.

This operation can be used to test whether two words are equal or not, for example,

```
if (x ^ y)
    ...          /* different */
```

Shift Operations
The *left-shift* operation

```
x << n
```

shifts the bits of x to the *left* by n positions, with the n leftmost bits being discarded, and the n rightmost bits being set to 0. Thus

```
x = x << 1;
```

or simply

```
x <<= 1;
```

is equivalent to multiplication by 2, and similarly,

    x <<= 2;

is equivalent to multiplication by 4, and so on.
   The *right-shift* operation

    x >> n

shifts the bits of x to the *right* by n positions, with the n rightmost bits
being discarded, and the n leftmost bits being set to 0.
   Thus

    x >>= 1;

is equivalent to division by 2, and similarly,

    x >>=2;

is equivalent to division by 4, and so on.

Example 11.1.1   The following function returns the value of the ith bit in a word:

```
#define ERROR      (−1)
#define CLEAR      1
#define BITSinCHAR 8
int bit(x, i)
unsigned x, i;
{
    if (i < 0 ¦¦ i >= sizeof(x) * BITSinCHAR)
        return(ERROR);
    return((x >> i) & CLEAR);
}
```

The *right-shift* operation

    x >> i

has the effect of moving the ith bit to the rightmost bit position. *And*-
ing this with the word CLEAR, which has the rightmost bit set and all
others cleared, yields the value of the ith bit in x.   ∎

Bitwise Negation
The last operation is bitwise *negation*:

    ~ x

yields the one's complement of x; that is, each bit in the result is the
complement of the corresponding bit in x (0's become 1's, 1's become

0's). This operator can be used in situations that depend on the word length of the target machine so that the resulting code is portable. For example, the operation

```
x &= 0xfff8;
```

can be used to clear the low-order 3 bits of the word x. However, this would work only on computers having 16-bit words. If the size of a word were, for example, 32 bits, the result would be different. A portable solution is to determine the complement of the desired mask, in this case,

```
0x7
```

and then use the ~ operator to recomplement this value when the program is executed so that the original mask is extended to the full length of the word, whatever it may be:

```
x &= ~0x7;
```

Example 11.1.2   As one more application of bitwise operations, let us consider the hash function hashpjw [Aho86]. (If you are unfamiliar with hashing, we suggest you refer to Section 13.1.3 for an explanation.)

The function hashpjw is applied to a string value and returns an integer result. The main problem is finding a hash function that yields values uniformly distributed in a certain interval $[0, B-1]$, where B is some constant.

A common technique is to add up the ASCII codes of the characters in the string and return this value modulo B. To get a better distribution, the cumulative value is multiplied by a certain constant A before adding another character.

Consider 32-bit integers, and use the constant $A = 16$. Since the result may overflow, before adding in the value of the next character, we check the high-order nibble of the current sum. If any bit in this nibble is set, we shift the nibble right 24 bits so that it becomes the second lowest nibble, exclusive-or it with the result so far, and then clear the high-order nibble:

```
#define B     255                /* or something else */
#define EOS '\0'
#define MASK 0xf0000000
int hashpjw(s)
char *s;
{
    char *p;
    unsigned h = 0,
             g;
```

```
for (p = s; *p != EOS; p++) {
    h = (h << 4 ) + (*p);
    if (g = h & MASK) {
        h ^= (g >> 24);
        h ^= g;
    }
}
return(h % B);
}
```                                                    ■

Another common use of bitwise operations is to deal with *groups* of bits that, for example, represent status flags:

```
unsigned status;
```

First, define constants that determine positions of flag bits within a status word. For example, assume we want to use bits 4, 5, and 6 as flags:

```
#define FLAG1   0x8
#define FLAG2   0x20
#define FLAG3   0x40
```

To turn all flags on, we would use

```
status != FLAG1 | FLAG2 | FLAG3;
```

To turn only FLAG1 and FLAG3 on:

```
status != FLAG1 | FLAG3;
```

To turn all flags off:

```
status &= ~(FLAG1 | FLAG2 | FLAG3);
```

To test whether FLAG2 and FLAG3 are both off:

```
if (!(status & (FLAG2 | FLAG3))) ...
```

We show another application of bitwise operations to define a data type SET in Section 13.4.3.

11.2 BIT FIELDS

Bit fields can be used to pack integer components into a single machine word. In most cases, the use of bit fields is nonportable and must be described separately for each implementation.

The preceding discussion on status flags shows that bitwise operations can be cumbersome. In these situations, bit fields can be used to simplify coding. Using bit fields, it is possible to specify that some variables are to be allocated at specific bit offsets within a given structure:

```
struct {
    unsigned leading  : 3;
    unsigned FLAG1    : 1;
    unsigned FLAG2    : 1;
    unsigned FLAG3    : 1;
    unsigned trailing : 11;
} flags;
```

Each field is specified by a name and the field length in bits. For this definition, the component leading will be allocated the first (highest) 3 bits of the structure, then each of the flags will be allocated 1 bit, and the component trailing will be allocated 11 bits. All the components are unsigned.

By using this definition of the structure flags, we can rewrite the operations given at the end of Section 11.1 so that the bits are assigned to directly; for example, to turn all the flags on, we would use

```
flags.FLAG1 = flags.FLAG2 = flags.FLAG3 = 1;
```

An equivalent way of defining the structure is to specify the keyword unsigned once only, and separate the definitions by commas:

```
struct {
    unsigned leading  : 3,
             FLAG1    : 1,
             FLAG2    : 1,
             FLAG3    : 1,
             trailing : 11;
} flags;
```

The name of a component may be omitted. This is useful because we often are concerned only with certain interior fields. In the preceding example, if we were concerned with only the three flag fields, we could define the structure as

```
struct {
    unsigned       : 3;
    unsigned FLAG1 : 1;
    unsigned FLAG2 : 1;
    unsigned FLAG3 : 1;
    unsigned       : 11;
} flags;
```

If the total size of all fields is greater than the size of a word, a new word is started. Thus, a field cannot be wider than a word. A bit field length also may be zero, which means the following component should start on the next alignment boundary appropriate to its type. For example, if the structure

```
struct {
     unsigned F1 : 1;
     unsigned    : 0;
     unsigned F2 : 2;
     unsigned F3 : 4;
     unsigned F4 : 3;
} example;
```

is allocated at memory address 98, the memory map for this structure would be as follows. We assume the word size is 8 bits and represent this by eight b's, with the bits making up each field indicated appropriately.

```
 98:  b b b b b b b b
      ‿
      F1
 99:  b b b b b b b b
      ‿‿ ‿‿‿‿‿‿
      F2    F3
100:  b b b b b b b b
      ‿‿‿
       F4
```

Arrays of fields and *&field* are not allowed. Also, fields cannot be pointed to by pointers.

EXERCISES

1. Write a function that reverses the bits in a byte.

2. Write a procedure bin(i) that prints a binary representation of the integer i using shift instructions.

3. Write a procedure octal(i) that prints a base-8 representation of the integer i using shift instructions.

4. Write a procedure swap(c) that swaps the low-order nibble of character c with the high-order nibble of character c and returns the result through c.

5. Write a procedure

```
void compress(str, mask)
char *str;
char mask;
```

that compresses the string `str` according to the specified 8-bit `mask`. For example, if `str` is

```
The quick red fox jumped
```

and the binary representation of mask is

```
10110011
```

the resulting value of `str` would be

```
Te ickrefoxjued
```

This result is determined by duplicating the mask for every group of eight characters and eliminating characters masked by a 0 bit:

```
The quick red fox jumped
101100111011001110110011
```

Note: The string being compressed might not be a multiple of eight characters in length as it is in this example.

6. Write a procedure `hex(i)` that outputs the 32-bit integer `i` as eight hexadecimal digits using bit fields.

12 File I/O Revisited

PREVIEW   *This chapter continues the presentation of file operations that we began in Chapter 4. We illustrate how files containing structured information such as arrays and structures can be managed in C. We also present several examples, including a linear search of a file of structures, a binary search of a file, and saving a linked list in a file. The terminal and file I/O operations we describe in this chapter are part of the system library. Other essential system library routines are the memory operations (see Chapter 7) and the string operations (see Chapter 10).*

REVIEW OF PASCAL CONSTRUCTS

Standard Pascal defines two kinds of files: text files and binary files. A **text file** consists of characters separated into lines of varying lengths by end-of-line characters, whereas a **binary file** consists of information organized into fixed-size components, each of the same type.

A file in standard Pascal, either text or binary, may be accessed only **sequentially**, and the mode of access may either be input or output, but not both. When a file is open for input, a search for a particular component must start at the current component (initially, the beginning of the file) and continue, component by component, until the required one is found or end-of-file is encountered. When a file is open for output, writing a new component appends it to the end of the file. To switch from one mode to another, a file must be closed and then reopened in the desired mode.

Many implementations of Pascal support **random-access** binary files in which the current position in a file can be updated by calling a routine such as SEEK(file, position); this allows a specific component to be read from a file or a new component to be stored at any position in the file, not just at the end. Moreover, a file may be stored for reading and writing at the same time.

Some implementations provide additional file operations:

FLUSH(file)	Empties the internal file buffer and writes its contents to disk (in most Pascal systems, the CLOSE routine performs this operation automatically)

FILEPOS(file)	Returns an integer value corresponding to the current position in the specified file
ERASE(file)	Deletes the indicated file
RENAME(file, name)	Renames a file to the specified name

C CONSTRUCTS

In C, a **file** is a sequence of bytes, and *no* distinction is made between text files and binary files. Nor is any distinction made between data files and devices such as terminals or printers; thus the term **stream**, which is commonly used to refer to a file in C, could mean a disk-based file or some other sort of I/O device. By default, streams in C are random access when applicable. For example, disk I/O is random access, but standard keyboard input is not.

The stdio.h Header File

The C header file stdio.h defines the data type FILE. This data type is a structure that holds information about a stream. The actual contents of stdio.h and the structure FILE depends on the implementation because it forms the interface between the language's run-time system and the operating system. Although our description may not apply to all existing C implementations, we try, in the following paragraphs, to present the general contents of stdio.h with respect to file I/O.

In operating systems like MS-DOS and Unix, a FILE object stores the location of a buffer, the current position in the buffer, and the current position within the file, as well as other information. As we explained in Chapter 4, most file I/O operations are *buffered;* this buffer is provided by the run-time system and so is transparent to the user.

Moreover, a table of FILE structures is sometimes defined in stdio.h; the size of this table corresponds to the maximum number of files that can be open at one time.

The user does not explicitly allocate objects of type FILE but instead calls function fopen, which returns a pointer to an object in the table of FILE structures.

When a program starts executing, three predefined variables are initialized:

```
FILE *stdin;
FILE *stdout;
FILE *stderr;
```

These three file pointers usually point to the first three objects in the system file table. Thus they should not be modified by the user. In most implementations, these "variables" are actually macros that expand to the appropriate file table reference and, despite their formal definitions, are *not* l-values.

The first variable, stdin, is a file pointer representing the input stream associated with the standard input, usually the terminal keyboard. The second variable, stdout, represents the standard output stream, in most cases, the terminal screen. The last variable, stderr, is a file pointer associated with some output stream, again usually the terminal. As we explain in Chapter 14, in some implementations, standard I/O can be redirected, and in these cases, any error messages produced by the program must be written to the standard error stream; otherwise, they do not appear on the screen.

The macro EOF is usually defined in stdio.h to be −1; this value is returned when end-of-file is encountered. Another macro NULL is usually defined to be 0.

The remaining part of stdio.h contains various macros and declarations of library functions; for example, the declaration

```
FILE *fopen();
```

would be in stdio.h.

File operations that operate on objects of type FILE are called **high-level** file operations, or simply file operations. Most C implementations provide so-called **low-level** file operations that operate on file descriptors. A **file descriptor** is an integer index into internal table describing currently open files.

In this chapter, we deal with high-level file operations that are defined for standard C and thus are *portable*. In Chapter 14, we introduce some low-level file operations available under the MS-DOS, Unix, and Macintosh operating systems.

12.1 FILE OPERATIONS

In this section, we introduce additional I/O operations defined in the C run-time library to manage random-access files (for the sake of completeness, those operations we introduced in Chapter 4 are also included here).

12.1.1 Error Checking

There are two ways to test whether or not file operations are successful. First, most operations return a value that may be examined to determine whether the operation was successful; for example, fclose returns EOF if it fails. Second, a global variable errno stores a nonzero error code if an operation fails. Because the values of these error codes depend on the system implementation, we do not describe them here.

Two routines deal with error checking:

```
void clearerr(f)
FILE *f;
```

clears any error indication in the variable errno, and

```
int ferror(f)
FILE *f;
```

returns 0 if no error occurred during the last I/O operation on the stream f; otherwise, it returns a nonzero value. A call to ferror does not reset the variable errno; this may be achieved using clearerr or by closing the file.

12.1.2 Current Position in a File

Four routines either get or set a file's position indicator:

```
ftell(f)
fseek(f, offset, mode)
rewind(f)
feof(f)
```

To determine the current position in a file, the function

```
long ftell(f)
FILE *f;
```

may be used. The stream f must be open for I/O. The current position in the file is returned as a long, for example,

```
FILE *f;
...
printf("The current position is %ld\n", ftell(f));
...
```

To change the current position in a file, the routine fseek may be used:

```
int fseek(f, offset, mode)
FILE *f;
long offset;
int mode;
```

The stream f must have been previously opened. If the operation is successful, 0 is returned; otherwise, a nonzero value is returned. A call to fseek sets the current position to

- The *absolute value* of offset if mode = 0
- The value of offset *relative to the current position* (the current position plus the signed offset) if mode = 1
- The value of offset relative to the *end of the file* if mode = 2

Note that offset is a long and the position of the first component in a file is 0; a call such as fseek(f, 0L, 0) would be needed to seek to the first component in the file (note the need to use the L suffix).

The effect of the call fseek(f, 0L, 0) can also be achieved using

```
void rewind(f)
FILE *f;
```

This is identical to the previous fseek call except that it is a procedure, and so no error can be indicated on return.

Example 12.1.1   The following function FileSize computes the size of a file. It returns EOF if an error is detected.

```
long FileSize(f)
FILE *f;
{
   if (fseek(f,0L,2)!=0) /* set position relative to end */
        return EOF;
   return ftell(f);
}                                                              ∎
```

To test for end-of-file, the function feof may be used:

```
int feof(f)
FILE *f;
```

The stream f must be open for input. This function returns a nonzero value if end-of-file has been reached; otherwise, it returns 0.

12.1.3   Opening and Closing Files

To open and close files or, more generally, streams, there are three routines:

```
fopen(fname, mode)
fclose(f)
freopen(fname, mode, f)
```

To **open** a stream, the function fopen may be used:

```
FILE *fopen(fname, mode)
char *fname;
char *mode;
```

fname and mode are strings. If the operation is successful, a new file pointer is returned; if unsuccessful, the value NULL is returned. The commonly permissible modes are

"r"	To open existing file for input
"w"	To open for output
"a"	To open for appending
"r+"	To open for input/output
"w+"	To open for input/output
"a+"	To open for input/output

All modes that open the file for output or input/output create a *new* file if the file with the name indicated by fname does not exist. If the file does already exist, the "a" and "a+" modes append to it, and "w" and "w+" erase the file and create a new one. If the file is open for input and output, both read and write operations may be performed; however, if an input operation is to be followed by an output operation, an intervening fseek or rewind *must* be executed. Similarly, an output operation may be followed by an input operation only if a call to fseek or rewind is first performed.

To **close** the stream f, the function fclose is used:

```
int fclose(f)
FILE *f;
```

flushing the internal buffer in the process. It returns EOF if it fails, and it returns 0 otherwise.

Another routine, freopen, is a combination of fopen and fclose:

```
FILE *freopen(fname, mode, f)
char *fname;
char *mode;
FILE *f;
```

The stream f must be open. First, freopen closes the stream f and then **reopens** it under the name fname in the mode specified by the second parameter. If the operation is successful, a file pointer is returned through both the third parameter and the function identifier; if an error occurs, the value of the third parameter is undetermined, and the value returned by the function is NULL. In the latter case, the corresponding error code is stored in the variable errno.

The exact format of the name fname depends on the implementation; usually, it is simply a filename, but it may also specify the device and directory where the file is to be opened. The function freopen has application in programs in which, for example, we want to redirect standard output to a file and then reset this stream to its usual value. The call

```
freopen("tmpout", "w", stdout)
```

will close the standard output stream and then use the same FILE object in the system table to open the file tmpout for output. Therefore, any output statements that write to the standard output stream will actually write to the file tmpout. A similar call to freopen can be used to reset the standard input stream; the specific details on how to do this once again depend on the implementation; we illustrate an example of how it can be done under Unix in Example 14.1.2.

12.1.4   File Input and Output

The fourth group of operations deals with I/O. There are four kinds of I/O operations:

- Single character I/O
- Formatted I/O
- String I/O
- Block I/O

12.1.4.1   Single Character I/O
To read a single character, there are two routines: getc and fgetc. The only difference between the two is that getc is usually implemented as a macro, and fgetc is usually implemented as a function.

```
int fgetc(f)       int getc(f)
FILE *f;           FILE *f;
```

The stream f must be open for input. The routines return EOF if end-of-file is encountered (or an error occurs), otherwise they return the ordinal value of the current character in the stream f.

Similarly, to output a single character, there are two routines: fputc and putc. Again, putc is usually implemented as a macro and fputc as a function.

```
int fputc(c, f)    int putc(c, f)
char c;            char c;
FILE *f;           FILE *f;
```

The stream f must be open for output. This routine writes the character c to the stream f and returns the ordinal value of this character if the operation is successful; it returns EOF otherwise.

Function ungetc pushes a single character back onto the specified stream:

```
int ungetc(c, f)
char c;
FILE *f;
```

The stream f must be open for input. The character c is pushed back on f so that the next call to a character input routine will read this character. If the character c can be pushed back, it is returned by ungetc; if not, ungetc returns the value EOF. The call is successful if

- The stream f is buffered
- At least one character has been read
- There were no calls to fseek or freopen since the last read

The value EOF cannot be pushed back. Moreover, there is usually a limit on how many characters may be restored to the input stream; in some systems, the limit is one.

One more operation is useful with buffered I/O operations. In some applications, we may wish to manually *flush* a file's output buffer. For example, we could be creating a file with important information in it and want to force all currently buffered data to be written to disk, or we might have a program that sends command sequences to a printer to configure it in some mode and want to send characters to the printer immediately rather than have them remain in the buffer. This ability is provided through the standard system library operation fflush:

```
int fflush(f)
FILE *f;
```

The stream f must be open for output. The internal buffer associated with f is emptied and 0 is returned. If an error occurs, EOF is returned.

12.1.4.2 Formatted File I/O

Two routines are defined for formatted I/O:

```
int fscanf(f, format, arg1, ..., argk)
FILE *f;
char *format;
int fprintf(f, format, arg1, ..., argk)
FILE *f;
char *format;
```

These routines are similar to the routines `scanf` and `printf`. We describe them in briefly Chapter 4 and in detail in Appendix C.

12.1.4.3 String I/O

Two routines are defined for string I/O:

```
char *fgets(buf, max, f)
char *buf;
int max;
FILE *f;

int fputs(buf, f)
char *buf;
FILE *f;
```

We describe both routines in detail in Section 10.3.

12.1.4.4 Block Character I/O

Block character I/O deals with the reading or writing of large *blocks* of characters in a single operation. Although the same effect could be achieved using character I/O, it would be much less efficient. Usually, this block of characters (or bytes) represents a complex object such as a structure or an array. Two operations are provided to perform block character I/O: `fread` and `fwrite`. Each of these routines is designed to read or write a number of consecutive blocks in a single call; this facilitates, for example, reading an array of structures.

```
int fread(buf, siz, count, f)
char *buf;
unsigned siz;
int count;
FILE *f;
```

The stream f must be open for input, and the pointer buf must point to a memory block allocated by the user (a character array or a block obtained using `malloc`, for example). When called, `fread` *inputs* count blocks from the stream f, each containing siz characters. The number of blocks successfully read is returned through the function identifier.

```
int fwrite(buf, siz, count, f)
char *buf;
unsigned siz;
int count;
FILE *f;
```

The stream f must be open for output, and the pointer buf must point to the user-defined buffer to be copied to the file. As in the `fread` operation, count blocks, each of size siz, are *output*. The actual number of items written is returned.

Because the types of pointers passed as actual parameters must match their corresponding formal parameter specifications (as we described in Chapter 7), in a call to fread or fwrite, the actual parameter corresponding to buf must be cast as a pointer to character (see Example 12.2.1).

12.1.5   Terminal I/O Operations

For the sake of completeness, we provide a complete list of terminal I/O operations. Since many are analogous to corresponding file operations, their meanings are obvious and so not described in detail here.

Single Character I/O

```
int getchar( )

int putchar(c)
char c;
```

String I/O

```
char *gets(s)
char *s;

int puts(s)
char *s;
```

Formatted I/O

```
int scanf(format, arg1, ..., argk)
char *format;

int printf(format, arg1, ..., argk)
char *format;
```

12.2   APPLICATIONS

In this section, we show through several examples how complex structures such as arrays and linked lists can be saved in files and then retrieved.

The operations fread and fwrite are useful for reading and writing complex objects. They are most efficient if the size of the object is a multiple of the physical sector size of the disk. The nature of these routines does not permit blocks of varying sizes to be read. If a file is organized in this manner, it would have to be processed using character I/O routines; often, however, more efficient, lower level operations are available; since these depend on the implementation, we describe them in Section 14.1.2.

12.2.1 Saving and Retrieving an Array of Structures

In this section, we show the implementation of two functions, one to save an array of structures in a file, and one to retrieve an array of structures from a file. A file that stores data in this manner we call a *binary* file to distinguish it from a *text* file. We then show a routine to initialize an array of structures from a text file. Finally, we provide a sample program that makes use of all these functions. As a part of this, we also demonstrate a technique for *error processing* using enumeration types.

Example 12.2.1   Consider an array of structures containing information about students:

```
#include <stdio.h>
#define NAMELEN  20
#define STUDNUM  100
typedef struct {
             char name[NAMELEN + 1];
             long studNum;
             double GPA;      /* grade point average */
         } INFO;
INFO registrar[STUDNUM];
```

The function fsave illustrates how an array of INFO structures can be saved in a file:

```
ERROR fsave(fname, r, num, mode)
char *fname;
INFO r[];
int num;
char *mode;
```

The parameter fname is the name of the file in which the array will be stored, the parameter r is the array itself, and the parameter num specifies how many elements of the array are to be stored. Whether the records being output should overwrite the existing information in the file or be appended to the end of the file is specified by the parameter mode.

What should the actual parameters of fwrite be? Since the structures in the array r are stored in consecutive memory blocks, we can transfer all num structures in a single call to fwrite:

```
fwrite((char *)r, sizeof(*r), num, f)
```

The first parameter must be cast to char *. The second parameter is the size of *r, which is the size of an INFO structure. An alternative solution is

```
fwrite((char *)r, sizeof(INFO), num, f)
```

The result type, ERROR, is an enumeration type defined to facilitate error handling. It lists the different kinds of errors that may occur:

```
typedef enum {
              PARS, WOPEN,  WRITE, WCLOSE, ROPEN,
              READ, RCLOSE, TOPEN, TREAD,  TCLOSE, OK
        } ERROR;
```

The function `diserr` will be used to display error messages corresponding to these codes:

```
void diserr(e)
ERROR e;
{
      switch (e) {
      case PARS   : printf("Incorrect parameters\n");
                    return;
      case WOPEN  : printf("Cannot open file for output\n");
                    return;
      case WRITE  : printf("File write error\n");
                    return;
      case WCLOSE : printf("Cannot close output file\n");
                    return;
      case ROPEN  : printf("Cannot open file for input\n");
                    return;
      case READ   : printf("File read error\n");
                    return;
      case RCLOSE : printf("Cannot close input file\n");
                    return;
      case TOPEN  : printf("Cannot open text file\n");
                    return;
      case TREAD  : printf("Text file read error\n");
                    return;
      case TCLOSE : printf("Cannot close text file\n");
                    return;
      }
}
```

The complete code of `fsave` follows; the logic of this code should make the meanings of the preceding error messages clear:

```
ERROR fsave(fname, r, num, mode)
char *fname;
INFO r[];
int num;
char *mode;
{
      FILE *f;

      if (fname == NULL || r == NULL )
            return(PARS);          /* wrong parameters */
```

```
        if ((f = fopen(fname, mode)) == NULL )
            return(WOPEN);        /* can't open for output */
        if (num > STUDNUM)
            num = STUDNUM;

        if (fwrite( (char*)r, sizeof(*r), num, f) < num)
            return(WRITE);        /* write error */

        if (fclose(f) == EOF)
            return(WCLOSE);       /* close error */
        return(OK);
    }
```

The next function needed for this example demonstrates how an array
of structures may be read from a file. Its header is

```
    ERROR fretrieve(fname, r, siz)
    char *fname;
    INFO r[];
    int *siz;
```

This function retrieves up to siz INFO structures from the file fname
and stores them in the array r. On entry to the function, the value of
siz represents the limit of how many structures are to be read; on exit,
siz returns the actual number of structures read. The function assumes
the size of the file being read is a multiple of the size of an INFO structure.

Since we generally do not know how many structures are in the file f,
we must read a single structure at a time until either siz structures
have been read or end-of-file is encountered:

```
    for (i=0; i<*siz && fread((char*)r, sizeof(INFO), 1, f);
                        i++,r++)
        ;
    if (i < *siz && !feof(f))
        return(READ);
```

The array identifier r is treated as a pointer—in each step of the loop, it
is incremented by 1 so that it will point to the following structure in the
array for the next fread operation.

The for statement terminates either when siz records have been
read, end-of-file has been reached, or a read error has occurred. The
complete code follows:

```
    ERROR fretrieve(fname, r, siz)
    char *fname;
    INFO r[];
    int *siz;
    {
        int i;
        FILE *f;
```

```
    if (fname == NULL !! r == NULL)
        return(PARS);
    if ((f = fopen(fname, "r")) == NULL)
        return(ROPEN);

    for (i=0; i<*siz && fread((char*)r,sizeof(INFO),1,f); i++,r++)
        ;
    *siz = i;

    if (fclose(f) == EOF)
        return(RCLOSE);
    return(OK);
}
```

To illustrate how an array of structures can be initialized from file data, assume we have a text file with lines of the form

name whitespace student-number whitespace GPA

The function input(fname, r, siz) reads the text file fname containing lines as we have described, stores the information in an array of INFO structures, and returns through siz the number of structures read. The main loop of this function,

```
    for (*siz = 0; *siz < STUDNUM && fscanf(f,"%20s%ld%lf",
            r->name,&(r->studNum),&(r->GPA))==3; (*siz)++,  r++)
        ;
    if (!feof(f))
        return(TREAD);
```

terminates when STUDNUM items have been read or when fscanf fails to read the three specified values; we therefore make an additional check after exiting from the loop. As in the previous function, r is treated as a pointer that moves along to each structure in the array during the loop; thus we can reference the components of the current structure directly through r. The number of successfully read items is returned through siz. The complete function follows:

```
ERROR input(fname, r, siz)
char *fname;
INFO r[];
int *siz;
{
    FILE *f;

    if (fname == NULL !! r == NULL)
        return(PARS);
```

```
        if ((f = fopen(fname, "r")) == NULL)
            return(TOPEN);

        for (*siz = 0; *siz < STUDNUM && fscanf(f,"%20s%ld%lf",
            r->name,&(r->studNum),&(r->GPA))==3;(*siz)++,r++)
            ;

        if (!feof(f))
            return(TREAD);
        if (fclose(f) == EOF)
            return(TCLOSE);
        return(OK);
}
```

We now present the main program. The name of the text file is passed
on the command line. The program loads the (previously defined) global
array registrar from this text file and then saves it in a binary file as
a number of INFO structures. The base name of this file is the same as
that of the input file but with an extension .bin. For example, if the
name of the text file is test.dat, the name of the binary file will be
test.bin. This modification is done through the function update.
Next, the contents of the binary file are retrieved and stored in the local
array reg, and eventually the information in this array is displayed.
This program serves no useful purpose other than to demonstrate the
operations we have defined.

```
#define FILELEN 20
main(argc, argv)
int argc;
char *argv[];
{
    extern void update();
    ERROR err;
    extern ERROR fsave();
    extern ERROR fretrieve();
    extern ERROR input();
    int siz;
    INFO reg[STUDNUM], *aux;
    char modified[FILELEN + 1];
    extern INFO registrar[];

    if (argc != 2) {
        printf("usage: %s filename\n", argv[0]);
        return;
    }

    if ((err = input(argv[1], registrar, &siz)) != OK) {
        diserr(err);
        return;
    }
    printf("%d elements read from the file %s\n",
            siz, argv[1]);
```

```
      update(modified, argv[1]);
      if ((err = fsave(modified,registrar,siz,"w")) != OK) {
            diserr(err);
            return;
      }

      if ((err = fretrieve(modified, reg, &siz)) != OK) {
            diserr(err);
            return;
      }
      printf("%d elements retrieved from the file %s\n",
                  siz, modified);
      printf("These elements are\n");
      for (aux = reg; siz; aux++, siz--)
            printf("%20s\t%ld\t%f\n", aux->name,
                        aux->studNum, aux->GPA);
}
```

To complete this example, the function `update` must be defined. This function is used to create the name of the binary file from the name of the text file given on the command line. If this filename has an extension (we assume there is only one), `strchr` would return a pointer to the position where the dot is in the name; by storing a \0 at this point, we effectively remove the extension.

```
#include <string.h>
#define DOT '.'
void update(s1, s2)
char *s1, *s2;
{
      char *s,
            *ext = ".bin";

      strncpy(s1, s2, FILELEN);
#ifdef unix
      if ((s = rindex(s1, DOT)) != NULL)
#else
      if ((s = strchr(s1, DOT)) != NULL)
#endif
            *s = '\0';
      strcat(sl, ext);
}
```

We use conditional compilation because in some Unix C implementations, the function `strchr` is called `rindex`. The macro `unix` is predefined only on Unix systems.   ∎

Example 12.2.2   In Example 12.2.1, we were using an array of structures that could be dealt with efficiently because they were allocated one contiguous block of memory. If, however, we had an array of *pointers* to structures, the memory for the various structures would not be contiguous, and the same technique could not be used. Instead, each structure would have to be output separately in a loop. Consider the definition

```
typedef INFO* PINFO;
```

where INFO is defined as in Example 12.2.1. The following function saves an array of siz pointers to INFO structures in the file fname. To shorten the code, we omit error checking in this example.

```
void fsavel(fname, r, siz)
char *fname;
PINFO r[];
int siz;
{
    FILE *f;

    f = fopen(fname, "w");
    while (siz--) {
        if (*r != NULL)
            fwrite((char *)(*r), sizeof(INFO), 1, f);
        r++;
    }
    fclose(f);
}
```

Here, *r is a pointer of type PINFO, and in the loop, we check whether or not the current element in the array is a NULL pointer before attempting to do output. By incrementing r by 1, we make it point to the next element of the array, since r is of type pointer to INFO.   ■

12.2.2 Saving and Retrieving Linked Lists

Example 12.2.3   This example shows how a linked list can be saved in a file and then retrieved. We use here a list of strings. Consider the definition

```
typedef struct ITEM   {
            char *value;
            struct ITEM *next;
        } ITEM, *PITEM;
```

The function fsave(f, h) takes two parameters—a FILE pointer f and a pointer h to the first element of the list. It assumes the file f has been open for output and stores the consecutive strings from the list in the file. To simplify the code, we limit error checking. If successful, fsave returns 1; if not, it returns 0.

```
int fsave(f, h)
FILE *f;
PITEM h;
{
   if (f == NULL)
        return(0);
   for (; h != NULL; h = h->next)
        if (fwrite(h->value,strlen(h->value)+1,1,f)<1)
              return(0);
   return(1);
}
```

In this example, `fwrite` returns 0 if an error occurs; it returns 1 if the call is successful. The `fwrite` routine considers that a single item, a string, is being written, not several bytes. We output all the bytes stored in a string, *including* the terminating \0.

Since the strings in the list may be of *different* lengths, once they are stored in the file, they must be retrieved using single character input. There is a solution that would allow us to use block input, but we would have to change the method used to output the strings. For example, we could have assumed none of the strings is longer than MAXL (some constant), and, at the price of wasted file space, write blocks of length MAXL. Since the code for this approach would be similar to that in Section 12.2.1, we choose not make this assumption and use single character input as suggested. (One possible solution that would allow block I/O to be used is to read in blocks of some fixed size and manually reconstruct the strings from these blocks as they are read. Since the ideal size of these blocks depends on the file system's characteristics, this approach depends on the system, and we postpone discussing the technique until Chapter 14.)

The function `fretrieve(f)` assumes that the file pointer f has been opened for input and creates a linked list by making repeated calls to the function `creeat` to allocate new elements for the list. The code for `creeat` follows:

```
int creeat(h)
PITEM *h;
{
    char *malloc();

    if ((*h = (PITEM)malloc(sizeof(ITEM))) == NULL)
        return(0);
    return(1);
}
```

The function `fretrieve` returns a pointer to the first element in the list it creates; a NULL pointer is returned if an error occurs. We assume the length of a string is limited to STRLIM. The function `strsave`, which we defined in Example 10.2.5, is used to make a copy of a string.

Let us begin by explaining the technique we use in this example. First of all, we check whether the file f is empty, and if it is not, we create the first element of the list; a pointer to this element will be returned as the value of the function if the entire operation can be completed successfully. Space for a new object is obtained using

```
if (creeat(&h))
     haux = h;
```

Here, haux is an auxiliary pointer that will point to the current element in the list, and h is the head of the list. A string recovered from the file will be copied to the current element in the list. The main loop reads characters from the file one at a time:

```
while ((i = fgetc(f)) != EOF)
```

and characters making up a string are copied into an auxiliary array aux:

```
char aux[STRLIM + 1];
```

To facilitate copying, we use a pointer paux initialized to aux; every time the null character that terminates a string is encountered, the pointer paux will be reset to aux:

```
if ((*paux++ = i) == '\0') {
     paux = aux;
```

Next, we must allocate memory for the string in the current element of the list and copy the string from the array aux to the newly obtained string. For this, we can use the function strsave

```
if ((haux->value = strsave(aux)) == NULL)
     return(NULL);
```

After having copied a complete string, we check whether anything is left in the file. If there is, we create a new list element linked to the "old" current element and move the pointer haux:

```
if (!feof(f)) {
     if (creeat(&haux->next))
          haux = haux->next;
}
```

After the end-of-file is encountered, we perform the additional error check:

```
if (paux != aux)
     return(NULL);
```

which verifies whether the last' string in the file has been terminated by
\0. Our error checking has a weakness: If something goes wrong, objects have been allocated that will never be used. This could be easily
corrected by calling the following recursive procedure `freeAll`, which
would free all elements:

```
void freeAll(h)
PITEM h;
{
     if (h != NULL) {
          freeAll(h->next);
          free((char *)h);
     }
}
```

The complete code follows:

```
#define STRLIM 100

PITEM fretrieve(f)
FILE *f;
{
     PITEM h, haux;
     char aux[STRLIM + 1],
          *paux = aux,
          *strsave();
     int i;

     if (f == NULL !! (rewind(f),feof(f))
     else if (paux == aux+STRLIM+1)
          error...
          return(NULL);
     if (!creeat(&h))
          return(NULL);

     haux = h;
     while ((i = fgetc(f)) != EOF)
          if ((*paux++ = i) == '\0') {
               paux = aux;
               if ((haux->value=strsave(aux))==NULL)
                    return(NULL);
               if (!feof(f)) {
                    if (!creeat(&haux->next))
                         return(NULL);
                    haux = haux->next;
               }
          }
     haux->next = NULL;
     if (paux != aux)
          return(NULL);
     else return(h);
}
```

12.2.3   Random Access Operations

We conclude this chapter by giving two examples that make use of C's random-access file capabilities.

This first example shows that input and output can be performed *simultaneously* on the same file. The only limitation is that if an input operation immediately follows an output operation, or vice versa, an intervening *seek* operation must be performed.

Example 12.2.4   Consider a file containing an unsorted sequence of records with information about students:

```
#define NAMELEN   20
typedef struct {
               char name[NAMELEN + 1];
               long studNum;
               int age;
          } STUDENT;
#define SIZE sizeof(STUDENT)
```

Assume no two records have the same value for studNum. The following function retrieve uses a *linear* search to find the student in the file f with the specified student number. If the record is found, the position of this record in the file is returned; otherwise, the value EOF is returned. To simplify the code, we omit error checking.

```
long retrieve(f, num)
FILE *f;
long num;
{
      STUDENT curr;

      rewind(f);
      while (fread((char *) &curr, SIZE, 1, f))
           if (curr.studNum == num)
                 return(ftell(f) - SIZE);
      return(EOF);
}
```

We want retrieve to return the first byte of the record that has been found; therefore, the value returned by ftell is decreased by the value SIZE. The function retrieve performs only input. The following function modify uses retrieve to find a particular student, changes the age field of this record, and then updates the file; modify returns 0 if successful, and it returns EOF if not.

As we explained before, the read and write operations must be separated by at least one call to fseek or rewind. Since the function modify, as its final action, writes to the file, it would be dangerous not to follow the write with the rewind; if the routine that calls modify tries to read from the same file immediately after calling modify, this call would fail.

```
#define RETURN(stat) { rewind(f); return(stat); }

int modify(f, num, age)
FILE *f;
long num;
int age;
{
    STUDENT curr;
    long retrieve(), offset;

    if ((offset = retrieve(f, num)) == EOF)
        RETURN(EOF)
    fseek(f, offset, 0);
    if (fread((char*) &curr, SIZE, 1, f) == 0)
        RETURN(EOF)

    curr.age = age;
    fseek(f, offset, 0);
    if (fwrite((char*) &curr, SIZE, 1, f) == 0)
        RETURN(EOF)
    RETURN(0)
}
```

■

Example 12.2.5   In this last example, we present an alternative implementation of the retrieve function given in Example 12.2.4. In this version, we assume the file is sorted according to the studNum field and can therefore use a *binary* search to locate the specified student. We make use of the function FileSize implemented in Example 12.1.1, and we omit error checking.

```
#define SIZE sizeof(STUDENT)
long retrieve(f, num)
FILE *f;
long num;
{
    STUDENT curr;
    long bottom, top, middle;
    extern long FileSize();

    bottom = 0;
    top = FileSize(f) / SIZE;
    while (bottom <= top) {
        middle = (bottom + top) / 2;
        fseek(f, middle * SIZE, 0);
        fread( (char *) &curr, SIZE, 1, f);
        if (curr.studNum == num)
            return(middle * SIZE);
        if (curr.studNum < num)
            bottom = middle + 1;
        else top = middle - 1;
    }
    return(EOF);
}
```

Since `retrieve` and `FileSize` return the position of a record as its byte offset within a file, we had to "scale" the calculations by SIZE.

Finally, remember that the file to be used by the preceding operations must be opened for *both* input and output, using, for example, the `"w+"` mode, rather than the `"w"` mode.

We discuss more advanced file structures, such as files organized as linked lists and binary search trees, in Chapter 13.

EXERCISES   In the following exercises, assume STUDENT is defined as

```
typedef struct {
            char name[30];
            int age;
            float GPA;
        } STUDENT;
```

1. Write a procedure COPY(`fil1`, `fil2`, `limit`) that reads structures of type STUDENT from the file `fil1` and copies those structures whose age field is less than `limit` to the file `fil2`.

2. Write an integer function More(`stufile`, `aver`) that returns 1 if the file `stufile` contains a STUDENT structure whose age field is less than `aver` and that returns 0 otherwise.

3. Write a function update(`stufile`) that increases by 10 percent the GPA of all those students in the file `stufile` who are at least 30 years old.

4. Write a program that reads a text file containing lines of the form

   age GPA name

   and creates a binary file containing corresponding STUDENT structures.

5. Write a program that reads a binary file containing STUDENT structures and creates a text file having lines of the form

   age GPA name

   corresponding to each STUDENT structure.

6. Write a function test(`stufile`) that finds the oldest and youngest students in the file `stufile` and swaps the structures containing

these students. The function returns 1 if two students with different ages exist; it returns 0 otherwise.

7. Write a function `remove(stufile, limit)` that removes from the STUDENT file `stufile` all students whose GPA is less than `limit`. Assume records are deleted by setting the name field to `"***"`.

8. Write a procedure `insert(stufile, name, age, GPA)` that inserts a STUDENT structure with its three fields set to name, age, and GPA, respectively, into the file `stufile`. Assume the file is sorted in ascending order by the name field, and insert the new structure so that the resulting file is still sorted.

9. Write a function `average(stufile)` that returns the average GPA of all students in the STUDENT file `stufile`.

13 Applications to Data Structures

PREVIEW   *This chapter does not introduce any new C constructs. It is an introduction to the implementation of Abstract Data Types (ADTs) in C. By an ADT, we mean an abstract set of operations defined on a certain model. We do not elaborate on Abstract Data Types but refer you to [Aho83] for details. We show three application programs that use some important data structures: a **calculator** with user-defined variables and built-in functions, the Dijkstra algorithm to find the **shortest path** in a graph, and a **database** program.*

*These programs use a variety of data structures, including **linked lists, stacks, hash tables, sets,** and file-based **binary search trees.** We discuss the implementation of these data structures in C. We also show how to implement a linked list of variable size records and discuss a **memory management** system with compaction.*

Even if you are not particularly interested in the three application programs, you should study this chapter carefully because our goal is to demonstrate C implementations of some ADTs and how to use them. Moreover, the programs shown here are larger, complete C programs.

13.1   A CALCULATOR WITH USER-DEFINED VARIABLES

In this section, we describe a program that implements a simple calculator. A "production" version of a program like this would likely use more advanced techniques, such as parsing and interpretation. Since it is beyond the scope of this book to cover these topics, the version we present uses data structures and algorithms either already known to you or easy to understand. The primary purpose here is to present an example of a larger C program and to demonstrate an application of the data structures that have been chosen.

To simplify the implementation, we assume expressions given to the calculator are in **postfix Polish notation** (see [Łuk29]). In postfix notation, there are no parentheses, and operators follow their operands. For example, the infix expression

2 * 3 + 5

is represented as

    2 3 * 5 +

in postfix notation, and

    (2 + 4) * 7

is represented as

    2 4 + 7 *

in postfix notation. If you are interested in the translation of expressions from infix to postfix notation, see [Kru84]. The reason for using postfix notation rather than the more common infix notation is that postfix expressions are easier to evaluate. Moreover, to avoid complications not relevant to this chapter's subject, we consider only binary operators +, −, *, /. We also assume all constants are of type double.

We will design the calculator program in two steps. In this section, we consider a version in which postfix expressions may be entered from the keyboard and their values displayed on the screen, or alternatively, the user may assign expressions to variables. In Section 13.2, we extend this version to allow built-in functions, such as an exponential function, to be used in expressions.

A sample dialog with the first version of the calculator follows:

    > 2 3 * 5 + =
      11.000

Here, > is the prompt displayed by the calculator. Each line should be terminated with =, and values are printed in fixed-point notation, with three digits after the decimal point.

The user can define variables in essentially the same way as in BASIC or FORTRAN, except a postfix notation is used:

    > 2 4 - = a

The variable a defined here may be used later in expressions, for example,

    > 2 a + =
      0.000

Two operators facilitate the use of variables. The first operator @ displays all variables that have been defined along with their current values:

```
> @
  a    -2.000
```

The second operator ! undefines a variable and can be applied to a variable name using a postfix notation:

```
> a!
> a 3 + =
  ? a is undefined
```

This example shows a portion of the error checking provided by the calculator program—if an undefined variable occurs in an expression, a message is displayed, and the entire line is skipped. We later describe the other kinds of error checking provided by this program.

To quit the program, the user enters an empty line. If any variables have been defined, the user is given the option of saving them in a file. These variables can be retrieved from the file when the calculator program is run again:

```
calc filename
```

What data structures are needed in this program? To deal with user-defined variables, we need some kind of table or *dictionary* in which variable names and values will be stored, with the following operations supported:

member(varname)	Return 1 if *varname* is in the dictionary, and 0 otherwise
insert(varname, val)	If *varname* is in the dictionary, change its value to *val*; otherwise, store *varname* and its value in the dictionary
delete(varname)	If *varname* is in the dictionary, remove it and return 1; otherwise, return 0
show	Show all variables and their values
save	Save a dictionary in a file
load	Load a dictionary from a file

To implement the *member* operation, we have to identify the *key* that uniquely determines the object being searched for. In our example, an object in the dictionary contains a variable's name and its value, with the name being the key.

There are many well-known implementations of dictionaries. In our program, we use an **open hash table.** This is an array of linked lists called the bucket table (each list is called a bucket). We therefore need to describe an implementation of ADT LIST, and we choose a pointer-based, singly linked data structure.

We have chosen some particular ADTs to discuss in this chapter but do not intend to provide all possible implementations of these. If you are interested in other versions, see [Aho83], which describes various Pascal implementations that can be translated into C.

To evaluate expressions in postfix notation, the following algorithm may be used:

> *while not end of line*
>   *get a "word"*
>
>   *if the word is a @, show all variables*
>   *if the word is a !, undefine a variable*
>   *if the word is a =, display expression's value, or store it in a variable*
>   *if the word is a number, save it*
>   *if the word is a user-defined variable, save its value*
>   *if the word is an operator, retrieve two most recently saved values,*
>   *apply the operator to these values and save the result*

We thus need a data structure in which we can operate on data in a Last-In-First-Out manner using the following operations:

push(value)	Save a value
pop()	Retrieve the most recently saved value

An ADT that provides these operations is called a STACK. In the following pages, we describe an array-based implementation of a stack, using the concept of dynamic arrays introduced in Chapter 8.

The complete calculator program will consist of four separately compiled files:

`list.c`	Defines list operations
`hash.c`	Defines hash table operations
`stack.c`	Defines stack operations
`calc.c`	Defines the main program for the calculator

There also will be a corresponding header file for each of these ADTs that may be included in any program module that uses a particular ADT. These header files will contain declarations of the operations available for an ADT and associated type definitions. For example, a program that uses the list ADT would include the file `list.h`.

13.1.1 A Pointer Implementation of Singly Linked Lists

There are three basic LIST operations: *insert, delete,* and *member.* We implement these basic operations, as well as an auxiliary function, `ListCr`, which is used to create a new list element. As is typical with pointer-based linked lists, the last element's next field is always NULL; if the list is empty, the variable representing it is NULL.

The list operations defined in list.c that are available to the user are declared in the file list.h:

```
#ifndef MAXS
#define MAXS  20      /* or whatever */
typedef struct ELEM {
            double value;
            struct ELEM *next;
            char name[MAXS + 1];
        } ELEM, *PELEM;
#endif
#ifndef TRUE
typedef int bool;
#define TRUE  1
#define FALSE 0
#endif
extern PELEM ListMem();
extern bool  ListIns();
extern bool  ListDel();
```

Thus if a programmer needs to use the routines defined in list.c to manage linked lists, the user needs to include only the header file list.h in a program to declare these functions and define the types and constants associated with them, and then link this program (after it is compiled) with the compiled version of list.c.

We have used conditional compilation to avoid including the same definitions more than once. (This is required because the header files associated with the other ADTs we describe define some symbols that are the same as those defined in list.h. If conditional compilation were not used and the header files of more than one ADT were included in the same program module, the compiler would complain that the user was trying to define an identifier that has already been defined.)

The first part of list.c lists the include files that it needs, as well as other definitions; specifically,

```
#include <stdio.h>
#include <string.h>
#include <ctype.h>
#include "list.h"
#define NIL    '\0'
```

list.h is included here because it requires the macro and type definitions that are defined in this header file.

The first function we describe is ListCr(name, value). This routine creates a new list element and returns a pointer to this element; if it fails for any reason, it returns NULL. The routine copies the value and the name passed as parameters to the appropriate fields of the new element. The name passed to the function is truncated to MAXS characters if necessary. Since this function is to be used only in the file list.c, its declaration is not included in list.h. Moreover, to limit the scope of this function to list.c, it is defined as static.

```
static PELEM ListCr(name, value)
char name[];
double value;
{
      PELEM aux;
      char *malloc();

      if (name == NULL)
          return(NULL);
      if ((aux = (PELEM) malloc(sizeof(ELEM))) == NULL)
          return(NULL);

      strncpy(aux->name, name, MAXS);
      if (strlen(name) > MAXS)
          name[MAXS + 1] = NIL;
      aux->value = value;
      aux->next = NULL;

      return(aux);
}
```

The next function is ListMem(head, name). This function implements the *member* operation; it searches for the specified name in the list pointed to by head and returns a pointer to the list element containing that name, or if the name is not in the list, it returns NULL.

```
PELEM ListMem(head, name)
PELEM head;
char name[];
{
      if (name == NULL)
          return(NULL);

      for (; head != NULL && strcmp(head->name, name);
          head = head->next)
          ;
      return(head);
}
```

The stop condition evaluates to false either if head is NULL (indicating the end of the list has been encountered) or if the string name is found.

The function ListIns(head, name, value) inserts an element containing the specified name and value in front of the list pointed to by head. It returns TRUE if successful and FALSE otherwise. The parameter head must be passed by reference because it will be modified.

```
bool ListIns(head, name, value)
PELEM *head;
char name[];
double value;
{
      PELEM first;

      if ((first = ListCr(name, value)) == NULL)
            return(FALSE);

      first->next = *head;
      *head = first;
      return(TRUE);
}
```

The last function ListDel(head, name) removes the element containing the given name from the list pointed to by head and returns TRUE; it returns FALSE if the name is not in the list.

```
bool ListDel(head, name)
PELEM *head;
char name[];
{
      PELEM curr = *head,
            pred = *head;

      if (curr == NULL || name == NULL)
            return(FALSE);

      /* check the first element */
      if (strcmp(curr->name, name) == 0) {
            *head = curr->next;
            free((char *)curr);
            return(TRUE);
      }

      /* search */
      for (curr = curr->next; curr != NULL; pred = curr,
            curr = curr->next)
            if (strcmp(curr->name, name) == 0) {
                  pred->next = curr->next;
                  free((char *)curr);
                  return(TRUE);
            }
      return(FALSE);
}
```

The for statement is used here if at least one element is in the list, and the first element is not the one we want to delete. The search for the value to delete is implemented using two pointers—one pointing to the current element and the other pointing to the current element's predecessor. Both pointers are maintained during the search because, when the required element is found, we need to modify its predecessor.

13.1.2 Linked Lists of Objects of Variable Sizes

The definition of ELEM provided in list.h wastes memory when names
are less than MAXS characters long. An alternative solution would be to
use a pointer to character:

```
typedef struct ELEM {
            double value;
            struct ELEM *next;
            char *name;
        } ELEM1, *PELEM1;
```

A disadvantage of this approach is that when a new list element is created, memory must be allocated twice—for the structure and for the
string contained in the structure. Similarly, when an element is deleted
from the list, two memory blocks must be freed. Because of this increased number of memory allocation and deallocation operations, the
system heap may become **fragmented**, that is, divided into a number of
small blocks of used and unused memory. Thus a memory allocation operation may fail because no single memory block on the heap is large
enough to satisfy the request, although much unused memory may exist. Some operating systems implement so-called **heap compaction**—all
available blocks of memory are shifted to one end of the heap and combined into a single block.

   Unfortunately, simple memory management systems cannot provide
memory compaction. Suppose p is a pointer, and a call to a memory allocation operation initialized p to point to the base of a block in the heap.
When the heap is compacted, the allocated block may be shifted, and so
the value of p (which still points to the same place) would become meaningless.

   An implementation of a memory management system with a compaction scheme as described here is presented in Section 13.3. For now,
we use C's malloc function to allocate memory.

   The problem at hand is to create a linked list of variable size objects.
Let us recall the definition of the type ELEM:

```
typedef struct ELEM {
            double value;
            struct ELEM *next;
            char name[MAXS + 1];
        } ELEM, *PELEM;
```

The first two components occupy a fixed number of bytes, and the last
component occupies a variable number of bytes depending on the length
of the name. Therefore, it is important that we place name as the last
component of the structure. When a list element is to be created, we
will not allocate sizeof(ELEM) bytes; instead, we will allocate the exact number of bytes needed to store the components, recognizing that

the `name` component is variable in size. Thus the size specified for the array name will not necessarily be MAXS+1 characters. The total number of bytes we need can be computed using the macro

```
#define ELEMSIZE(str)    (sizeof(ELEM) - MAXS + \
                             strlen(str))
```

where `str` is a pointer to character that represents the string to be stored in the structure.

The definition of the function `ListCr`, assuming variable size elements, follows:

```
PELEM ListCr(name, value)
char name[];
double *value;
{
     PELEM aux;
     char *malloc();

     if (name == NULL)
          return(NULL);
     if ((aux = (PELEM) malloc(ELEMSIZE(name))) == NULL)
               return(NULL);
     ...
```

The rest of the function is identical to the previous version of `ListCr`, which created fixed-size objects. The only required change in this version is the memory allocation statement.

13.1.3 Open Hash Table

As we mentioned, an open hash table is an appropriate data structure for representing a DICTIONARY. The main idea of a hash table is to use a function, called a **hash** function, that maps key values to nonnegative integer values less than a certain integer constant B. The value generated by the hash function is then used to index into the bucket table; if the value being searched for is in the dictionary, it must be in this bucket. Therefore, the size of the bucket table is B.

As before, we create a header file `hash.h` that may be included in a user's program to provide the definitions needed for using the hash operations:

```
#ifndef MAXS
#define MAXS  20     /* or whatever */
typedef struct ELEM {
          double value;
          struct ELEM *next;
          char name[MAXS + 1];
     } ELEM, *PELEM;
```

```
#endif
#ifndef TRUE
typedef int bool;
#define TRUE   1
#define FALSE  0
#endif
extern PELEM HashMem();
extern bool  HashVal();
extern bool  HashIns();
extern void  HashSh();
extern bool  HashSav();
extern bool  HashLoa();
extern void  HashIni();
```

Again, we use conditional compilation here to avoid defining symbols that have already been defined.

The file hash.c starts out much like list.c, listing the necessary include files and other related definitions. Since the hash routines we describe here use the list operations discussed previously, the header file list.h is included:

```
#include <stdio.h>
#include <string.h>
#include <ctype.h>
#include "list.h"
#include "hash.h"
#define NIL     '\0'

#define B   117                    /* or whatever */
static PELEM BuckTab[B];
```

Although both header files list.h and hash.h contain some identical definitions, for example, the type bool, only one of these definitions will be actually compiled because of the conditional compilation used in these header files.

The array BuckTab is defined as static to restrict its scope to the file hash.c; access to this array from within program modules other than hash.c will be provided indirectly through operations defined in hash.h and visible externally.

A hash function can be implemented in many ways. We provided a relatively sophisticated example in Example 11.1.2; here we use a simpler version:

```
static int hash(name)
char name[];
{
     int aux;

     for (aux = 0; *name; aux += *name++)
          ;
     return aux % B;
}
```

The value returned by the function is in the range 0 to B−1.

Now for the functions that manage the open hash table. The first function, HashMem(name), returns a pointer to the record containing the specified name if it is in the hash table; otherwise, it returns NULL:

```
PELEM HashMem(name)
char name[];
{
      return ListMem(BuckTab[hash(name)], name);
}
```

In the calculator program, this function has limited application; we include it here because, in general, it is an essential component of a DICTIONARY ADT.

The next function, HashVal(name, val), returns TRUE if the specified name is in the hash table and passes the value of this variable back through the parameter val; if the name is not there, the function returns FALSE:

```
bool HashVal(name, val)
char name[];
double *val;
{
      PELEM aux;

      if ((aux = HashMem(name)) == NULL)
            return FALSE;

      *val = aux->value;
      return TRUE;
}
```

The function HashIns(name, val) checks if name is already in a table, and if so, updates its value to val; otherwise, it stores the new name and its value in the dictionary. The operation returns TRUE if successful and FALSE otherwise:

```
bool HashIns(name, val)
char name[];
double val;
{
      int h;
      PELEM el;

      el = ListMem(BuckTab[h = hash(name)], name);
      if (el != NULL) {
            el->value = val;
            return TRUE;
      }
      return ListIns(&BuckTab[h], name, val);
}
```

The function HashDel(name) checks whether name is in the dictionary, and if so, removes it and returns TRUE; otherwise it returns FALSE:

```
bool HashDel(name)
char name[];
{
    return ListDel(&BuckTab[hash(name)], name);
}
```

The function HashSh() shows all variables that have been defined along with their current values:

```
void HashSh()
{
    PELEM aux, *haux;

    for (haux = BuckTab; haux < BuckTab + B; haux++)
        for (aux = *haux; aux; aux = aux->next)
            printf("%20s%20.3f\n",aux->name,aux->value);
}
```

We have used the pointer haux here to traverse the array BuckTab rather than an integer index.

The function HashSav(fname) saves the hash table in the file fname. To implement this operation, we assume the buckets hold fixed-size elements. Of the three fields in the ELEM structure, only two are stored in the file—the value of the pointer next would be meaningless when later retrieved from the file. Therefore, we define another structure that will be used to extract, and later to retrieve, these two fields:

```
typedef struct {
            double value1;
            char name1[MAXS + 1];
        } ELEM1, *PELEM1;

bool HashSav(fname)
char fname[];
{
    FILE *f;
    PELEM aux, *haux;
    ELEM1 kopy;

    if (fname == NULL || (f = fopen(fname, "w")) == NULL)
        return FALSE;
```

```
                /* for each bucket in the table */
                for (haux = BuckTab; haux < BuckTab + B; haux++)
                        /* for each element in a bucket */
                        for (aux = *haux; aux; aux = aux->next) {
                                /* copy the value and name fields to kopy */
                                kopy.value1 = aux->value;
                                strcpy(kopy.name1, aux->name);
                                if (fwrite((char*)&kopy,sizeof(ELEM1),1,f) == 0)
                                        return FALSE;
                        }

                if (fclose(f) == EOF)
                        return FALSE;
                return TRUE;
        }
```

The function HashLoa(fname) loads the hash table from the file fname:

```
        bool HashLoa(fname)
        char fname[];
        {
                FILE *f;
                ELEM1 kopy;

                if (fname == NULL !! (f = fopen(fname, "r")) == NULL)
                        return FALSE;

                /* for each record in the file */
                while (fread((char *)&kopy, sizeof(ELEM1), 1, f))
                        /* insert it into the hash table */
                        if (!HashIns(kopy.name1, kopy.value1))
                                return FALSE;

                if (fclose(f) == EOF)
                        return FALSE;
                return TRUE;
        }
```

The last operation, HashIni(), initializes the table:

```
        void HashIni()
        {
                PELEM *haux;

                for (haux = BuckTab; haux < BuckTab + B; haux++)
                        *haux = NULL;
        }
```

13.1.4 Array Implementation of ADT Stack

As with the list and hash structures, two files are associated with our STACK ADT. The file stack.h declares the associated constants, types, and operations available to manipulate stacks of real numbers:

```
#define STACKINIT 50              /* initial size */
#define MEMORY  1                 /* error codes */
#define EMPTY   2
extern int StackErr;
#ifndef TRUE
typedef int bool;
#define TRUE  1
#define FALSE 0
#endif
extern bool StackIni();
extern void push();
extern double pop();
extern bool empty();
```

The file stack.c contains the code for the routines declared in stack.h. We now describe how these routines are implemented. In the implementation we have chosen, as we mentioned, a stack will be stored in an array. To avoid problems with overflowing the stack, we increase the size of the array that it is stored in every time it becomes full, and we decrease it when it has grown more than twice its original size and a large part of it is not being used.

To handle errors that may occur (for example, trying to pop an item from an empty stack), the global variable StackErr will be used; this variable will be set either to 0 if an operation is successful or to the code of the error if not.

```
#include <stdio.h>
#include <string.h>
#include <ctype.h>
#include "stack.h"
static unsigned size = STACKINIT;
static double *stack;
static double *top;
int StackErr = 0;

extern char *calloc();
#define GET(st, siz) if (((st) =  \
        (double*)calloc(sizeof(double), (siz))) == NULL) \
              { StackErr = MEMORY;  return FALSE; }
```

The macro GET is used to get memory if the stack needs to be increased in size. The variable StackErr is not defined as static because it may be accessed in the main program to determine the cause of a failure.

The function StackIni() initializes the stack:

```
bool StackIni()
{
    GET(stack, size)
    top = stack;
    return TRUE;
}
```

The function pop() removes the value on top of the stack and returns this value. If the stack happens to be empty, pop returns 0 (strictly as a dummy value) and sets the variable StackErr to EMPTY. This solution is a compromise to simplify the implementation of the calculator. For example, to perform addition, we will have to say

```
push(pop() + pop());
if (!StackErr)
        . . .
```

In the code of pop, we check if the stack is more than twice its original size and is 90% empty; if so, we decrease the size of the stack by half. We use the function expand to change the size of the stack. If the third argument to this routine is LESS, the stack is decreased in size, and if it is MORE, it is increased in size, where LESS and MORE are values of an enumeration type:

```
enum expan {
    LESS, MORE
};

double pop()
{
    if (top == stack) {  /* empty */
        StackErr = EMPTY;
        return 0;
    }
    if (size > 2*STACKINIT && (top - stack) < size / 10 + 1)
        if (!expand(&stack, &size, LESS))
                return 0;
    return *--top;
}
```

The routine push(val) adds the item val to the stack. It is defined as

```
void push(val)
double val;
{
    if (top == stack + size)  /* full */
        if (!expand(&stack, &size, MORE))
                return;
  *top++ = val;
}
```

The function expand allocates an array either twice or half the size of the current stack, copies the stack to the new area, frees the old stack, and reassigns the top pointer:

```
static bool expand(st, siz, e)
double **st;
int *siz;
enum expan e;
{
      double *newst, *aux1, *aux2;

      *siz = (e == MORE) ? *siz * 2 : *siz / 2;
      GET(newst, *siz)
      for (aux1 = newst, aux2 = *st; aux2 <= top;
                  *aux1++ = *aux2++)
            ;
      top = aux1 - 1;
      free((char *)*st);
      *st = newst;
      return TRUE;
}
```

This dynamic changing of the size of the stack is *transparent* to the user. In a well-designed ADT, however, hiding details like this from the user is important. Static variables and functions often play a major role in achieving this transparency.

The last simple function we need is

```
bool empty()
{
      return top == stack;
}
```

13.1.5 The Main Program

In this section, we describe the contents of the file calc.c, which implements the auxiliary and main functions for the calculator program. To process each input line, we read a word at a time, and depending on the kind of word, perform some action.

A **word** is not simply a sequence of non-whitespace characters; for example,

```
10PI+
```

consists of three words—10, PI, and +. We therefore use the term **token** to describe a sequence of characters that forms a single meaningful symbol in an expression. Extracting tokens from the input stream is called **scanning**. Two global variables will be used for scanning: The character array input will store the current input line, and the character pointer `curr` will point to the current character in the input array. We assume a user-defined name is a sequence of letters and digits, starting with a letter.

The function `GetTok()` skips whitespace and copies a single token from the array `input` into the global array `TokName` and updates the pointer `curr`. It returns the kind of token found. We define an enumeration type `TOKEN` to identify the kind of token:

```
typedef enum {
            EOS, SHOW, UNDEFINE, EQUAL,
            CONSTANT, OPERATOR, NAME, OTHER
        } TOKEN;
```

where the individual values represent the following tokens:

EOS	End of string encountered
SHOW	@
UNDEFINE	!
EQUAL	=
CONSTANT	A double number
OPERATOR	+, −, *, /
NAME	Identifier
OTHER	Anything else

The tokens `CONSTANT`, `OPERATOR`, and `NAME` also have a value associated with them: For a `CONSTANT`, `GetTok` stores its value in the global `double` variable `TokValue`; for a `NAME`, `GetTok` stores its value in the global character array `TokName`; and for an `OPERATOR`, `GetTok` stores its ordinal value in the global integer `TokOper`.

In the main program, the hash table and the stack are initialized. If the command line used to invoke the program contains a filename, this file is assumed to contain a hash table saved from a previous execution, and this table is loaded into the internal dictionary. The processing of input lines then begins. The main loop is

```
while (PROMPT, gets(input) && input[0])
        ...
```

and so in each step, a prompt is displayed and a new line is read into the array `input`. The loop terminates either if end-of-file is encountered (`gets` returns NULL) or if an empty line is entered by the user (which would mean `input[0]` is equal to \0). Now the input line is stored in the array `input` and can be scanned.

The scanning is performed by the loop:

```
while ((t = GetTok()) != EOS)
```

which terminates when the end-of-string is encountered.

The main program follows:

```c
#include <stdio.h>
#include <ctype.h>
#include "stack.h"
#include "hash.h"
#define NIL '\0'

char input[MAXS + 1];
char *curr;
char TokName[MAXS + 1];
double TokValue;
int TokOper;

#define PROMPT          printf("> ")
#define ERROR1(mes)     printf((mes))
#define ERROR2(tok)     printf("? %s undefined\n", (tok))
#define CLEAR           while (!empty()) pop()
#define PR(arg)         printf("%.3f\n", (arg))

typedef enum {
            EOS, SHOW, UNDEFINE, EQUAL,
            CONSTANT, OPERATOR, NAME, OTHER
        } TOKEN;

main(argc, argv)
int argc;
char *argv[];
{
    double val;
    TOKEN GetTok(), t;
    bool error;
    extern bool process();

    if (argc > 2) {
        printf("usage: %s filename\n", *argv);
        return;
    }

    HashIni();
    StackIni();
    if (argc == 2 && !HashLoa(argv[1]) )
        printf("Cannot read file %s\n", argv[1]);

    while (PROMPT, gets(input) && input[0]) {
        CLEAR;          /* empty stack in case of errors */
        curr = input; /* set current character pointer */
        error = FALSE;

        while ((t = GetTok()) != EOS) {
            switch (t) {
            case SHOW  : /* display variables and values */
                    HashSh();
                    goto end; /* do not read more tokens */
            case UNDEFINE : /* delete identifier from table */
```

```
                               if (!HashDel(TokName))
                                       error = TRUE;
                               goto end;
                case EQUAL :
                               goto end;
                case CONSTANT : /* save constants on the stack */
                               push(TokValue);
                               break;
                case OPERATOR : /* process operator token */
                               if (!process(TokOper)) {
                                       error = TRUE;
                                       goto end;
                               }
                               break;
                case NAME : /* retrieve its value */
                               if (!HashVal(TokName,&val)) {
                                       error = TRUE;
                                       ERROR2(TokName);
                                       goto end;
                               }
                               push(val);
                               break;
                case OTHER : /* error detected */
                               error = TRUE;
                               break;
                }
        }

        /* check if there was an error */
        end: if (error) {
                       ERROR1("error occurred\n")
                       continue;
        }
        /* an input line can be of the form "... =" or "... = name" */
        if (t == EQUAL) { /* get next token */
                if ((t = GetTok()) == EOS) {
                        val = pop(); /* output expression value if EOLN */
                        PR(val);
                }
                else if (t == NAME) {
                        val = pop();  /* save value in hash table if name */
                        if (!HashIns(TokName, val))
                                ERROR1("cannot insert to hash table\n")
                } else ERROR2(TokName);
        }
}

/* save hash table if necessary */
if (argc == 2 && !HashSav(argv[1]))
        printf("? cannot save the hash table\n");
}
```

All constant values are pushed on the stack. Similarly, when names are encountered, their current values are pushed on the stack. If an operator is encountered, the function `process` performs the corresponding action.

Error processing is rather limited. A boolean variable `error` is used as an error flag, and it is set if any error occurs. We have used `goto` statements because `break` used within a `switch` would not terminate the `while` statement that encloses this `switch`. These `goto` statements are used when an error occurs, when an end-of-line is expected (for example, after a @), and when a = is encountered. In this last case, outside the scanning loop, we check whether the = is the last token on the input line, and if so, print the value on top of the stack. Otherwise, a name is expected, and so the value from the stack is stored in the hash table as the current value of that name.

The function `process` is used to perform the indicated operation. It pops two values off the stack and applies the operator to them. The result is pushed onto the stack.

```
bool process(oper)
int oper;
{
        double aux;

        switch (oper) {
        case '+': push(pop() + pop());
                  break;
        case '*': push(pop() * pop());
                  break;
        case '-': aux = pop();
                  push(pop() - aux);
                  break;
        case '/': aux = pop();
                  if (aux == 0) {
                          printf("division by 0\n");
                          return FALSE;
                  }
                  push(pop() / aux);
                  break;
        default : printf("unknown operator\n");
                  return FALSE;
        }

        return TRUE;
}
```

To simplify the code, the function does not use certain facilities provided in our implementation of stacks. For example, we could have used the variable `StackErr` to issue an error message when an attempt to pop a value from an empty stack is made (this may happen, for example, for an input line

```
2 3 + *
```

in which the multiplication operation would pop two values when one only is available). We encourage you to add the code for more complete error processing and recovery.

Finally, let us look at the code for *scanning*. Recall that GetTok extracts tokens from the global array input, using a pointer curr. We define an auxiliary macro GETCHAR to extract a single character from this array:

```
#define GETCHAR    (*curr == NIL ? *curr : *curr++)
```

When extracting some kinds of tokens, for example, numbers, we have to "unget" one character. This action is performed by another macro:

```
#define UNGETCHAR    if (curr >= input && c != NIL ) curr--;
```

Here, c is the current character (defined in the function GetTok). Let us explain the reason for the test

```
c != NIL
```

used in this macro. GETCHAR will be called using

```
c = GETCHAR
```

and so curr is pointing one character ahead in the array input. In some cases, for example, when a digit is the last character in input, the value of c is identical to the value pointed to by curr, and ungetting one character would restore a character that has already been processed (and may lead to an infinite loop).

The code for GetTok, described previously, follows:

```
TOKEN GetTok()
{
    int c;

    /* skip leading whitespace */
    do
        c = GETCHAR;
    while (isspace(c));

    switch (c) {
    case NIL : return EOS;
    case '@' : return SHOW;
    case '=' : return EQUAL;
    case '!' : return UNDEFINE;
    case '+' :
    case '-' :
    case '*' :
    case '/' : TokOper = c;
               return OPERATOR;
```

```
default   : { /* numeric or alphanumeric token */
             char *p = TokName;
             if (isalpha(c)) {   /* identifier */
                 while (isalnum(c)) {
                     *p++ = c;
                     c = GETCHAR;
                 }
                 *p = NIL;
                 UNGETCHAR
                 return NAME;
             }
             else if (isdigit(c)) {   /* numeric */
                 while (isdigit(c)) {
                     *p++ = c;
                     c = GETCHAR;
                 }
                 if (c == '.') {
                     *p++ = c;
                     c = GETCHAR;
                     while (isdigit(c)) {
                         *p++ = c;
                         c = GETCHAR;
                     }
                 }

                 *p = NIL;
                 UNGETCHAR
                 sscanf(TokName, "%lf", &TokValue);
                 return CONSTANT;
             }
             else return OTHER; /* unknown token kind */
         }
     }
}
```

13.2   A CALCULATOR WITH BUILT-IN FUNCTIONS

In this section, we describe an extension of the calculator program that includes *built-in* functions. The input line may now contain calls to some built-in functions using the same postfix notation used for regular operators, for example,

```
> 2 4 pow
  16.000
```

where pow is a power function. Since the calculator uses postfix notation, x y pow is x to the power y.

To support this new feature, we extend the hash table so that it may contain both user-defined names and built-in functions. We do not discuss how expressions in this extended calculator are evaluated; this we leave for you to do as an exercise.

For simplicity, we assume all built-in functions are of type `double` and have one or two arguments. A built-in function will be stored in a bucket corresponding to the hash value of its name. Therefore, two kinds of bucket elements will be in a list: One kind will be used to store built-in functions, and each of these elements will contain the function name, the number of parameters this function takes, and a pointer to the actual code that implements the function's actions. The other kind will be used to store user-defined variables and will be essentially identical to that given in Section 13.1.3.

To begin with, we describe the modified lists. The enumerated type `KIND` will be used to determine whether the element contains a function or a variable:

```
typedef enum {
        FKIND, VKIND
    } KIND;
```

The structure `ELEM` will now contain a common part and two variants, defined using a `union`:

```
typedef struct ELEM {
        KIND    kind;
        char    name[MAXS + 1];
        struct  ELEM *next;
        union {
            struct {
                    int    fpars;
                    double (*fptr)();
            } f;
            double value;
        } v;
    } ELEM, *PELEM;
```

The types of the nested `union` and `structure` do not have names because we will not need them.

Since list elements may be one of two possible variants, we need two separate functions to create list objects. The first one, `ListCrV`, is used to create a new list element for a user-defined variable and is essentially identical to `ListCr` defined in Section 13.1.1. The other function, `ListCrF`, is used to create a list element representing a built-in function:

```
static PELEM ListCrF(fname, fpars, fptr)
char fname[];
int fpars;
double (*fptr)();
{
    PELEM aux;
    char *malloc();
```

```
         if (fname == NULL)
             return(NULL);
         if ((aux = (PELEM) malloc(sizeof(ELEM))) == NULL)
             return(NULL);
         if (strlen(fname) > MAXS)
             fname[MAXS] = NIL;
         aux->kind = FKIND;
         strncpy(aux->name, fname, MAXS);
         aux->next = NULL;
         aux->v.f.fpars = fpars;
         aux->v.f.fptr  = fptr;
         return(aux);
}
```

The only other list operation that has to be redefined is *insert*. Again, we have two operations: ListInsV, to insert a new element containing a user-defined name, and ListInsF, to insert a new element containing a built-in function:

```
bool ListInsF(head, fname, fpars, fptr)
PELEM *head;
char fname[];
int fpars;
double (*fptr)();
{
     PELEM first;

     first = *head;
     if ((*head = ListCrF(fname, fpars, fptr)) == NULL)
             return(FALSE);
     (*head)->next = first;
     return(TRUE);
}
```

Now we outline the *hash* operations. As before, there are operations to insert a new function or user variable and operations to retrieve the value of an existing function or user variable:

```
bool HashInsF(fname, fpars, fptr)        bool HashInsV(name, val)
char fname[];                            char name[];
int fpars;                               double val;
double (*fptr)();

bool HashValF(fname, fpars, fptr)        bool HashValV(name, val)
char fname[];                            char name[];
int *fpars;                              double *val;
double (*fptr)();
```

The two following examples show how basic mathematical functions can be added to the hash table. To install the exponential function, the call

```
HashInsF("exp", 1, exp);
```

would be made. The first parameter represents the function name, the second parameter represents the number of arguments the function takes, and the third parameter represents the function itself. Similarly, to include the function pow, the call

```
HashInsF("pow", 2, pow);
```

would be given. To use C's mathematical functions, the header math.h should be included.

To demonstrate yet another C programming technique, let us consider a variation of the calculator program in which there are built-in functions but no user-defined variables.

Since there are only a few functions, a simple array rather than a hash table can be used to represent the function table, with the functions defined sorted by name to speed up search time:

```
typedef struct {
            char    *fname;
            int     fpars;
            double  (*fptr)();
        } FELEM;

static FELEM table[] = {
    { "exp", 1, exp },
    { "log", 1, log },
    { "pow", 2, pow },
    ...
}
```

The size of the array table has not been specified in the definition—it will be calculated by the compiler using the list of initializers. If the size of this array is needed in the program, a macro could be used:

```
#define TSIZE       (sizeof(table) / sizeof(FELEM))
```

Since most of the routines to implement this calculator program are nearly identical to those we have already looked at, we show only one function, eval(fname, val), which returns through the parameter val the value of the function fname. We assume the actual parameters have been pushed on the calculator's stack, with the first parameter being on top. As before, we assume the built-in functions have either one or two arguments.

The first action of the function eval is to find the entry representing the function fname in the array table. Since the array is assumed to be sorted on function names, we may use a binary search:

```
bool eval (fname, val)
char fname[];
double *val;
{
     FELEM *b, *e, *m;
     int notdone;
     double par1, par2;

     if (fname == NULL)
          return(FALSE);

     /* search the array table */
     for (b = table, e = table + TSIZE - 1; b <= e; ) {
          m = b + (e - b) / 2;
          notdone = strcmp(m->fname, fname);
          if (notdone == 0)
               break;
          else if (notdone < 0)
               b = m + 1;
          else e = m - 1;
     }

     if (notdone)
          return(FALSE);
     par1 = pop();
     if (StackErr)
          return(FALSE);
     switch (m->fpars) {
     case 1 : *val = (*m->fptr)(par1);
               return(TRUE);
     case 2 : par2 = pop();
               if (StackErr)
                    return(FALSE);
               *val = (*m->fptr)(par1, par2);
               return(TRUE);
     }
}
```

We have used pointers to implement the binary search. The pointer b
points to the beginning of the array, and the pointer e points to the end.
In each step of the loop, the pointer m is set to b+(e−b)/2. This expression is valid because e−b is the integer distance between e and b,
and so b+(e−b)/2 is a pointer pointing to a point halfway between b
and e. Note how the function fptr is called.

13.3 A MEMORY MANAGEMENT SYSTEM WITH COMPACTION

In this section, we describe a user-defined memory management system
that supports heap compaction. A simpler system without compaction is
described in [Ker78]. We first describe the memory management system
and then show some possible applications. The system presented here
may seem rather cumbersome. Still, implementing this system gives us

a chance to introduce several interesting concepts, and the system itself may indeed prove useful in some applications.

In a typical memory management system, a **heap** is a contiguous area of memory divided into blocks of used and unused memory. The system maintains a list of the unused blocks (the **free list**). Initially, the heap consists of a single large block. Associated with a heap are two basic functions:

getmem(size)   Get a block of length size from the heap and return a pointer to the beginning of this block

freemem(p)   Return the block pointed to by p to the free list

These two routines have to deal with several issues. When a block of memory is returned to the free list, it should be checked whether or not it can be combined with either of its neighboring blocks. When a new block is to be allocated, one can be selected from the free list using the first-fit, best-fit, or worst-fit algorithm. The **first-fit** algorithm chooses the first free block large enough to satisfy the request. The **best-fit** algorithm looks for the smallest block that satisfies the request. The **worst-fit** algorithm looks for the largest block in the free list that satisfies the request. For more details about these algorithms, see [Aho83].

This system cannot support compaction (as described in 13.1.2) because the pointers obtained by calls to getmem point directly to the heap—if a block in the heap is moved, any pointers being used to access this block still point to where the block used to be, not to where it has been moved. To allow compaction, an intermediate or **master** array is required. Pointers returned by getmem will never point directly to the heap; instead, they will point to the master array, which in turn, will contain pointers to the heap.

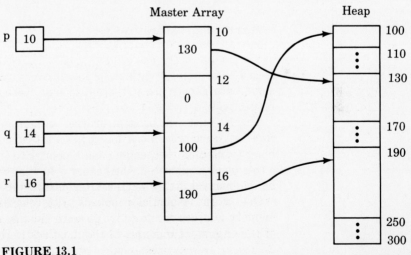

FIGURE 13.1

We assume the size of the blocks allocated on the heap are 10, 40, and 60 bytes, respectively. Compaction is now possible because moving blocks within the heap will not change the values of the user's pointers—they will still point to the same entries in the master array. Only the pointers in the master array will change.

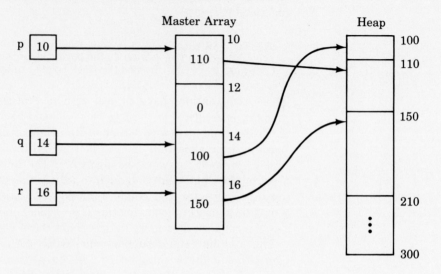

FIGURE 13.2

In the later part of this section, we describe some rules that must be followed when using this kind of system. Some basic definitions follow:

```
#define HEAPS        1000      /* size of the heap */
#define MASTERS      50        /* number of master pointers */

static char heap[HEAPS];
static char *master[MASTERS];
```

Recall that a static variable is initialized to zero; we can therefore assume both arrays are initialized to null characters and NULL pointers, respectively.

The free list will be kept ordered in storage order. To maintain the free list, each free block has a header that contains the length of the block (excluding the header) and a pointer to the next free block. When a free block is allocated, the header is kept so that the block's length can be determined if this block is later deallocated.

One of the essential problems with allocating memory is that the memory address returned by ge tmem must be adjusted to be a multiple of the alignment modulus of the most restrictive type (see Chapter 7).

Each block in the heap will be aligned to this type. In our example, we assume int is the most restrictive type (this is the case on the PDP-11 and VAX 11/780, as well as others).

```
typedef int  ALIGNED;
typedef union head {
     struct {
          union head *next;
          unsigned   len;
     } h;
     ALIGNED r;   /* this definition forces alignment */
} HEADER;
#define SIZEH  (sizeof(HEADER))
```

The free list will have a header:

```
static HEADER head;
```

The header's next field points to the first free block; the header's len field will not be used. A macro EMPTY is used to test whether or not the free list is empty:

```
#define EMPTY   (head.h.next == NULL)
```

Each element on the free list will start with a header, and similarly, each block allocated for the user will start with a header. In both cases, the value of the len field in a header will not include the size of a header.

The procedure MemIni is used to initialize the heap and the master array:

```
void MemIni()
{
     head.h.len = 0;                       /* not really needed */
     head.h.next = (HEADER*) heap;
     head.h.next->h.len = HEAPS - SIZEH;
     head.h.next->h.next = NULL;
}
```

The header's next field is now pointing to the heap. In the heap itself, one header has been allocated. Its length is the size of the heap decreased by the size of the header, and its next field is NULL.

The function MasNext returns the next available entry in the master array or EOF if it fails. The global variable nextav points one entry beyond where the previous available entry was determined to be and is used to start this new search:

```
static int nextav = 0;
```

```
int MasNext()
{
    int i, res;

    for (i = 0; i < MASTERS; i++)  {
        res = nextav++;
        nextav %= MASTERS;
        if (!master[res])
            return(res);
    }
    return(EOF);
}
```

The function getmem(size) allocates an unused entry in the master array, takes a block (or a part of it) from the free list, saves the base address of this block in the master array, and returns a pointer to this entry in the master array. Thus the type of getmem is a pointer to pointer to char.

The block allocated on the heap is preceded by the header that contains the length of this block; the value of the pointer in the master array is the address immediately beyond the header.

The requested size is rounded up to the nearest alignment multiple using the following macro:

```
#define round(arg) ((sizeof(ALIGNED)-1+(unsigned)(arg)) & \
                     (~(sizeof(ALIGNED)-1)))

char **getmem(size)
unsigned size;
{
    HEADER *curr, *pred, *left;
    int fit = 0,
        i;

    if (size == 0 || EMPTY)
        return(NULL);
    size = round(size);

    /* use first-fit to find a block of the requested size */
    /* If found, pred points to its predecessor on the */
    /* free list */
    for (pred = &head, curr = head.h.next; curr != NULL;
                pred = curr, curr = curr->h.next)
        if ((fit = curr->h.len - size) >= 0) { /* found */
            fit = (fit < SIZEH) ? 1 : 0;
            /* check leftover */
            break;
        }
```

```
        if (fit < 0)    /* not found, compact  */
            if (!compact())  /* no compaction was possible */
                return(NULL);
            else return(getmem(size)); /* check new free list */
    else  { /* block found, allocate master array entry */
        if ((i = MasNext()) == EOF)
            return(NULL);
        if (fit == 1)        /* perfect match  */
            pred->h.next = curr->h.next;
        else {       /* try to merge with neighbors */
            /* update predecessor's next */
            pred->h.next = left =
              (HEADER *)( (char *)curr + size + SIZEH);
            /* set up fields in leftover part */
            left->h.next = curr->h.next;
            left->h.len  = curr->h.len - size - SIZEH;
            /* set length of new block */
            curr->h.len = size;
        }
        /* skip the header */
        master[i] = (char *)(curr + 1);
        return(&master[i]);
    }
}
```

We have used the *first-fit* algorithm to look for a block of the requested size. Since the free list is to be updated, the search uses two pointers, one pointing to the current block and another pointing to its predecessor. If a block large enough to satisfy the request is found, we check whether or not the space that would be left over from this block after allocating memory for the requested block is smaller than a header; if it is, fit is set to 1; otherwise, it is set to 0. If the leftover is smaller than a header, it would never be allocated by later calls to getmem; thus it is better to include this small amount of additional space into the block being allocated. If the leftover is larger than a header, it is added to the free list.

If the first-fit algorithm fails to find an appropriate block, a function compact is called to compact the memory in the heap. This function returns FALSE if it cannot improve the free list; otherwise, it returns TRUE. After a successful compaction, getmem is called recursively to try once more to get the required block of memory.

The algorithm for compact is somewhat involved, and so we describe it first in pseudo-code:

if there is at most 1 element on the free list
    return 0
destination = first free block

> *for each element p on the free list do*
>   *source = the used block B following p in the heap*
>   *size   = the size of B*
>   *move size bytes from the source to the destination*
>   *update all pointers from the master array*
>   *update all pointers from the master array pointing to the block B*
>   *increase destination by the size*

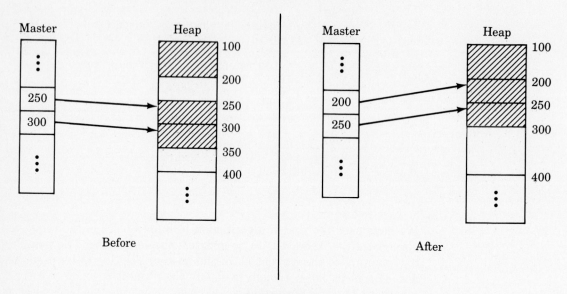

Compaction
(shaded areas are used, others are free)

FIGURE 13.3

Some implementations provide an efficient way of moving a block of memory using an optimized assembly code routine; this operation is usually called movmem. For the sake of those implementations that do not provide this nonstandard function, we provide a (less efficient) C version:

```
static void movmem(source, destin, size)
char *source, *destin;
unsigned size;
{
        if (destin < source + size && destin > source)
                for (source += size-1, destin += size-1;
                        size--; *destin-- = *source--)
                        ;
        else while (size--)
                        *destin++ = *source++;
}
```

The first of these two cases is when a block to be moved overlaps with the original block.

The function update(low, high, size) increments by size the values of all pointers from the master array into the memory block between the values of low and high. To optimize the code, a variable front is maintained to point to the first entry in the master array that may be subject to update. This function will be called in compact every time a block in the heap is moved to update the master array. In the first call of update in compact, any unused entries in the master array are skipped, and front points to the first used entry. In successive calls, front is incremented when appropriate.

```c
static int front = 0;

static void update(low, high, size)
char *low, *high;
unsigned size;
{
    int aux;

    if (size == 0 || low >= high)
        return;

    for (; master[front] == NULL;  front++)
        if (front == MASTERS - 1)
            /* nothing to update */
            return;

    for (aux = front; aux < MASTERS; aux++)
        if (master[aux] >= low && master[aux] < high) {
            master[aux] -= size;
            if (aux == front)
                front++;
        }
}
```

In the code for compact, two pointers are used to scan the free list. The current element being examined is pointed to by the pointer curr, and its successor is pointed to by the pointer succ. The loop terminates when current or its successor is NULL.

```c
static bool compact()
{
    HEADER *curr, *succ;
    char *source, *destin;
    unsigned size;

    curr = head.h.next;
    if (curr == NULL || curr->h.next == NULL)
        return(FALSE); /* free list contains 0 or 1 block */
```

```
destin = (char *)curr;
do {
    succ = curr->h.next;
    source = (char*)curr + curr->h.len + SIZEH;
    size=(succ==NULL?heap+HEAPS:(char*)succ)-source;
    /* move block up in heap */
    movmem(source, destin, size);
    /* update master array */
    update(source, source + size, source - destin);
    /* update destination for the next step */
    destin += size;
    curr = succ;
} while (succ != NULL);

front = 0;              /* for the next call of compact */
/* update free list */
head.h.next = curr = (HEADER *)destin;
curr->h.next = NULL;
curr->h.len = HEAPS - SIZEH - (destin - heap);

return(TRUE);
}
```

The next function is freemem. When the call freemem(p) is made, the
header of the block in the heap pointed to by p can be used to determine
the size of the block to be freed. The code consists of two parts. After
the initial error checking is done, the free list is searched to find the two
blocks on the left and right side of the block that is being released to determine if either of them is a free block that can be coalesced with this
block.

```
void freemem(p)
char **p;
{
    HEADER *left, *right, *aux;
    char **masterp;
    unsigned size;

    masterp = p;
    if (p == NULL !! p < master !! p >= master + MASTERS)
        return;

    *p = (char*)((HEADER*)*p-1); /* move p beyond header */
    size = (aux = (HEADER *)*p)->h.len;
    /* search the free list */
    for (left = &head, right = head.h.next;
                right != NULL && (char *)right < *p;
                left = right, right = right->h.next)
        ;
```

```
            /* check if merging with left neighbor */
            if (left!=&head&&(char*)left+left->h.len+SIZEH == *p) {
                    aux = left;
                    left->h.len += size + SIZEH;
            }
            else {  /* add block to free list */
                    /* size is already stored in header */
                    aux->h.next  = right;
                    left->h.next = aux;
            }

            /* check if merging with right neighbor */
            if ((char *)aux+aux->h.len+SIZEH == (char *)right) {
                    aux->h.len += right->h.len + SIZEH;
                    aux->h.next = right->h.next;
            }

            /* set corresponding master pointer to null */
            *masterp = NULL;
    }
```

Another useful function would be one that corresponds to the standard
C routine realloc(p, siz); this function assumes memory has been
allocated for p calling getmem, and it changes the size of that block to
siz. Allocating an entirely new memory region is done only when necessary—if possible, the size of the block is increased or decreased in
place. We leave the implementation of this function for you to do as an
exercise.

We now describe the set of rules that specify how this memory management system may be used. In this description, we use the term
xpointers to describe pointers that are allocated memory blocks using
getmem. As an example, consider a linked list of integer values. We
start with the definition of a list element:

```
typedef struct ELEM {
    int value;
    struct ELEM **next;
} ELEM, *PELEM;
```

Here, next has been defined as a pointer to pointer to structure. This is
the first rule:

1. Define an *xpointer* as a pointer to a pointer to the base type.
   To obtain memory, we can use a statement similar to the one that
   would be used with malloc:

```
PELEM *p;
p = (PELEM *)getmem(sizeof(ELEM));
```

For the integrity of our memory system, xpointers must not be directly assigned any values. For example, the statement

```
p = exp
```

would be incorrect. This leads to the second rule:

2. Access the heap only through the singly dereferenced xpointers.

For example, to initialize the element p, we could say

```
(*p)->val = 3;
(*p)->next = NULL;
```

If we have q defined as

```
char *q;
```

and do

```
q = *p;
```

we cannot rely on the value of q because if compaction occurs this value will become meaningless. However, the value of

```
(*p)->val
```

after compaction is still valid because the value of *p is automatically updated. This leads to the third rule:

3. Use *p wherever you would use p in an ordinary system.

The complete code of the list operation ListCr using this memory system follows. We leave the remaining list operations as an exercise.

```
PELEM *ListCr(val)
int val;
{
    PELEM *aux;
    char **getmem();

    if ((aux = (PELEM*)getmem(sizeof(ELEM))  == NULL)
        return(NULL);

    (*aux)->value = val;
    (*aux)->next = NULL;

    return(aux);
}
```

13.4   DIJKSTRA'S SHORTEST PATHS ALGORITHM

In this section, we implement a well-known algorithm by Dijkstra to find the shortest path in a directed graph from a designated vertex called the **source** to each other vertex (for complete details, see [Aho83]). The arcs of the graph are labeled by nonnegative integers, called **costs**, and the **shortest path** to a vertex is the one with the least total cost.

The main idea of this algorithm is to maintain a set S that contains the vertices whose shortest distance from the source is known. Initially, this set contains the source only. In each step of the algorithm, a new vertex is added to the set S. When S contains all vertices, the algorithm terminates. To determine which vertex should be added to S, an array D is used that holds the costs of paths from the source to each other vertex, passing only through vertices in the set S (excluding the endpoint vertices).

After the algorithm has terminated, we want to display the paths going from the source to any other vertex. For this purpose, another array, P, is maintained. $P[w]$ contains the vertex immediately before w in shortest path.

We assume a graph has N vertices numbered 0 to $N-1$, and the vertex 0 is the source. The outline of the Dijkstra algorithm is

```
initialize S to contain the source (vertex 0)
for i = 1 to N - 1 do
    choose vertex w which is not in S such that
            D[w] is minimum;
    add w to S
    update D: for each v that is not in S do
            if (m = min(D[v], D[w] + cost(w,v))) < D[v]
            then
                    D[v] = m
                    P[v] = w
```

To implement this algorithm, we need to implement two data types: an ADT GRAPH and an ADT SET. As we did in Section 13.1, we choose particular implementations to represent these data types to show some features of C. The ADT GRAPH will be implemented using cursor-based **adjacency lists**, and the ADT SET will be implemented using a **bit-vector** data structure.

In the following three sections, we describe how these data structures are implemented; we describe the main program in Section 13.4.4. The complete program consists of three separately compiled files and three header files:

graph.h	Header file declaring the data structures for the ADT GRAPH
clist.h	Declares the LIST data type and associated operations

```
set.h          Declares the SET data type and related operations
clist.c        Defines some LIST operations
set.c          Defines some SET operations
dijkstra.c     Contains the main program
```

13.4.1   Adjacency List Implementation of ADT Graph

We do not attempt to show a complete implementation of the ADT
GRAPH; rather, we just describe the routines needed to implement the
Dijkstra algorithm. The following definitions are stored in the file
graph.h, which includes clist.h (described in Section 13.4.2):

```
#include "clist.h"
```

We assume the graph has at most MAXVER vertices:

```
#define MAXVER   20        /* or whatever */
```

The graph is represented by an array G of lists; the list G[v] is the list
of vertices adjacent to v:

```
typedef LIST GRAPH[MAXVER];
```

where LIST is defined in list.h. No graph operations are declared in
graph.h, since our application does not require any.

13.4.2   Cursor Implementation of ADT List

We have already described one implementation of an ADT LIST in Section 13.1.1. We describe another one here because in some applications,
a pointer implementation is unsuitable. For example, to implement a
linked list in a file, pointers are not applicable, and another approach
must be taken. A **cursor** implementation of an ADT LIST is a simple
transformation of a pointer implementation (see [Aho83]). A single array, called SPACE, is used to hold all lists. An element of a list can be
referred to using a cursor—an index into SPACE—in the same way
pointers are used in a pointer implementation.

The array SPACE essentially represents a *heap*; thus a linked list of
the available elements in SPACE is maintained. When a new element is
to be inserted in a list, an element from the available list is removed and
used; when an element is deleted from a list, it is added to the available
list for future reuse.

We first describe the file clist.h. Integer values are used to denote cursors into the array SPACE, and thus to denote lists stored in SPACE. To improve the readability of the program, we define data types CURSOR, VERTEX, and LIST as synonyms of int:

```
typedef int CURSOR, LIST, VERTEX;
```

For the sake of our example, we define lists containing not only vertices but also arc costs.

```
typedef struct {
            VERTEX vertex;
            int    cost;
            CURSOR next;
        } NODE;
```

The remaining code in clist.h is

```
#ifndef TRUE
typedef int bool;
#define TRUE 1
#define FALSE 0
#endif
extern void ListIni();
extern CURSOR ListRet();
extern bool ListIns();
extern int ListCost();
```

Now, the file clist.c: The first part of this file contains the following definitions:

```
#include <stdio.h>
#include "clist.h"
#define MAXNOD    100        /* or whatever */
#define  NIL      (-1)
static NODE SPACE[MAXNOD];
static int avail;
```

To facilitate the implementation of the LIST operations, three macros are also defined:

```
#define NEXT(i)    (SPACE[(i)].next)
#define VAL(i)     (SPACE[(i)].vertex)
#define COST(i)    (SPACE[(i)].cost)
```

Since we intend to discuss only those LIST operations that are useful in implementing the Dijkstra algorithm, we do not, for example, discuss the *delete* operation.

The remaining part of clist.c contains a variety of functions for managing a cursor-based list. First, we present the function ListIni, which initializes SPACE by placing all of its elements on the available list:

```
void ListIni()
{
      for (avail = 0; avail < MAXNOD - 1; avail++)
            NEXT(avail) = avail + 1;
      NEXT(avail) = NIL;
      avail = 0;
}
```

The next function, ListRet(L, v), returns a cursor to the element of list L that contains the vertex v, or NIL if v is not in L.

```
CURSOR ListRet(L, v)
LIST L;
VERTEX v;
{
      CURSOR aux;

      for (aux = L; aux != NIL; aux = NEXT(aux))
            if (VAL(aux) == v)
                  return(aux);
      return(NIL);
}
```

To implement the function ListIns, which inserts a new element in front of the list, we first need a function that allocates a new element in SPACE and returns a cursor to this element:

```
static CURSOR new()
{
      CURSOR i;

      if (avail == NIL)
            return(NIL);

      i = avail;
      avail = NEXT(avail);
      return(i);
}
```

The code of ListIns follows:

```
bool ListIns(L, vertex, cost)
LIST *L;
VERTEX vertex;
int cost;
{
      CURSOR aux;
```

```
        if ((aux = new()) == NIL)
            return(FALSE);
    NEXT(aux) = *L;
    COST(aux) = cost;
    VAL(aux) = vertex;
    *L = aux;
    return(TRUE);
}
```

The last function returns the cost stored in a node:

```
int ListCost(v)
VERTEX v;
{
    return(COST(v));
}
```

We define this function because we will need to access cost values in the main program but will not have direct access to the array SPACE, since it is defined as static.

13.4.3 Bit-Vector Implementation of ADT Set

We consider an ADT SET with the following operations:

SetUnion(A, B, C)	Returns through C the union of the sets A and B
SetInt(A, B, C)	Returns through C the intersection of the sets A and B
SetDif(A, B, C)	Returns through C the difference of the sets A and B
SetCompl(A, B)	Returns through B the complement of the set A
SetMem(x, A)	Returns 1 if x is a member of A; returns 0 otherwise.
SetIns(x, A)	Inserts x to the set A
SetDel(x, A)	Deletes x from the set A

We assume the set elements are nonnegative integers less than a certain constant SETL. These set operations are defined in the file set.c and use the so-called **bit-vector** implementation of an ADT SET. In this implementation, a set is represented by a boolean array; the integer i is in the set if the ith element of this array is true. We use a block of consecutive memory words and consider this block to be an array of bits. The header file set.h contains the basic definitions and declarations associated with the ADT SET:

```
#ifndef BYTEL
#define BYTEL 8
#define SETL 128                              /* or whatever */
typedef char SET[SETL / BYTEL];
#endif
```

```
extern void SetUnion();
extern void SetInt();
extern void SetDif();
extern void SetCompl();
extern int  SetMem();
extern void SetIns();
extern void SetDel();
```

Thus the maximum size of a set is SETL. Our implementation does not depend on the length of a word, but it *does* depend on the length of a byte. If a byte has 9 bits (as it does on some computers), the constant BYTEL must be modified. (Our model also assumes each memory location holds a *single* byte.) If we use the values as defined here, a variable of type SET would occupy 16 consecutive bytes of memory.

We consider a variable s of type SET an array of bits, with the individual bits numbered from 0 to SETL−1 and stored in bytes s[0] to s[SETL/BYTEL−1]. Moreover, the bits in a byte are considered ordered from *right to left*. These assumptions do not impose any restrictions on the implementation; they merely state how the SET implementation views objects of type SET. To define an initially empty set, we would say, for example,

```
static SET s = {0};
```

As we indicated in Section 8.3, array initialization is valid if it is either a global or static local array. Since in this example, the number of initializers is less than the number of set elements, all elements are set to 0.

We now define some functions to manipulate set variables. They are defined in set.c, which includes set.h. The first operation is union:

```
void SetUnion(a, b, c)
SET a, b, c;
{
    int i;

    for (i = 0; i < SETL / BYTEL; i++)
        c[i] = a[i] | b[i];
}
```

The consecutive bytes in c are set by *or*ing the corresponding bytes in sets a and b.

The implementations of intersection, difference, and complement are similar:

```
void SetInt(a, b, c)
SET a, b, c;
{
    int i;
```

```
        for (i = 0; i < SETL / BYTEL; i++)
            c[i] = a[i] & b[i];
}

void SetDif(a, b, c)
SET a, b, c;
{
    int i;

    for (i = 0; i < SETL / BYTEL; i++)
        c[i] = (a[i] ^ b[i]) & a[i];
}

void SetCompl(a, b)
SET a, b;
{
    int i;

    for (i = 0; i < SETL / BYTEL; i++)
        b[i] = ~a[i];
}
```

To implement the remaining SET operations, we have to implement routines to perform the following actions:

- Return the value of the ith bit in s
- Set the ith bit in s to 1
- Set the ith bit in s to 0

It can be determined that the ith bit in a set is at position i%BYTEL in the byte at index i/BYTEL in the array. To facilitate these operations, we define two macros:

```
#define BYTE(s, i)    ( (s)[(i) / BYTEL] )
#define BIT(i)        ( ((i) % BYTEL) )
```

We start with the function SetMem(s, i). The byte at index BYTE (s, i) is shifted to the right by BIT(i) positions, and then *and*ed with 1 to get the value at the ith position:

```
int SetMem(s, i)
SET s;
int i;
{
    return(BYTE(s, i) >> BIT(i) & 1);
}
```

Recall that the >> operation has higher precedence than the & operation.

To set the ith bit in s, the bit at BYTE(s, i) is set to 1 by shifting the value 1 left BIT(i) positions using

```
1 << BIT(i)
```

and *or*ing it with this byte

```
void SetIns(s, i)
SET s;
int i;
{
    BYTE(s, i) != 1 << BIT(i);
}
```

The last function, SetDel, is the complement of SetIns:

```
void SetDel(s, i)
SET s;
int i;
{
    BYTE(s, i) &= ~(1 << BIT(i));
}
```

If a set is needed to hold, for example, strings, these strings can be mapped onto the interval [0, SETL−1].

13.4.4 The Main Program

The main program (stored in the file dijkstra.c) includes the header files graph.h and set.h:

```
#include <stdio.h>
#include "graph.h"
#include "set.h"
```

The data structures used are as follows:

```
#define MAXINT    32767      /* or whatever */
#define NIL       (-1)

GRAPH G;
static SET S = {0};
int D[MAXVER];
int P[MAXVER];
int maxver;
FILE *gdat;
```

The constant MAXINT is used to denote the cost if there is no arc between two vertices. The last variable, maxver, represents the actual number of vertices in a given graph.

The first function we describe is pcost(v, w), which returns the cost of the arc from the vertex v to w, or MAXINT if there is no such arc.

```
int pcost(v, w)
VERTEX v, w;
{
        CURSOR p;

        if ((p = ListRet(G[v], w)) == NIL)
             return(MAXINT);
        return(ListCost(p));
}
```

To *initialize* the graph being used, we assume it is read from a file organized in the following manner: The first line contains the number of vertices in the graph. Each subsequent line contains an integer representing a vertex v, followed by the number of vertices adjacent to this vertex, followed by pairs of integers representing vertices adjacent to v and the costs of the arcs they define. For example,

```
3
2    1   1      5
1    0
0    2   1      4    2    8
```

represents the graph shown in Figure 13.4.

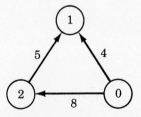

FIGURE 13.4

The procedure init initializes the data structures. We assume the input data are read from the file gdat and are in the format just described. The macro R is defined to read an integer variable and return the value read; thus R can be used both as an instruction and as an expression.

```
#define R(arg)        (fscanf(gdat, "%d", &(arg)), (arg))
void init()
{
     VERTEX i, j, v, c, vert;
     int adjnum;

     ListIni();

     for (i = 0; i < MAXVER; i++) {
         G[i] = NIL;
         P[i] = 0;
     }

     R(maxver);
     for (i = 0; i < maxver; i++) {
         R(vert);
         R(adjnum);
         for (j = 0; j < adjnum; j++)
             ListIns(&(G[vert]), R(v), R(c));
     }

     D[0] = 0;
     for (i = 1; i < maxver; i++)
         D[i] = pcost(0, i);
}
```

The next function looks for a vertex v that does not belong to the set S such that D[v] is minimum:

```
VERTEX minD()
{
     VERTEX i, minim;

     /* find the first vertex not in S */
     for (i = 0; i < maxver; i++)
         if (!SetMem(S, i)) {
             minim = i;
             break;
         }

     /* now see if any has a smaller D value */
     for (; i < maxver; i++)
         if (!SetMem(S, i) && D[i] < D[minim])
             minim = i;

     return(minim);
}
```

The last function we present before the main program is shown is the recursive function print, which recovers the shortest paths from the array P:

```
void print(v)
VERTEX v;
{
    if (P[v])
        print(P[v]);
    printf(" %d ", v);
}
```

The code of the main program follows:

```
main()
{
    VERTEX i, v, w;
    int aux;
    char fname[20];

    printf("Enter file name: ");
    gets(fname);
    if ((gdat = fopen(fname, "r")) == NULL) {
        printf("File %s does not exist\n", fname);
        return;
    }

    init();
    SetIns(S, 0);   /* put in source vertex 0 */

    for (i = 0; i < maxver - 1; i++) {
        w = minD();
        SetIns(S, w);
        for (v = 0; v < maxver; v++)
            if (!SetMem(S,v) && (aux = pcost(w,v)) < MAXINT)
                if (aux + D[w] < D[v]) {
                    P[v] = w;
                    D[v] = aux + D[w];
                }
    }

    printf("The shortest paths are as follows:\n");
    for (i = 1; i < maxver; i++) {
        printf("\n0->%d : cost %d 0", i, D[i]);
        print(i);
    }
    putchar('\n');

    if (fclose(gdat) == EOF)
        printf("File %s cannot be closed\n", fname);
}
```

13.5   A SIMPLE DATABASE

In this section, we present an example of a *file-based* DICTIONARY
ADT, which means operations are performed on disk storage rather
than in internal memory.

This ADT has several applications, particularly with respect to database programs. As an example, we consider a database of employees with just three attributes—name, salary, and employee number, the last being the *key* used for searches. Extensions to this example to include other attributes or to have other keys would require only simple changes in the program.

Several data structures could be used to implement this database—open and closed hash tables, binary search trees (BSTs), B-trees, and others. We demonstrate a BST implementation.

A **binary search tree** is a binary tree labeled by an ordered set so that the label of each node is less than the label of every node in the right subtree of this node and greater than the label of every node in the left subtree of this node.

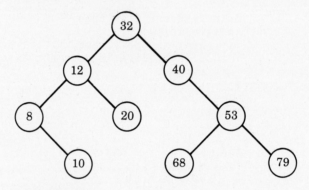

FIGURE 13.5

A BST is a generalization of an ordered set, and it speeds up search times because a version of a binary search can be used. A search for an element x starts from the root of the tree and then continues in the left or the right subtree, depending on whether x is less than or greater than the value stored in the root. This search is most efficient if the tree is *balanced*, but on this subject, we do not go into details.

On the one hand, there is little difference between searching internal memory and searching external memory, since files in C are random access and can therefore be conceptualized as open-ended arrays; on the other hand, any updates performed on information read from the file into internal memory must be written *back* to the file to record the change in the external structure.

13.5.1   A File Organized as a Binary Search Tree

A pointer implementation of an internal binary search tree is straightforward. Pointer-based structures, however, cannot be directly represented in external storage; instead, an approach similar to the *cursor-*

based implementation of an ADT LIST (see Section 13.4.2) is used. The file being used is treated as an open-ended array of structures, numbered from 0. Using integer cursors, lists can be implemented by linking structures in the file. The values of these cursors are indices of other structures in the file, or 0 if the link is null.

We present only brief descriptions of the algorithms needed to implement *member*, *insert*, and *delete* on BSTs; for complete details, see [Aho83].

In the database program implemented, the following commands will be available to the user:

Load fname	To load the database from the file fname
Add info	To add information about a single employee
Del empno	To delete from the database an employee
Info empno	To display information about an employee
Show low high	To list all employees having salaries between low and high
Print	To list all employees sorted according to employee number
Cleanup	To compact and rebuild the database file

We start with the data structures that will be used. The file containing the database will be a file of structures with three possible variants:

- A structure containing data about an employee with links to its left and right children
- A structure to store the root of the tree and a pointer to the available list; this structure is always the first structure (number 0) in the file
- A structure representing an element on the available list with a single link next pointing to the next structure in this list

```
#define NAMELEN    30
typedef union {
    struct {
        int empno;
        char name[NAMELEN + 1];
        float salary;
        long lchild;
        long rchild;
    } emp;
    struct {
        long root;
        long avail;
    } header;
    struct {
        long next;
    } unused;
} emprec;
```

As in the cursor-based list that we described in Section 13.4.2, the *available* list is maintained by the program itself. The main difference between an available list implemented in a file and one in internal memory is that in a file the available list is logically never empty, since the file can be extended in size indefinitely. For clarity, we have defined the unused variant as a structure even though it contains only a single attribute next.

Since the structure at position 0 in the file is always used to point to the root of the tree and indicates the start of the available list, it can never be a node in the tree; thus the value 0 can be used to indicate a null cursor.

We now describe the basic BST file operations. The remaining functions and the complete program we leave for you as an exercise.

The following macros are used in this program to facilitate I/O operations:

```
#define SIZE                    sizeof(emprec)

#define SREAD(base, rec, pos)                           \
    { fseek((base), (long)(SIZE * (pos)), 0);   \
        fread((char *)&(rec), SIZE, 1, (base)) ; }

#define SWRITE(base, rec, pos)                          \
    { fseek((base), (long)(SIZE * (pos)), 0);   \
        fwrite((char *)&(rec), SIZE, 1, (base)) ; }
```

The first function, makebase(fname), is used to initialize the database file fname; it sets the root field of record 0 to 0 (to indicate the binary tree is empty) and the avail field to 1 (which represents the record beyond the current end of the file and will be the record where the first tree node is allocated). This function returns NULL if it fails; otherwise, it returns a file pointer.

```
FILE *makebase(fname)
char *fname;
{
    FILE *base;
    emprec rec0;

    rec0.header.root  = 0;
    rec0.header.avail = 1;
    if ((base = fopen(fname, "w+")) == NULL)
        return(NULL);
    SWRITE(base, rec0, 0)
    return(base);
}
```

The second function, member(base, empno, lc, par), is an implementation of a nonrecursive search on a BST. The first parameter, base, is a file pointer that represents the database being searched; the second parameter, empno, is the key used for the search; the last two parameters (passed by reference) return, respectively, the index of the parent of the structure found in the file and a flag indicating whether the structure found is the left or right child of this parent. The function itself is a boolean function that returns the value TRUE if the node with the given key has been found and that returns FALSE otherwise.

Since in many cases, a variable rec of type emprec is used, the following macros are defined to be used as abbreviations for several dotted expressions:

```
#define EMPNO    rec.emp.empno
#define EMPSAL   rec.emp.salary
#define EMPNAME  rec.emp.name
#define EMPLC    rec.emp.lchild
#define EMPRC    rec.emp.rchild
```

The code for member follows; it is a generalization of a binary search on a sorted array:

```
bool member(base, empno, lc, par)
FILE *base;
int empno;
bool *lc;
long *par;
{
    emprec rec;
    long node;

    SREAD(base, rec, 0)
    *par = 0;
    *lc  = FALSE;

    /* search the tree */
    for (node=rec.header.root;node;node=(*lc?EMPLC:EMPRC)) {
        SREAD(base, rec, node)
        if (empno == EMPNO)
            return(TRUE);
        *par = node;
        *lc  = empno < EMPNO;
    }

    return(FALSE);
}
```

In the next function, the size of the database file must be determined. In Chapter 12, we presented a function that could be used for this purpose; here, we use a macro.

```
#define FSIZE(fil)  (fseek((fil), 0L, 2),  \
                     ((ftell(fil) + 1) / SIZE))
```

The size of the file is computed in records, not bytes.

To add an object to the BST file, member is first called to determine whether this object already exists. If it does not exist, member returns all the necessary information about where the new object should be inserted—specifically, the index of this node's prospective parent and whether it will be the left or right child of this node.

The additional difficulty in implementing insert is that a structure to store the new object has to be retrieved from the available list. To properly update the available list, two cases must be considered: the available list starts beyond the end of the file, or the available list starts somewhere within the file.

```
bool insert(base, empno, name, salary)
FILE *base;
int empno;
char name[];
float salary;
{
    bool isleft;
    long parent, oldavl;
    emprec newrec, rec0, rec, prec;

    if (member(base, empno, &isleft, &parent))
        return(FALSE);

    /* initialize new record */
    newrec.emp.empno = empno;
    strcpy(newrec.emp.name, name);
    newrec.emp.salary = salary;
    newrec.emp.lchild = newrec.emp.rchild = 0;

    /* get root and parent structures */
    SREAD(base, rec0, 0)
    SREAD(base, prec, parent)

    /* update avail, consider two cases */
    oldavl = rec0.header.avail;
    if (oldavl == FSIZE(base))
        rec0.header.avail++;
    else {
        SREAD(base, rec, oldavl)
        rec0.header.avail = rec.unused.next;
    }

    /* update new node's parent */
    if (parent == 0)    /* new root */
        rec0.header.root = oldavl;
    else if (isleft)
            prec.emp.lchild = oldavl;
    else prec.emp.rchild = oldavl;
```

```
      /* write back to file */
      SWRITE(base, newrec, oldavl)
      SWRITE(base, rec0, 0)
      if (parent != 0)
          SWRITE(base, prec, parent)
      return(TRUE);
}
```

To implement delete, it is again necessary to first check if the object already exists. If it does, the number of children belonging to this node is determined. There are three cases: there are no children, there is only one child, or there are two children. The first two cases are easy to handle. In the third case, the node containing the *minimum* value in the right subtree of the node being removed is deleted by calling the function deletemin; then, its data is copied to the node that was to be deleted.

```
bool delete(base, empno)
FILE *base;
int empno;
{
      long parent, todelete, newchild, deletemin();
      bool lc;
      emprec rec0, rec, prec, drec;

      if (!member(base, empno, &lc, &parent))
          return(FALSE);

      /* get the header and parent structures */
      SREAD(base, rec0, 0)
      SREAD(base, prec, parent)

      /* determine the index of the structure with empno */
      todelete=parent?(lc?prec.emp.lchild:prec.emp.rchild)
                     : rec0.header.root;
      SREAD(base, rec, todelete)

      /* depending on the number of children */
      if (EMPLC && EMPRC) {      /* there are 2 children */
          newchild = todelete;
          todelete = deletemin(base, newchild, EMPRC);
          /* copy employee data to the node being deleted */
          SREAD(base, drec, todelete)
          EMPNO = drec.emp.empno;
          strcpy(EMPNAME, drec.emp.name);
          EMPSAL = drec.emp.salary;
          SWRITE(base, rec, newchild)
      }
      else newchild=(!EMPLC&&!EMPRC)?0:(!EMPLC?EMPRC:EMPLC);
```

```
               /* update deleted node's parent */
               if (parent == 0)
                    rec0.header.root = newchild;
               else if (lc)
                    prec.emp.lchild = newchild;
               else prec.emp.rchild = newchild;

               /* update the available list */
               SREAD(base, drec, todelete)
               drec.unused.next = rec0.header.avail;
               rec0.header.avail = todelete;
               /* write back to file */
               SWRITE(base, rec0, 0)
               SWRITE(base, drec, todelete)
               if (parent)
                    SWRITE(base, prec, parent)

               return(TRUE);
     }
```

In the function deletemin(base, parent, child), the second
parameter is always the parent of the third parameter. This function is
called recursively until it reaches a node with no left child; since the tree
is a BST, this node must contain the minimum value. Once this node is
found, it is deleted by changing its parent link to this node's right child.

```
     long deletemin(base, parent, child)
     FILE *base;
     long parent, child;
     {
          emprec rec, prec;

          SREAD(base, rec, child)
          if (!EMPLC) {
               SREAD(base, prec, parent)
               if (prec.emp.rchild == child)
                    prec.emp.rchild = EMPRC;
               else prec.emp.lchild = EMPRC;
               SWRITE(base, prec, parent)
               return(child);
          }
          else return(deletemin(base, child, EMPLC));
     }
```

After several insert and delete operations have been performed,
the available list may become quite long. Since the objects on the available list take up space in the file, it is reasonable to periodically *compact*
the file, eliminating the space occupied by the available list. This operation is provided by the cleanup function; it copies the tree from the
database file to a temporary file, erases the database file, and then re-
copies the temporary file back to the original. This sequence of actions is
the only way of removing the elements on the available list, since there

is no file operation to remove a part of a file. A database system could
be designed so that this cleanup operation is called automatically if the
length of the available list becomes too large. In our example, we de-
cided to leave cleanup as an option called at the user's convenience because cleanup is a time-consuming operation, and this would allow the
user to do the operation when time is not critical.

During cleanup, it might also be appropriate to restructure the tree
so that it is optimally balanced. Ideally, this should be considered, but
we do not do so in the program. Instead, our implementation of
cleanup will retain the structure of a tree and remove all elements
from the available list.

The main part of cleanup is done by a recursive function,
rebuild(root, base, newbase, filepos), which traverses the
tree based at root in the file base and copies the nodes into a new file
indicated by newbase. The parameter filepos is passed by reference,
and it returns the current position in the new file.

```
static void rebuild(root, base, newbase, filepos)
long root;
FILE *base, *newbase;
long *filepos;
{
    long left, right, pos;
    emprec rec;

    if (root) {
        /* get a root node */
        SREAD(base, rec, root)

        /* save current file position */
        pos = (*filepos)++;

        /* root will be stored at position pos */
        if (EMPLC) {
            /* save index where left child will go */
            left = *filepos;
            /* go into recursion */
            rebuild(EMPLC, base, newbase, filepos);
            /* update left child */
            EMPLC = left;
        }

        if (EMPRC) {
            right = *filepos;
            rebuild(EMPRC, base, newbase, filepos);
            EMPRC = right;
        }

        /* write back changes made to root */
        SWRITE(newbase, rec, pos)
    }
}
```

Notice that `filepos` is an index in the new file; as the tree is traversed, the positions of where a given node's children will be written is determined using `filepos`. The code for `cleanup` follows; `fname` is the name used originally to open the database, and `base` is a file pointer pointing to the currently opened database. The tree is copied to a temporary file called `_temp`. Some systems, for example Unix, provide special means to create temporary filenames, but here we want to use only standard C; for this reason, too, we do not try to delete the temporary file after it is copied back to the original file. In Chapter 14, we show some nonstandard C file operations that can be used in these cases.

```c
bool cleanup(fname, base)
char fname[];
FILE *base;
{
    emprec rec0;
    long filepos, i;
    FILE *newbase;

    if ((newbase = makebase("_temp")) == NULL)
        return(FALSE);

    filepos = 1;
    /* get the root */
    SREAD(base, rec0, 0)

    rebuild(rec0.header.root, base, newbase, &filepos);

    /* update the root */
    rec0.header.root = (filepos == 1) ? 0 : 1;
    rec0.header.avail = filepos;
    SWRITE(newbase, rec0, 0)
    printf("\n%ld record(s) removed\n", FSIZE(base) - filepos);

    freopen(fname, "w+", base);
    /* copy to old file */
    for (i = 0; i < filepos; i++) {
        SREAD(newbase, rec0, i)
        SWRITE(base, rec0, i)
    }
    fclose(newbase);
    return(TRUE);
}
```

We leave the remaining part of this program as an exercise.

EXERCISES

1. Write a recursive procedure that prints all elements on a singly linked list containing integers.

2. Consider the following data structures to implement a binary tree:

```
typedef struct node {
          struct node *left, *right;
          int val;
      } NODE, *TREE;
```

   a. Write a recursive integer function sum(t) that returns the sum of all values stored in the leaves of the tree t.
   b. Write a recursive procedure prune(t) that removes all leaves from the tree t.

3. Consider the following definition:

```
typedef struct str {
      char val;
      struct str *next;
  } *str;
```

   This structure can be used to create a linked list of characters. Write the function

```
int from(s, y)
char *s;
str **y;
```

   which converts the string s into the list y and returns 1 if successful, 0 otherwise. Also, write the function

```
void into(y, s)
str *y;
char *s;
```

   which converts the list y into the string s. Test these functions in an appropriate main program.

4. Give the data structures needed to implement a pointer-based singly linked list of real values. Then implement

```
append(L, f)
```

   which appends the real value f to the list L (inserts it at the end), and

```
remove(L, f)
```

which removes the first element from the list L and returns the value stored in this element through the real parameter f. In this operation, remember to deallocate the element that has been removed. Error checking is required.

5. Implement operations to create a linked list of text lines, where the characters in each line are also a linked list (thus we have a linked list of linked lists of characters). Test your operations by reading in several lines and storing them in this fashion. Write some additional functions to edit these lines, for example, routines to insert or delete a word in some line.

6. Implement closed hash table operations (see [Aho83]).

7. Implement internal BST operations (see [Aho83]).

8. Implement ADT TREE, using the leftmost-child, right-sibling representation (see [Aho83]).

9. Implement some internal sorting algorithms, for example, insertion sort, heapsort, and quicksort.

14 Some Real Systems

PREVIEW   *Up to now, we have avoided discussions of nonstandard C operations even if they are supported by several implementations. This chapter describes various useful functions available in different C systems. In particular, we look at implementations of C under three different operating systems:* **Unix** *[Rit78],* **MS-DOS** *(Lattice C [Lat85] and Instant-C [Ins86]), and the* **Macintosh** *(Aztec C [Man84] and LightspeedC [Thi86]). Since the Lattice C compiler implements many of the ANSI C recommendations [ANS86], we devote one section of this chapter to the* **ANSI C** *standard.*

We do not intend to cover all the system-specific features of these different implementations—the Unix environment alone could be the subject of a complete book. We concentrate on those additional features that seem to be supported by most of the popular implementations. The value of these extensions is that if complete portability (across all C systems) is not a concern, many programs can be written in a more efficient and still almost portable way.

In the Unix section, we concentrate on **I/O redirection**, **error processing**, *and* **low-level file I/O**. *Since the history of Unix is closely related to C, most of the features described in this section will also be found in other C implementations; strictly speaking, however, they are not defined in standard C, and this is why we describe them here. In the MS-DOS section, we describe how to access* **MS-DOS services** *and show two useful applications: a program to move a file from one directory to another and a simple version of Unix's make facility to recompile a file if it was updated since its last compilation. We also describe briefly an MS-DOS C* **interpreter**. *In the Macintosh section, we describe how to work with* **windows** *and* **menus**.*

14.1   UNIX

We begin this section with a brief description of how to use the C compiler under the Unix operating system.

All C *source* files must have the suffix `.c`. The C compiler is called up by issuing the `cc` command, and by default, it invokes the loader automatically after compilation has completed. For example, the command

```
cc file.c
```

preprocesses `file.c`, compiles it, links it with the C library, and eventually produces an executable object code file called `a.out`. The −o option can be used to store the object code in a file other than `a.out`. For example,

```
cc file.c −o main
```

stores the object code in the file `main`. To suppress the loading phase, the −c option can be used:

```
cc −c file.c
```

This option does not link the compiled code with the system library but leaves it in a file with the extension `.o`, `file.o` in our example. It is particularly useful if the program is divided into several modules that are to be separately compiled. The `cc` command can also be used solely as a linker. For example,

```
cc f1.o f2.o f3.o −o prog
```

links the specified object code files and stores the executable code in a single file called `prog`.

14.1.1   I/O Redirection and Environment Strings

If the file `test` contains executable code, the command

```
test argument1 argument2
```

passes the values *argument1* and *argument2* to the program. These would be accessed in a C program through the `main` function arguments, as we discussed in Section 10.5.

The command line can be used not only to pass arguments to a program but also to redirect the standard I/O streams. Any program that reads from the keyboard (`stdin`) or writes to the screen (`stdout`) can specify that either, or both, of these streams be **redirected**—that is, standard input to come from a file rather than the keyboard and standard output to be sent to a file rather than to the screen. This is done when a program is invoked: a > on the command line denotes redirection of *output*, and a < denotes redirection of *input*. For example, the command

```
test <file1
```

would cause standard input to be redirected to come from the file file1 rather than the keyboard; the command

```
test >file2
```

would cause standard output to be redirected to the file file2; the command

```
test <file1 >file2
```

would cause both standard input and standard output to be redirected. In all cases, the code of the program test does not need to be modified for the I/O redirection to work.

The redirection specifiers are *not* considered arguments of the command line. For example,

```
test <file1 >file2 hello
```

has one argument hello on the command line.

Programs that read a single input file and create a single output file from it are often called **filters**. Under Unix, filters are frequently implemented using I/O redirection.

Example 14.1.1   Assume the code of the following program is stored in the file examp:

```
#include <stdio.h>
main()
{
     register int i;

     while ((i = getchar()) != EOF)
          putchar(i);
}
```

To speed up execution, we have specified that the variable i be placed in a register. The invocation of this program using

```
examp >TEST <TEST1
```

would copy the file TEST1 to the file TEST.   ∎

I/O redirection can also be set up explicitly by the user within a C program. This is done with the function freopen, (see Section 12.1.3). The first parameter of this function specifies the name of file (or device) corresponding to the interactive console. To redirect, for example, standard output to the file specified by the variable fname, the code

```
    FILE *out;
    if ((out = freopen(fname, "w", stdout)) == NULL)
        /* error */
        ...
```

could be used. To reconnect it to the console, the statement

```
    out = freopen("/dev/tty", "r", out);
```

is needed because, under Unix, /dev/tty is the device that represents the standard input stream.

Example 14.1.2   The following program reads from the standard input stream and writes to the standard output stream that has been redirected to the file called tmpout:

```
    #include <stdio.h>
    main()
    {
        FILE *out;
        register int i;

        if ((out = freopen("tmpout", "w", stdout)) == NULL) {
            fprintf(stderr, "cannot redirect to tmpout\n");
            return;
        }

        while ((i = getchar()) != EOF)
            putchar(i);

        out = freopen("/dev/tty", "r", out);
    }
```

Error messages should be printed using

```
    fprintf(stderr, ... );
```

as in this example because the standard output may be redirected.   ∎

C programs under Unix can access the command line arguments in the same way that we described in Section 10.5. Besides the standard argc and argv parameters, a third parameter may be specified. This parameter represents an array of strings that corresponds to the current settings of the **environment** that the program is running in. Unlike command line arguments, the values of environment variables may be set at any time, not just when a program is loaded.

Example 14.1.3   The following program prints the values of all environment variables:

```
#include <stdio.h>
main(argc, argv, envp)
int argc;
char *argv[];
char *envp[];
{
    for (; **envp; envp++)
        printf("%s\n", *envp);
}
```

The loop terminates because the last element of the array `envp` is a null string. ∎

Finally, under Unix macros may be defined and undefined on the command line:

$-\mathrm{D}Name = def$

defines the macro *Name*, and

$-\mathrm{U}Name$

undefines the macro *Name*.

14.1.2 Abnormal Termination

Standard C does not provide a way to halt the execution of a program at any arbitrary point; in Unix C, the function `exit` can be used for this. (Recall that `return` terminates the execution of only the current function.) The function `exit` has a single integer parameter:

```
exit(code)
```

`code`, as a matter of a convention, is 0 if the termination is successful; otherwise, it is nonzero. The value of the environment variable `status` is equal to the exit code of the program that has most recently terminated and can be tested either in shell procedures or by accessing the environment in a C program. This is a useful feature if a group of programs is running in sequence, and one of them wants to determine whether or not its predecessor terminated successfully.

Thus if programs are meant to be used in this manner, a program that terminates successfully should always use the call

```
exit(0)
```

Example 14.1.4   The following program copies one file to another file. The names of the files are passed on the command line:

```
#include <stdio.h>
void copy(name1, name2)
char *name1, *name2;
{
    register int i;
    FILE *f1, *f2;

    if ((f1 = fopen(name1, "r")) == NULL ¦¦
        (f2 = fopen(name2, "w")) == NULL)
        exit(1);

    while ((i = fgetc(f1)) != EOF)
        fputc(i, f2);

    if (fclose(f1) == EOF ¦¦ fclose(f2) == EOF)
        exit(1);
}

main(argc, argv)
int argc;
char *argv[];
{
    if (argc != 3)
        exit(1);

    copy(argv[1], argv[2]);
    exit(0);
}
```

∎

The function `exit` is useful to abort a program, but often we wish to terminate some function call, or a sequence of function calls, and return to a function that can decide how to proceed. This is often referred to as **exception handling**. For example, in an editor program, if one of its commands fails, the program, instead of aborting, should turn control over to a central **error handler**, which would dispatch the error and then return to the editor command level to accept the next comand. In general, an exception may be the result of either a success or a failure, but in both cases, we want to return control to a specific place in the program—possibly back through several levels of procedure calls—and we do not want to use a `goto` statement to do this.

A typical way of achieving this effect is to have each function return some error code, which is checked by the calling function; if it finds the code returned by the called function indicates that an exception has occurred, it also terminates and returns this code. This is rather cumbersome because it requires a check for each call. To return from a sequence of calls, we need to *save* the state of the system stack in the function where control is to be returned in the event of an exception and then *restore* the stack to this state when an exception occurs in some other function. In C, this facility is provided by two functions, `setjmp` and `longjmp`.

To use these functions, the programmer has to include the following header file:

```
#include <setjmp.h>
```

which defines a type `jmp_buf`. Assume `env` is a variable of this type:

```
jmp_buf env;
```

The call

```
setjmp(env)
```

saves the current environment (the state of the stack) in the structure env and returns 0. A later call to `longjmp`, for example,

```
longjmp(env, val)
```

returns control to the `setjmp` call that saved the environment in env and causes `setjmp`, in this instance, to return the value val. Therefore, `setjmp` would usually be called like

```
if ((i = setjmp(env)) == 0)
    /* case when setjmp is called directly */
    ...
else /* case when returning from longjmp */
    ...
```

To avoid possible confusion, `setjmp` is implemented so that it returns 0 only when called directly; on an indirect invocation via `longjmp`, `setjmp` returns the value passed as a parameter to `longjmp` unless this value is 0, in which case `setjmp` returns the value 1.

Example 14.1.5   The following program demonstrates a recursive factorial function `fact(n, i)` that accumulates the result in the second parameter according to the definition

```
fact(n, i):  if (n == 1)
                  return the value of i to main program;
             else call fact(n-1, i*n);
```

Eventually, the value passed along through the second parameter is returned to the main program:

```
#include <stdio.h>
#include <setjmp.h>
jmp_buf env;
main()
{
    int i, j;
    extern void fact();
```

```
        printf("Enter a number between 1 and 6: ");
        scanf("%d", &j);
        if (j < 1 !! j > 6) {
                printf("Incorrect value\n");
                exit(1);
        }

        if ((i = setjmp(env)) == 0)
            fact(j, 1);
        else printf("Its factorial is %d\n", i);
        exit(0);
    }
```

In the `if` statement, the case when `i` is equal to 0 is the case when `setjmp` is *called*, and the case when `i` is different from 0 is the case when `setjmp` *returns* from `fact` via a `longjmp` call:

```
    void fact(n, i)
    int n, i;
    {
        if (n <= 1)
            longjmp(env, i);
        fact(n - 1, i * n);
    }
```

Although the second actual parameter is passed by value, as a result of the call to `longjmp`, the value of this parameter is returned to `main`. The variable env used in this routine is a global variable.   ∎

The main difference between a "classical" recursive implementation of factorial and the preceding one is that in the classical implementation, if n is equal to 1, the execution completes through a chain of returns from recursive calls, whereas in the example, it terminates *immediately* by executing a single jump back to the caller.

Example 14.1.6   The following program demonstrates a recursive implementation of member on an internal binary search tree (see [Aho83]):

```
    #include <stdio.h>
    #include <setjmp.h>
    #define NIL     (-1)
    #define MAXEL   100

    struct node {
        int value;
        int left, right;
    } SPACE[MAXEL];

    jmp_buf env;
```

```
void member(nod, val)
int nod, val;
{
    if (nod == NIL)
        longjmp(env, nod);
    else if (val == SPACE[nod].value)
        longjmp(env, nod);
    else if (val < SPACE[nod].value)
        member(SPACE[nod].left, val);
    else member(SPACE[nod].right, val);
}
```

The value NIL is used to indicate an unsuccessful search. The routine would be called using

```
if ((i = setjmp(env)) == 0)
    member(root, val);
else if (i == NIL)
    printf("%d not found\n", val);
else printf("%d found\n", val);
```

The result of the search is returned through setjmp and assigned to i.

■

Examples 14.1.5 and 14.1.6 are somewhat artificial because the setjmp/longjmp combination is usually used for *recovering* from errors, not for speeding up returns from recursive procedures. Lack of space prevents us from showing an example that demonstrates these routines' intended application.

14.1.3 Low-Level File Operations

The file operations we described in Chapter 12 are completely portable but may be inefficient in applications. The low-level file operations that we describe here are usually more efficient, since they read and write physical blocks of data.

These low-level file operations function at a level where a file is referred to by its integer **file descriptor**, which is an index in some system file table. From the user's viewpoint, the actual contents of this table are unimportant; when a file is opened, its file descriptor is returned and used in later file operations. By default, when a program is executed, three files are opened:

- Standard input, descriptor 0
- Standard output, descriptor 1
- Standard error output, descriptor 2

I/O redirection is therefore accomplished by simply reassigning the values of some fields of descriptors 0 and 1 in this table.

The file operations that work with files through file descriptors rather than FILE variables follows:

```
open(fname, rwmode, permissions)
close(fd)
read(fd, buf, size)
write(fd, buf, size)
lseek(fd, offset, mode)
unlink(fname)
```

The open function opens a file or creates a new file:

```
int open(fname, rwmode, permissions)
char *fname;
int rwmode, permissions;
```

This routine opens the file fname for

- Input, if rwmode = 0
- Output, if rwmode = 1
- I/O,   if rwmode = 2

Most implementations provide a header file called fcntl.h, which defines symbolic constants for the various modes that may be specified. Typical constants are

```
O_CREAT      create file if it does not exist
O_RDONLY     open for input
O_WRONLY     open for output
O_RDWR       open for input/output
```

These flags can be combined using bitwise *or*, for example,

```
O_CREAT | O_WRONLY
```

The third parameter specifies the **permission mode**, for example 0600 gives read and write permission for the owner. For a complete list of permission modes that are allowed under Unix, consult the appropriate Unix system manual.

The function open returns −1 if it fails and an integer file descriptor otherwise.

The function close closes the file with the file descriptor fd:

```
int close(fd)
int fd;
```

It returns −1 if it fails and 0 otherwise.

The function read reads size bytes from the file with the descriptor fd and stores them in the buffer buf:

```
int read(fd, buf, size)
int fd;
char buf[];
int size;
```

It returns the number of bytes actually read (which may be fewer than size if end-of-file is encountered).

The function write copies size bytes from the buffer buf to the file with the descriptor fd:

```
int write(fd, buf, size)
int fd;
char buf[];
int size;
```

It returns the number of bytes actually written (which may be fewer than size if some kind of error occurs).

The function lseek is identical to fseek, except the first parameter is a file descriptor rather than a file pointer:

```
long lseek(fd, offset, mode)
int fd;
long offset;
int mode;
```

The function unlink deletes the file with the name fname:

```
unlink(fname)
char fname[];
```

We now show some applications of these operations. In all these examples, we use the constant BUFSIZE, which corresponds to the most common size of a disk block on Unix systems.

Example 14.1.7 The following program shows an efficient way to make a copy of a file:

```
#define BUFSIZE    512
#include <stdio.h>
main()
{
      char buf[BUFSIZE];
      register int i;

      while (i = read(0, buf, BUFSIZE))
            if (i != write(1, buf, i)) {
                  fprintf(stderr, "Error in writing\n");
                  exit(1);
            }
      exit(0);
}
```

This program is a *filter*: It reads from standard input and writes to standard output. To copy the file TEST1 to the file TEST2, the program would be invoked using the command

```
copy <TEST1 >TEST2
```

assuming the executable code is stored in the file copy.   ∎

Example 14.1.8 The following program shows how to save a linked list of variable length strings in a file and how to retrieve this list (compare this with Example 12.2.3).

```
typedef int bool;
#define TRUE   1
#define FALSE  0
typedef struct temp {
            char *value;
            struct temp *next;
        } ITEM, *PITEM;
```

The function fsave(fname, h) saves the list h in the file fname. It traverses the list copying each string to a buffer. When the buffer becomes full, it is copied to the file. The function returns TRUE if successful, and it returns FALSE if any error occurs.

```
#include <stdio.h>
#include <fcntl.h>
#define BUFSIZE   512
#define MODE      0600        /* permission code  */
bool fsave(fname, h)
char fname[];
PITEM h;
/* saves the list h in the file fname */
{
    int fd;
    unsigned len;
    char buf[BUFSIZE],
         *lim    = buf + BUFSIZE -1,
         *bufcur = buf,
         *strcur;

    if ((fd = open(fname, O_CREAT | O_WRONLY, MODE)) == EOF)
        return(FALSE);

    for (; h != NULL; h = h->next) {
        for (strcur = h->value; ; strcur++) {
            *bufcur++ = *strcur;
            if (bufcur > lim) {     /* write to file */
                if (write(fd, buf, BUFSIZE) != BUFSIZE)
                    return(FALSE);
```

```
                                /* reset pointer   */
                                bufcur = buf;
                        }
                        if (*strcur == '\0')
                                break;
                }
        }

        /* write the last block */
        if (len = (unsigned)(bufcur - buf))
                if (write(fd, buf, len) != len)
                        return(FALSE);

        if (close(fd) == EOF)
                return(FALSE);

        return(TRUE);
}
```

The pointer lim points to the last element of the buffer, and the pointer
bufcur points to the current element of the buffer. The terminating
null characters are also written to the file; this is the reason the stop
condition had to be placed within the inner for statement.

The function fretriv (which follows) retrieves a list of variable
length strings from a file. In this function, we use the routine creeat
(see Example 12.2.3). We assume the maximum length of a string is
STRLIM. We also use strsave (see Example 10.2.5).

Using low-level file input, it is not possible to check whether or not
end-of-file has been reached until *after* the read function returns 0. Thus
when a string is added to the list and the current file block is empty, a
new block is read from the file, and only if this succeeds is a new list element created. The array aux is used to collect the current string being
recovered from the file, and the pointer paux is moved along the array
to copy characters from the buffer to that array.

The function fretriv returns NULL if it fails for any reason; otherwise, it returns a pointer to the head of the list.

```
#define STRLIM 100          /* or whatever */

PITEM fretriv(fname)
char fname[];
{
        int fd, n, i;
        PITEM h, haux;
        char buf[BUFSIZE],
                aux[STRLIM + 1],
                *paux = aux,
                *strsave();

        if ((fd = open(fname, O_RDONLY, MODE)) == EOF)
                return(NULL);
```

```
                /* initial read */
                if (n = read(fd, buf, BUFSIZE)) {
                        if (!creeat(&h))
                                return(NULL);
                        haux = h;
                }
                else /* empty file */
                        return(NULL);

                while (n)
                        for (i = 0; ; i++) {
                                if (i == n) {     /* get new block */
                                        n = read(fd, buf, BUFSIZE);
                                        break;
                                }

                                /* collect characters from a string */
                                if ((*paux++ = buf[i]) == '\0') {
                                        /* end-of-string, reset paux */
                                        paux = aux;

                                        /* save in the list */
                                        if ((haux->value = strsave(aux)) == NULL)
                                                return(NULL);

                                        if (i < n-1) {   /* more in the buffer */
                                                if (!creeat(&haux->next))
                                                        return(NULL);
                                                haux = haux->next;
                                        }
                                        else { /* possibly end-of-file */
                                                if (n = read(fd, buf, BUFSIZE)) {
                                                        if (!creeat(&haux->next))
                                                                return(NULL);
                                                        haux = haux->next;
                                                }
                                                break;
                                        }
                                }
                        }

        haux->next = NULL;
        if (paux != aux)
                return(NULL);
        else if (close(fd) == EOF)
                return(NULL);
        else return(h);
}
```

In each step of the main loop, a new block is read from the file into a
buffer represented by the array buf, and then the characters in this
buffer are copied to the array aux. When the terminating \0 character

is encountered, the string is saved in the current list element. If any characters are left in the buffer, a new list element is created; otherwise, a new block is read from the file, and if this read is successful, a new list element is created. ∎

These low-level file operations do not read just ASCII text; they can also be used to read arbitrary *binary* data. This allows many types of applications to be written that require this sort of access, such as binary file editors and installation programs.

14.2 MS-DOS

In this section, we first describe programming in C under the MS-DOS operating system, using the Lattice C compiler [Lat85], version 3.0. We chose this implementation because it is a generic MS-DOS implementation that runs on any MS-DOS machine. Moreover, the Lattice C implementation supports the full Kernighan and Ritchie standard, and its extensions comply to those suggested in the ANSI C standard [Ans86]. We describe some of these extensions in Section 14.2.1.1. We also give a brief description of Instant-C [Ins86], a C interpreter.

14.2.1 Lattice C

Lattice C provides many extensions to standard C to assist program development under MS-DOS, but unfortunately, space does not permit our describing all of them here. Instead, we present several small programs to illustrate some particular features of Lattice C.

The architecture of the 8086 and 8088 is such that direct access to its full megabyte address space is possible only through special **segment registers**. Since the use of these segment registers involves a certain amount of overhead, the compiler comes in four versions, or models, that allow varying amounts of memory to be accessed. This affects how large the code portion of a program and how large the data portion of a program (static variables, the stack, and the heap) may be. If the amount of memory needed for the program code is less than 64K, access to it is more efficient, since NEAR subroutine calls and returns may be used; if the program code exceeds 64K, less efficient FAR calls and returns must be used to manage subroutines. Similarly, if the data used by the program take up less than 64K, pointers 2 bytes in size are sufficient to access any portion of this space; if more than 64K is needed for data, pointers have to be 4 bytes long. The four models are

Model	Code space	Data space
S	64K	64K
P	1M	64K

Model	Code space	Data space
D	64K	1M
L	1M	1M

The versions that allow 1M of memory to be used may not actually be able to obtain this maximum, since code and data must reside in the same address space. For example, if model L is used, and the data space requires 0.2M, the code space may be no larger than 0.8M. In the following examples, we assume the *small* model S is used.

In some memory models, care must be taken when using pointers because sizes of the various pointers may be *different*. For example, in the P memory model with 64K of data memory and 1M of code memory, pointers to data are 2 bytes long, whereas pointers to functions are 4 bytes long.

The Lattice C compiler comes with an `install` program that simplifies the task of setting up a disk for using the compiler on. This is especially useful if the system is being loaded onto a hard disk. By default, the `install` program sets up a directory called `lc`, in which there are subdirectories to store various portions of the Lattice C system; for example,

```
\lc\s          Contains files needed for S model
\lc\source     Contains source code files
```

To compile a program stored in the file `test.c`, you would issue the command

```
lc -ms test
```

The `lc` program is a two-pass compiler; a successful compilation places the object code in a file with an `.obj` extension, `test.obj` in the previous example. The option `-m` specifies which compiler model to select, model S (small) in this case. Alternatively, one of the command files provided with the system may be used. In this case, the user could issue the command

```
lcs test
```

to invoke the command file `lcs.bat`, which is stored under the `lc` directory. A version of this command file is provided for each of the compiler models.

The compiler consults the MS-DOS environment variable INCLUDE to locate files specified in an `#include` command. For example, if this variable is set using

```
SET INCLUDE = \LC\I;\LC\II
```

and the directive

```
#include "stdio.h"
```

is used in a program, the file stdio.h is first looked for in the current directory, and if necessary, the directories listed in INCLUDE (\LC\I and \LC\II in this case) are then searched. If angle brackets are used, for example,

```
#include <stdio.h>
```

the search is limited to those directories listed in INCLUDE.

Lattice C uses Microsoft's link program, which is provided on most MS-DOS systems. To simplify the link command, Lattice again supplies a variety of command files. To link an S model object code file, such as test in the preceding example, the command

```
links test
```

could be given. This results in the command

```
link \lc\s\c+test, test,test/m,\lc\s\ls
```

being executed, which ensures that the necessary libraries are specified for the linker. This command places the executable code in a file with a .exe extension, test.exe in the example. Equivalent link command files are provided for each of the models of the system.

If several object files need to be linked, a second parameter may be specified. For example, the command

```
links test t1+t2+t3
```

would link the object modules test.obj, t1.obj, t2.obj, and t3.obj and place the executable code in the file test.exe.

As we mentioned, we do not try to describe all aspects of the Lattice C system. If you want additional details on the operation of the compiler or the other utilities of the system, see the Lattice C documentation. We describe in detail the following topics:

- Lattice C extensions that comply with the ANSI C standard
- Access to MS-DOS services
- Access to MS-DOS directories
- Access to file attributes (time and archive)
- Memory utility functions

14.2.1.1   The ANSI C Standard

Lattice C implements several extensions suggested by the ANSI C standard:

1. The `void` data type is supported. The compiler will issue a warning if a function that is not `void` does not return a value. ANSI C defines `void` as an empty set of values, not as a synonym for `int`.
2. Enumeration types are supported.
3. Structures and unions may be used in assignment statements, and functions may return structure types. Structures and unions may also be passed as value parameters.
4. External function declarations may include a list of specifiers indicating the types of the formal parameters. For example,

   ```
   extern int * cop(char *, char *);
   ```

   declares `cop` as an external function that takes two parameters of type pointer to character and returns a pointer to integer. This allows the compiler to check whether the number and types of actual parameters correspond to the external declaration and to issue a warning if they do not.
5. The `assert` macro can be used to test the validity of your code:

   ```
   assert(x)
   ```

   checks whether `x` is 0 (false), and if it is, calls the function `_assert(exp,file,line)`, which displays a textual representation of the expression x along with the source file name and line number where the `assert` occurs and aborts execution. To use this macro, the file `assert.h` must be included. You may find it helpful to look at a part of this include file:

   ```
   #ifndef NDEBUG
   #define assert(x) {if(x); \
                       else _assert("x",__FILE__,__LINE__);}
   #else
   #define assert(x)
   #endif
   ```

   This shows that if the symbol NDEBUG is not defined (as would be the default case), debugging should be performed, and the `assert` macro is defined to call the system function `_assert` with the indicated parameters. (The symbols __FILE__ and __LINE__ are special compiler macros that, at any point, are equal to the current file being compiled and current line number in that file, respectively.) If NDEBUG is defined when `assert.h` is included, the `assert` macro value is empty; thus calls to assert would have no effect. The NDEBUG symbol could be defined using

```
#define NDEBUG
```

or by invoking the compiler with the −d option. The programmer could also define his or her own assert macro.

Using assert allows requests for memory, for example, to be easily monitored. Consider the following statements:

```
p = malloc(10);
assert(p);
```

In this example, if malloc returns NULL, the assert on p will result in the call

```
_assert("p",__FILE__,__LINE__);
```

which will print the message

```
Assertion (p) failed in file ... line ...
```

This is assuming NDEBUG is not defined and the user has not redefined the assert macro. A memory allocation check like this would normally be done using an if statement, for example,

```
if ((p = malloc(10)) == NULL)
    error("...");
```

where error would have to be defined by the programmer.
If NDEBUG is defined, no actions will take place when assert is called, since the body of this macro in this instance is *void*. This must be considered when assert is being used in a program. For example, if the statement

```
assert(p = malloc(10));
```

is used and the symbol NDEBUG is defined, this will not be correct, since the assert macro in this case is void, and consequently the call to malloc will not be made. Therefore, only expressions that do not produce side effects should be used with assert. This is consistent with our recommendation in Chapter 5, suggesting that *side effects* in macro calls be avoided. Of course, another possibility is to define the nondebugging version of this macro as follows:

```
#define assert(x)        {(x);}
```

In this version, the call would expand to

```
{p = malloc(10);}
```

Several library functions can be used with assert. For example,

```
isdptr(ptr)
```

returns 0 if ptr is not a valid data pointer. A valid data pointer points
to a cell in the static, automatic, or heap data areas.

Lattice C supports the exit function (see Section 14.1.2). The value
of the argument specified in a call to exit is passed back to the operating system, where it can be used in batch files. For example, a batch file
to run the preceding program may look like

```
IF ERRORLEVEL 1 GOTO ERROR
...
:ERROR
...
```

If a program terminates as a result of calling exit(i), ERRORLEVEL n
is true for i >= n. Thus if the program successfully terminates using
exit(0), its exit code is 0, and ERRORLEVEL 1 would be false. On the
other hand, if the exit(1) is executed, its exit code is 1, and
ERRORLEVEL 1 would be true.

14.2.1.2 MS-DOS Services

In this section, we describe, through two examples, how MS-DOS services may be accessed in Lattice C. We assume you are familiar with
the MS-DOS BDOS and have a manual available.

The header file dos.h defines the union REGS

```
union REGS {
      struct XREG x;
      struct HREG h;
}
```

where XREG defines variables (of type short) to correspond to the
8086's general-purpose 16-bit registers, and HREG defines the corresponding high/low halves of these registers. Another structure, SREGS,
defines short integers to represent the various segment registers of
the 8086.

Support for the 8086's **software interrupts** is provided through the
following functions:

```
int int86(intno, inregs, outregs)
int int86x(intno, inregs, outregs, segsin)
int int86s(intno, segsin, segsout)
```

```
int          intno;
union REGS   *inregs;
union REGS   *outregs;
struct SREGS *segsin, *segsout;
```

The first parameter specifies the interrupt number; `inregs` and `segsin` should be loaded with the appropriate values before the interrupt is issued. After the function terminates, `outregs` and `segsout` will contain result values as defined for the particular interrupt. If the interrupt request requires specific values for the segment registers, `int86x` or `int86s` must be used; otherwise, `int86` is adequate. The current values of the segment registers can be obtained using the function `segread`:

```
segread(segregs)
struct SREGS *segregs;
```

All the interrupt routines return the processor flags as the result of the function.

The MS-DOS services customarily invoked through interrupt number 21 (hexadecimal) may also be accessed through the functions `intdos`, `intdosx`, and `intdoss`. These functions do not specify `intno`, since it is always 21.

Example 14.2.1   To find the amount of free disk space in a specified drive, function 36 may be used. The type `byte` used here is defined in `dos.h` as a synonym for type `char`.

```c
#include "stdio.h"
#include "dos.h"

long dsksize(drive)
int drive;
{
    union REGS inregs, outregs;

    inregs.h.ah = (byte)0x36;
    inregs.h.dl = (byte)drive;
    intdos(&inregs, &outregs);

    if (outregs.x.ax == 0xFFFF) {
        fprintf(stderr, "error in dsksize\n");
        exit(1);
    }

    return (long)outregs.x.bx * (long)outregs.x.cx *
                                (long)outregs.x.ax;
}
```

Both parameters of `intdos` are passed by reference.   ∎

Version 3.0 of Lattice C also provides access to the MS-DOS services through individual functions for each of the services. These functions set up the appropriate `intdos` call themselves, simplifying the programmer's task. For example, to determine the free disk space, the function

```
int getdfs(drive, info)
int drive;
struct DISKINFO *info;
```

may be used. This function returns −1 if it fails, and it returns 0 otherwise. The first parameter is 1 for drive A, 2 for drive B, and so on. The type of the second parameter is defined in `dos.h`:

```
struct DISKINFO {
    unsigned short free, cpd, spc, bps;
}
```

where `free` is the number of free clusters, `cpd` is the number of clusters per drive, `spc` is the number of sectors per cluster, and `bps` is the number of bytes per sector.

Example 14.2.2   The following program expects a single drive character on the command line. If no argument is provided, the current drive is assumed. It prints the number of free bytes on this drive. To test whether the specified drive is an existing drive, the library function `chgdsk(dr)` is used. This function returns the highest allowable drive, and if possible, changes the current drive to `dr`. If `dr` is out of range, `chgdsk` returns the highest allowable drive. If no drive is specified on the command line, the program uses the library function `getdsk` to get the current drive. This function returns 0 for drive A, 1 for drive B, and so on.

```
#include "dos.h"
#include "stdio.h"

main(argc, argv)
int argc;
char *argv[];
{
    struct DISKINFO info;
    int dr, high;

    high = chgdsk(100);
    switch (argc) {
    case 1: dr = getdsk();
            if (getdfs(dr + 1, &info) == 0) {
                printf("Drive %c has %ld free bytes\n",
                        dr + 'A', (long)(info.free) *
                        (long)(info.spc) * (long)(info.bps)
                exit(0);
            }
            fprintf(stderr, "error in getdfs\n");
            exit(1);
```

```
          case 2: if (high < (dr = argv[1][0] - 'A' + 1)) {
                  fprintf(stderr, "Drive %c does not exist\n",
                                  argv[1][0]);
                  exit(1);
                  }
                  if (getdfs(dr, &info) == 0) {
                  printf("Drive %c has %ld free bytes\n",
                                  argv[1][0], (long)(info.free) *
                                  (long)(info.spc) * (long)(info.bps));
                  exit(0);
                  }
                  fprintf(stderr, "error in getdfs\n");
                  exit(1);

          default:fprintf(stderr, "usage: dsk [drive]\n");
                  exit(1);
                  }
  }
```
∎

14.2.1.3 MS-DOS Directories

Version 3.0 of Lattice C supports most of the MS-DOS directory operations. These include

```
    int getcd(drive, path)
```

stores the current directory path in the parameter path. Parameter drive is 0 for the current drive, 1 for A, and so on.

```
    int chdir(path)
```

changes the current directory to the specified path.

```
    int mkdir(path)
```

creates a new directory in the specified path.

```
    int rmdir(path)
```

removes the directory in the specified path.

Example 14.2.3 demonstrates how some of these functions can be used. It also shows the use of some the library string functions that operate on filenames:

```
    int stcgfn(node, name)
```

finds the node portion of a filename path and stores it in the array node. The size of node (the number of characters) is returned as the result of the function. For example,

```
    i = stcgfn(node, "\\a\\b\\nam.c")
```

stores nam.c in node and 5 in i.

```
void strmfp(name, path, node)
```

creates a filename from the specified path and node. For example,

```
strmfp(name, "\\a\\b", "test.c")
```

stores \a\b\test.c in name.

Example 14.2.3 The following program moves the file specified on the command line either from the indicated directory to the current directory or from the current directory to another directory, depending on how the program is invoked. In either case, the name of the file is retained. For example,

```
move \a\b\test
```

executed in the directory \x\y will move the file test in the directory \a\b to the directory \x\y, deleting the file \a\b\test and creating this file as \x\y\test. If move is executed with two parameters, a file can be moved from the current directory to another directory. For example,

```
move fname \a\b
```

moves the file fname from the current directory to \a\b\fname. First, the function move is defined. This function "moves" a directory entry, that is, it deletes from one directory and places in another. The function takes two parameters that represent path names; both paths must be on the same device.

```
#include "stdio.h"
#include "dos.h"
#include "string.h"

void move(fname1, fname2)
char *fname1, *fname2;
{
    union REGS inregs, outregs;
    struct SREGS sregs;

    inregs.h.ah = (byte)0x56; /* dos 56 - move dir entry */
    segread(&sregs);
    inregs.x.dx = (short)fname1;
    inregs.x.di = (short)fname2;
    intdosx(&inregs, &outregs, &sregs);
```

```
            /* check for errors */
            if (outregs.x.ax == 2) {
                fprintf(stderr, "error in move\n");
                exit(1);
            }
    }
```

The constant FMSIZE used in the main program (which follows) is defined in the file dos.h to be a "safe" length for a filename path. The maximum length of a path under MS-DOS version 2 is 64.

The library function getcd, which gets the path to the current directory from the root, is also used in the main program. Because an initial \ is not included, an empty string is returned if the current directory is the root. The library string operation strins(s, t) inserts t in front of s.

```
main(argc, argv)
int  argc;
char *argv[];
{
        char path[65], node[FMSIZE],
             fname[FMSIZE], fname2[FMSIZE];
        int  size;

        /* get current dir */
        if (getcd(getdsk() + 1, path) != 0) {
            fprintf(stderr, "error in getcd\n");
            exit(1);
        }

        switch(argc) {
        case 2 : /* move \a\b\fname */
                 /* get node */
                 if ((size = stcgfn(node, argv[1])) == 0) {
                     fprintf(stderr, "incorrect name\n");
                     exit(1);
                 }
                 /* concat with curdir */
                 if (path[0] != '\0')    /* not in root */
                     strmfp(fname, path, node);
                 strins(fname, "\\");
                 move(argv[1], fname);
                 exit(0);

        case 3 : /* move name \a\b (directory) */
                 /* create a fname to copy to */
                 strmfp(fname, argv[2], argv[1]);
                 /* create a name to copy to */
                 if (path[0] == '\0')   /* in root */
                     strcpy(fname2, argv[1]);
                 else strmfp(fname2, path, argv[1]);
                 strins(fname2, "\\");
                 move(fname2, fname);
                 exit(0);
```

```
          default: fprintf(stderr, "usage:\t move pathname\n");
                   fprintf(stderr, "or\tmove fname directory\n");
                   exit(1);
          }
}                                                                          ■
```

14.2.1.4   File Attributes

An MS-DOS file has several attributes associated with it. In this section, we demonstrate how two of these attributes—the **archive** ("A") attribute and the file creation time stamp—may be accessed.

The "A" attribute is set when a file is created or updated and is intended to be used by incremental backup programs to determine whether a file has to be backed up.

The **creation time** attribute can be used to determine whether a file has been modified since the last time it was compiled by comparing it to the time stamp of the corresponding object code file.

Example 14.2.4   The following program can be used to back up files. It checks the "A" attribute, and if it is on, copies the file to another drive and clears this attribute. The program can be called in three ways:

back	To back up all files on the current drive and directory to drive A
back fname	To back up file fname (wild cards allowed) to drive A
back fname drive	To back up file fname to the specified drive

Two useful functions provided by Lattice C are used to implement the program back:

```
int getfnl(filpat, names, siz, attr)
char *filpat, *names;
int siz, attr;
```

This function finds all files in the current directory that match filpat, and have attributes indicated by attr, and stores their names in the siz byte memory area pointed to by names. The function returns the number of files that matched the search criteria. Each filename is terminated by \0, and the last string is empty. Strings stored in this manner can be easily separated using

```
int strbpl(pointer, max, names)
char *pointer[];
int max;
char *names;
```

The function strbpl returns a value that indicates how many pointers to strings have been placed in the array pointer (at most max). For example, if the code

```
char days[] = {"Monday", "Tuesday", "Wednesday", "Thursday",
               "Friday", "Saturday", "Sunday", '\0'};
char *pdays[7];
int n;
n = strbpl(pdays, 7, days);
```

is executed, n would be set to 7, and the individual elements of pdays
would contain pointers to the seven strings in the character array days.

The backup program follows. Since large arrays are used to store the
filenames that match the pattern provided by the user, the size of the
user's stack area is increased.

```
unsigned _STACK =  20000;
#include "stdio.h"
#include "string.h"
#include "dos.h"
#include "fcntl.h"
#define NOFFILES 512
#define ALLSIZE (NOFFILES * 20)
#define ARCH 32    /* indicates bit 5, archive bit */

main(argc, argv)
int argc;
char *argv[];
{
     extern int cop(char *, char );
     char names[ALLSIZE], *fnames[NOFFILES], *curr,
          drive, *name;
     int i, count;

     if (argc > 3) {
          fprintf(stderr, "usage: back [filpat [drive]]\n");
          exit(1);
     }

     switch(argc) {
     case 1 : name = "*.*";
              drive = 'A';
              break;
     case 2 : name = argv[1];
              drive = 'A';
              break;
     case 3 : name = argv[1];
              drive = argv[2][0];
              if (toupper(drive) - 'A' > chgdsk(100)) {
                   fprintf(stderr, "Incorrect drive %c\n",
                                    drive);
                   exit(1);
              }
     }

     if ((count = getfnl(name,names,ALLSIZE,ARCH)) == 0)
          exit(0);
```

```
    if (strbpl(fnames, NOFFILES, names) != count) {
        fprintf(stderr, "Too many files\n");
        exit(1);
    }

    for (i = 0, count--; count + 1; count--)
        if (getfa(current = fnames[count]) == ARCH) {
            printf("Backing up\t%s\n", curr);
            if (cop(curr, drive) == EOF)
                fprintf(stderr, "Cannot back up %s\n", curr)
            else i++;
            if (chgfa(curr, 0) == -1)
                fprintf(stderr,
                    "Cannot reset A attribute in %s\n", curr);
        }

    printf("%d file(s) backed up\n", i);
}
```

The function cop(fname, dr) copies the file fname to the file with the same name on drive dr and returns EOF if it fails; otherwise, it returns 0. It uses the low-level file operations (see Section 14.1.3); under MS-DOS, there are no file permissions, so the third argument of open is always 0.

```
int cop(fname, dr)
char *fname;
char dr;
{
    int f1, f2, n;
    char drive[25], b[512];

    drive[0] = dr;
    drive[1] = ':';
    drive[2] = '\0';
    if ((f1 = open(fname, O_RDONLY ¦ O_RAW, 0)) == -1)
        return(EOF);

    strcat(drive, fname);
    if ((f2 = open(drive,O_CREAT¦O_WRONLY¦O_RAW,0)) == -1) {
        fprintf(stderr, "Cannot open output file:%s\n", fname
        return(EOF);
    }

    while ((n = read(f1, b, 512)) > 0)
        if (write(f2, b, n) != n) {
            fprintf(stderr,
                "Write error in output file: %s\n", fname);
            return(EOF);
        }
```

```
            close(f1);
            close(f2);
            return(0);
      }
```

Example 14.2.5   The following program compares the creation times of two files passed on the command line and prints a message indicating which was created first. To do this, the library function

```
int dfind(info, filpat, attr)
struct FILEINFO *info;
char *filpat;
int attr;
```

is used, which searches the current directory for the first file that matches filpat and has attributes attr and, if successful, returns 0 through dfind and information about the file through info. The companion function dnext can be used to search for other files matching the pattern.

The structure FILEINFO is defined in the file dos.h

```
struct FILEINFO {
      char reserved[21];
      char attr;
      long time;
      long size;
      char fname[13];
};
```

The creation time and date are packed in the long (32-bit) integer time, which can be unpacked and stored in a character array x using the function

```
ftunpk(time, x)
```

where x is a 6-byte array mapped as follows:

x[0]	contains	year−1980
x[1]	contains	month
x[2]	contains	day
x[3]	contains	hour
x[4]	contains	minute
x[5]	contains	second

This unpacked version can be converted into a manageable form using two other functions, stpdate and stptime.

The function stpdate has three parameters defined as follows:

```
char *stpdate(p, mode, date)
char *p;
int mode;
char *date;
```

It converts the file date stored in the 3-byte array `date` as

date[0]	contains	year−1980
date[1]	contains	month
date[2]	contains	day

into a string. The resulting string is stored in memory in either ASCII or BCD format, starting at the address pointed to by p. The actual format depends on the value of `mode`; for example, if `mode` is 2, the format is a 9-byte ASCII string (including a terminating \0):

mm/*dd*/*yy*

The function `stpdate` returns a pointer to the first byte beyond the result string (the \0 character). For example, assume we define an array

```
char stamp[6];
```

which (as the result of a call to `ftunpk`) contains

stamp[0]	stamp[1]	stamp[2]	stamp[3]	stamp[4]	stamp[5]
06	05	11	18	32	45

If we have the variables

```
char b[22], *np;
```

defined, after the call

```
np = stpdate(b, 2, stamp);
```

the string b would contain

```
05/11/86
```

terminated by a null, and np would point to this null character.
A similar function, `stptime`, is defined as

```
char *stptime(p, mode, time)
char *p;
int mode;
char time[4];
```

It converts the array `time` stored in the form

time[0]	hour
time[1]	minute

```
time[2]      second
time[3]      hundredth
```

to a string. The parameter mode specifies how the time is to be converted. For example, if mode is 6, the time is returned in a format that can be easily displayed as

hh:mm:ss AP

where *AP* is either AM or PM.

The ordinal values of the entries in the array time are used, not their character representations. The function returns a pointer to the first byte past the result string.

Continuing the example in which the call to stpdata stored the date in the array b, assume a blank has been subsequently stored in b immediately after the date 05/11/86, using

```
*np++ = ' ';
```

and the following call to the function stptime has been made:

```
np = stptime(np, 6, &stamp[3]);
```

The last argument in this call may be somewhat puzzling to you. Recall that in the definition of stptime, the parameter time is defined as a four-element character array. This is equivalent to specifying time as a pointer to char. That is, the array size 4 in this specification is merely for documentation and is actually ignored by the compiler. The actual parameter &stamp[3] is simply a pointer to character and is therefore correct. This call to stptime inserts the time, currently stored in stamp[3] through stamp[6], in the remaining part of the array b. The contents of b would now be

```
05/11/86 6:32:45 PM
```

The function ftime(fname, stamp) returns the creation time and date of the file fname as 6 bytes through parameter stamp and as a string in the format

mm/dd/yy hh:mm:ss AP

through function ftime:

```
#include "dos.h"
#include "stdio.h"
#include "string.h"
```

```
char *ftime(fname, stamp)
char *fname, *stamp;
{
     struct FILEINFO info;
     char *p, *b, *malloc();

     if (dfind(&info, fname, 0))
          return(NULL);

     if ((b = malloc(22)) == NULL)
          return(NULL);

     ftunpk(info.time, stamp);
     p = stpdate(b, 2, stamp);
     *p++ = ' ';
     p = stptime(p, 6, &stamp[3]);

     return(b);
}
```

The main program prints the last access times of both files and then
compares them:

```
main(argc, argv)
int argc;
char *argv[];
{
     char stamp1[7], stamp2[7], *b1, *b2;
     int res;
     extern char *ftime(char *, char *);

     if (argc != 3) {
          fprintf(stderr, "usage: compare fname1 fname2\n");
          exit(1);
     }

     if ((b1 = ftime(argv[1], stamp1)) == NULL ||
         (b2 = ftime(argv[2], stamp2)) == NULL) {
               fprintf(stderr, "error in ftime\n");
               exit(1);
     }

     stamp1[6] = stamp2[6] = '\0';

     printf("Time of %s is %s\n", argv[1], b1);
     printf("Time of %s is %s\n", argv[2], b2);
     if ((res = strcmp(stamp1, stamp2)) < 0)
          printf("%s is older than %s\n", argv[1], argv[2]);
     else if (res > 0)
          printf("%s is older than %s\n", argv[2], argv[1]);
     else printf("%s and %s were created at the same time\n",
                    argv[1], argv[2]);
     exit(0);
}
```

Note that stamp1 and stamp2 have been defined as arrays of seven elements so that they could be treated as strings and, after adding the terminating null character, be compared using strcmp. ∎

Example 14.2.6   The following program shows a simple version of the **make** program available under Unix that checks whether a file has been updated since its last compilation and recompiles it if necessary. The function ftime is used as well as the library function system(cmd), which executes the specified MS-DOS command. Two new library string operations are also used:

```
int stcgfe(ext, name)
```

stores in ext the extension of the filename passed in name and returns the length of this extension. For example, the call

```
stcgfe(ext, "\\a\\b\\f.c");
```

places the string c in ext. And

```
void strmfe(newname, oldname, ext)
```

stores in the string newname the value of oldname with its extension changed to ext.

The complete program follows:

```
#include "dos.h"
#include "stdio.h"
#include "string.h"

main(argc, argv)
int argc;
char *argv[];
{
    char stamp1[7], stamp2[7], *b1, *b2,
        fname[FMSIZE+7], objnam[FMSIZE];
    extern char *ftime(char *, char *);
    int res;

    if (argc != 2) {
        fprintf(stderr, "usage: make fname\n");
        exit(1);
    }

    if (stcgfe(fname, argv[1]) == 0)
        strmfe(fname, argv[1], "c");
    else strcpy(fname, argv[1]);

    /* creates .obj name */
    strmfe(objnam, fname, "obj");
```

```
    /* check if it exists */
    if ((b1 = ftime(fname, stamp1)) == NULL) {
        fprintf(stderr, "error in ftime\n");
        exit(1);
    }
    if ((b2 = ftime(objnam, stamp2)) == NULL) {
        fprintf(stderr, "%s does not exist\n", objnam);
        exit(1);
    }

    stamp1[6] = stamp2[6] = '\0';
    if ((res = strcmp(stamp1, stamp2)) > 0) {
        /* recompile */
        strins(fname, "lc -ms ");
        if (system(fname) != 0) {
            fprintf(stderr, "Cannot run compiler\n");
            exit(1);
        }
    }
    exit(0);
}
```

14.2.1.5 Memory Operations

Several functions are designed to allow efficient manipulation of blocks of memory, for example,

```
movmem(source, destin, siz)
char *source, *destin;
unsigned siz;
```

which moves a block of memory of the size siz from the address source to the address destin. This routine is implemented in optimized assembly code and thus is very fast.

Example 14.2.7   In applications such as editors it is often necessary to insert a character into a memory buffer, requiring a (possibly large) portion of the buffer to be shifted down to make space for the character (or characters) being inserted. This could be done directly in C using a loop, but if a large amount of data is being moved, a loop may be inefficient; thus movmem should be used. The following function assumes the size of the buffer is defined by the constant SIZE. The function

```
insert(buf, last, pos, c)
```

which inserts the character c at position pos in the buffer buf and updates the variable last, is implemented. The variable last points to the last element of the buffer that has been used. If no room is left in the array, the function returns 0; otherwise, it returns 1.

```
#define SIZE   65000L   /* or whatever */

int insert(buf, last, pos, c)
char buf[];
char **last, *pos;
char c;
{
     if (pos>=buf&&pos<buf+SIZE &&*last < buf+SIZE-1) {
          /* make room */
          movmem(pos, pos + 1, (unsigned)(*last - pos));
          *pos = c;
          (*last)++;
          return(1);
     }
     return(0);
}
```

Other memory functions provided by the Lattice C system include

memchr	To find a character in a memory block
memcmp	To compare two memory blocks
memset	To set a memory block to a particular value

Additional useful Lattice C functions are

argopt	Get options from argument list
chkml	Check for largest memory block available
getenv	Get environment variable
putenv	Add or replace environment string
onbreak	Plant break trap
onerror	MS-DOS critical error trap
onexit	Exit trap

There is also a complete set of routines for dealing with Unix-like "handle" file I/O.

14.2.2 Instant-C

In this section, we describe Instant-C [Ins86], an integrated environment consisting of a full-screen editor, linker, and interpreter. This system is useful for learning C and debugging C programs. Instant-C is implemented to work on an IBM-PC compatible microcomputer, but it will also work on any computer running MS-DOS (although we did encounter several small problems when using a non-PC compatible).

The basic file, ic.exe, is rather large—279040 bytes. Instant-C requires at least 512K bytes of internal memory, but more is recommended. After loading Instant-C, the user is running the interpreter, and typing any C expression will cause its *interpretation*, for example,

```
# int i;
```

(# is Instant-C's prompt).

```
# i = 4;
# printf("value of %d\n", i);
4
```

The static error checking performed by Instant-C is not as good as an interpreted language could provide. For example, the statement

```
# printf("%d", i, i);
```

will be accepted. The main strength of Instant-C lies in *run-time* checks, especially when calling functions.

The Instant-C editor operates on functions rather than on files. To create a new function, for example, test, the user types

```
ed test
```

which initiates the editor and creates a function text called test.c. All currently used function texts are stored in internal memory and may be edited as needed. The editor has an option of compiling the function, and if the compilation is successful, the user is back at interpreter level. At this level, the function can be interpreted. The execution of a function can be *interrupted* if a call to a special breakpoint function _() is inserted in the function. A run-time error will also terminate the execution of a function.

The execution stack at the point of the interruption may be examined, allowing all variables within the scope of the current function (those on the top of the stack) to be displayed or changed. To access variables in the scope of any other function currently on the stack, the user can issue the command

```
local function-name
```

to change the current context. Another command,

```
back
```

shows the name of the routine that called the function that has been interrupted. There are other debugging mechanisms, for example, trace, to start tracing a function, or watch, to start watching changes in a variable. We demonstrate the use of Instant-C on a sample program that creates a linked list of integers. We intentionally put errors in the code and debug them as part of this exercise.

Consider the following version:

```c
typedef struct elem {
    struct elem *next;
    int val;
} ELEM, *PELEM;

void new(p)
PELEM p;
{
    if ((p = (PELEM) malloc(sizeof(ELEM))) == NULL)
        exit(0);
}

main()
{
    int i, j;
    PELEM c, h;

    new(h);
    c = h;
    for (i = 0;  i < 9;  i++) {
        printf("Another integer please: ");
        scanf("%d", &j);
        new(c->next);
        c = c->next;
        c->val = j;
    }
    c->next = NULL;

    for (c = h;  c;  c = c->next)
        printf("%d ", c->val);
}
```

When this program was executed, Instant-C interrupted its execution with the message:

```
Execution interrupted: Reference through NULL pointer at
"main" line 11:

      scanf("%d", &j);
=>    new(c->next);
      c = c->next;
```

The value of c was inspected:

```
# c
     address 0x0000
```

From this error, it was clear that the cause of the interruption was an attempt to perform a remote access using –> on a NULL pointer. The formal parameter p was changed to *p, and a breakpoint was inserted in new:

```
void new(p)
PELEM *p;
{
     _();
     if ((*p = (PELEM) malloc(sizeof(ELEM))) == NULL)
          exit(0);
}
```

and the execution was restarted. This time the first interrupt was caused by the call to _():

```
Execution interrupted: breakpoint at "new" line 4:

     {
=>       _();
         if ((*p = (PELEM) malloc(sizeof(ELEM))) == NULL)
              exit(0);
```

From this point, the execution was continued step by step using the Instant-C command step. After executing two consecutive steps, the execution was again interrupted:

```
Execution interrupted: Reference through NULL pointer at
"new" line 5:

     {
         _();
=>       if ((*p = (PELEM) malloc(sizeof(ELEM))) == NULL)
              exit(0);
```

To find the value of h, the command

```
local main
```

was issued, since h was invisible in new. The value of h (the actual parameter supposed to be passed by reference) turned out to be 0, which made it possible to make another correction.

This description should give you some sense of how Instant-C can be used for both learning C and debugging C programs.

14.3 THE MACINTOSH

In this section, we discuss programming in C on the Apple Macintosh microcomputer. First, we briefly describe the Macintosh environment and comment on aspects of this environment relevant to C programmers. Then, we describe two existing C systems—Aztec C by Manx Software Systems, Inc. [Man84] and LightspeedC by THINK Technologies, Inc. [Thi86]. Unfortunately, because of the complexity of the Macintosh environment, presenting anything more than an overview of this system is impossible. We hope, however, that our discussion gives you a sense of what programming in C on the Macintosh is like. If you are interested in further details, see *Inside Macintosh* [App86].

14.3.1 Macintosh Programming Issues

Designing and using a C system for the Macintosh poses some problems not normally encountered for more traditional microcomputers. Because the full power of the Macintosh cannot be realized without making use of the vast assortment of routines available within the Macintosh's ROM **Toolbox**, any program development system must provide the user with complete and direct access to this Toolbox.

It is, of course, the implementor's responsibility to ensure that this interface is reasonably supported. To this end, when developing a C programming system for the Macintosh, the implementor has to solve certain problems that result directly from the origins of this machine.

The forerunner of Macintosh was the **Apple Lisa**, a 68000-based high-end microcomputer. Its ROM Toolbox was written in Lisa Pascal, and its routines were designed to be directly callable from Lisa Pascal. When the Macintosh was developed, the Lisa's ROM Toolbox was rewritten in optimized 68000 assembly code to improve its performance and used in the Macintosh. However, this new ROM's compatibility with Lisa Pascal was maintained, which allowed programs written in Lisa Pascal on the Lisa to run with little or no modification on the Macintosh.

Even though the heart of the Macintosh's operating system has Pascal origins, this does not mean the Macintosh must be programmed in Pascal. More C-based development systems than Pascal-based systems have been designed for the Macintosh. However, because of the differences between Pascal and C, the Pascal-based Toolbox routines pose certain problems for a standard C compiler; thus the compiler must provide some mechanism to help the programmer use the Toolbox.

Available C development systems tackle the problem in one of two ways. One approach is to provide special "glue" routines for each of the

Toolbox services that make the necessary conversions when a Toolbox request is made from a C program. From the user's viewpoint, this provides a basically transparent interface to the Toolbox, but it is at the cost of increased overhead each time a Toolbox call is made. Rather than use this glued interface, several systems provide mechanisms that allow calls to the Toolbox routines to be made directly, with any necessary conversions being made either by the compiler or by the user. This direct interface maximizes the performance of C programs that use the Toolbox, but it is more difficult for the compiler implementor to support and is not entirely hidden from the user. Moreover, the direct approach requires that certain nonstandard features be provided by the C compiler, which might upset some C purists.

There are two aspects of Pascal and C implementations that cause these interface problems: *parameter passing* and *strings*.

Parameter Passing

Standard C generally uses the system stack to pass parameters to functions and procedures. The order in which these parameters are pushed on the stack is usually from right to left so that on entry to a subroutine, the parameter on top of the stack is the first parameter of the subroutine. Most Pascal systems also use the stack for passing parameters, but the order in which the parameters are pushed on the stack is usually from *left to right*—the exact opposite of C. This does not create any problems if the subroutine being called has no more than one parameter. However, if a C subroutine has more than one parameter, when the routine is called, the parameters are in reverse order on the stack when compared to an equivalent Pascal function.

Since the Toolbox routines are Pascal-based, when they are called by a C function, the parameters are not in the order expected by the Toolbox. Reversing these parameters is one of the tasks performed by the glue-based interface and obviously involves a fair amount of overhead each time a Toolbox routine is called. The direct interface solves the problem by having the compiler push the parameters on the stack in the order opposite from how it normally would whenever a Toolbox routine is called. This eliminates the overhead but requires a special compiler feature.

An obvious solution would be to simply reverse the order of the parameters when one of these Toolbox routines is called from C. However, all the documents describing the Macintosh environment, and the Toolbox in particular, use the Pascal order for describing the operating system functions. Thus the programmer would have to consciously make the proper adjustments when calling these routines from a C program. Since it would be easy to forget to do this, it is not an attractive solution to the problem.

Strings

Many of the Toolbox routines manipulate character strings. In C, strings are sequences of characters terminated by a null byte. Lisa Pascal, on the other hand, defines a string as a sequence of characters *preceded* by a byte indicating its length. Since the Toolbox routines expect strings to be in the latter form, C programs that pass strings to the Toolbox must convert them to the Pascal format. In the case of the glued interface, this can again be handled transparently by having the glue routines make the necessary conversion before calling the Toolbox. However, this would mean the string conversion would be performed every time a call is made. In the direct interface, the approach is to provide the user with a mechanism to convert C strings to Pascal strings and to require that the user make the necessary conversions before calling the Toolbox. This means the conversion has to be done only once for a given call, but the burden is placed on the user to ensure that it is done.

Another aspect of programming on the Macintosh that presents problems to the user is the **window-based** user interface. Although applications may be written that use a more traditional line-oriented user interface, it is recommended that a specific set of guidelines be followed when developing a Macintosh application so that the user interface is supported in a consistent manner. This standard Macintosh interface uses a mouse as its principal input device along with such things as pulldown menus, dialog boxes, and multiple windows. Unfortunately, the programming effort required to support this interface is significant and is often more involved than the application being developed.

It is therefore difficult to present programs that demonstrate features of the Macintosh, since even the simplest of examples can be several pages long. The programs we have chosen in this section are indeed simple, but they illustrate what typical Macintosh applications are like.

14.3.2 AZTEC C

In this section, we describe programming on the Macintosh using the Aztec C development system. We chose this particular system because we felt, of the systems available at the time of this writing, it was the most complete application development system.

Aztec C provides the Macintosh programmer with a Unix-like environment through a program called the SHELL. Unlike typical Macintosh applications, this environment uses a traditional line-oriented user interface rather than a mouse driven one. Since this shell is Unix-based, it provides the user with many of the facilities typically available under Unix to assist program development. For example, the Aztec compiler, assembler, and linker are known as cc, as, and ln, respectively, and offer many of the same options as their Unix equivalents.

Even though the environment presented to the user is Unix-based, the Macintosh's Toolbox is completely supported, allowing the development of standard Macintosh applications. On the other hand, while in this environment, traditional Unix-like programs, supporting command line arguments, I/O redirection, shell variables, and so on, may be written. This allows a programmer to write C programs without having to deal with the complexities of the Macintosh user interface. Some of the sample programs in this book were tested using Aztec C on a Macintosh and required little or no modification.

14.3.2.1   The Compiler

The Aztec C compiler is a one-pass compiler implemented according to the language definition found in [Ker78]. To compile a program, a command of the form

cc [−*options*] *filename.c*

is given, where [−*options*] specifies optional parameters. The output of the compiler is an assembly language program that must be assembled using the Manx assembler. By default, this assembler is automatically called by the compiler when it has completed compiling a program. The option −A tells the compiler not to start the assembler. Output from the assembler is an object code file that must be linked using the Manx linker.

The Aztec compiler maintains a high degree of compatibility with many C systems. Unfortunately, the version of the compiler that we reviewed did not support several commonly found extensions to the C language, including bit fields, enumeration types, and passing structures by value.

The compiler supports several extensions to assist the user in accessing the Toolbox. One of these is the #asm directive, which allows 68000 assembly code to be interspersed within C source code, for example,

```
main()
{
... C code ...
#asm
... assembly language code ...
#endasm
... C code ...
}
```

The Aztec compiler supports a direct interface to the Toolbox. This is made possible by a special declaration syntax that identifies a function or procedure as Pascal-based. Thus when such a routine is called, the parameters are pushed on the stack in the reverse order. The form of this type of declaration is

```
pascal type func ( ) = 0xnnnn;
```

where *type* is the type of value returned by the function, *func* is the name of the function, and 0x*nnnn* is its trap value. (A **trap** is a special type of 68000 machine instruction that causes a jump to take place; each of the Toolbox routines has a unique trap value and is normally called using this trap instruction.) To assist the user in this, the Aztec system provides several include files that declare each of the Toolbox routines along with related constants, structures, and so on. For example, if the user plans to write an application that uses menus, the header file menu.h should be included.

To complete the interface, the Aztec compiler provides the user with a mechanism to manage Pascal format strings. To specify a Pascal format string constant, it must start with the sequence \P. For example, if the string constant

```
"\Pstring"
```

is used, the compiler will create a string consisting of these characters and generate a length byte as the first character of the string (the zeroth character). The string will still be null terminated so that it can be used with the standard C string functions. The length byte does *not* include the terminating null.

In addition to this, two functions are provided to convert C strings into Pascal strings and vice versa:

```
char *ctop(cstr)
char *cstr;

char *ptoc(pstr)
char *pstr;
```

The function ctop converts a C format string into an equivalent Pascal format string, overlaying the original. A pointer to the converted string is returned. The function ptoc performs the opposite conversion.

14.3.2.2 Writing Macintosh Applications with Aztec C
As we mentioned, it is possible to write standard Unix-like C programs to run under the Aztec shell environment. For example,

```
main()
{
    printf("Hello, world!\n");
}
```

would compile and run under the shell without any further change. However, by default, the executable file created by the linker for an example like this would run only under this special shell environment, not under the **Finder**, Macintosh's normal user interface. This obviously is not acceptable if stand-alone applications are to be developed for the Macintosh for users who do not have the Aztec shell environment. Aztec C solves this problem by allowing the user to create three different types of executable code files.

When an Aztec C program is loaded for execution, control is first given to a special function called `Croot`. This function performs initialization activities that select the program's characteristics, and then calls the program's `main` function. The Aztec system provides three different versions of the `Croot` function that determine the way in which a program may interact with the outside environment. The three versions of this function and the characteristics they give a program are

shcroot   With this version of `Croot`, programs may be executed only within the Aztec shell, not from the Finder. Typical Unix-like features, such as command line arguments, I/O redirection, and so on are supported.

sacroot   This version of `Croot` allows an application to run stand-alone, that is, under the Finder or the shell. Standard C console I/O routines, such as `scanf` and `printf`, and Unix-style features, such as I/O redirection and command line arguments, are not supported.

mixcroot   Programs using this version of `Croot` may be activated by the Finder or the shell, and standard I/O functions may be used. Other Unix-style features, such as I/O redirection are not supported.

By default, the linker uses the `shroot` version of `Croot`, so programs may be used only within the shell environment. If programs are to be used outside the Aztec system, they must be linked with either `sacroot` or `mixcroot`, depending on whether or not standard I/O functions are needed. The sample program that uses `printf` must be linked with `mixcroot` if it is to be activated from the Finder:

```
ln hello.o -M mixcroot.o -lc
```

The -M option tells the linker a specific version of `Croot` is to be linked, in this case `mixcroot`. The -1 option is used to link a program with a library. This particular example tells the linker to search the standard C library c.lib; if floating point operations are used in a program, the option −lm is also needed so that the math library m.lib is searched.

The appearance of this program when it executes is not the same as the previous example; in that case, the program essentially mimics how the equivalent program under Unix would act when it was executed:

```
-? hello
Hello, world!

-?
```

The −? is the standard prompt under the Aztec system. Although the mixcroot version of the program still supports the standard I/O functions, it now begins to act more like a Macintosh application. The program starts out by clearing the screen, then displays the message in the top-left corner, and finally returns to either the shell or the Finder, depending on where the program was launched from. The message itself will appear on the screen only briefly, for as soon as the program terminates, the screen is cleared. To have the message stay on the screen longer, the following addition could be made to the program:

```
#include <event.h>
main()
{
     printf("Hello, world!\n");
     while (!Button())
          ;
}
```

Since the key to the Macintosh interface is the mouse, it is sensible to make use of it, even in a simple example like this. The function Button is a Toolbox routine that returns true if the button on the mouse is pressed. So in this example, after the message is displayed on the screen, it will simply loop until the user presses the mouse button, and the screen will stay intact until that time.

Since this function is one of the Toolbox routines, it must be declared as a Pascal type function, and its trap number must be specified. As we indicated, to simplify the programmer's task, several include files are provided that define certain groups of Toolbox functions along with associated types and constants. The function Button belongs to a group of routines responsible for the management of events under the Macintosh environment. In fact, **event management** is the most important principle of effective programming on the Macintosh, since the Macintosh environment is event driven, with many of the actions performed by the user being recorded in a system event queue. For example, whenever the user presses the mouse button, types on the keyboard, or inserts a disk in a disk drive, the application running is notified by means of an event placed in the event queue. Moreover, a special "update screen" event is posted whenever a window that had been overlapping another window is closed.

An item may be removed from the event queue using the function

```
Boolean GetNextEvent(eventMask,theEventPtr)
short eventMask;
EventRecord *theEventPtr;
```

where `EventRecord` is defined in `event.h` as

```
typedef struct {
          short   what;
          long    message;
          long    when;
          Point   where;
          short   modifiers;
    } EventRecord;
```

`Point` is a structure type defined in the header file, `quickdraw.h` which is automatically included when `event.h` is included. We discuss this further below.

When `GetNextEvent` is called from a program, an event record of the type specified by `eventMask` is returned through the pointer `theEventPtr`. The event manager always returns the highest priority event available of the requested types, so strictly speaking, the event queue is a priority queue (for example, a mouse event has higher priority than a keyboard event). It returns true if the event returned has to be processed further. The type of the event returned is indicated by the attribute `what` in the event record. If no event of the indicated type is available, a special "null" event is returned, and the function returns false.

The parameter `eventMask` allows the user to specify the types of events to be examined. Although this mask could be specified as a numeric value, this is rarely done, since special constants are defined in `event.h` to represent the different types of event. Some of these are

```
#define mDownMask     0x0002    /* mouse button down */
#define mUpMask       0x0004    /* mouse button up */
#define keyDownMask   0x0008    /* key pressed */
#define keyUpMask     0x0010    /* key released */
#define autoKeyMask   0x0020    /* auto key repeat */
#define diskMask      0x0080    /* disk inserted */
#define everyEvent    0xffff    /* select all events */
```

The mask `everyEvent` is frequently used, since this will tell the function `GetNextEvent` to examine all currently available events and returns the one with the highest priority.

The following example illustrates how events may be managed; it is an extended version of the previous example, which now waits for either the mouse button or a key to be pressed by examining the event queue:

```
#include <event.h>
main()
{
    EventRecord theEvent;

    FlushEvents(everyEvent,0);

    printf("Hello, world!\n");
    printf("\nPress mouse or key to end\n");

    while (1) if (GetNextEvent(everyEvent,&theEvent))
        switch (theEvent.what) {

        case mouseDown:
            printf("Mouse button pressed, aborting\n");
            exit(0);

        case keyDown:
            printf("Key pressed, aborting\n");
            exit(0);

        default:
            printf("Press mouse or key to end\n");
        }

}
```

This program introduces another function, FlushEvents, which is passed an event mask and clears the queue of any pending events of the type specified. The call made in the preceding example is commonly used in a Macintosh application at the start of execution to clear all events from the event queue. This program also makes use of two constants, mouseDown and keyDown, that are defined in event.h to select the type of event. There are constants like these for each of the possible types of events, so the programmer does not have to remember the numeric codes that these constants represent.

Although trivial, this program illustrates the basic structure of a typical Macintosh application: a loop examining events and performing tasks as indicated by the events. Lacking from this example are windows and menus, two other features of the Macintosh that are a must for a Macintosh application.

The screen of the Macintosh is bit-mapped and may be used for graphics. It is 342 bits (pixels) tall by 512 bits wide. A wide collection of routines are defined in quickdraw.h for doing graphics—such as drawing lines, circles, and filled polygons—as well as for related constants and types, such as the type `Point`, which is used in an event record:

```
typedef struct {
            short   v;
            short   h;
        } Point;
```

This structure is used by quickdraw routines to represent a point on the Macintosh screen in terms of its vertical and horizontal coordinates (0 to 341 vertically and 0 to 511 horizontally).

A window on the Macintosh is a defined rectangular area of the screen in which text and graphics information may be displayed. Any number of windows may be created (within limits), and each is independent of the others. Windows may actually overlap on the screen, in which case one of the windows is considered the current window and hides the other windows (or a part of them) that share the same area of the screen. When a window is created, its top-left and bottom-right corners must be specified in screen coordinates. This will determine its initial size and position. It is possible to change the position of a window on the screen by selecting it with the mouse and "dragging" it to a new location, although this must be done under the control of a program. Similarly, the size of a window can be modified.

The routines and other definitions associated with creating and managing windows are defined primarily in the `window.h` header file. One of the functions that may be used to create a new window is

```
WindowPtr NewWindow(wStorage, boundsRecPtr, title,
                    visible, procID, behind,
                    goAwayFlag, refCon)
Ptr wStorage;          Rect *boundsRecPtr;    Str255 title;
Boolean visible;       int procID;            WindowPtr behind;
Boolean goAwayFlag;    long refCon;
```

To adequately describe the purposes of all the parameters is beyond the scope of our discussion on the Macintosh environment. Most parameters are given default values in any case, and can therefore be ignored. The result type, `WindowPtr`, is a pointer to a structure describing a window. The parameters that may be discussed without much difficulty are `boundsRecPtr`, `title`, and `procID`. The types `Rect` and `Str255` are defined in `quickdraw.h` as

```
typedef struct {
            short   top;
            short   left;
            short   bottom;
            short   right;
        } Rect;

typedef char * Str255;
```

Each window may be given a name, and this is specified through the `title` parameter. This string must be a Pascal format string and so must be specified using the \P modifier, for example,

```
"\PTest Window"
```

The initial size and position of a window must be indicated, and this is the purpose of `boundRecPtr`. This parameter specifies the upper-left and lower-right corners of the window being created. To simplify operations on `Rect` type variables, several routines are defined in the function `quickdraw.h`. One of these is

```
void SetRect(rPtr, left, top, right, bottom)
Rect *rPtr;
short left, top, right, bottom;
```

Thus to initialize a `Rect` type variable, the following could be used:

```
Rect r;
...
SetRect(&r, 10, 10, 100, 150);
```

Finally, `procID` indicates the type of window being created. Again, various constants are defined (in `window.h`) that may be used, and we recommend that they be used to improve the readability of the code.

As a final example, the following program illustrates how windows may be used in a program and, in particular, how windows are independent of one another. Three different types of windows are created using appropriate type constants.

```
#include <quickdraw.h>
#include <window.h>
#include <event.h>
#include <font.h>
main()
{
    EventRecord theEvent;
    WindowPtr mouseWind, keyWind, autoWind;
    Rect r;

    InitGraf(&thePort);
    InitFonts();
    InitWindows();
    FlushEvents(everyEvent, 0);

    SetRect(&r, 20, 50, 200, 180);
    mouseWind = NewWindow
        (0L,&r,"\PMouse",TRUE,documentProc,-1L, FALSE, 0L);
    SetPort(mouseWind);
    TextFont(monaco);
    TextSize(12);
```

```
SetRect(&r, 300, 50, 500, 180);
keyWind = NewWindow(
    OL,&r,"\PKeyboard",TRUE,rDocProc,-1L, FALSE, OL);
SetPort(keyWind);
TextFont(newYork);
TextSize(18);

SetRect(&r, 150, 250, 400, 300);
autoWind = NewWindow(
    OL,&r,"\PAuto",TRUE,dBoxProc, -1L, FALSE, OL);
SetPort(autoWind);
TextFont(geneva);
TextSize(9);

while (1) if (GetNextEvent(everyEvent, &theEvent))
    switch (theEvent.what) {

    case mouseDown:
        SetPort(mouseWind);
        printf("Mouse button pressed\n");
        if (theEvent.where.v < 50)
            exit(0);
        continue;

    case keyDown:
        SetPort(keyWind);
        printf("Key pressed\n");
        continue;

    case autoKey:
        SetPort(autoWind);
        printf("Key repeat event\n");
        continue;
    }

}
```

This program demonstrates several new concepts. It first performs the necessary initialization calls (not all of them are required with every version of Croot, but it is safer to specify them anyway) and then creates three windows at different positions on the screen and sets a specific character type (called a **font**) and size for each window. This is done with the routines TextFont and TextSize. The names of the fonts used in this example—monaco, newYork, and geneva—are constants defined in the font.h header file. The program monitors events, and when one is detected, it displays a message in the window being used to report occurrences of that event, using SetPort to select the appropriate window. The message displayed is in the font type and size that has been set for that window. The program terminates when a mouseDown event is detected and the vertical position of the cursor on the screen at that time is less than 50 (the top part of the screen). A sample execution follows; notice the mouse arrow at the lower-left corner of the screen:

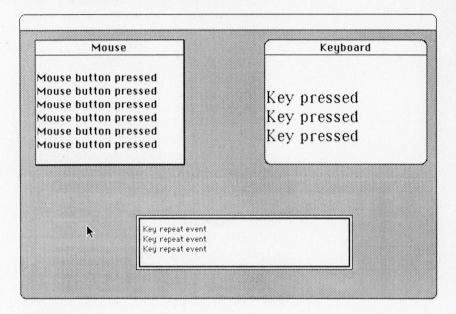

FIGURE 14.1

This concludes our discussion of programming on the Macintosh using Aztec C. In the next section, we describe Macintosh's menu manager and file I/O routines.

14.3.3   LightspeedC

LightspeedC is another of the breed of optimized memory-based compilers that have surfaced since Turbo Pascal [Bor85] was introduced a few years ago. The system is aptly named on two counts: The letter "c" is the standard abbreviation for the speed of light constant, and it is very fast—benchmarks have rated it at more than ten times faster than Aztec C.

The programming environment presented by LightspeedC is as different from the shell environment of Aztec C as the Macintosh is different from the IBM-PC. Whereas the Aztec interface uses a more traditional line-oriented approach, LightspeedC takes full advantage of the Macintosh system and offers a menu-driven, mouse-controlled environment. For someone wanting to use C on a Macintosh who is already fa-

miliar with C on a Unix-like system, Aztec C would likely be easier to
start with simply because of its familiar environment. However, because LightspeedC is so fast (roughly 250 to 500 lines per second), it is
much more suited to experimentation than Aztec C. That is, a programmer will not be discouraged from making a small change in a program, since he or she will be able to see the results quickly, without
having to sit through a long compile. This can be an important advantage when programming on the Macintosh.

14.3.3.1   The Compiler

The LightspeedC compiler supports the full C language definition as described in [Ker78] as well as several of the more recent features of C
that we have described in this book. These features include enumeration
types, bitfield operations, structure assignment, structures passed as
arguments, and structures returned from functions. The compiler also
provides a special "anonymous" pointer type, void *.

Toolbox Interface

LightspeedC uses a direct interface to the Toolbox routines, although
its approach is slightly different from Aztec C's. Include files similar to
those of Aztec C (though with different names) are provided to define
the necessary constants and types, but the declarations of the Toolbox
functions are not part of these files. This is because all the Toolbox and
operating system interface routines are built in to the compiler and will
automatically be called using the required Pascal conventions. That is,
the compiler knows the names of each of the routines and can thus take
the necessary actions whenever it encounters one of these names in a
program. This differs from Aztec C in that the routines are not built in
to the compiler but must instead be explicitly declared as Pascal type
functions. This increases the sizes of the Toolbox include files as compared to LightspeedC.

Not only are the names of the routines built in to the compiler, LightspeedC also knows the number of arguments and the sizes of each of the
arguments and will issue appropriate errors if a call is incorrect. Only
the sizes of the parameters are known, not their types. Similarly, the
result types of the functions are not known, only their sizes, and the result types are therefore treated as integers (char, int, or long). To
prevent problems of type compatibility, the Toolbox include files contain
macro definitions that cast the result types of those functions that do not
return integral values to their proper types. For example, the file
WindowMgr.h (corresponding to the file window.h in Aztec C) contains the line

```
#define NewWindow        (WindowPtr) NewWindow
```

to cast the result type of the function NewWindow as WindowPtr. (A C preprocessor generally does not allow a definition like this, since it is a self-referential macro; however, this construct is special to LightspeedC and does not result in unbounded expansion.)

Strings are handled similarly to strings in Aztec C, with the control sequence \p or \P being used to indicate a Pascal format string. The string is *not* null terminated, as it is in Aztec C. Two functions are provided to convert strings from Pascal format to C format and vice versa. These are called PtoCstr and CtoPstr.

The version of LightspeedC we tested does not provide an in-line assembler, nor is an assembler provided with the system. Instead, if the programmer needs to interface an assembly routine with a program, he or she must use Apple's MDS assembler and convert the object code produced by that system to a form compatible with LightspeedC object libraries, using the program Relconv, which is provided with LightspeedC. We discuss more on this matter in the next section.

Projects

A key feature of LightspeedC is its concept of a **project**. As we discussed in Chapter 6, a common practice when writing C programs is to divide a program into several modules containing related functions and procedures, compile them separately, and then link the object modules. LightspeedC takes advantage of the Macintosh environment to perfect this concept.

LightspeedC visualizes each application as a so-called project. When a new project is started, LightspeedC requires that a name be given to it. The programmer may then create individual source code modules and add them to the project. LightspeedC keeps a list of all source code modules that have been added to the project. When a user wishes to continue work on an existing project, he or she is shown a complete list of the files that are part of that project. The user can select any one of them for editing, create a new module, or request that a particular one be compiled.

Not only does the compiler remember which files belong to a project, it also remembers whether or not a file has been modified since the last time it was compiled. This allows the user to simply request that the project be run, and the compiler will automatically compile all the modules that have been changed.

The object code files that are created are also kept as part of the project document. Moreover, the user may create object libraries and have them added to the project or add one of the libraries provided with the system. MDS assembly modules may be added as libraries by using the Relconv application. In this respect, LightspeedC is little awkward; it would have been better if LightspeedC had provided an integrated assembler and if it had allowed assembly source modules to be added to a project in the same manner as C source modules. When a project is rebuilt, any assembly modules would be assembled and the C modules would be compiled. This addition would be a logical extension to LightspeedC's project concept and perhaps a later version will support it. (As of press time, the latest version of LightspeedC features an in-line assembly directive.)

To be fair, Aztec C does provide a project mechanism through a program called make. This is similar to the make facility provided on Unix systems. However, the make facility is neither as flexible nor as intuitive as the project facility of LightspeedC. This is primarily because LightspeedC's project facility is built around the Macintosh user interface rather than the traditional line-oriented interface used by Aztec's make facility. Many applications are simply better suited to the window-based, menu-driven Macintosh environment, and the project facility is a good example.

14.3.3.2 Writing Macintosh Applications with LightspeedC

To demonstrate some further features of LightspeedC and the Macintosh, we will develop a complete application. The function of this program is simple: Convert a specified input file to either uppercase or lowercase. This normally is a trivial exercise in C under a Unix-like system, but as this example demonstrates, writing an application for the Macintosh and having it appear Mac-like creates another whole set of responsibilities for the programmer.

Menus

This program makes use of menus. A **menu** is a special type of window that an application may provide to allow a user to communicate with it. From the user's viewpoint, menus are controlled through the mouse. With the mouse, the user moves the cursor to the so-called **menu bar** (a region at the top of the screen that lists the names of the available menus), positions it over one of the menu names listed there, and presses the mouse button. The selected menu then "pulls down," revealing a list of menu options. With the mouse button still depressed, the user slides the arrow down the menu list. As each item is reached, it is highlighted. When the desired option is found, the user simply releases the mouse button and the running application is sent information indicating which menu and which option within that menu has been selected.

The constants and types associated with menus are defined in the LightspeedC header MenuMgr.h. Several functions to manage menus are also defined. One of the first things a program must do is set up the menus to be presented to the user when the program is run. The first routine that must be called is

```
void InitMenus()
```

The procedure InitMenus must be called by any application that plans to use menus to initialize the menu manager. Once this is done, the other menu routines may be used. The function NewMenu is used to create a menu data structure and return a "handle" to it (a pointer to a pointer). Its definition is

```
MenuHandle NewMenu(menuID, menuTitle)
int menuID;
Str255 menuTitle;

void AppendMenu(menu, data)
MenuHandle menu;
Str255 data;

void InsertMenu(menu, beforeId)
MenuHandle menu;
int beforeId;

void DrawMenuBar()
```

where

```
typedef struct {
    int     menuID;      /* ID of menu */
    int     menuWidth;   /* menu width in pixels */
    int     menuHeight;  /* menu height in pixels */
    Handle  menuProc;    /* menu definition proc */
    long    enableFlags; /* flags enabled items */
    Str255  menuData;    /* menu title */
} MenuInfo;

typedef MenuInfo  *MenuPtr;
typedef MenuPtr   *MenuHandle;
```

Most of these attributes are self-explanatory. The attribute menuProc is pointer to a pointer to a function and is defined only if the user wants to write a customized menu manager routine. Menu items may be enabled and disabled, and enableFlags simply indicates each item's current state.

The function is straightforward to use. For example, to create a new menu entitled File, the following could be used:

```
MenuHandle fileMenu;
fileMenu = NewMenu(fileMenu,"\PFile");
```

To add options to an existing menu, the procedure

```
void AppendMenu(theMenu, data)
MenuHandle theMenu;
Str255 data;
```

For example, to add the options `Open` and `Close` to `fileMenu`, the call

```
AppendMenu(fileMenu, "\POpen;Close");
```

could be made; the semicolons separate the individual options. Alternatively, this could have been done using two separate calls to the procedure `AppendMenu`, first with `"\POpen"` and then with `"\PClose"`.

Once menu data structures have been created, they have to be added to the menu bar. This is done with the procedure

```
void InsertMenu(theMenu, beforeID)
MenuHandle theMenu;
int beforeID;
```

where `beforeID` is the number of the menu (numbering from 1) before which the new menu is to be inserted. If 0 is specified for `beforeID`, the menu is added at the end of all existing menus.

Finally, once the desired menus have been created and added to the menu bar, the menu bar must be drawn. This is done with

```
void DrawMenuBar()
```

For this program, we use two separate menus, one with three options and another with two. The procedure `SetUpMenus` is called to create these menus:

```
#define fileMenu   1
#define optionMenu 2
MenuHandle menus[3];

void SetupMenus()
{
    menus[fileMenu] = NewMenu(fileMenu, "\PFile");
    AppendMenu(menus[fileMenu], "\PInfo;(-;Open;Quit");
    menus[optionMenu] = NewMenu(optionMenu, "\POptions");
    AppendMenu(menus[optionMenu],"\P To UPPER! ;To lower! ");
    InsertMenu(menus[fileMenu], 0);
    InsertMenu(menus[optionMenu], 0);
    DrawMenuBar();
}
```

(menus is defined to have three elements, but entry 0 is not used. This is again because of the Pascal origins of the Toolbox routines. The C program is written in this manner to avoid having to convert index expressions that are intended to be used in arrays indexed from 1, not 0.) This code sets up two menus, one called `File` and the other called `Options`. The exclamation mark after the `To UPPER` and `To lower` items of the `Options` menu is used to indicate that these are "flagged" items; when a menu is pulled down, a flag character (a check mark in this program) appears to the left of each flagged item. This is used here to indicate whether uppercase or lowercase conversion is being performed. By default, the input file will be converted to uppercase, so when the `Options` menu is pulled down, it should appear as

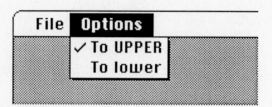

FIGURE 14.2

If the user selects lowercase conversion, a check mark will appear beside this item in the menu and be removed from the uppercase item. Two procedures are used to handle this:

```
void toUpper()
{
    SetItemMark(menus[optionMenu], 2, noMark);
    SetItemMark(menus[optionMenu], 1, checkMark);
    upperCase = TRUE;
}

void toLower()
{
    SetItemMark(menus[optionMenu], 1, noMark);
    SetItemMark(menus[optionMenu], 2, checkMark);
    upperCase = FALSE;
}
```

where `upperCase` is a global boolean used to indicate which type of case conversion to be performed, and `noMark` and `checkMark` are constants defined in `MenuMgr.h`; they are simply the Macintosh character codes of a space and a check mark, respectively.

The File menu contains four options, but the second item, indicated by `"(-"`, represents a disabled item and is simply used as a separator. This menu appears as shown in Fig. 14.3

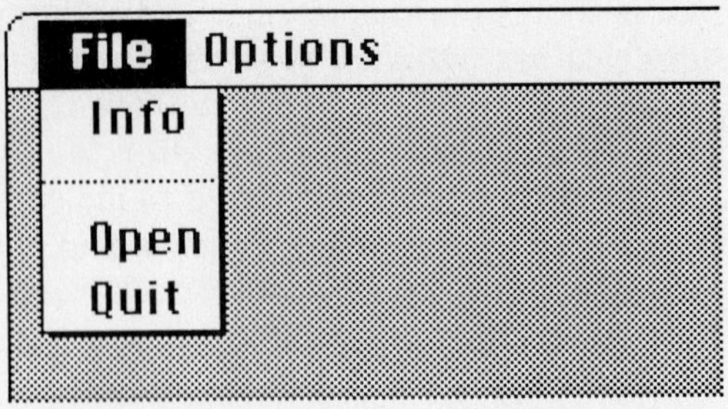

FIGURE 14.3

when it is pulled down. The Info item simply displays a brief description of the program in a window (see Fig. 14.4).

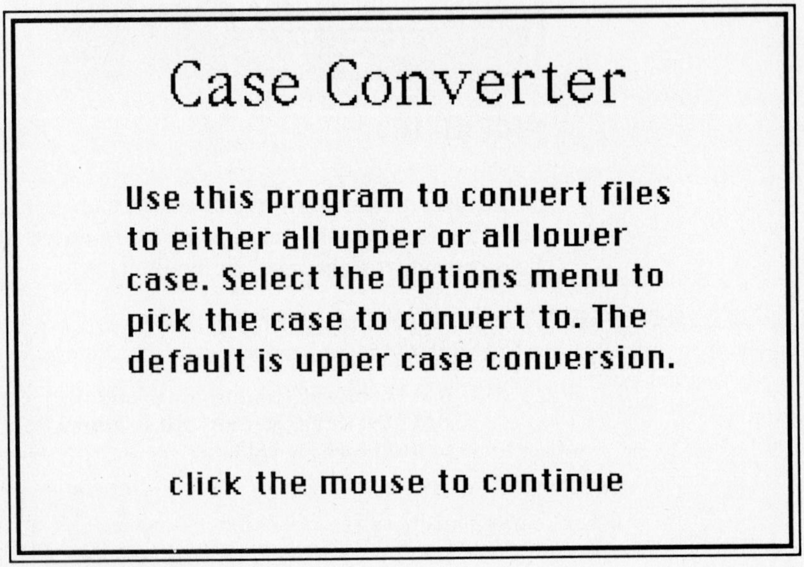

Case Converter

Use this program to convert files to either all upper or all lower case. Select the Options menu to pick the case to convert to. The default is upper case conversion.

click the mouse to continue

FIGURE 14.4

This is done using the following procedure:

```
void info()
{
    WindowPtr infoWindow;
    Rect      r;
    static char *msg[] = {
        "\PCase Converter",
        "\PUse this program to convert files",
        "\Pto either all upper or all lower",
        "\Pcase. Select the Options menu to",
```

```
                "\Ppick the case to convert to. The",
                "\Pdefault is uppercase conversion.",
                "\P",
                "\P",
                "\P    click the mouse to continue",
                NULL
        };
        char **p = msg;
        int  vert;

        SetRect(&r, 105, 72, 405, 272);
        infoWindow = NewWindow
                    (0L, &r, "\P", TRUE, dBoxProc, -1L, FALSE, 0L);
        SetPort(infoWindow);
        TextFont(newYork);
        TextSize(24);
        MoveTo(150-StringWidth(msg[0])/2, 30);
        DrawString(msg[0]);
        TextFont(systemFont);
        TextSize(12);
        vert = 70;
        while (*++p) {
                MoveTo(40, vert);
                DrawString(*p);
                vert += 16;
        }
        while (!Button())
                ;
        DisposeWindow(infoWindow);
}
```

Note the use of the graphics routines MoveTo, StringWidth, and
DrawString (defined in quickdraw.h). The purposes of these routines should be clear, so we do not describe them further.

The Quit option is selected to end the program. Choosing the Open
item causes the routine convert to be called; this prompts for the file to
convert and then performs the case switch. By case switch we mean
switch from upper to lower case and vice versa. Although LightspeedC
supports all standard C file operations, we recommend that the special
Macintosh file manager routines be used directly to improve efficiency
and to present a consistent dialog with the user when filenames are requested. The routines used by convert are

```
(a)    void SFGetFile(where, prompt, fileFilter, numTypes,
                    typeList, dlgHook, reply)
       Point where;
       Str255 prompt;
       ProcPtr fileFilter;
       int numTypes;
       SFTypeList typelist;
       ProcPtr dlgHook;
       SFReply reply;
```

This routine opens a special type of window called a "dialog" that allows a user to easily select which file to have processed. Its basic appearance is as shown in Figure 14.5.

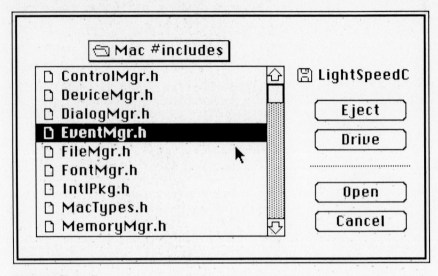

FIGURE 14.5

Again, it is pointless to describe each of these parameters in detail. The most important parameter is `reply`, which returns a record indicating which file the user selected. It is defined as

```
typedef struct {
        Boolean good;       /* false if canceled */
        Boolean copy;       /* not used */
        OSType  fType;      /* file type */
        int     vRefNum;    /* volume reference number */
        int     version;    /* file's version number */
        Str255  fName;      /* filename */
} SFReply;
```

```
(b)  OSErr FSOpen(fileName, vRefNum, refNum)
     Str255 fileName;
     int vRefNum;
     int *refNum;
```

This routine is used to open the specified file on the indicated volume (drive). It returns a **reference number**, which is used for later access to the file. `OSErr` is an integer code indicating a variety of possible errors.

```
(c)  OSErr FSClose(refNum)
     int refNum;
```

This routine is used to close the file with the indicated reference number.

```
(d)  OSErr FSRead(refNum, count, buffPtr)
     int refNum;
     int *count;
     Ptr buffPtr;
```

This routine reads in `count` characters from the file with the indicated reference number and stores them in the buffer pointed to by `buffPtr`. The actual number read is returned in `count`.

```
(e)  OSErr FSWrite(refNum, count, buffPtr)
     int refNum;
     int *count;
     Ptr buffPtr;
```

This routine writes `count` characters stored in the buffer pointed to by `buffPtr` to the file with the indicated reference number. The actual number written is returned in `count`.

```
(f)  OSErr GetEof(refNum, logEOF)
     int refNum;
     long *logEOF;
```

This routine returns the logical size of the file in `logEOF`.

```
(g)  OSErr SetFPos(refNum, posMode, posOff)
     int refNum;
     int posMode;
     long posOff;
```

This routine is used to set the file read/write pointer to the indicated position within the file with reference number `refNum`. `posMode` is used to indicate whether the offset `posOff` is relative to the beginning of the file, the end of the file, or the current position.

The routine `convert` follows:

```
void convert()
{
     static Point    topleft = {80,80};
     SFReply         reply;
     int             i, fRef;
     unsigned long   fSize, cCount, curPos;
     char            fBuf[512];

     SFGetFile(topleft, "", NULL, 1, "TEXT", NULL, &reply);
     if (!reply.good)
          return; /* Cancel button pressed */
```

```
        FSOpen(reply.fName, reply.vRefNum, &fRef);
        GetEOF(fRef, &fSize);


        for (curPos=0, cCount=512; cCount==512; curPos +=512) {
            SetFPos(fRef, fsFromStart, curPos);
            FSRead(fRef, &cCount, fBuf);
            for (i = 0; i < cCount; i++)
                if (upperCase) {
                    if (islower(fBuf[i]))
                        fBuf[i] = toupper(fBuf[i]);
                } else
                    if (isupper(fBuf[i]))
                        fBuf[i] = tolower(fBuf[i]);
            SetFPos(fRef, fsFromStart, curPos);
            FSWrite(fRef, &cCount, fBuf);
        }

        FSClose(fRef);
    }
```

The routines used to perform the indicated menu options are called through procedure doCommand, which itself is called from the main program when a menu item is selected. The rest of the program follows:

```
  void doCommand(theMenu,theItem)
  int theMenu, theItem;
  {
        switch (theMenu) {

        case fileMenu:
            switch (theItem) {
            case 1: info();
                    break;
            case 3: convert();
                    break;
            case 4: notDone = FALSE;
                    break;
            }
            break;

        case optionMenu:
            switch (theItem) {
            case 1: toUpper();
                    break;
            case 2: toLower();
                    break;
            }
        }
        HiliteMenu(0); /* Unhighlight menu */
  }

Boolean notDone = TRUE;
Boolean upperCase;
```

```
main()
{
    EventRecord event;
    WindowPtr   whichWindow;
    int         code;

    InitGraf(&thePort);
    InitFonts();
    InitWindows();
    InitMenus();
    InitDialogs(NULL);
    InitCursor();
    FlushEvents(everyEvent, 0);

    SetupMenus();
    toUpper();   /* set default case switch */
    while (notDone) {
        GetNextEvent(everyEvent,&event);
        switch (event.what) {

        case mouseDown:
                code = FindWindow(&event.where,&whichWindow);
                switch (code) {
                case inMenuBar:
                    doCommand(MenuSelect(&event.where));
                    break;
                default: ;
                /* ignore other clicks */
                }

        default: ;
        /* ignore other events */
        }
    }
}
```

FindWindow is a Toolbox routine used to determine which window the
mouse was in when it was pressed; here, the only window is the menu
bar, so only that is considered. Finally, the routine MenuSelect is
used to open up the menu that the mouse selected so that the user may
choose an item from that menu. The result of this routine is a long integer containing the menu number and item number selected as its two
halves. This 32-bit long integer is automatically split into two 16-bit integers when doCommand is called.

   Although the program itself is only a little more than 100 lines long, a
variety of include files are required:

```
#include <stdio.h>
#include <QuickDraw.h>
#include <WindowMgr.h>
```

```
#include <EventMgr.h>
#include <MenuMgr.h>
#include <FontMgr.h>
#include <FileMgr.h>
#include <StdFilePkg.h>
```

making the effective length of the program more than 1000 lines. Fortunately, the LightspeedC compiler is fast—only two or three seconds are needed to compile this program.

14.3.4   Final Words

This completes our discussion of programming in C under the Macintosh environment. We have described only a small fraction of the available routines and features, but the complexity and power of the environment should be clear.

The two C systems we discussed are both excellent tools for program development. If you are a Unix advocate or plan to develop software that is to be ported to non-Macintosh environments, Aztec C would be a good choice; if you like a more standard Macintosh interface and want fast compile speeds and increased productivity, LightspeedC is the one to choose.

References

[Ada83] United States Department of Defense. *Reference Manual for the Ada Programming Language*. American National Standards Institute, Inc. 1983.

[Aho83] Aho, Alfred V., John E. Hopcroft, and Jeffrey D. Ullman. *Data Structures and Algorithms*. Addison-Wesley, Reading, Mass., 1983.

[Aho86] Aho, Alfred V., Ravi Sethi, and Jeffrey D. Ullman. *Compilers. Principles, Techniques, and Tools*. Addison-Wesley, Reading, Mass., 1986.

[Ans86] *ANSI Draft Programming Language C*. X3 Secretariat: Computer and Business Equipment Manufacturers Association, 311 First NW, Suite 500, Washington D.C. 20001 (July 1986).

[App86] Apple Corporation. *Inside Macintosh*, volumes I through V. Addison-Wesley, Reading, Mass., 1986.

[Bor85] Borland International Inc. *Turbo Pascal Reference Manual* (version 3.0), Borland International Inc., Scotts Valley, Calif., 1985.

[Bow77] Bowles, Kenneth L. *Microcomputer Problem Solving Using Pascal*. Springer-Verlag, New York, 1977.

[Com84] Comer, Douglas. *Operating System Design. The XINU Approach*. Prentice-Hall, Englewood Cliffs, N.J., 1984.

[Coo83] Cooper, Doug. *Standard Pascal. User Reference Manual*. W. W. Norton & Company, New York, 1983.

[Har84] Harbison, Samuel P., and Guy L. Steele. *C: A Reference Manual*. Prentice-Hall, Englewood Cliffs, N.J., 1984.

[Ins86] Rational Systems, Inc. *Instant-C User's Manual* (version 1.93). Rational Systems, Inc., Natick, Mass., 1986.

[Jen78] Jensen, Kathleen, and Niklaus Wirth. *Pascal User Manual and Report*, 2nd ed. Springer-Verlag, New York, 1978.

[Joh78] Johnson, S. C. *Yacc: Yet Another Compiler-Compiler*. Bell Laboratories, Computing Science Technical Report #32 (July 1978).

[Ker78] Kernighan, Brian W., and Dennis M. Ritchie. *The C Programming Language*. Prentice-Hall, Englewood Cliffs, N.J., 1978.

[Kru84] Kruse, Robert L. *Data Structures and Program Design*. Prentice-Hall, Englewood Cliffs, N.J., 1984.

[Lat85] Lattice Incorporated. *Lattice C Compiler for MS-DOS* (version 3.00E). Lattice Incorporated, 1985.

[Łuk29] Łukasiewicz, Jan. *Elementy Logiki Matematycznej*. Warsaw 1929; English translation: *Elements of Mathematical Logic*. Pergamon Press, Oxford, England, 1963.

[Man84] Manx Software Systems, Inc. *Aztec C for the Macintosh*. Manx Software Systems, Inc., 1984.

[Mei80] Meissner, Loren P., and Elliott I. Organick. *Fortran 77*. Addison-Wesley, Reading, Mass., 1980.

[Plu84] Plum, Thomas. *C Programming Guidelines*. Prentice-Hall, Englewood Cliffs, N.J., 1984.

[Pra84] Pratt, Terrence W. *Programming Languages. Design and Implementation*, 2nd ed. Prentice-Hall, Englewood Cliffs, N.J., 1984.

[Rit78] Ritchie, D. M., S. C. Johnson, M. E. Lesk, and B. W. Kernighan. *Unix Time-Sharing System: The C Programming Language*. Bell System Technical J., 57, no. 6 (Oct. 1978), pp. 1991-2019.

[Ste86] Steele, Peter W., and Ivan Tomek. *Z80 Assembly Language Programming*. Computer Science Press, Rockville, Maryland, 1986.

[Thi86] THINK Technologies, Inc. *LightspeedC User's Manual* (version 1). THINK Technologies, Inc., 1986.

Special Characters, Keywords, and Syntax

Operators and separators:

```
;     }     ,     {     :     =     (     )     ]     *     [     .     #
_     \     |     "     %     -     &     !     ~     /     +     ->    ++
--    <<    >>    <     <=    >=    >     ==    !=    ^     |     &&    | |
?     +=    -=    *=    /=    %=    >>=   <<=   &=    |=    ^=
```

Reserved words:

Storage classes	*Data types*	*Statements*
auto	char	break
extern	double	case
register	enum	continue
static	float	default
	int	do
Miscellanous	long	else
	short	for
typedef	struct	goto
sizeof	union	if
	unsigned	return
	void	switch
		while

C Syntax:

The C syntax is described below using an extended form of the Backus-Naur notation. The definitions of identifiers, constants, and strings are not given, but the syntax of these constructs should be clear.

item?	Denotes an optional *item*
item*	Denotes 0 or more repetitions of the *item*
item+	Denotes 1 or more repetitions of the *item*

Terminal symbols are enclosed in single quotation marks. The grammar is context sensitive; that is, some expressions that can be generated from the description given are not actually correct. These context-dependencies are described in the text.

program ::= *external-def**

The remaining definitions are sorted alphabetically.

$$
\begin{array}{ll}
\textit{abstract-decl} & ::= \textit{empty} \mid \text{'('} \textit{ abstract-decl } \text{')'} \mid \\
& \quad \text{'*'} \textit{ abstract-decl } \mid \\
& \quad \textit{abstract-decl } \text{'('} \text{ ')'} \mid \\
& \quad \textit{abstract-decl } \text{'['} \textit{ expression? } \text{']'}
\end{array}
$$

Here, *empty* stands for an empty string.

$$
\begin{array}{ll}
\textit{arg-list} & ::= \textit{identifier} \ (\text{','} \textit{ identifier })* \\
\textit{assign-operator} & ::= \quad \text{'='} \mid \text{'+='} \mid \text{'-='} \mid \text{'*='} \mid \\
& \quad \text{'/='} \mid \text{'\%='} \mid \text{'<<='} \mid \text{'>>='} \mid \\
& \quad \text{'\&='} \mid \text{'|='} \mid \text{'\^{}='} \\[1em]
\textit{binary-operator} & ::= \quad \text{'<'} \mid \text{'<='} \mid \text{'>'} \mid \text{'>='} \mid \\
& \quad \text{'<<'} \mid \text{'>>'} \mid \text{'=='} \mid \text{'!='} \mid \\
& \quad \text{','} \mid \text{'/'} \mid \text{'\%'} \mid \text{'+'} \mid \text{'-'} \mid \text{'*'} \mid \\
& \quad \text{'\&'} \mid \text{'|'} \mid \text{'\^{}'} \mid \text{'\&\&'} \mid \text{'||'} \mid \\
& \quad \text{'?'} \textit{ expression } \text{':'} \\[1em]
\textit{char-type} & ::= \text{'unsigned'? 'char'} \\
\textit{compound} & ::= \text{'\{'} \textit{ declaration* statement* } \text{'\}'} \\
\textit{data-def} & ::= \textit{declaration} \\
\textit{declaration} & ::= \textit{storage? type init-decl-list? } \text{';'} \\
\textit{declarator} & ::= \textit{identifier} \mid \text{'('} \textit{ declarator } \text{')'} \mid \\
& \quad \text{'*'} \textit{ declarator } \mid \\
& \quad \textit{declarator } \text{'('} \textit{ arg-list? } \text{')'} \mid \\
& \quad \textit{declarator } \text{'['} \textit{ expression } \text{']'} \\[1em]
\textit{enum-field} & ::= \textit{identifier} \ (\text{'='} \textit{ expression})? \\
\textit{enum-field-list} & ::= \textit{enum-field} \ (\text{','} \textit{ enum-field})* \\
\textit{enum-spec} & ::= \text{'enum'} \textit{ identifier?} \\
& \quad\quad \text{'\{'} \textit{ enum-field-list } \text{'\}'} \mid \\
& \quad \text{'enum'} \textit{ identifier} \\[1em]
\textit{expression} & ::= \textit{primary} \mid \textit{unary} \mid \\
& \quad \textit{expression binary-operator expression} \mid \\
& \quad \textit{l-value assign-operator expression} \\[1em]
\textit{expression-list} & ::= \textit{expression} \ (\text{','} \textit{ expression }) * \\
\textit{external-def} & ::= \textit{function-def} \mid \textit{data-def} \\
\textit{field-decl} & ::= \textit{type field-declarator} \\
& \quad\quad (\text{','} \textit{ field-declarator})* \ \text{';'}
\end{array}
$$

field-declarator   ::= *declarator* ¦ *declarator*? ':' *expression*

field-list   ::= *field-decl* (',' *field-decl*)*

function-def   ::= *storage*? *type*? *declarator*
           par-specs* *compound*

i-list   ::= *expression* ¦ *i-list* ',' *i-list* ¦
        '{' *i-list* '}'

initializer   ::= '=' *expression* ¦ '=' '{' *i-list* '}'

init-decl   ::= *declarator* ('=' *initializer*)?

init-decl-list   ::= *init-decl* (',' *init-decl*)* ';'

int-type   ::= 'unsigned'? ('short'? ¦ 'long'?) 'int'?

l-value   ::= *identifier* ¦ '(' *l-value* ')' ¦
        primary '[' *expression* ']' ¦
        l-value '.' *identifier* ¦
        primary '->' *identifier* ¦
        '*' *expression*

par-specs   ::= *type declarator* ';'

primary   ::= *identifier* ¦ *constant* ¦ *string* ¦
        '(' *expression* ')' ¦
        primary '[' *expression* ']' ¦
        primary '(' *expression-list*? ')' ¦
        l-value '.' *identifier* ¦
        primary '->' *identifier*

statement   ::= *expression* ';' ¦ *compound* ¦
        'if' '(' *expression* ')' *statement*
           ('else' *statement*)? ¦
        'while' '(' *expression* ')' *statement* ¦
        'do' *statement* 'while'
          '(' *expression* ')' ';' ¦
        'for''('*expression*?':'*expression*?';
          '*expression*?')' *statement*
        'switch' '(' *expression* ')' *statement* ¦
        'case' *expression* ':' *statement* ¦
        'default' ':' *statement* ¦
        'break' ';' ¦ 'continue' ';' ¦
        'return' (*expression*)? ';' ¦
        'goto' *identifier* ';' ¦
        identifier ':' *statement* ¦ ';'

storage   ::= `'auto'` ¦ `'static'` ¦ `'extern'` ¦
                            `'register'` ¦ `'typedef'`

str-union-enum-spec::= *str-union-spec* ¦ *enum-spec*

str-union-spec   ::= (`'struct'` ¦ `'union'`) *identifier*?
                            (`'{'` *field-list* `'}'`)?

type   ::= *int-type* ¦ *char-type* ¦ `'float'` ¦ `'double'`
                            ¦ *str-union-enum-spec* ¦ `'void'` ¦ *identifier*

type-name   ::= *type abstract-decl*

unary   ::= *unary-operator expression* ¦ `'&'` *l-value* ¦
                            `'++'` *l-value* ¦ `'--'` *l-value* ¦
                            l-value `'++'` ¦ *l-value* `'--'` ¦
                            `'('` *type-name* `')'` *expression* ¦
                            `'sizeof'` `'('` *type-name* `')'` ¦
                            `'sizeof'` *expression*

unary-operator   ::= `'*'` ¦ `'-'` ¦ `'!'` ¦ `'~'`

Precedence and Associativity Tables

Precedence determines the order in which the operators are evaluated in expressions in the absence of explicit parentheses. The following table lists the operators in order of decreasing precedence; operators with higher precedence are evaluated first in expressions.

If the two operators have the same precedence, **associativity** rules are used to decide the order of evaluation. There are two possible associativity rules: *left to right* and *right to left*. For example, in the expression

```
a = b = c
```

the associativity rule must be used to determine the order of evaluation. If the rule is right to left, this expression is equivalent to

```
a = (b = c)
```

In the table, all operators within the same box have the same precedence and associativity rule.

Operator	Meaning	Associativity
( )	function call	left to right
[ ]	indexing	
.	dotted access	
–>	dotted access using pointers	
!	not	right to left
~	one's complement	
–	negation	
++	increment	
––	decrement	
&	address	
*	contents	
(*type-name*)	casting	
sizeof	size of an object	
*	multiplication	left to right
/	division	
%	modulo	
+	addition	left to right
–	subtraction	

Operator	Meaning	Associativity
<< >>	left shift right shift	left to right
< <= > >=	less than less than or equal to greater than greater than or equal to	left to right
== !=	equality inequality	left to right
&	bitwise and	left to right
∧	bitwise exclusive or	left to right
¦	bitwise or	left to right
&&	and	left to right
¦¦	or	left to right
?:	conditional expression	right to left
= *= /= %= += −= <<= >>= &= ¦= ∧=	assignment	right to left
,	comma expression	left to right

Formatted Input and Output

C.1 FORMATTED INPUT

There are three input functions:

```
int scanf(format control string, arg1, ..., argk)
```

to read from standard input,

```
int fscanf(f, format control string, arg1, ..., argk)
```

to read from file *f*, and

```
int sscanf(s, format control string, arg1, ..., argk)
```

to read from string *s*.

Each of these functions returns the number of successful assignments of input sequences to arguments. This number may be less than the number of given arguments in two cases:

- End-of-file (or, for `sscanf`, end-of-string) is reached before all arguments are read; in this case, the value `EOF` is returned.
- Input data do not match specifications given in the control string; in this case, the number of successful assignments is returned.

Thus, for example, to read from the file *f* until end-of-file is encountered, the following loop could be used:

```
while (fscanf(f, format, arg1, ..., argk) != EOF)
    ...
```

This loop would not terminate if an error occurred, for example, when reading a file of integers and a nondigit is encountered. To take this case into account, the loop can be rewritten as follows:

```
while ((i = fscanf(f, format, arg1, ... , argk)) != EOF)
    if (i < k)
        - print error message or something ...
```

All arguments will receive some values as a result of the call, so they must be passed by reference. In other words, all arguments must be pointers.

The *format control string* determines the interpretation of input sequences as they are read, and it may contain

- Conversion specifications starting with %
- Whitespace characters
- Ordinary characters

The number of conversion specifications that are not *suppressed* and the number of arguments must be equal. Moreover, the type of an argument must match its corresponding conversion specification; for example, the argument type for the conversion character d (which specifies a signed integer conversion) must be pointer to integer.

A conversion specification is of the form

% * *width size conversion-character*

where the *, *width*, and *size* fields are optional. This specification determines how the input data is converted. The converted value is placed in the location pointed to by the corresponding argument. An input data is defined as a string of consecutive non-whitespace characters, so it extends to the next whitespace character. This may be limited by the specification of the conversion or the *width*. Whitespace characters (line boundaries in particular) are skipped when an input function is looking for an input field that matches the specification. For example, if a conversion specifies an integer input, all whitespace, including end-of-lines, are skipped when looking for the integer value (with two exceptions, which we describe later).

The optional asterisk is an **assignment suppress character**; that is, the input data is read, but it is *not* assigned to the argument. Instead, it is discarded.

The field *width* must be an unsigned positive decimal constant. It specifies the maximum input field width.

There are two possible *size* flags: the letter h and the letter l (both in lowercase).

The size flag h causes the argument involved to be treated as short and can be used with any of the conversion characters for

signed decimal
unsigned decimal
unsigned octal
unsigned hexadecimal

The size flag l causes the argument involved to be treated as long and can be used with the same conversion specification as allowed for the size flag h as well as with the conversion specification %f used for signed float to indicate a conversion of type double. A complete list of conversion specifications follows:

d	A signed decimal integer
u	An unsigned decimal integer
o	An unsigned octal integer (with or without a leading 0)
x, X	An unsigned hexadecimal integer (with or without a leading 0x)
c	A single character
s	A character string
f, e, E, g, G	A floating point number in the form [−]*ddd.ddd*[E[*sign*]*dd*] where the portions in square brackets are optional. A lowercase e may also be used to specify the exponent part. All these operations are identical.
[ ]	A character class

A character class resembles a Pascal set constant, being enclosed by square brackets. There are four forms of character classes:

- A list of characters; for example,

      [AbC]

  denotes four characters: a blank and letters A, b, and C

- An ASCII range of characters specified as in Pascal but with a hyphen rather than two dots; for example,

      [a−z]

  denotes all lowercase letters
- The complement of a range, with a circumflex $^\wedge$ as the character; for example,

      [$^\wedge$a−z]

  denotes all characters that are *not* lowercase letters
- Combinations of these; for example,

      [0−9a−z]

  denotes all digits and lowercase letters

A character class conversion specification specifies a string, so the corresponding argument must be of type pointer to character. An input field will consist of all consecutive characters that match any of the characters in the class.

There are only two cases in which whitespace characters are not skipped when looking for an input field: a character and a character class conversion specification.

The remaining characters allowed in format control strings are whitespace characters and ordinary characters. According to [Ker78], whitespace characters are simply ignored. According to more recent descriptions, such as [Har84], any number of consecutive whitespace characters in the format control string means the same number of whitespace characters in the input is read and discarded. Ordinary characters require an an exact match.

Examples

```
char      c;
unsigned  ui;
int       i;
float     f;
char      x[5],
          y[5];
```

Assume input stream is

```
21  3456
1.2 abcd367Z
```

The call

```
scanf("%c%u%2o%*d%f%4s%4[0-9]", &c, &ui, &i, &f, x, y);
```

assigns

- The character 2 to c
- The integer value 1 to ui
- The octal value 34 (28 decimal) to i (only two digits are read), then the value 56 is read and discarded
- The value 1.2 to f
- The string abcd to x (this string is terminated by the null character, so reading five characters would cause an error; also, the blank preceding the string is skipped)
- The value 367 to y

Another example:

```
int    i;
char   x[10],
       y[20];
```

Assume the initial value of x is

```
123AZCa54
```

(terminated by a null character). The call

```
sscanf(x, "%*d%19[^a-z]%*c%d", y, &i);
```

assigns

- The string AZC to y (123 is skipped, and the first character that is not a lowercase letter is the A)
- The value 54 to i

C.2   FORMATTED OUTPUT

There are three output functions:

```
printf(format control string, arg1, ..., argk)
```

to write to standard input;

```
fprintf(f, format control string, arg1, ..., argk)
```

to write to file f;

```
sprintf(s, format control string , arg1, ..., argk)
```

to write to string s.

The value returned by the functions is EOF if an error occurred and a value different from EOF otherwise (this latter value depends on the implementation).

A format control string contains:

- Conversion specifications starting with %
- Ordinary characters

Conversion specifications specify the conversion and formatting of arguments. The number of arguments (k) must be equal to the number of conversion specifications. Moreover, the type of an argument must be identical with the specification given in the corresponding conversion specification. A conversion specification is of the form:

% modifier width precision size conversion-character

All flags preceding the *conversion-character* are optional. The list of conversion characters is identical to that for formatted input. The allowed flags are modifier flags, field width flags, precision flags, and size flags.

Modifier Flags

- Minus: −
  By default a value is right justified in the field; this flag specifies left justification. For example,

  ```
  char s[6];
  sprintf(s, "%-5s", "hey");
  ```

  will place in s the string

  ```
  "hey  "
  ```

- Zero: 0
  Causes 0's to be used for padding rather than spaces.

- Signed integer control: '+' or ' '
  An occurrence of a '+' or ' ' (blank) flag causes this flag to be prefixed to the output value if the value is nonnegative. It is relevant only for the following flags: d, e, E, f, g, G. For example,

  ```
  int i = 10;
  printf("%+d", i);
  ```

  prints

  ```
  +10
  ```

- Unsigned integer control: #
  Causes a leading 0 or 0x, respectively, to be prefixed to the octal or hexadecimal value displayed. For example,

  ```
  printf("%#x", 56);
  ```

prints

```
0x38
```

Field Width Flag
This is specified by an unsigned integer constant. The field *width* will be automatically expanded if necessary. The field width may be specified as a *, in which case an additional argument to printf must be provided to specify the field width to use. For example, the statement

```
printf("!%*s!", 7, "Hello");
```

outputs

```
!Hello  !
```

Precision Flag
This is specified by an unsigned integer constant preceded by a dot. For real values, it indicates the number of digits in the fractional part; for a string, it indicates the maximum length of the string to be printed. For example,

```
char str[] = "university";
printf("!%-6.3s!", str);
```

prints

```
!uni   !
```

Size Flags
As for input, the flag l specifies long. It may only be used with the following conversion specifications: %d, %o, %u, %x, %X. To output a % character, it must be preceded by another % character.

Conversion specifications have meanings similar to those described for scanf. Conversion characters e, f, E, g, and G have slightly different meanings here. The form of output depends on the character:

f	[−] *ddd.ddd*
e	[−] *d.ddddd* e*{sign}dd*
E	[−] *d.ddddd* E*{sign}dd*
g	shorter of f and e
G	shorter of f and E

Thus e specifies scientific notation. The default precision is 6. For example,

```
float x = 12.3455;
printf("%f, %.1f, %e, %.2E", x, x, x, x);
```

prints

```
12.345500, 12.3, 1.234550e+01, 1.23E+01
```

If you are interested in learning more about how the conversions are performed, see the implementation of printf in [Com84].

The ASCII Character Set

Binary	Hex	Octal	Decimal	ASCII	Ctrl	C Format
00000000	00	000	000	NUL	@	'\0'
00000001	01	001	001	SOH	A	'\001'
00000010	02	002	002	STX	B	'\002'
00000011	03	003	003	ETX	C	'\003'
00000100	04	004	004	EOT	D	'\004'
00000101	05	005	005	ENQ	E	'\005'
00000110	06	006	006	ACK	F	'\006'
00000111	07	007	007	BEL	G	'\007'
00001000	08	010	008	BS	H	'\b'
00001001	09	011	009	HT	I	'\i'
00001010	0A	012	010	LF	J	'\n'
00001011	0B	013	011	VT	K	'\v'
00001100	0C	014	012	FF	L	'\f'
00001101	0D	015	013	CR	M	'\r'
00001110	0E	016	014	SO	N	'\016'
00001111	0F	017	015	SI	O	'\017'
00010000	10	020	016	DLE	P	'\020'
00010001	11	021	017	DC1	Q	'\021'
00010010	12	022	018	DC2	R	'\022'
00010011	13	023	019	DC3	S	'\023'
00010100	14	024	020	DC4	T	'\024'
00010101	15	025	021	NAK	U	'\025'
00010110	16	026	022	SYN	V	'\026'
00010111	17	027	023	ETB	W	'\027'
00011000	18	030	024	CAN	X	'\030'
00011001	19	031	025	EM	Y	'\031'
00011010	1A	032	026	SUB	Z	'\032'
00011011	1B	033	027	ESC	[	'\033'
00011100	1C	034	028	FS	\	'\034'
00011101	1D	035	029	GS	]	'\035'
00011110	1E	036	030	RS	^	'\036'
00011111	1F	037	031	US	_	'\037'
00100000	20	040	032	space		' '
00100001	21	041	033	!		
00100010	22	042	034	"		'\"'
00100011	23	043	035	#		
00100100	24	044	036	$		
00100101	25	045	037	%		
00100110	26	046	038	&		
00100111	27	047	039	'		'\''
00101000	28	050	040	(		
00101001	29	051	041	)		
00101010	2A	052	042	*		

Binary	Hex	Octal	Decimal	ASCII	Ctrl	C Format
00101011	2B	053	043	+		
00101100	2C	054	044	,		
00101101	2D	055	045	−		
00101110	2E	056	046	.		
00101111	2F	057	047	/		
00110000	30	060	048	0		
00110001	31	061	049	1		
00110010	32	062	050	2		
00110011	33	063	051	3		
00110100	34	064	052	4		
00110101	35	065	053	5		
00110110	36	066	054	6		
00110111	37	067	055	7		
00111000	38	070	056	8		
00111001	39	071	057	9		
00111010	3A	072	058	:		
00111011	3B	073	059	;		
00111100	3C	074	060	<		
00111101	3D	075	061	=		
00111110	3E	076	062	>		
00111111	3F	077	063	?		
01000000	40	100	064	@		
01000001	41	101	065	A		
01000010	42	102	066	B		
01000011	43	103	067	C		
01000100	44	104	068	D		
01000101	45	105	069	E		
01000110	46	106	070	F		
01000111	47	107	071	G		
01001000	48	110	072	H		
01001001	49	111	073	I		
01001010	4A	112	074	J		
01001011	4B	113	075	K		
01001100	4C	114	076	L		
01001101	4D	115	077	M		
01001110	4E	116	078	N		
01001111	4F	117	079	O		
01010000	50	120	080	P		
01010001	51	121	081	Q		
01010010	52	122	082	R		
01010011	53	123	083	S		
01010100	54	124	084	T		
01010101	55	125	085	U		
01010110	56	126	086	V		
01010111	57	127	087	W		
01011000	58	130	088	X		
01011001	59	131	089	Y		
01011010	5A	132	090	Z		
01011011	5B	133	091	[		
01011100	5C	134	092	\		'\\'
01011101	5D	135	093	]		
01011110	5E	136	094	^		

Binary	Hex	Octal	Decimal	ASCII	Ctrl	C Format
01011111	5F	137	095	_		
01100000	60	140	096	'		
01100001	61	141	097	a		
01100010	62	142	098	b		
01100011	63	143	099	c		
01100100	64	144	100	d		
01100101	65	145	101	e		
01100110	66	146	102	f		
01100111	67	147	103	g		
01101000	68	150	104	h		
01101001	69	151	105	i		
01101010	6A	152	106	j		
01101011	6B	153	107	k		
01101100	6C	154	108	l		
01101101	6D	155	109	m		
01101110	6E	156	110	n		
01101111	6F	157	111	o		
01110000	70	160	112	p		
01110001	71	161	113	q		
01110010	72	162	114	r		
01110011	73	163	115	s		
01110100	74	164	116	t		
01110101	75	165	117	u		
01110110	76	166	118	v		
01110111	77	167	119	w		
01111000	78	170	120	x		
01111001	79	171	121	y		
01111010	7A	172	122	z		
01111011	7B	173	123	{		
01111100	7C	174	124	¦		
01111101	7D	175	125	}		
01111110	7E	176	126	~		
01111111	7F	177	127	DEL		'\177'

Answers to Odd-Numbered Exercises

E.1 CHAPTER 2

1.
a.

```
main()
{
    int i;

    i = 2;
}
```

b.

```
main()
{
    int i = 3, k = 4;

    i = k = 3;
}
```

3.
a. 5, i = 3, j = 5
b. 6, i = 3, j = 5
c. −1, i = 4, j = 4
d. 6, i = 6, j = 6

5.

```
printf("J. Bond \\ Apt. #645 N.Y.,N.Y. ");
printf("\\ \"Agent 007\"\nUSA\n");
```

7.

```
66 43.5 A
66 43 65
B 65
```

9.

```c
#include <stdio.h>
main()
{
     int c;

     c = getchar();
     putchar(c + 1);
}
```

11.

```c
#include <stdio.h>
main()
{
     double price;

     printf("\nEnter the price: ");
     scanf("%lf", &price);
     printf("\nThe price including sales tax (10%%) is %.2f\n",
          price *= 1.1);
}
```

13.

```c
#include <stdio.h>
main()
{
     double length, width, area;

     printf("\nEnter the length and the width of the floor: ");
     scanf("%lf%lf", &length, &width);
     printf("The area of the floor is %5.2f square meters",
                    area = length * width);
     printf("\nThe cost for the carpet is $%5.2f\n",
                    area * 10.0);
}
```

15.

```c
#include <stdio.h>
main()
{
     char c1, c2, c3;

     scanf("%c%c%c", &c1, &c2, &c3);
     printf("%c%c%c\n", c1 + 'a' - 'A', c2 + 'a' - 'A',
          c3 + 'a' - 'A');
}
```

E.2   CHAPTER 3

1.

a. 0

b. i = 1
   i = 3
   i = 4

3.

```c
#include <stdio.h>
main()
{
      char  letter;
      int     i;
      double mark, exam, final,
               test   = 0,
               assign = 0;

      printf("\nEnter four test marks: ");

      for (i = 0; i++ < 4; test += mark)
            scanf("%lf", &mark);

      printf("Enter five assignment marks: ");
      for (i = 0; i++ < 5; assign += mark)
            scanf("%lf", &mark);

      printf("Enter exam mark: ");
      scanf("%lf", &exam);

      final = test * .1 + assign * .03 + exam * .45;
      if (final >= 79.5)
            letter = 'A';
      else if (final >= 69.5)
            letter = 'B';
      else if (final >= 59.5)
            letter = 'C';
      else if (final >= 49.5)
            letter = 'D';
      else letter = 'E';

      printf("Final grade = %f = %c = ", final, letter);
      switch (letter) {
      case 'A' : printf("excellent.");
                  break;
      case 'B' : printf("good.");
                  break;
      case 'C' : printf("fair.");
                  break;
      case 'D' : printf("poor.");
                  break;
      case 'E' : printf("failure.");
                  break;
      }
      putchar('\n');
}
```

5.

```c
#include <stdio.h>
main()
{
    int    i, exp, power;
    double val = 1,
           num;

    printf("\nEnter a number: ");
    scanf("%lf", &num);
    do  {
        printf("Enter its exponent, (>= 0): ");
        scanf("%d", &exp);
        if (exp < 0)
            printf("That's not positive\n");
    }
    while (exp < 0);
    if (exp % 2 == 0) {
        power = exp / 2;
        for (i = 0; i < power; i++)
            val *= num;
        val *= val;
    }
    else {
        power = exp - 1;
        power /= 2;
        for (i = 0; i < power; i++)
            val *= num;
        val *= val * num;
    }

    printf("%f to the power of %d is %f\n", num, exp, val);
}
```

7.

```c
#include <stdio.h>
main()
{
    int i, n;
    long fact = 1;

    while (1) {
        printf("\nEnter a positive integer: ");
        scanf("%d", &n);
        if (n > 0)
            break;
    }

    for (i = 1; i <= n; i++)
        fact *= i;
    printf("The factorial of %d is %ld\n", n, fact);
}
```

9.

```c
#include <stdio.h>
main()
{
      long i, dig, aux = 1;

      while (1) {
            printf("Please enter a positive integer value: ");
            scanf("%ld", &i);
            if (i > 0)
                  break;
            else printf("Incorrect value, please reenter\n");
      }

      printf("In hex, %ld is ", i);
      for (dig = i; dig >= 1; dig /= 16)
            aux *= 16;
      for (aux /= 16; aux != 0; aux /= 16) {
            dig = i / aux;
            i -= dig * aux;
            printf("%c", dig + '0' + ((dig < 10) ? 0 : 7));
      }
      putchar('\n');
}
```

11.

```c
#include <stdio.h>
main()
{
      int maxc, minc, c;

      for (maxc=minc=c=getchar(); c != '*'; c=getchar())
            if (c > maxc)
                  maxc = c;
            else if (c < minc)
                  minc = c;

      printf("Maximum char is %c\tminimum char is %c\n",
                        maxc, minc);
}
```

13.

```c
#include <stdio.h>
main()
{
      int i, N,
            res = 1;
```

```
        while (1) {
                printf("Please enter a positive integer value: ");
                scanf("%d", &N);
                if (N > 0)
                        break;
                else printf("Incorrect value, please reenter\n");
        }
        for (i = 2; i <= N * 2; i += 2)
                res *= i;
        printf("The result is %d\n", res * res);
}
```

15.

```
/* This program works reliably up to n = 12.
   Change long to double for larger values.
*/

#include <stdio.h>
main()
{
        long n,         /* n is the row to stop at */
                i, r, f, ifact, imrfact, rfact;

        do {
                printf("Please enter an integer >= 0: ");
                scanf("%ld", &n);
                if (n < 0)
                        printf("Incorrect value, try again\n");
        }
        while (n < 0);

        for (i = 0; i <= n; i++) {
                for (ifact = 1, f = 2; f <= i; f++)
                        ifact *= f;
                for (r = 0; r <= i; r++) {
                        for (imrfact = 1, f = 2; f <= i - r; f++)
                                imrfact *= f;
                        for (rfact = 1, f = 2; f <= r; f++)
                                rfact *= f;
                        printf("%ld ", ifact / (imrfact * rfact));
                }
                putchar('\n');
        }
}
```

E.3   CHAPTER 4

1.

```
#include <stdio.h>
main()
```

```
    {
        double salary,
               maxsal = 0,
               total  = 0;

        while (scanf("%lf",&salary) != EOF) {
            maxsal = (salary > maxsal) ? salary : maxsal;
            total += salary;
            while (getchar() != '\n')
                  ;
        }

        prinf("Total of salaries is %f\n", total);
        printf("Maximum salary is %f\n", maxsal);
    }
```

3.

```
    #include <stdio.h>
    main()
    {
        int     c,
                len     = 0,
                maxlen  = 0;
        long    longest = 0,
                line    = 0;
        FILE    *f;

        if ((f = fopen("TEST", "r")) == NULL) {
            printf("The file TEST cannot be opened\n");
            return;
        }
        while ((c = getc(f)) != EOF)
            if (c == '\n') {
                ++line;
                if (len > maxlen) {
                    maxlen = len;
                    longest = line;
                }
                len = 0;
            }
            else ++len;

        if (fclose(f) == EOF)
            printf("File cannot be closed\n");
        else {
            printf("\nThe longest line is line \# %ld, ",
                longest);
            printf("it has %d characters\n", maxlen);
        }
    }
```

5.

```c
#include <stdio.h>
main()
{
    int c, key, before,
        after = 0;
    long line = 1;

    printf("\nEnter character to look for: ");
    key = getchar();
    getchar();

    while ((c = getchar()) != EOF) {
      if (c == '\n') {
            ++line;
            before = 0;
      }
      else if (c == key) {
            printf("\n%c found in line \# %ld", key, line);
            printf("\nNumber of chars before is %d", before);
            while ((c = getchar()) != '\n' && c != EOF)
                ++after;
            printf("\nNumber of chars after is %d\n", after);
            return;
      }
      else ++before;
    }

    printf("\n%c not found in text\n", key);
}
```

7.

```c
#include <stdio.h>
main()
{
  int c1,
      c2     = ' ',
      win1   = 0,
      win2   = 0,
      gameno = 1;

  while ((c1 = getchar()) != EOF) {

        while (c1 == ' ')
            c1 = getchar();
        putchar(c1);
```

```
        while ((c2 = getchar()) == ' ')
            ;
        putchar(c2);

        putchar('\n');

        if ((c1 != 'P' && c1 != 'R' && c1 != 'S')
                || (c2 != 'P' && c2 != 'R' && c2 != 'S'))
            printf("Play not legal in game \# %d\n", gameno);
        else if (c1 == c2)
            printf("Tie game, no winner for game \# %d\n", gameno);
        else if ((c1 == 'P' && c2 == 'R') || (c1 == 'R' && c2 == 'S')
                || (c1 == 'S' && c2 == 'P')) {
            printf("First player wins game \# %d\n", gameno);
            ++win1;
        }
        else {
            printf("Second player wins game \# %d\n", gameno);
            ++win2;
        }
        ++gameno;
        while ((c1 = getchar()) != '\n' && c1 != EOF)
            ;
    }

    printf("First player won %d games ", win1);
    printf("and second player won %d games\n", win2);
    if (win1 == win2)
        printf("There is no overall winner\n");
    else if (win1 > win2)
        printf("The overall winner is the first player\n");
    else printf("The overall winner is the second player\n");
}
```

9.

```
#include <stdio.h>
main()
{
    FILE *f1, *f2;
    int c1, c2;
    long line = 1,
         chpos = 1;

    if ((f1 = fopen("TEST1", "r")) == NULL ||
            (f2 = fopen("TEST2", "r")) == NULL)
        printf("Cannot open input file\n");
```

```
      else {
          for (c1 = getc(f1), c2 = getc(f2);
                   c1 != EOF && c2 != EOF && c1 == c2;
                   c1 = getc(f1), c2 = getc(f2))
              if (c1 == '\n') {
                  chpos = 1;
                  line++;
              }
              else chpos++;

          if (c1 == c2)
              printf("Files are identical\n");
          else {
            printf("Files differ on line #%ld, pos #%ld\n",
                         line, chpos);

            printf("Character from TEST1");
            if (c1 < 32) {
                printf(" is a nonprintable character:\n");
                printf("\tASCII code: %d\n", c1);
            }
            else printf(":\n\t%c\n", c1);

            printf("Character from TEST2");
            if (c2 < 32) {
                printf(" is a nonprintable character:\n");
                printf("\tASCII code: %d\n", c2);
            }
            else printf(":\n\t%c\n", c2);
          }

          if (fclose(f1) == EOF !! fclose(f2) == EOF)
              printf("Cannot close input file\n");
      }
  }
```

11.

```
#include <stdio.h>
main()
{
    FILE *f;
    int c;
    long len = 0,
         N;

    if ((f = fopen("TEST", "r")) == NULL)
        printf("File TEST does not exist\n");
    else {
        do {
            printf("Enter line number > 0 : ");
            scanf("%ld", &N);
        }
```

```
                while (N < 1);

                while (N != 1 && (c = getc(f)) != EOF) {
                        while (c != EOF && c != '\n')
                                c = getc(f);
                        if (c == EOF)
                                break;
                        else N--;
                }

                if (N != 1)
                        printf("That line does not exist\n");
                else {
                        while ((c = getc(f)) != EOF && c != '\n')
                                len++;
                        if (c == EOF)
                                printf("That line does not exist\n");
                        else printf("Line length is %ld\n", len);
                }

                if (fclose(f) == EOF)
                        printf("Cannot close file TEST\n");
        }
}
```

13.

```
#include <stdio.h>
main()
{
        int oper;
        long line = 0;
        float num1, num2, num3;

        while ((oper = getchar()) != EOF) {
                line++;
                scanf("%f%f%f%*c", &num1, &num2, &num3);
                if (num1 < 0 || num2 < 0 || num3 < 0)
                        printf("LINE # %ld: wrong data\n", line);
                else if (oper == 'S')
                        printf("%.1f SUM\n", num1 + num2 + num3);
                else printf("%.1f PRODUCT\n", num1 * num2 * num3);
        }
}
```

E.4   CHAPTER 5

1.

```
#define W(c) ((c) == ' ' || (c) == '\t' || (c) == '\n')
#define R(x) scanf("%d",&(x));
```

3.

```
 -2
  2
 -2
  1
```

5.

```
#define ISNPRINT(c) ((c) < 32 !! (c) > 126)
```

7.

```
#define GETINT(x) (scanf("%d",&(x)), (x))
```

E.5   CHAPTER 6

1.

```
#include <stdio.h>

char up(c)
char c;
{
    return((c >= 'a' && c <= 'z') ? c - 'a' + 'A' : c);
}

main()
{
    char letter;

    printf("Enter a letter to convert - ");
    scanf("%c", &letter);

    printf("The letter %c in uppercase is %c\n", letter,
            up(letter));
}
```

3.

```
#include <stdio.h>
void show(r, n)
double r;
int n;
{
    int i;
    double aux = 1;

    printf("%5.2f to power      is\n", r);
```

```
                for (i = 1; i <= n; i++) {
                    aux *= r;
                    printf("\t\t%d\t%5.2f\n", i, aux);
                }
        }

    main()
    {
            double f;
            int n;

            printf("Enter a real and an integer value: ");
            scanf("%lf%d", &f, &n);
            if (n <= 0) {
                    printf("%d is not positive, terminating... \n",n);
                    return;
            }

            show(f, n);
    }
```

5.

```
    #include <stdio.h>

    void triangle(c, n)
    char c;
    int n;
    {
            int i, j;

            for (i = 1; i <= n; i++)  {
                    for (j = 1; j <= i; j++)
                            putchar(c);
                    putchar('\n');
            }
    }

    main()
    {
            int n;
            char c;

            printf("Enter an integer and a character: ");
            scanf("%d%c", &n, &c);

            triangle(c, n);
    }
```

7.

```
    #include <stdio.h>

    long occur(f, c)
```

```
FILE *f;
char c;
{
     int i;
     long occ = 0;

     while ((i = getc(f)) != EOF)
          if (i == c)
               occ++;
     return(occ);
}

main()
{
     FILE *f;
     char c;
     extern long occur();

     if ((f = fopen("TEST", "r")) == NULL) {
          printf("Cannot open TEST\n");
          return;
     }

     printf("Please enter a character: ");
     c = getchar();

     printf("There are %ld occurrences of %c in TEST\n",
               occur(f, c), c);
     if (fclose(f) == EOF)
          printf("Cannot close TEST\n");
}
```

E.6   CHAPTER 7

1.

```
main()
{
     int j = 2,
          *p, i;
     char *malloc();

     *i = 1;                       − i is not a pointer
     *p = 1;                       − p is not initialized
     p = malloc(sizeof(int))       − malloc returns pointer to char
     *p = &i                       − *p is of type integer
     p = &j;                       − OK
     *p  = i;                      − value of i undetermined
     *p = j++;                     − OK
```

3.

```
pc  += 6;                    – pc = 900 + 6 = 906
pi1 += 6;                    – pi1 = 1000 + 6(2) = 1012
pf1 += 6;                    – pf1 = 1100 + 6(4) = 1124
*pf1 = pi1 – pi2;            – *(1124) = (1012 – 1012) / 2 = 0
*pi1 = pf1 – pf2;            – *(1012) = (1124 – 1112) / 4 = 3
pi1 –= *pi2;                 – pi1 = 1012 – 3(2) = 1006
```

5.

```
#include <stdio.h>
#define SIZE 15
main()
{
     float *pf, *temppf, *min,
           sum = 0;
     char *malloc();

     if ((min = temppf = pf =
                (float*)malloc(SIZE*sizeof(float))) == NULL)
          printf("Cannot allocate memory\n");
     else {
          for (; temppf – pf < SIZE; temppf++)
               scanf("%f", temppf);
          for (temppf--; temppf >= pf; temppf--) {
               min = (*min > *temppf) ? temppf : min;
               sum += *temppf;
          }
          printf("Sum is %f, minimum is %f\n", sum, *min);
     }
}
```

7.

a.

b.
```
for (aux = p1; aux < p1 + SIZE; aux++)
     scanf("%u", aux);
```

c.

d. 400
200
3
408
208
5
8
        /* aux == 212 */
3

9.

```c
#define SIZE 10
#include <stdio.h>
main()
{
    char *malloc(), *word;
    int i, j, k, c;

    if ((word = malloc(SIZE)) == NULL)  {
        printf("\nCould not allocate memory\n");
        return;
    }

    while ((c = getchar()) != EOF)  {
        while (c == ' ' || c == '\t' || c == '\n')
            c = getchar();
        if (c == EOF)
            break;

        for (i = 0; i<SIZE && c!=' ' && c!='\t' &&
            c!='\n' && c!=EOF; i++, c = getchar())
            *(word + i) = c;
        k = --i;

        for (j = 0; j < k && *(word + j) == *(word + k);
            j++ ,k--)
            ;                        /* palindrome? */
        if (j >= k) {                /* was a palindrome */
            for (j = 0; j <= i; putchar(*(word + j++)))
                ;                    /* output it */
            putchar('\n');
        }
    }
}
```

11.

```c
#define SIZE 10
#include <stdio.h>
main()
{
```

```
        char *malloc();
        int i, j, k, num, *pint,
            prod = 1,
            sum = 0;

        if ((pint = (int*)malloc(SIZE * sizeof(int))) == NULL) {
            printf("\nCould not allocate memory\n");
            return;
        }
        for (i = 0; i < SIZE; i++) {
            scanf("%d", pint + i);
            if (*(pint + i) == 0)
                break;
        }

        /* sort in ascending order */
        for (j = 0; j < i - 1; j++)
            for (k = j + 1; k < i; k++)
                if (*(pint + k) < *(pint + j)) {
                    num = *(pint + k);
                    *(pint + k) = *(pint + j);
                    *(pint + j) = num;

                }

        /* sum integers in odd positions */
        for (j = 0; j < i; j += 2)
            sum += *(pint + j);
        if (i <= 1)
            prod = 0;
        else /* multiply integers at even positions */
            for (j = 1; j < i; j += 2)
                prod *= *(pint+j);

        printf("Sum is %d\n", sum);
        printf("Product is %d\n", prod);
}
```

13.

```
    #include <stdio.h>
    main()
    {
        char *malloc(), *curr, **names;
        int i, c,
            count = 0;

        if ((names=(char**)malloc(sizeof(char*)*50)) == NULL) {
            printf("\nCould not allocate memory\n");
            return;
        }

        while (count < 50 && (c = getchar()) != EOF) {
```

```
            while (c == ' ' || c == '\n' || c == '\t')
                  c = getchar();
            if(c == EOF)
                  break;
            if (c >= 'A' && c <= 'Z') {
                  if ((curr = malloc(11)) == NULL) {
                        printf("\nCould not allocate memory\n");
                        return;
                  }
                  for (i = 0; i < 10; ++i, c = getchar())
                        if (c!=' '&&c!='\n'&&c!='\t'&&c!= EOF)
                              *(curr + i) = c;
                        else break;
                  *(curr + i) = '\0';
                  /* keep a pointer to the word */
                  *names++ = curr;
                  ++count;
            }
      }

      --names;         /* points to last word */
      if (count > 0)
            /* output words in reverse order */
            for (i = 1; i <= count; ++i) {
                  curr = *names;
                  while (*curr != '\0')
                        putchar(*curr++);
                  putchar('\n');
                  --names;  /* points to previous word */
            }
}
```

15.

```
#include <stdio.h>

void alter(x, y)
double *x, *y;
{
      double temp;

      temp = *x;
      *x += *y;
      *y *= temp;
}

main()
{
      double x = 10,
             y = 20;

      printf("x and y before are %f and %f\n", x, y);
      alter(&x, &y);
```

```
        printf("x and y after are %f and %f\n", x, y);
}
```

17.

```
double f(x)
double x;
{
    return(x * x * x);
}

#include <stdio.h>
#define LINELEN 80
void graph(f, a, b, step)
double (*f)();
double a, b, step;
{
    double fmax, fmin, scale, res, i;
    int x;

    fmax = fmin = (*f)(a);

    /* find minimum and maximum value of the function */
    for (i = a; i <= b; i += step) {
        res = (*f)(i);
        fmax = (fmax < res) ? res : fmax;
        fmin = (fmin > res) ? res : fmin;
    }
    scale = ((fmax-fmin)== 0) ? 1 : LINELEN / (fmax - fmin);

    for (i = a; i <= b; i += step) {
        res = (*f)(i);
        for (x = 1; x < (int)(res * scale); x++)
            putchar(' ');
        printf("*\n");
    }
}

main()
{
    graph(f, -1.0, 1.0, .1);
}
```

E.7 CHAPTER 8

1.

```
#include <stdio.h>
main()
{
```

```
        int i;
        char line[80];

        for (i=0; i < 80 && (line[i]=getchar())!='\n';i++)
            ;
        for (i = 0; i < 80 && line[i] != '\n'; i++)
            if (line[i]!=' ' &&line[i]<'0' !! line[i] > '9')
                putchar(line[i]);
        putchar('\n');
}
```

3.

```
    #include <stdio.h>
    main()
    {
        float arr[50],
              sum = 0,
              prod = 1;
        int i;

        for (i = 0; i < 50; i++) {
            scanf("%f", &arr[i]);
            if (arr[i] == 0)
                break;
        }

        for (i = 0; i < 50 && arr[i] != 0; i++) {
            sum += arr[i];
            prod *= arr[i];
        }

        printf("The product is %f, the sum is %f\n",
            prod, sum);
    }
```

5.

```
    #include <stdio.h>
    main()
    {
        FILE *f;
        int marks[100];
        char initials[100];
        int Bnumb = 0,
            count = 0,
            mark = 1;
        char initial;

        if ((f = fopen("TEST", "r")) == NULL) {
```

```
                    printf("Cannot open TEST\n");
                    return;
            }

            do
                    fscanf(f,"%d%*c%c",&marks[Bnumb], &initials[Bnumb]);
            while (marks[Bnumb++]);

            Bnumb -= 2;
            /* number of students in section B */

            while (fscanf(f, "%d%*c%c",&mark, &initial) != EOF) {
                    for (; mark>marks[count]&&count<=Bnumb; count++)
                        printf("%d %c B\n", marks[count], initials[count]);
                    printf("%d %c C\n", mark, initial);
            }

            /* now process the "tail" of the arrays */

            for (; count <= Bnumb; count++)
                printf("%d %c B\n", marks[count], initials[count]);
            if (fclose(f) == EOF)
                    printf("Cannot close TEST\n");
    }
```

7.

```
    int FIND(F, x, n)
    float F[], x;
    int n;
    {
            int mid, bottom = 0,
                top = n - 1;

            while (bottom <= top) {
                    mid = (bottom + top) / 2;
                    if (F[mid] == x)
                            return(1);
                    else if (F[mid] < x)
                            bottom = mid + 1;
                    else top = mid - 1;
            }
            return(0);
    }
```

9.

```
    #include <stdio.h>

    void PRO(F, x, n)
    float F[], *x;
```

```
int n;
{
        int i;

        *x = F[0];
        for (i = 1; i < n; i++)
                *x *= F[i];
}

main()
{
        float nums[10], product;
           . . .
        /* initialize or whatever */
           . . .
        PRO(nums, &product, 5);
           . . .
}
```

11.

```
#include <stdio.h>
#define ERROR { printf("Memory allocation failed\n"); \
                return; }
int shrink(a)
float *a[];
{
        static int size = 10;
        float *new, *aux, *aux1;
        char *malloc();

        size = (size <= 0) ? 0 : size - 2;
        if ((new=(float*)malloc(size*sizeof(float))) == NULL)
                return(0);

        for (aux=new, aux1=*a; aux<new+size; *aux++ = *aux1++)
                ;
        free((char*)*a);
        *a = new;
        printf("Size is now %d\n", size);
        return(1);
}

main()
{
        float *reals;
        char *malloc();
        int i;

        if ((reals=(float*)malloc(10*sizeof(float))) == NULL)
                ERROR
```

```
      else {
            printf("Enter 10 reals : ");
            for (i = 0; i < 10; i++)
                  scanf("%f", &reals[i]);
            for (i = 0; i < 3; i++)
                  if (!shrink(&reals))
                        ERROR
            for (i = 0; i < 4; i++)
                  printf("%f ", reals[i]);
            putchar('\n');
      }
}
```

13.

```
#include <stdio.h>

float *mult(a, b, n)
float *a, *b;
int n;
{
      float *res;
      int i;
      char *malloc();

      if ((res = (float*) malloc(n * sizeof(float))) == NULL)
            return(NULL);
      for (i = 0; i < n; i++)
            res[i] = a[i] * b[i];
      return(res);
}

main()
{
      float a[10], b[10], *result;
      int i;

      printf("Enter values for two 10 element vectors\n");
      for (i = 0; i < 10; i++)
            scanf("%f", &a[i]);

      for (i = 0; i < 10; i++)
            scanf("%f", &b[i]);

      if ((result = mult(a, b, 10)) == NULL)
            printf("Memory allocation failed\n");
      else {
            printf("The product of the vectors is:\n");
            for (i = 0; i < 10; i++)
                  printf("%f ", result[i]);
            putchar('\n');
      }
}
```

15.

```
double value(x, p, n)
double x, p[ ];
int n;
{
      double res = 0;

      for (; n >= 0; n--)
            res = p[n] + x * res;
      return(res);
}
```

E.8   CHAPTER 9

1.

```
complex subtract(x, y)          /*  x - y  */
complex x, y;
{
      complex z;

      z.re = x.re - y.re;
      z.im = x.im - y.im;
      return(z);
}

complex multiply(x, y)          /*  x * y  */
complex x, y;
{
      complex z;

      z.re = x.re * y.re - x.im * y.im;
      z.im = x.re * y.im + x.im * y.re;
      return(z);
}

complex divide(x, y)            /*  x / y  */
complex x, y;
{
      complex z;
      double denom;

      denom = y.re * y.re + y.im * y.im;
      if (denom == 0)
            denom = 1;

      z.re = (x.re * y.re + x.im * y.im) / denom;
      z.im = (x.im * y.re + x.re * y.im) / denom;

      return(z);
}
```

3.

```
#define MAXINT 32767

void info(a, fage, eage)
struct agent a;
int *fage, *eage;
{
    int i;

    *fage = MAXINT;   /* initial very old friend */
    *eage = -1;       /* initial very young enemy */
    for (i = 0; i < 10; i++) {
      if (a.friends[i].sex==female&&a.friends[i].age<*fage)
            *fage = a.friends[i].age;
      if (a.enemies[i].sex==male&&a.enemies[i].age>*eage)
            *eage = a.enemies[i].age;
    }

    if (*fage == MAXINT)
        *fage = -1;
}
```

5.

a.

```
struct el *newel()
{
    char *malloc();

    return((struct el *) malloc(sizeof(struct el)));
}
```

b.

```
void newel(ptr)
struct el **ptr;
{
    char *malloc();

    *ptr = (struct el *) malloc(sizeof(struct el));
}
```

7.
a.

```
void update(comp, id, nage, nsal)
PEMP comp[];
int id, nage;
```

```
 float nsal;
{
     char *malloc();
     PEMP emp;

     if ((emp=(PEMP)malloc(sizeof(struct employee))) == NULL)
          return;

     emp->age = nage;
     emp->salary = nsal;
     comp[id] = emp;
}
```

b.

```
double total(comp)
PEMP comp[];
{
     int i;
     double sum = 0;

     for (i = 0; i < 100; i++)
          if (comp[i] != NULL && (comp[i])->age >= 50)
               sum += (comp[i])->salary;
     return(sum);
}
```

9.

```
#include <stdio.h>

typedef struct elem{
          int data;
          struct elem *next;
     } LISTEL, *LIST;

typedef int bool;
#define TRUE 1
#define FALSE 0

bool ins(lst, n)
LIST *lst;
int n;
/* Insert n at the front of lst */
{
     LIST temp;
     char *malloc();

     if ((temp = (LIST)malloc(sizeof(LISTEL))) == NULL)
          return(FALSE);
     temp->next = *lst;
     temp->data = n;
     *lst = temp;
     return(TRUE);
}
```

```
      void del(lst)
      LIST *lst;
      /* Delete an element from the front of lst */
      {
            LIST temp;

            if (*lst == NULL)
                  return;
            temp = *lst;
            *lst = (*lst)->next;
            free((char*)temp);
      }

      #define N 1000
      main()
      {
            LIST prev, aux, first = NULL;
            int num;

            for (num = N; num > 1; num--)
                  if (!ins(&first, num))
                        break;

            if (num != 1)
                  printf("Cannot allocate memory\n");
            else {
                  for (num = 2; num <= N; num++)
                        for (prev = first, aux = first->next; aux;)
                              if (aux->data!=num&&aux->data%num==0) {
                                    del(&prev->next);
                                    aux = prev->next;
                              }
                              else {
                                    prev = aux;
                                    aux = aux->next;
                              }
                  for (aux = first; aux; aux = aux->next)
                        printf("%d ", aux->data);
                  putchar('\n');
            }
      }
```

E.9 CHAPTER 10

1.

```
      void strip(s, t)
      char *s, *t;
      {
            for (; *s == ' '; s++)
                  ;
```

```
        while (*t++ = *s++)
                ;
}
```

3.

```
    int strcmp(s1, s2)
    char *s1, *s2;
    {
        for (; *s1 && *s1 == *s2; s1++, s2++)
                ;
        return (*s1 == *s2) ? 0 : (*s1 < *s2) ? -1 : 1;
    }
```

5.

```
    #include <stdio.h>
    #include <string.h>
    main(argc, argv)
    int argc;
    char *argv[];
    {
        char *aux;
        FILE *f;

        if (argc != 2 ) {
            printf("usage: %s filename\n", argv[0]);
            return;
        }

        if ((aux = strrchr(argv[1], '.')) == NULL ||
            (*(aux + 1) != 'c' || *(aux + 2) != '\0'))
            printf("No .c extension\n");
        else {
            /* change extension to 'o' */
            *(aux + 1) = 'o';
            if ((f = fopen(argv[1], "r")) == NULL)
                printf("NO OBJECT FILE\n");
            else {
                fclose(f);
                printf("OK\n");
            }
        }
    }
```

7.

```
    #include <stdio.h>
    main(argc, argv)
    int argc;
    char *argv[];
```

```
    {
        char first[31], last[51];
        FILE *fil;

        if (argc != 2) {
            printf("usage: %s filename\n", argv[0]);
            return;
        }

        if ((fil = fopen(argv[1], "r")) == NULL) {
            printf("File not found\n");
            return;
        }

        while(fscanf(fil, "%30s", first) != EOF) {
            fscanf(fil, "%50s", last);
            printf("%s %c\n", last, first[0]);
        }

        if (fclose(fil) == EOF)
            printf("Cannot close file\n");
    }
```

9.

```
test-number
est-number
st-number
t-number
I
like
to
program
```

11.

```
fine
bad
bad
```

13.

```
#include <stdio.h>
#include <ctype.h>
main(argc, argv)
int argc;
char *argv[];
{
    FILE *in, *out;
    int c, tofile,
        PosInfile = 0,
        PosInline;
    char line[17];
```

```
      if (argc > 3 || argc < 2) {
          printf("usage: %s filename [filename2]\n", argv[0]);
          return;
      }

  line[16] = '\0';
  out = stdout;   /* set default output device */
  tofile = (argc == 3);
  if ((in = fopen(argv[1], "r")) == NULL ||
              (tofile && (out=fopen(argv[2],"w"))==NULL)) {
      printf("Cannot open files\n");
      return;
  }

  while ((c = getc(in)) != EOF) {
      PosInline = PosInfile % 16;
      if (PosInline == 0)
          fprintf(out,"%04x:", PosInfile);
      fprintf(out," %02x", c);
      line[PosInline] = (isprint(c)) ? c : '.';
      if (PosInline == 15)
          fprintf(out," %s\n", line);
      PosInfile++;
  }

  if (PosInfile % 16 != 0) {
      line[PosInfile % 16] = '\0';
      fprintf(out,"  %s\n", line);
  }

  if (fclose(in) == EOF || (tofile && fclose(out) == EOF))
      printf("Cannot close files\n");
}
```

E.10 CHAPTER 11

1.

```
#define BYTESIZE 8
#define CHARSIZE (sizeof(char)*BYTESIZE)

char reverse(b)
char b;
{
    unsigned b1 = b,
             b2 = 0;
    int i;
```

```
            for (i = 0; i < CHARSIZE; i++) {
                    b2 <<= 1;
                    b2 += (b1 & 1);
                    b1 >>= 1;
            }
            return(b2);
    }
```

3.

```
#define BYTESIZE    8
#define INTSIZE     (sizeof(int)*BYTESIZE)
#define NUMDIGS     (INTSIZE/3 + (INTSIZE%3 != 0))
#define MASK        7

void octal(num)
unsigned num;
{
    int nonzero, d, msdigit;

    nonzero = 0;
    for (d = NUMDIGS-1; d >= 0; d--) {
        msdigit = num >> d * 3 & MASK;
        nonzero = nonzero || msdigit;
        if (nonzero)
                putchar(msdigit + '0');
    }

    if (!nonzero)
            putchar('0');
}
```

5.

```
#define BYTESIZE 8

void compress(str, mask)
char *str;
unsigned char mask;
{
    unsigned msbit;
    char *ptr;

    for (ptr = str; *ptr; ptr++) {
        msbit = mask >> BYTESIZE - 1;
        mask = mask << 1 | msbit;
        if (msbit)
                *str++ = *ptr;
    }
    *str++ = '\0';
}
```

E.11 CHAPTER 12

1.

```
void COPY(fil1, fil2, limit)
FILE *fil1, *fil2;
int limit;
{
    STUDENT srec;

    rewind(fil1);
    while (fread((char*)&srec,sizeof(STUDENT),1,fil1)) {
        if (srec.age < limit)
            fwrite((char*)&srec,sizeof(STUDENT),1,fil2);
    }
}
```

3.

```
void update(stufile)
FILE *stufile;
{
    STUDENT srec;
    long counter = 0;

    while (1) {
      fseek(stufile, counter * sizeof(STUDENT), 0);
      if (!fread((char*)&srec,sizeof(STUDENT),1,stufile))
          return;
      if (srec.age >= 30) {
          srec.GPA *= 1.1;
          fseek(stufile, counter * sizeof(STUDENT), 0);
          fwrite((char*)&srec,sizeof(STUDENT),1,stufile);
      }
      counter++;
    }
}
```

5.

```
#include <stdio.h>

typedef struct {
            char name[30];
            int age;
            float GPA;
        } STUDENT;
```

```
main(argc, argv)
int argc;
char *argv[];
{
     FILE *stufile, *datafile;
     STUDENT srec;

     if ((stufile = fopen(argv[1], "r")) == NULL ||
            (datafile=fopen(argv[2],"w"))==NULL) {
         printf("Cannot open files\n");
         return;
     }

     while (fread((char*)&srec,sizeof(STUDENT), 1,stufile))
         fprintf(datafile, "%d\t%0.2f\t%s\n",
                    srec.age, srec.GPA, srec.name);

     if (fclose(stufile) == EOF || fclose(datafile) == EOF)
         printf("Cannot close files\n");
}
```

7.

```
void remove(stufile, limit)
FILE *stufile;
float limit;
{
     STUDENT srec;
     long counter = 0;
     char *deleted = "***";

     rewind(stufile);
     while (1) {
         fseek(stufile, counter * sizeof(STUDENT), 0);
         if (!fread((char*)&srec,sizeof(STUDENT),1,stufile))
             return;

         if (strcmp(srec.name,deleted)!=0&&srec.GPA < limit) {
             strcpy(srec.name, deleted);
             fseek(stufile, counter * sizeof(STUDENT), 0);
             fwrite((char*)&srec,sizeof(STUDENT),1,stufile);
         }
         counter++;
     }
}
```

9.

```
float average(stufile)
FILE *stufile;
{
    STUDENT srec;
    int snum = 0;
    float total = 0;

    for (rewind(stufile);
      fread((char*)&srec,sizeof(STUDENT),1,stufile);
        snum++)
          total += srec.GPA;
    return(snum ? total / snum : 0);
}
```

E.12   CHAPTER 13

1.

```
void lprint(lst)
LIST lst;
{
    if (lst != NULL) {
        printf("%d\t", lst->data);
        lprint(lst->next);
    }
}
```

3.

```
#include <stdio.h>
#include <string.h>

typedef struct str {
    char val;
    struct str *next;
} str;

/* Macro to allocate new list element */
#define NEW(aux) if ((aux = (struct str *)\
  malloc(sizeof(struct str))) == NULL) return(0);
```

```
/* Function which converts a string into a linked list.
   Returns 1 if successful and 0 otherwise
 */
int from(s, y)
char *s;
str **y;
{
    str *aux;
    int len;
    char *malloc();

    NEW(aux)
    *y = aux;
    aux->val = s[0];
    for (len = 1; len <= strlen(s); len++) {
        NEW(aux->next)
        aux = aux->next;
        aux->val = s[len];
    }
    aux->next = NULL;
    return(1);
}


/* Procedure which converts list into string */
void into(y, s)
str *y;
char *s;
{
    for (; y; *s++ = y->val, y = y->next)
        ;
}

/* Main program to test the preceding function.
   Error checking is limited
 */
main()
{
    char test[30], newstring[30];
    str *first;


    printf("Input a test string (len < 30): ");
    gets(test);
    printf("Converting to a linked list\n");
    if (!from(test, &first)) {
        printf("Error in conversion to linked-list\n");
        return;
    }
    printf("Converting back to a string\n");
    into(first, newstring);
    printf("The string is : %s\n", newstring);
}
```

5.

```
/* Operations to create a linked list of text lines */
#include <stdio.h>

/* main data structures */
typedef struct charlist {
               char ch;
               struct charlist *next;
        } charlist, *Pcharlist;

typedef struct strlist {
               Pcharlist string;
               struct strlist *next;
        } strlist, *Pstrlist;

char *malloc();

/* Insert character into list */
int cins(c, l)
char c;
Pcharlist *l;
{
     Pcharlist rec;

     if ((rec = (charlist) malloc(sizeof(charlist))) == NULL)
          return(0);
     rec-> = c;
     rec->chnext = *l;
     *l = rec;
     return(1);
}


/* Delete first element from list */
void cdel(l)
Pcharlist *l;
{
     Pcharlist temp;

     if (*l != NULL) {
          temp = *l;
          *l = (*l)->next;
          free((char*)temp);
     }
}

/* Following are operations for linked lists of strings */

/* insert string into list */
int sins(s, l)
Pcharlist s;
Pstrlist *l;
{
     Pstrlist rec;
```

```
     if ((rec = (Pstrlist) malloc(sizeof(strlist))) == NULL)
          return(0);
     rec->string = s;
     rec->next = *l;
     *l = rec;
     return(1);
}

/* Delete string from list */
void sdel(l)
Pstrlist *l;

{
     Pstrlist temp;

     if (*l != NULL) {
          temp = *l;
          *l = (*l)->next;
          while (temp->string)
               cdel(&(temp->string));
          free((char*)temp);
     }
}


/* Following are functions for editing the linked lists
   Print every string, prefixed by a line number,
   contained in the given linked list of char lists
 */
void prtxt(text)
Pstrlist text;
{
     Pcharlist aux;
     int linnum = 1;

     for (; text; text = text->next, linnum++) {
          printf("%3d ", linnum);
          for (aux = text->string; aux; aux = aux->next)
               putchar(aux->ch);
          putchar('\n');
     }
}


/* Make a linked list out of the character string pline
   and insert it before line linnum in text (a linked list
   of char lists). If the given line does not exist, insert
   at the end of text
 */
void inslin(text, pline, linnum)
Pstrlist *text;
char *pline;
int linnum;
{
     Pcharlist line = NULL;
     Pstrlist aux, pred;
     int i;
```

```c
        /* find predecessor of the required line */
        for (pred=NULL, aux=*text; linnum>1&&aux != NULL;
                   linnum--, pred = aux, aux = aux->next)
            ;
        /* insert each character into a new line */
        for (i = strlen(pline); 1; i--)
            cins(pline[i - 1], &line);
        /* insert a new line */
        sins(line, &aux);
        if (pred != NULL)  /* modify predecessor */
            pred->next = aux;
        else *text = aux;
}

/* If list linnum exists in text, it is deleted,
   otherwise, text is left untouched
 */
void dellin(text, linnum)
Pstrlist *text;
int linnum;

{
        Pstrlist aux, pred;

        /* find predecessor of the required line */
        for (pred=NULL, aux=*text; linnum>1&&aux != NULL;
                   linnum--, pred = aux, aux = aux->next)
            ;
        if (aux != NULL)
            sdel(&aux);
        else return;
        if (pred != NULL)
            pred->next = aux;
        else *text = aux;
}

/* Characters from the string chars are inserted
   in line linnum at position. If either linnum
   or position is nonexistent, text is left untouched
 */
void insstr(text, linnum, position, chars)
Pstrlist text;
int linnum, position;
char *chars;
{
    Pstrlist aux;
    Pcharlist line, pred;
    int i;

    for (aux=text;linnum>1&&aux!=NULL;aux=aux->next,linnum--)
        ;
    if (aux != NULL) {
            /* find predecessor of the required line */
```

```
            for (pred=NULL,line=aux->string;position>0&&line!=NULL;
                        position--, pred=line, line=line->next)
                ;
            if (line != NULL) {
                /* inserts characters into a new line */
                for (i = strlen(chars); i; i--)
                    cins(chars[i - 1], &line);
                if (pred != NULL)  /* modify predecessor */
                    pred->next = line;
                else aux->string = line;
            }
        }
}

/* Num characters from line linnum beginning at
   position are deleted from text. If either linnum
   or position do not exist, text is left untouched
 */
void delstr(text, linnum, position, num)
Pstrlist text;
int linnum, position, num;
{
    Pstrlist aux;
    Pcharlist line, pred;

    for (aux=text; linnum>1&&aux!=NULL; aux=aux->next, linnum--)
        ;
    if (aux != NULL) {
        /* find predecessor of the required line */
        for (pred=NULL,line=aux->string;position>0&&line!=NULL;
            position--, pred = line, line = line->next)
            ;

        if (line != NULL) {
            while (num--)      /* delete all characters */
                cdel(&line);
            if (pred != NULL)
                pred->next = line;
            else aux->string = line;
        }
    }
}

/* Main program to test the preceding functions.
   Error checking is limited
 */
main()
{
    char line[50], comm[2], *gets();
    int linnum, pos, num;
    Pstrlist test = NULL;
```

```
    do {
      printf("Linked List Editor\n\n");
      printf("Commands are --\n\nD\tdelete line\nI\tinsert line");
      printf("\nX\tdelete part of line\nN\tinsert part of line");
      printf("\nP\tprint all lines\nQ\tquit\n\n");
      scanf("%1s%*c", comm);
      switch (comm[0]) {
            case 'D' : printf("which line -- ");
                       scanf("%d%*c", &linnum);
                       if (linnum > 0)
                             dellin(&text, linnum);
                       break;
            case 'I' : printf("which line -- ");
                       scanf("%d%*c", &linnum);
                       if (linnum > 0) {
                             printf( "enter line (len < 50) -- ");
                             gets(line);
                             inslin(&text, line, linnum);
                       }
                       break;
            case 'X' : printf("which line -- ");
                       scanf("%d", &linnum);
                       printf("which position -- ");
                       scanf("%d", &pos);
                       printf("how many -- ");
                       scanf("%d%*c", &num);
                       if (linnum > 0 &&
                             pos >= 0 && num > 0)
                             delstr(text,linnum, pos,num);
                       break;
            case 'N' : printf("which line -- ");
                       scanf("%d", &linnum);
                       printf("which position -- ");
                       scanf("%d%*c", &pos);
                       if (linnum > 0 && pos >= 0) {
                             printf( "enter string (len < 50) -- ");
                             gets(line);
                             insstr(text,linnum, pos,line);
                       }
                       break;
            case 'P' :  printf("printing\n"); prtxt(text);
                       break;
      }
    }
  while (comm[0] != 'Q');
}
```

7.

```
/* For simplicity, we assume the elements in
   the tree are chars. No error checking is performed.
*/
```

```c
#include <stdio.h>

typedef char eltype;
typedef struct nodetype {
            eltype element;
            struct nodetype *left, *right;
        } NODE, *PNODE;

typedef PNODE TREE;

int member(x, T)
eltype x;
TREE T;
{
    if (T == NULL)
        return(0);
    else if (x == T->element)
        return(1);
    else if (x < T->element)
        return(member(x, T->left));
    else return(member(x, T->right));
}

void insert(x, T)
eltype x;
TREE *T;
{
    char *malloc();

    if (*T == NULL) {
        *T = (TREE)malloc(sizeof(NODE));
        (*T)->element = x;
        (*T)->left = (*T)->right = NULL;
    }
    else if (x < (*T)->element)
        insert(x, &((*T)->left));
    else if (x > (*T)->element)
        insert(x, &((*T)->right));
}

eltype deletemin(T)
TREE *T;
{
    PNODE tnode;
    eltype temp;

    if ((*T)->left == NULL) {
        temp = (*T)->element;
        tnode = *T;
        *T = (*T)->right;
        free((char*)tnode);
        return(temp);
    }
    else return(deletemin(&((*T)->left)));
}
```

```
void delete(x, T)
eltype x;
TREE *T;
{
    PNODE tnode;

    if (*T != NULL)
        if (x < (*T)->element)
            delete(x, &((*T)->left));
        else if (x > (*T)->element)
            delete(x, &((*T)->right));
        /* if we reach here, x is in the node */
        else if ((*T)->left==NULL&&(*T)->right == NULL) {
            tnode = *T;
            *T = NULL;
            free((char*)tnode);
        }
        else if ((*T)->left == NULL) {
            tnode = *T;
            *T = (*T)->right;
            free((char*)tnode);
        }
        else if ((*T)->right == NULL) {
            tnode = *T;
            *T = (*T)->left;
            free((char*)tnode);
        }
        else (*T)->element = deletemin(&((*T)->right));
}
```

9.

```
/* For these algorithms, we assume the elements
   to sort are n integers stored in an array.
 */

#define MININT (-32768) /* or whatever */

typedef int keytype;

void insertsort(arr, n)
int arr[];
int n;
{
    int i, j;
    keytype temp;

    arr[0] = MININT;
    for (i = 2; i <= n; i++)
        for (j = i; arr[j] < arr[j - 1]; j--) {
```

```
                        temp = arr[j];
                        arr[j] = arr[j - 1];
                        arr[j - 1] = temp;
                }
        }

        /* The following functions implement quicksort */

        int findpivot(arr, i, j)
        int arr[];
        int i, j;
        {
                keytype firstkey;
                int k;

                firstkey = arr[i];
                for (k = i + 1; k <= j; k++)
                        if (arr[k] > firstkey)
                                return(k);
                        else if (arr[k] < firstkey)
                                return(i);
                return(0);
        }

        int partition(arr, i, j, pivot)
        int arr[];
        int i, j;
        keytype pivot;
        {
                int l = i,
                    r = j;
                keytype temp;

                while (1) {
                        while (arr[l] < pivot)
                                l++;
                        while (arr[r] >= pivot)
                                r--;
                        if (l > r)
                                break;
                        temp = arr[l];
                        arr[l] = arr[r];
                        arr[r] = temp;
                }
                return(l);
        }

        void quicksort(arr, i, j)
        int arr[];
        int i, j;
        {
                keytype pivot;
                int pivotindex;
                int k;
```

```
pivotindex = findpivot(arr, i, j);
if (pivotindex != 0) {
     pivot = arr[pivotindex];
     k = partition(arr, i, j, pivot);
     if (i != k - 1)
          quicksort(arr, i, k - 1);
     if (k != j)
          quicksort(arr, k, j);
}
}
```

Comparison Between Pascal and C

Pascal	Construct	C
Sequence of letters and digits starting with a letter; case insensitive	Identifiers	Sequence of letters and digits starting with a letter or underscore; case sensitive
(* ... *)	Comments	/* ... */
INTEGER BOOLEAN CHAR REAL	Data types	int long int short int int char float double
VAR i : INTEGER; c, d : CHAR; x, y : REAL;	Declaration of variables	int i; char c, d; float x, y;

l-value := *exp*
i := 2;
c := 'a';
x := x + 2 * x;
	Assignment	*l-value* = *exp*
		i = 2;
		c = 'a';
		x = x + 2 * x;

PROGRAM TEST;
VAR
  i,j : INTEGER;
BEGIN
  i := 1;
  j := 3;
  i := i + j;
END.
	Main program	main()
		{
		  int i, j;
		
		  i = 1;
		  j = 3;
		  i = i + j;
		}

+ − * / + − DIV MOD	addition subtraction multiplication real division unary + unary − integer division modulo	+ − * / not defined − / %
READ(i);	Reading an integer value	scanf("%d", &i);

Pascal	Construct	C
`WRITE(i);`	Writing integer value	`printf("%d", i);`

Pascal	Construct	C
`<`	less than	`<`
`<=`	not greater	`<=`
`>`	greater than	`>`
`>=`	not less	`>=`
`=`	equality	`==`
`<>`	inequality	`!=`
`AND`	logical and	`&&`
`OR`	logical or	`¦¦`
`NOT`	negation	`!`

Pascal	Construct	C
`IF` *booleanExp* `THEN` *stmt*	if statement	`if (`*exp*`)` *stmt*
`IF` *booleanExp* `THEN` *stmt1* `ELSE` *stmt2*		`if (`*exp*`)` *stmt1* `else` *stmt2*
`IF x < 1` `THEN y := 2`		`if (x < 1)` `y = 2`
`IF x < 1` `THEN y := 2` `ELSE y := 3`		`if (x < 1)` `y = 2;` `else y = 3`

Pascal	Construct	C
`WHILE` *booleanExp* `DO` *stmt*	while statement	`while (`*exp*`)` *stmt*
`WHILE x < 1` `DO x := x + 1`		`while (x < 1) x++`

Pascal	Construct	C
`REPEAT` *stmt* `UNTIL` *condition*	repeat statement	`do` *stmt* `while (`*condition*`)`
`REPEAT x := x+1` `UNTIL x > 0`		`do x++;` `while (x <= 0)`

Pascal	Construct	C
`FOR` *controlVar* `:=` *start* `TO` *stop* `DO` *stmt*	for statement	`for (`*exp1*`; `*exp2*`; `*exp3*`)` *stmt*
`FOR i := 1 TO 10 DO` `    WRITE(i)`		`for (i=1; i<=10; i++)` `        printf("%d", i)`

Pascal	Construct	C

`CASE` *exp* `OF` *l1,l2,...,lk* :   *stmt1*;
 	
...
 	
m1,m2,...,mn : *stmtp*;
 	
`END;`
	case statement	`switch (`*exp*`) {` `case `*l1*`: ... case `*lk*`:` `        `*stmt1*`; break;`
		`    ...`
		`case `*m1*`: ... case `*mn*`:` `        `*stmtp*`; break;` `default: `*stmts*`; break;` `}`

Pascal	Construct	C

`READ(c);`
`CASE c OF`
`'a', 'b', 'c' :`
   `WRITE('1');`
`'d': WRITE('2');`
 `(* not defined *)`
`END;`
		`switch (c=getchar()) {`
		`case 'a': case 'b':`
		`case 'c': putchar('1'); break;`
		`case 'd': putchar('2'); break;`
		`default : putchar('3');`
		`}`

`ASSIGN(f, 'TEST');` `RESET(f);`	Open file for reading	`f = fopen("TEST", "r");`
`ASSIGN(f, 'TEST');` `REWRITE(f);`	Open file for writing	`f = fopen("TEST", "w");`
`WHILE NOT EOLN DO` `READ(C)`	Testing for end-of-line	`while ((c = getchar())` `!= '\n')`
`WHILE NOT EOF DO` `READ(c)`	Testing for end-of-file	`while ((c = getchar())` `!= EOF)`

`FUNCTION max(a, b : INTEGER):`
   `INTEGER;`
`BEGIN`
   `IF a > b THEN`
     `max := a`
   `ELSE max := b`
`END;`
	Function
	definition
		`int max(a, b)`
		`int a, b;`
		`{`
		   `return(a > b ? a : b);`
		`}`

`PROCEDURE test;`
`VAR i : INTEGER;`
`BEGIN`
   `i := 2;`
   `...`
`END;`
	Procedure
	definition
		`void test()`
		`{`
		   `int i;`
		   `i = 2;`
		   `...`
		`}`

`VAR id : ^typ;`
 	
`VAR p : ^INTEGER;`
	Pointer variable
	definition
		`typ *id;`
		
		`int *p;`

`TYPE pint =^INTEGER;`
 	
`VAR p : pint;`
	Pointer type	`typedef int * pint;`
		
		`pint p;`

`p^`	Dereferencing	`*p`
`NIL`	nil pointer	`NULL`
`VAR p: ^typ;` `NEW(p);`	Memory allocation	`typ *p;` `p = (typ *) malloc(sizeof(typ));`
`DISPOSE(p);`	deallocation	`free((char*)p);`

Pascal	Construct	C
VAR *a*: ARRAY[0..*size*−1] OF *T*;	Array	*T a*[*size*];
TYPE *newID* = ARRAY[0..*size*−1] OF *knownID*; VEC5 = ARRAY [0..4] OF INTEGER; VEC3 = ARRAY [0..2] OF INTEGER; FVEC = ARRAY [0..9] OF REAL; v5 : VEC5; v3 : VEC3; f : FVEC;	Array type	typedef *knownID newID*[*size*]; typedef int VEC5[5]; typedef int VEC3[3]; typedef float FVEC[10]; VEC5 v5; VEC3 v3; FVEC f;
VAR X : ARRAY[0..1,0..2] OF INTEGER;	Two-dimensional array	int x[2][3];
TYPE TWO = ARRAY[0..2,0..3] OF INTEGER; SINGLE = ARRAY[0..4] OF INTEGER; TWO = ARRAY[0..3] OF SINGLE;	Two-dimensional array type	typedef int TWO[3][4]; typedef int SINGLE[5]; typedef SINGLE TWO[4];
VAR *A* : RECORD *components*; END; VAR A : RECORD I :INTEGER; R : REAL; END;	Record variable	struct { *components*; } a; struct { int i; float f; } a;

TYPE *typ* = RECORD
components;
END;
 	
TYPE STUDENT = RECORD
  NAME:ARRAY[0..29] OF CHAR;
  StudNum : INTEGER;
END;
 	
TYPE CLASS =
  ARRAY[0..99] OF STUDENT;
VAR Stats : CLASS;
	Record type	typedef struct *typ* {
		   components;
		} *typ*;
		
		typedef struct student {
		    char name[30];
		    int StudNum;
		} STUDENT;
		
		typedef STUDENT CLASS[100];
		
		CLASS Stats;

pointer^.*field*	field access using pointers	*pointer*−>*field*

Pascal	Construct	C

TYPE *typ* = RECORD
  common attributes;
  CASE *varTyp* OF
  val1 : (*variant1*);
  ...
 	
  valk : (*variantk*);
END;
TYPE VARIANTS = RECORD
CASE BOOLEAN OF
TRUE : (i, j : INTEGER);
FALSE : (k, l : REAL);
END;
	Free unions	```typedef union typ {```
		
		  variant1;
		  ...
		  variantk;
		} *typ*;
		
		```typedef union {```
		  ```struct {```
		    ```int i, j;```
		  ```} v1;```
		  ```struct {```
		    ```float k, l;```
		  ```} v2;```
		```} VARIANTS;```

TYPE color =
  (blue, red, green);
	Enumeration
	type
		```typedef enum {```
		  ```blue, red, green```
		```} color;```

APPENDIX G System Library Summary

Three classes of library functions are described in this appendix:

- I/O functions
- String functions
- Memory functions

Within each class, function definitions are sorted alphabetically. A Pascal-like notation is used to specify the types of the formal parameters. Most of these functions return some special values to indicate success or failure; these values are indicated below. For a complete description, see the text.

G.1 I/O FUNCTIONS

```
void clearerr(FILE *fp)
```
Clears errors for fp

```
int fclose(FILE *fp)
```
Closes fp
Returns EOF if fails

```
int feof(FILE *fp)
```
Tests for end-of-file for fp
Returns 0 if fails

```
int ferror(FILE *fp)
```
Tests for errors for fp
Returns 0 if no errors

```
int fflush(FILE *fp)
```
Flushes buffer for fp
Returns EOF if fails

```
int fgetc(FILE *fp)
```
Reads next character from fp
Returns EOF if fails

```
char *fgets(char *s; int max; FILE *fp)
```
Reads from fp and stores in s, stops on end-of-line or when max bytes are read
End-of-line character is included
Returns NULL if fails

```
FILE *fopen(char *nam, *md)
```
Opens file nam in mode md
Returns NULL if fails

```
int fprintf(FILE *fp, char *fmt, arg1, ...)
```
Formatted output to fp with format fmt
Returns EOF if fails

```
int fputc(char c; FILE *fp)          Write c to fp
                                     Returns EOF if fails

int fputs(char *str; FILE *fp)       Writes string str to fp
                                     Returns EOF if fails

int fread(char *buf; unsigned siz; int count; FILE *fp)
                                     Reads from fp count blocks
                                     siz bytes in size
                                     Returns the number of
                                     items read

FILE *freopen(char *nam, *md; FILE *fp)
                                     Closes fp, reopens for file
                                     nam and mode md
                                     Returns NULL if fails

int fscanf(FILE *fp; char *fmt; &arg1, ...)
                                     Formatted read from fp
                                     with format fmt
                                     Returns EOF if fails

int fseek(FILE *fp; long offs; int t)
                                     Seeks in fp to an offset of
                                     offs bytes, according to t
                                     Returns 0 if succeeds

long ftell(FILE *fp)                 Returns position in fp

int fwrite(char *buf; unsigned siz; int count; FILE *fp)
                                     Copies from buf to fp count
                                     blocks, siz bytes each
                                     Returns the number of
                                     items written

int getc(FILE *fp)                   Reads from fp one character
                                     Returns EOF if fails

int getchar()                        Reads from stdio one
                                     character
                                     Returns EOF if fails

char *gets(char *s)                  Reads from stdio one line and
                                     stores in s
                                     Returns NULL if fails

int printf(char *fmt, arg1, ...)     Formatted output to stdout
                                     with format fmt
                                     Returns EOF if fails

int putc(char c; FILE *fp)           Writes c to fp
                                     Returns EOF if fails

int putchar(char c)                  Writes c to stdout
                                     Returns EOF if fails

int puts(char *s)                    Writes string s to stdout
                                     Returns EOF if fails

void rewind(FILE *fp)                Seeks to 0th byte of fp

int scanf(char *fmt; &arg1, ...)     formatted read from stdin with
                                     format fmt
                                     Returns EOF if fails
```

```
int sprintf(char *s, *fmt, arg1, ...)
```
Formatted output to string s
with format fmt
Returns EOF it fails

```
int sscanf(char *s, *fmt; &arg1, ...)
```
Formatted read from string s
with format fmt
Returns EOF if fails

```
int ungetc(char c; FILE *fp)
```
Pushes c back onto fp
Returns EOF if fails

G.2 STRING FUNCTIONS

G.2.1 Macros
```
int isalnum(char c)
```
Tests if c is alphanumeric
```
int isalpha(char c)
```
Tests if c is alphabetic
```
int isascii(char c)
```
Tests if if c is ASCII
```
int iscntrl(char c)
```
Tests if c is nonprintable
```
int isdigit(char c)
```
Tests if c is a digit
```
int isgraph(char c)
```
Tests if c is any printable character
except a space

```
int islower(char c)
```
Tests if c is a lowercase letter
```
int isodigit(char c)
```
Tests if c is an octal digit
```
int isprint(char c)
```
Tests if c is a printable character
including space

```
int isspace(char c)
```
Tests if c is a whitespace character
```
int isupper(char c)
```
Tests if c is an uppercase letter
```
int isxdigit(char c)
```
Tests if c is a hexadecimal digit
```
int toascii(char c)
```
Returns the low-order 7 bits of c
```
int toint(char c)
```
Returns the decimal value of the
hexadecimal digit c

```
int tolower(char c)
```
Returns lowercase of c
```
int toupper(char c)
```
Returns uppercase of c

G.2.2 Functions
```
char *strcat(char *s1, *s2)
```
Appends s2 to s1
Returns s1

```
char *strchr(char *s; char c)
```
Returns a pointer to the
first occurrence of the
character c in s, or NULL
Sometimes called index

```
int strcmp(char *s1, *s2)
```
Returns 0 if s1 = s2
        −1 if s1 < s2
         1 if s1 > s2

```
char *strcpy(char *s1, *s2)
```
Copies s2 to s1. Returns s1
```
int strcspn(char *s1, *s2)
```
Returns the length of the longest
initial segment of s1 that consists

	of characters not found in s2
`int strlen(char *s)`	Returns length of s
`char *strncat(char *s1, *s2; int n)`	Appends no more than n characters from s2 to s1
`int strncmp(char *s1, *s2; int n)`	As `strcmp`, but compares only n characters
`char *strncpy(char *s1, *s2; int n)`	Copies at most n characters from s2 to s1
`char *strpbrk(char *s1, *s2)`	Searches s1 for any of the characters in s2 Returns a pointer to first character, or NULL
`int strpos(char *s; char c)`	Returns the position of c in s, or −1
`char *strrchr(char *s; char c)`	As `strchr`, but searches for the last occurrence of character c in s Sometimes called `rindex`
`char *strrpbrk(char *s1, *s2)`	As `strpbrk`, but returns a pointer to the last occurrence
`int strrpos(char *s; char c)`	As `strpos`, but searches for the last occurrence of c in s
`int strspn(char *s1, *s2)`	As `strcspn`, but skips over characters that are in the set s2, and returns the longest initial segment of s1 that consists of characters found in s2

G.3   MEMORY FUNCTIONS

`char *calloc(unsigned n, siz)`	Allocates memory for n*siz bytes
`void cfree(char *p)`	Frees block p
`char *clalloc(unsigned long n, siz)`	Allocates memory for n*siz bytes
`void free(char *p)`	Frees block p
`char *malloc(unsigned n)`	Allocates memory object of n bytes in size
`char *mlalloc(unsigned long n)`	Allocates memory object of n bytes in size
`char *realloc(char *p; unsigned siz)`	Reallocates memory
`char *relalloc(char *p; unsigned long siz)`	Reallocates memory

Index

Index of Programs, Functions, and Procedures

The numbers listed in chapters 3 through 12 represent example numbers, whereas those listed in Chapter 13 and 14 represent section numbers.

POINTERS AND MEMORY MANAGEMENT

ONE-DIMENSIONAL ARRAYS

TWO-DIMENSIONAL ARRAYS

STRUCTURES

UNIONS

STRINGS

ARRAYS OF POINTERS TO STRINGS

COMMAND LINE ARGUMENTS

BITWISE OPERATIONS

ADVANCED FILE I/O OPERATIONS